Secret

&

Suppressed

SECRET AND SUPPRESSED

BANNED IDEAS & HIDDEN HISTORY

EDITED BY JIM KEITH

FERAL HOUSE

ISBN: 0-922915-14-8
9 8 7 6 5 4 3 2 1

For a free catalogue of Feral House books send SASE to:
Feral House
PO Box 3466
Portland, OR 97208

With appreciation to Adam Parfrey.

I would like to thank the following persons
for their contributions to the research:
Vicky Bolin, X. Sharks DeSpot, Hawthorne Abendsen,
Michael A. Hoffman II, Jerry Smith, Larry Nunn,
Wayne Henderson, James Shelby Downard, Greg Krupey,
Tim O'Neill, Ron Bonds, Tim Cridland, Kenn Thomas,
Howard Martenson, Ace Hayes, Len Bracken,
John Aes-Nihil and "The Franciscan."

The editor is always interested in contacting people who
have interesting information. I can be contacted care of
IllumiNet Press, PO Box 2808, Lilburn, GA, 30226.

—Jim Keith

Contents

The Disinformational Plague

The Elite Controllers

PREFACE

Careful examination of the facts will reveal something curious to the unbiased: America's electronic and print media are simultaneously "free" and heavily controlled.

The existence of books like this one proves that there is freedom of the press within the clipped-wing aviary of the "underground," where the ravings of radicals accomplish little more than provide comic relief. In the big buck, million-copy world of the mainstream, commentators on both Left and Right have discerned and decried the hand of censorship and manipulation for years while wittingly or otherwise playing a part in the mass deception. Conservatives like Limbaugh and Quayle prattle about the liberal slant of the news, while liberals like Chomsky and Vidal reveal the subtleties of an ongoing manipulation and redesign of our society by a cabal of the ruling elite who own the media, and their henchperson spin-doctors who tinker with the mind of the body politic.

How can the media be both free and controlled at the same time? And why?

FREEDOM IS SLAVERY. Every civilization has had slavery as an essential element of its economy —including our own. Have you attained the "American Dream" by making payments on your own home? But who owns your home, really? If you're still making payments, who owns your car? Washer/dryer? Refrigerator/freezer? Big screen TV? Just stop making payments and see what happens. Let's say you've paid off your car, paid off your home. What happens if you don't pay property taxes on time, or pay car insurance? What if you suddenly take ill?Ever hear of indentured servitude? Before the Civil War, free men who needed money could sell themselves into slavery for a period of time, usually seven years. Most Americans are way over their heads in debt. Daily they sell themselves into slavery — in forty hour weeks, eight hour shifts, if they can find them.

What has all this got to do with the media? The people who direct and control the world's financial resources are, to a very large extent, the same people who control and direct the world's media. Networks, cable stations, studios, theatre chains, publishing consortiums, newspapers, are owned by a handful of people, and those people either own the banks or are owned by the banks.

THE HORRIBLE TRUTH. Electronic and print media are a pacification program run by the Happyface Fun Enforcers. There is an ideal mental/emotional state for rabid consumerism, and that is the state of glad that the media promotes. The shock cuts and nervous camera succor a short attention span; so short, in fact, that your brain becomes a sieve, short-circuiting memory and logic. You are on IV TV, awaiting the next in-flow of shock or pacifying hypnotic to keep you hooked into the consumerist foodchain.

> Small robbers are put in prison;
> A great robber becomes a feudal lord;
> And in the gate of the feudal lord your righteous scholars will be found.
>
> — Man Kau-Teh

IGNORANCE IS STRENGTH. By now, most of America has heard the phrase "Politically Correct," a term that George Orwell would have relished. I means to speak, think and act within the mandates of a supposed worldview of compassion and tolerance. It also means that there are certain thoughts — a lot of them, actually — that you must not think.

I had a personal encounter with the unthinkable recently. It was at a recent convention for writers, publishers, and fans of "marginal" forms of literature, including science fiction, horror, comics, conspiracy politics, and other genres catering to the not-quite-right in the head. There, I chaired a panel discussion on the topic of "Censorship," prefacing the free-for-all with a thumbnail listing of a few things that you can't discuss in this society without facing the wrath of the self-appointed righteous. I was careful to state that by mentioning these dreadful subjects that I was not endorsing them, and **I am still not endorsing them**, but pointed out these were topics that one could not safely consider, regardless of the alleged protections of our much-touted First Amendment.

1. Racial correlation to IQ.

2. Homosexuality as pathology.

3. Holocaust revisionism (i.e., did 6 million die?).

4. AIDS as military bio-warfare.

5. Application of the same rules and procedures to AIDS victims as to victims of other communicable diseases.

While these subjects all seemed prosaic to a jaded figurine such as myself, they were not, as I had anticipated, old news to everyone. Still, I hardly expected such a stimulus-response convulsion from so-called free-thinkers and iconoclasts. As soon as I had totted off on my fingers the prime candidates for "things you can't think, much less talk about around here," a fellow panelist, a capable writer whom I had personally invited to participate in the discussion, threatened to walk if I didn't immediately shut my face!

And so, in this spirited panel discussion about "Censorship" — in which, over the course of the next hour, it was agreed that aforesaid practice was a Very Bad Thing indeed, engaged in only by the worst examples of a Puritanistic society like unto that of Saddam Hussein's — there were subjects, certain subjects that we dared not touch upon.

THE CHILD IS FATHER TO THE MANNEQUIN. Wrote H.L. Mencken in 1919:

> It is precisely here ... that the culture of the individual has been reduced to the most rigid and absurd regimentation. It is precisely here, of all civilized countries, that eccentricity in demeanor and opinion has come to bear the heaviest penalties. The whole drift of our law is toward the absolute prohibition of all ideas that diverge in the slightest from the accepted platitudes, and behind that drift of law there is a far more potent force of growing custom, and under that custom there is a national philosophy which erects conformity into the noblest of virtues and the free functioning of personality into a capital crime against society.

It is almost impossible to join the mainstream media without getting a BA in Journalism. One might think that this is done to ensure that the "cub reporter" has learned the basic technical skills needed for the job. It's not. It is to ensure that the new kids have been indoctrinated into the correct mindset. That they think right.

Objective reporting seems to be passé. Now the kids are given a lot of ideas about "social responsibility" and other buzzwords that sound awfully close to thought control in a do-good disguise. The indications are that the current crop of reporters are being taught not to tell us what happened, but how to think and feel about it, and how to put the event in a context of right and wrong. Inclinations, feelings, not facts. The distortion of reality if it doesn't fit the program. White lies. Gentle lies, and in some guises with "hated" personalities, vicious lies.

Secret and Suppressed is meant as a hopeful alternative to so much silence and so many lies. It is an anthology of documents and ideas hidden from view by people and institutions who know what's best for you. By virtue of being important enough to hide, this information has proven itself important enough to print. Culled from a wide variety of sources (including telephone poles), the articles in this collection span an enormous range of ideologies.

On occasion I have included a particular piece in this volume not for its absolute validity, which is often nigh-impossible to determine, but for its quotient of unacceptability in the reality tunnels of the mainstream. We refuse to patronize you by playing Time/Life and deciding what is real and what is bogus. That is for you to decide. Please do not confuse the map with the territory, nor the editor or publisher with the contents of the book.

To go beyond the brainwash requires only a modicum of curiosity and self-motivation. Picking up this book is perhaps not a bad start. It seems fair to warn you, however, that even a tentative scratching at the gargoyle-façade that passes for reality will likely unleash a clutch of demons from the far side of Truth.

This book, you might say, is an attempt to create doors for a few of those gibbering entities ... where once there were walls.

— Jim Keith

MENTICIDE

My Father Is A Clone

Gary Stollman

On August 19, 1987 a gun-carrying Gary Stollman entered the studio of Los Angeles's KNBC television, crashing consumer reporter David Horowitz's live newscast. Stollman handed Horowitz a written statement and ordered him to read it while holding a gun on him. Unbeknownst to Stollman, KNBC immediately switched to a commercial, not permitting the statement to be transmitted. When Horowitz finished reading the statement, Stollman surrendered his gun, which turned out to be a toy pistol. Stollman, the son of a pharmacist who appeared on KNBC newscasts as an expert on drugs, was sent to Los Angeles County Jail. This is the text of his message:

The man who has appeared on KNBC for the last 3 years is not my biological father. He is a clone, a double created by the Central Intelligence Agency and alien forces. It is only a small part of a greater plot to overthrow the United States government, and possibly the human race itself. The CIA has replaced and tried to destroy my family, and those of my friends.

Although I have known about this since 1981, I have not taken any action about it for fear of the lives of my family. I have been forced into CIA-run mental hospitals, such as Cedars-Sinai Thalians, where I am shown being interviewed by many different doctors, although I spoke to nobody there for two weeks. At UCLA-NPI, I attempted to have myself released by a court several times, but was asked by a Dr. Martin Zsuba to keep removing my requests for a writ-hearing. I have been unable to obtain records from several other hospitals, including Ben Taub Hospital in Cincinnati, where all the phones were turned off for 48 hours after I arrived.

I do not know where my real family or others are being held, but I believe it is somewhere in California. The records for Ben Taub Hospital, I have been informed, no longer exist, or have been misplaced.

I heard an interview a few weeks ago, on radio station KPFK, in which a former CIA official told a college audience in San Diego how the CIA has towed barges filled with diseases across New York Harbor, placed lightbulbs in the subways to create vertigo, and cameras to observe the reactions, and may have created the AIDS virus to wipe out the gay population.

He also spoke of secret teams that were created after World War II. I say that the CIA assassinated John F. Kennedy and the 22 material witnesses that day, who all died within 2 years of each other, a mathematical impossibility. What they are capable of, I know only too well. I demand the public release of all secret Air Force files concerning UFOs, which were kept secret even from Senator Barry Goldwater. On my way back from Expo 86 last year, I heard a broadcast in Oregon that he once asked to see the files and was told, "Hell, no!" I demand the release of information concerning the objects contained in Hangar 18 at Wright-Patterson Air Force Base, now obscurely referred to as the Environmental Control Building, the most highly guarded building in the world. Why has the knowledge of such advanced beings and equipment been kept so secret that even the United States Congress does not know?

I would have been satisfied to let my situation stand if it were only I and my family who were at stake here. However, I spoke to a girl at Florida Junior College two summers ago, who related the story to me of how seven of her friends had also been replaced. She said that she had written absence excuses for them when they weren't sick, then they disappeared for a week, only to come back with different personalities. Unless we act swiftly, there may not be very much hope for any of us. These people, or whatever they are, are taking over the phone services right now. The CIA is either doing this themselves, or are helping them.

I was warned in 1981 by someone with connections to the CIA to stay off computers, that they didn't trust people on computers. Then I began receiving disturbing calls from my parents, which led me to believe that something terrible was going on. I was forced into a mental hospital in Tallahassee, where I learned that my brother in law had been driven insane in the same manner that someone was trying to do to me. I eventually was released, but then my mom came down to visit me and I knew it was an imposter. I know that the secret service is involved in this as well, so who knows just how far this has gone in five years. I know of a counselor named Pat, who worked at the Optimist Boys School near Pasadena, who was involved in recruiting members for some secret group of people. Apparently they adopted orphans and gave them fake IDs and birth certificates. Since we already know of a secret group led by the President's own staff, someone had better find out what is going on and fast. I only know that there are beings around us now with the power to teleport instantaneously and do the same to others, who can read and control minds, and transform matter into other forms or create it at will.

I ask for a Congressional Investigation and Federal protection for my family, and those involved. There is no way I can harm anyone with an empty BB gun.

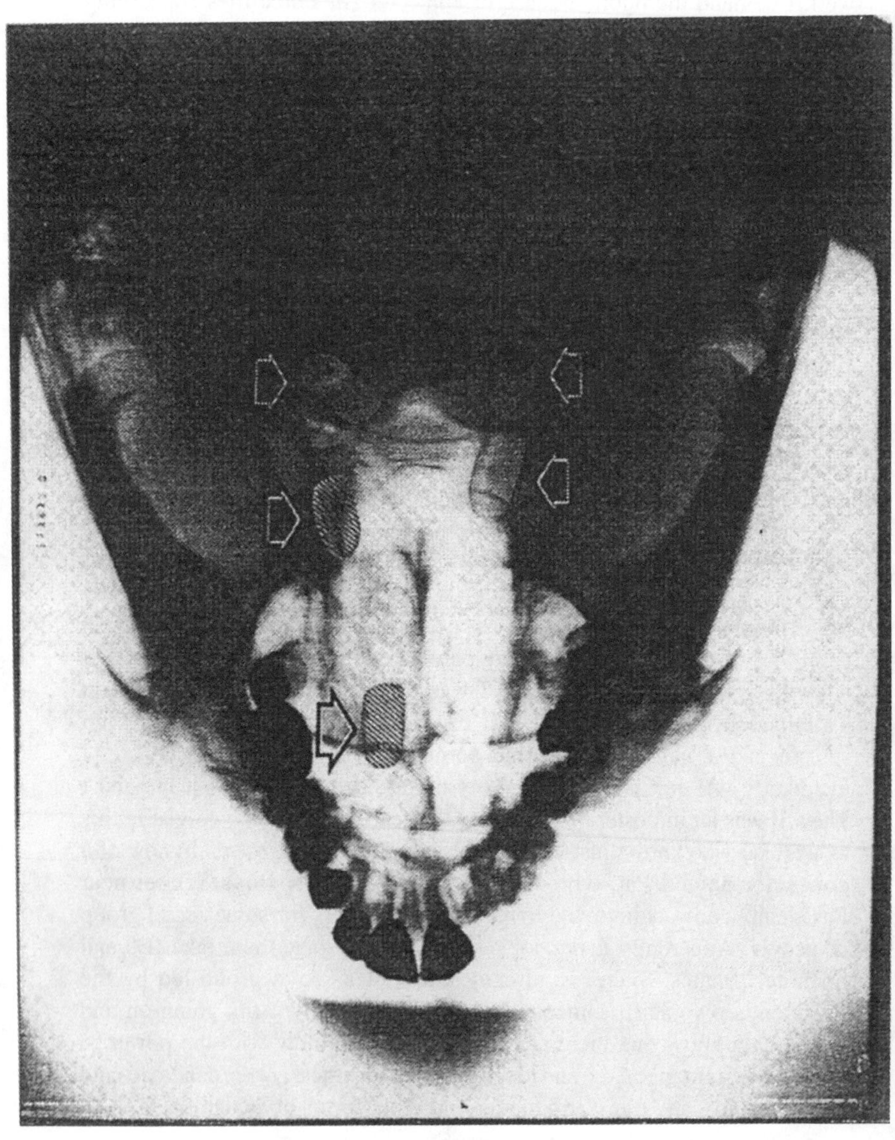

This X-ray shows five transmitters implanted in Robert Naeslund's brain.

An Open Letter to the Swedish Prime Minister Regarding Electromagnetic Terror

Robert Naeslund

November 19, 1992

Prime Minister Carl Bildt
Stockholm, Sweden

Ever since an operation at Söder Hospital in Stockholm at the end of the 1960s, I have been used in a medical experiment which has meant a lot of suffering and has been very painful. The operation was performed by Dr. Curt Strand, who inserted a foreign object, a so-called brain transmitter, into my head through the right nasal passage. For many years I have tried to get help from Swedish physicians and even from the National Board of Health and Welfare *(Socialstyrelsen).* However, I was confronted by doctors who became my enemies and I was, among other things, declared mentally ill and placed in a mental hospital. In 1983 I came in contact with Prof. P.A. Lindstrom at the University of California, San Diego, in the United States, who examined my x-rays. Many Swedish doctors had given written opinions about these, and stated that the x-rays were completely normal, that there were no foreign objects in my head.

Prof. Lindstrom wrote in one of his many statements that, "I can only confirm that some foreign objects, most likely brain transmitters, have been implanted at the base of your frontal brain and in the skull. In my opinion, there is no excuse for such implantations. I fully agree with Lincoln Lawrence who, in his book on page 27, wrote, "There are two particularly dreadful procedures which have been developed, those working and playing with them secretly call them R.H.I.C and E.D.O.M — Radio-Hypnotic Intracerebral Control and Electronic Dissolution of Memory." These, as well as ESB, Electronic Stimulation of the Brain, constitute what is included in biomedical telemetry, the complete mind control.

After Prof. Lindstrom wrote his opinion, about ten other doctors in different countries have given written statements which attest to the implanted transmitters in my head. The statements clearly show that Swedish doctors have given false reports concerning my case. Despite the evidence which proves the outrage, I cannot get surgical help in Sweden to remove the many transmitters implanted in my head, which are active day and night, year after year. This was the reason why I sought help in Djakarta when I visited Indonesia. But we will clearly see the few helpful physicians' intentions are worthless when secret police are acting on their information from mind control.

On August 4, 1987, I visited St. Carolus Hospital, Ji Salemba, Djakarta, and I met Professor Hendayo to whom I showed my x-rays, as well as reports from various doctors. He, obviously, could see the implanted foreign objects and more x-rays taken the same day confirmed the fact, so Dr. Hendayo agreed to operate. I stayed at the hospital until the following day. They took blood tests, etc., and informed me to come back on August 11th.

On the morning of the 12th, I was shown to the operating room. Right outside of the door, I met Dr. Hendayo. He told me that something had happened which would cause the postponement of the operation. He would not say why. Considering how important this was to me, I insisted that he keep his part of the agreement and do the operation. His behavior and attitude that morning was much different than earlier. The complaisance and friendliness of the previous meeting were gone, replaced by irritation and stress. But he changed his mind and agreed to perform the operation. As soon as we entered the operating ward, two people entered from another room; they were western middle-aged men. One of them had a syringe and gave me the sedative without a word or any preparation.

In the middle of the operation I awoke with a horrible pain in my head. My arms and legs were secured with straps. One person held my hand steady, while another held open the 5 cm. incision in my forehead with some sort of instrument. A third person held an object, resembling a branding iron used on animals, which he burned into my head. During the 45 seconds of the operation in which I was awake, I experienced the feeling that my head was being blown to bits. I screamed in pain and tried to free my arms and legs. I fell unconscious from the pain and shock. The next thing I knew, it was 2 a.m. and I could feel my brain on fire. This was 18 hours after the operation.

The next morning I went to the hospital's radiology department and asked the doctor to x-ray my head. The picture showed the injury and that there was a foreign object in the damaged area. I went to the chief physician and told him what had happened. Afterward, I visited Dr. Hendayo and he told me, "It wasn't my idea to do this ... I had no choice ... You should have listened to me and postponed the operation ... Your country's secret police was involved...."

The reason the operation turned out the way it did is quite clear. Prof. Hendayo was, at first, in favor of the operation. But the Swedish Secret Police (SÄPO) followed me via mind control and they knew every step I took. When Dr. Hendayo promised to operate on me, SÄPO also knew. In order to stop me, they informed their CIA colleagues in Indonesia, who forbade the doctor to help me, or they threatened to expose them. That was why the doctor could not say why he wanted to postpone the operation. SÄPO/CIA had obviously wanted to warn me and show that there were other powers behind the decision. Now, five years later, I have physical pain in the area which was damaged. In addition, my mental and psychological abilities have been greatly altered. The difficulty in finding a doctor who will operate on me is the great secret behind the use of mind control telemetry and doctors' international solidarity with colleagues who use people for experiments. These transmitters have changed my life in many ways and torment me through their constant use.

In a 1978 report entitled "ELF Magnetic Fields and EEG Entrainment" Dr. Robert Beck, Director of Biomedical Research in Los Angeles, writes, "The Canadians report alarming mood alterations in certain areas of eastern Canada which observers believe are linked to Soviet [electromagnetic transmissions]." In 1987, *Atlantic Monthly* magazine elaborated on how electromagnetic weaponry has been developed with the ability to both affect the nervous system and to induce death. This research has concentrated upon a much wider spectrum of frequencies from microwaves, gamma and laser beams, right down to the extremely low frequencies which the brain works by. As Robert Beck stated in an interview with the *Omni,* "It is easier to generate cancer in a person than it is to cure." The article continues to discuss the range of applications of these new radiation weapons: "Radio-frequency weapons that impair the nervous system might have uses in commando operations, anti-terrorist actions, and what the Pentagon calls 'low level conflicts' when more deadly weapons are being held back." The meaning of the term 'low level conflict' seems to be consistent wherever these conflicts occur, either in the USA, England, Sweden, or Russia.

That this arsenal is being used against the citizenry in the new Russia as in the former Soviet Union is quite apparent from a statement published at the end of 1991 by SovData DiaLine:

"Psychological warfare is still being used by state security agents against people in Russia, even after the abortive August coup," said Emilia Chirkova, a Deputy of the Zelenograd Soviet and member of the Human Rights Commission. She recalls the scandal surrounding the alleged bugging equipment installed close to Boris Yeltsin's office. KGB agents admitted then that the directional aerial in the equipment was designed for transmission, not for reception. She believes it was part of an attempt to affect the health of the Russian President using high-frequency electromagnetic radiation. '"The Human Rights Committee," Chirkova said, "had warned Yeltsin about such a possibility." She cited several further instances of the use of similar devices. Microwave equipment had been used in 1989 and 1990 in Vladivostok and Moscow prisons, in a mental hospital in Oryol, and in the Serbsky Institute in Moscow [also a mental hospital], she said. During his exile in Gorky, Andrei Sacharov noticed the presence of a high-tension electromagnetic field in his flat. It was reported recently in the press that Ruslan Khasbulatov, Speaker of the Russian Parliament, had had to move from his flat to another district of Moscow. High-level electromagnetic radiation has been included among the possible causes of the discomfort he felt in his flat.

Purported victims of psychological warfare have written to the paper. From Voronezh comes this letter: "They controlled my laughter, my thoughts, and caused pain in various parts of my body... It all started in October 1985, after I had openly criticized the first secretary of the City Committee of the Communist Party." "Sometimes voices can be heard in the head from the effect of microwave pulse radiation which causes acoustic oscillations in the brain," explained Gennady Shchelkunov, a radio electronics researcher from the Istok Association. Numerous sufferers from this alleged manipulation have set up a public movement. In June 1991, a group of Zelenograd deputies sent an appeal signed by 150 people to President Yeltsin, demanding an investigation into the use of bio-electronic weapons.

In Sweden there are clear signs that SÄPO/FOA uses unwitting people in very long-term research programs. At one of SÄPO's secret bases in Sweden, the so-called Tjädergarden in Söraker just outside Sundsvall, these weapons has been tested on residents in the nearby estates and the long-term effects of electromagnetic weapons and fields are being studied.

The following is an extract from a 15-page letter from Tjädergarden resident Ossian Andersson to the Swedish government: "...owing to the terror, harrowing persecution and gross violations of human rights which I have been subjected to for the last eight years, I hereby request the government to allow me to resume a normal human existence. I am completely without legal protection while the security police and military researchers toy with me at their whim. My letters are to no effect, the authorities shirk any responsibility... I am being used as a guinea pig for weapons of ultrasonic, electromagnetic field, acoustic and death-ray type, and my central nervous system has been seized so that they can control my brain with micro-electronic technology and microcomputers ... the symptoms of ultrasonic radiation are headaches, dizziness, disorientation and visual impairment. Other symptoms are a degeneration of intelligence with an additional effect on blood circulation and visceral pain ... acoustic weapons do not cause injury, rather they convey a nebulous disorientation which can shatter all one's organized activities. These weapons work by introducing chaos into one's life ... the radiation penetrates all types of material which I have used for protection. For instance, I built a case with a 2 mm thick lead insulation, under which I lay at night, to no avail... Microchips are also part of the picture, since I became aware that they were able to control my entire range of brain activity. These micro-devices must have been placed in my both without my knowledge... It is cruel to force a pensioner such as myself to suffer day after day and to prevent him to sleep no more than an hour now and then."

Since I myself have been in Söraker and know Ossian well, I can affirm that what he describes is but a fragment of the truly frightening nature of his torment. He is now 82 years old, and the terror meted out to him is completely bereft of humanitarian norms. He is being seriously exploited in a harrowing experiment conducted for periods of 22 hours during day and night in which he finds it impossible to snatch even a moment's sleep; and so it has been, with a persistent brutal intensity, for the last 20 years. Ossian has also undergone cranial radiographic examination from which the implantation of a foreign object with cerebral connections can be confirmed.

Edward Kelly was a journalist and came to Sweden in the mid 1970s, where, since 1984, he worked for an alternative news agency investigating the use, by medical institutions, of patients in various medical experiments. Kelly contacted the Socialstyrelsen/Board of Health and Welfare and several other state institutions in order to obtain certain information, at the same time informing them of his research, and a week later he fell seriously ill. It started with sharp pains in his back which rendered him bed-ridden; soon he had to be carried when he needed to visit the toilet. From the very beginning of the illness, strange phenomena were to be observed in his bedroom: papers stapled to the walls began to roll themselves up, those affixed with tape folded up and fell to the floor and several people noticed that they felt unwell after spending short time in his room. Kelly's cat, who used to like lying on his bed, now refused to enter and restricted itself to other rooms in the house.

Doctors examining Kelly diagnosed lumbago and by the middle of March he developed a bad cough; at the end of the month he was taken to hospital where his body was found riddled with cancer. Finally, on the 28th of May 1985 at Karolinska Hospital, he died.

A similar story concerns me. In 1985 I was behind the petition to the Director of Public Prosecutions, supported by 50 signatures, demanding a response to the question whether doctors should have the right to implant transmitters into the heads of unwitting patients during surgery. I was also one of those responsible for the following advertisement which was printed in 30 Swedish daily, weekly and monthly papers, and which exposed the above outrages taking place within all large Swedish hospitals. At about the same time the first advertisement was published, I noticed a radiation or frequency which seemed to rise up from below my flat. In the mornings it felt as though my face, shoulders and back had been sunburned. If I layed a sheet of paper on the floor, it would, after only a matter of hours, begin to roll itself up from both ends and all battery-operated equipment rapidly were quickly drained of power. The waves increased until I was forced to move out into a friend's flat.

I hired another flat at Kocksgatan 38 in Stockholm where, for the first two weeks, everything was fine. By the 1st of May, however, the trouble started again. The effects were much the same; the feelings of burning heat and noticeable burns on the face after just an hour and the spreading of the sensation into the palate, throat and lungs. Paper rolled itself up whether hanging on the wall or lying on the floor — but now I also experienced how my blood circulation was being affected. I wrote of my last days in the flat: "The radiation has increased for the last two weeks, and now, the 29th of May, it is completely unthinkable to sleep here. It is possible to be in the flat for at most two hours, but after that one has to leave because the pain in the lungs, the dehydration, the dry cough and general weakness."

Due to critical conditions caused by SÄPO's radiation, I was forced to abandon my efforts to expose their electromagnetic terrorism. It was to be five years before I resumed the fight. At the beginning of 1992 I came into contact with the International Network against Mind Control, and was involved in the drafting of the following letter to Prime Minister John Major. The day after it was sent and faxed to colleagues the world over, press agencies, and so on, SÄPO resumed its radiation so that after three days I was forced to again abandon my flat.

Prime Minister John Major
British Government
London SW1A OAA
England

Dear Sir,

Our international network of researchers has, for several years, been engaged in investigations into mind control and its widespread utilization around the world and we have become aware of several victims in Great Britain; reports received from exploited individuals refer to mental hospitals, police authorities and prisons as among the state institutions involved in the implantation of transmitters, electrodes of radio-transmitting crystals in people. The use of mind control is such a grave encroachment on civil liberty that, if allowed to develop further, it will threaten the freedom and integrity of all. Along with environmental problems, this is one of the most urgent issues to address if we are to ensure a more secure future.

The reason we are addressing this letter to you personally is that a meeting between Mr. John Austin-Walker, Member of the Parliament, and a victim of mind control, impressed on him the importance of pursuing investigations into the matter so much that he addressed a letter to you himself in August this year. Later writing to the injured party, a Mr. N'Tumba, he said: "Following your most recent visit to see me, I have written to the Prime Minister on your behalf. As you know, there is very little accountability of security services to the House of Commons and Members of Parliament have almost no power in relation to the activities of M15. As soon as I receive a response from the Prime Minister, I will be in touch with you again."

Just what happened to Mr. N'Tumba, he describes himself in a letter to us: "Concerning the brain transmitter in my head, it has been performing without my knowledge of consent...What's very outrageous is that I am sharing all my visions, thoughts, images, hearing...etc. with people around me as the security services are engaging in a large scale propaganda drive to smear my character, background, behavior, emotions and motives...I have no privacy at all...I am not a spy, I am not a criminal, I am not a terrorist. Being an innocent victim of M15 ... my persecution started in June 1988." What is more, there is no reason to suspect the validity of what he writes; we are overburdened with letters such as this one from the USA, Denmark, Sweden, Germany, New Zealand inter alia and our investigations in Sweden reveal a terrifying reality where the mental health services, police authorities and hospitals implant radio-transmitting devices in people's heads and brains. This reality is exposed by a vast amount of x-ray material to be a chilling and gloomy vision of the future, stage-managed for decades by the security forces in collaboration with medical and psychiatric institutions who together have created a secret power which transcends law and order, and which is beyond intrusive public control.

Brain-computer radio communication has long been considered impossible by the majority of people and has consequently been relegated to science-fiction, but the fact is that the technology had been developed into reality by at least the 1960s, during which time the initial experiments were being performed on unwitting subjects. The system has at different times been called Intra Cerebral Mind Control, ESB, Electronic Stimulation of Brain, Biological Radiocommunication or Bio-medical telemetry and in both the eastern and western worlds is the prevailing system of mind control, creating unlimited possibilities to influence and change an individual's behavior patterns and personality. By means of two-way radio communication, called telemetry or remote-control, an electromagnetic wave can be sent on a return trip to a receiver/transmitter located under the skull or in the brain; this signal records the activity of the brain and returns it to a computer for analysis, from which all aspects of the subject's life can be exposed. Radio transmitting crystals, which when injected into the bloodstream fasten themselves to the brain, have been under development for decades. They work on the same principle as a normal transmitter, use the same technology, and contain the same possibilities.

To analyze an EEG in a computer instead of a conventional printer provides an entirely fresh perspective on the conclusions which can be drawn, and gives a whole new perspective on what can be concluded. Cognitive manifestations and activity such as thoughts and visual impressions or emotions, behavior and psychological reactions can continually be registered making it possible for secret police authorities, medical scientists and the state to observe an individual in a deeper and more comprehensive way than the individual could possibly do him or herself. Through analysis and manipulation by the computer, it is even possible for changes in an individual's physical mental status to be effected. The potential of intracerebral remote control is limited only by the imagination of the investigator, especially when it is remembered that, since these frequencies travel at the speed of light, the system of control is not constrained by matters of range.

Concerning the case of Mr. N'Tumba, it is obvious that there is simply no justification for implanting the mind transmitter, whether for police surveillance or psychiatric research. We feel, furthermore, that this is yet another example of human rights violation as defined under the CSCE 1980-83 Madrid conference and as embodied in the Final Act of Helsinki. We also wish to note that such activities are also in contravention of several agreements, endorsed by Great Britain, within the United Nations system, including in particular the International Bill of Human Rights and Articles 3, 4, 5 and 12 of the Universal Declaration of Human Rights.

Recently, we received some X-ray pictures of Mr. N'Tumba and our medical experts in Stockholm have examined those of his skull and can confirm that a transmitter has been implanted in his left nostril.

Furthermore, it can be seen that electrodes placed in the occipital lobe are blocking the blood flow behind their delimitation where the oxygen depletion is caused and this is seen as well in his frontal brain just above the implanted transmitter. Among the changes caused by the frequencies affecting his brain, the reduced oxygen levels have induced an alteration of neurological functions, impaired cognitive abilities including that of memory. Moreover, he has obviously been anaesthetized without his knowledge so that this implantation could be performed.

We would greatly appreciate a statement regarding your views concerning this issue, and we urgently press you for all possible assistance which you can give to Mr. N'Tumba.

Yours faithfully,

Lennart Lindqvist
International Secretary

The first signs of radiation from electromagnetic weapons were noticed during the nights of the 11th October, the day after the letter [reproduced here in abbreviated form] was faxed worldwide. I was awakened at 3 a.m. by a blockage of the blood circulation in my hands, feet, forearms and parts of my legs, hands and feet swelled up and became numb. My face and back became sunburned as if I had been sunbathing on a hot summer's day. This was to be repeated night after night and it must be assumed that the electromagnetic waves were ultraviolet in nature, a radiation which affects the skin's pigmentation and which are known to cause cancer. The radiation continued during the following day and night and even though I tried to be at home as little as possible, it became quite clear that they still had the power to vary the spectrum and intensity of the radiation which they were using against me. From the first day, I experienced noticeable changes in my lungs and windpipe which resembled the symptoms following the radiation of 1985. The windpipe and respiratory passages became parched, my voice hoarse, and my lungs painful. I also suffered from acute amnesia whenever I crossed the threshold to my flat. By the third day, I considered it my safest move to leave my flat and so I went away for a week.

On returning, I found myself in a radiation chamber of considerably greater power than the one I had left in which it was possible to generate a multitude of destructively painful symptoms by varying the spectrum and intensity. I was kept awake at nights and sent into a kind of trance during the days, but by far the most frightening effect was that on the lungs which even after the first night had been severely impaired. When, after two days, I also began to suffer from backache and an almost crippling immobility, and when even the shortest possible time in my flat began to be unbearable, I felt that it was time to desist risking my life and moved in with friends. Since I had to return occasionally to my flat, I was able to establish that the radiation continued to penetrate my flat and on one fortunate occasion I was able to identify its source. The deteriorating winter found me at home one evening taking in some flowers from my balcony when I noticed in the block opposite, in the window of the flat directly under my own, was some apparatus, partially visible between the angled slats of a venetian blind. It was directed up at my flat. It was emitting no light but its surface was lustrous.

During the night I collected some infra-red film and some binoculars so that I could study it more closely. As early as the previous summer, being more often out on the balcony, I had noticed that there was never any light in that flat, just as there is none nowadays. The day after, I called on the flat at Verkstadsgatan 22 and rung the doorbell above the name Broman. No one answered, not surprisingly since I heard from the neighbors that he had passed away some months back. The same day, I had the film developed; the picture I obtained revealed the apparatus with startling clarity.

From here SÄPO was terrorizing me and enfeebling my health with their destructive radiation, and so together with some friends I contrived to break into the flat and seize the apparatus. However, by 8 p.m. the same evening when I was home monitoring the situation, I noticed that the apparatus was gone. They had been there and removed it and with it, the radiation. I was able to return home.

This letter has been written in English since so much of the material is already on disk in that language and since I feel it is a more practical language to use. The letter has not been written with the intention of prompting a written reply, since any answer you convey I am sure to notice. I would, however, appreciate acknowledgment of receipt.

Yours sincerely,

Robert Naeslund

Right: Another view of a brain implant X-ray

Remote Mind Control Technology

Anna Keeler

There had been an ongoing controversy over health effects of electromagnetic fields (EMF) for years (e.g., extremely low frequency radiation and the Navy's Project Seafarer; emissions of high power lines and video display terminals; radar and other military and industrial sources of radio frequencies and microwaves, such as plastic sealers and molders). Less is known of Department of Defense (DOD) and Central Intelligence Agency (CIA) interest in anti-personnel applications of the invisible energies. The ability of certain parameters of EMF to cause health effects, including neurological and behavioral disturbances, has been part of the military and CIA arsenal for years.

Capabilities of the energies to cause predictable and exploitable effects or damages can be gleaned from discussion of health effects from environmental exposures. Interestingly, some scientists funded by the DOD or CIA to research and develop invisible electromagnetic weapons have voiced strong concern (perhaps even superior knowledge or compensatory to guilt) over potentially serious consequences of environmental exposures.

Eldon Byrd who worked for Naval Surface Weapons, Office of Non-Lethal Weapons, was commissioned in 1981 to develop electromagnetic devices for purposes including "riot control," clandestine operations and hostage removal. In the context of a controversy over reproductive hazards to Video Display Terminal (VDT) operators, he wrote of alterations in brain function of animals exposed to low intensity fields. Offspring of exposed animals "exhibited a drastic degradation of intelligence later in life ... couldn't learn easy tasks ... indicating a very definite and irreversible damage to the central nervous system of the fetus." With VDT operators exposed to weak fields, there have been clusters of miscarriages and birth defects (with evidence of central nervous system damage to the fetus). Byrd also wrote of experiments where behavior of animals was controlled by exposure to weak electromagnetic fields. "At a certain frequency and power intensity, they could make the animal purr, lay down and roll over."

Jose Delgado, advocate of a psychocivilized society through mind control, no longer implants electrodes in the brains of mental patients and prisoners; he now induces profound behavioral changes (hyperactivity, passivity, etc.) by exposing animals to precisely tuned EMFs. He has also written of genetic damage produced by weak EMF fields, similar to those emitted by VDTs. Invariably, brain tissue damage and skeletal deformation was observed in new born chicks that had been exposed. He was concerned enough to check emissions from the appliances in his kitchen.

Ross Adey induces calcium efflux in brain tissue with low power level fields (a basis for the CIA and military's "confusion weaponry") and has done behavioral experiments with radar modulated at electro-encephalogram (EEG) rhythms. He is understandably concerned about environmental exposures within 1 to 30 Hz (cycles per second), either as a low frequency or an amplitude modulation on a microwave or radio frequency, as these can physiologically interact with the brain even at very low power densities.

Microwaves

Microwave health effects is a juncture where Department of Defense and environmental concerns collide and part ways. Security concerns, according to Sam Koslov of Defense Advanced Research Projects Agency (DARPA), first prompted U.S. study of health effects of low intensity (or non-thermal) microwaves. At times, up to 70-80% of the research was funded by the military. From 1965 to 1970, a study dubbed Project Pandora was undertaken to determine the health and psychological effects of low intensity microwaves, the so-called "Moscow signal" registered at the American Embassy in Moscow. Initially, there was confusion over whether the signal was an attempt to activate bugging devices or for some other purpose. There was suspicion that the microwave irradiation was being used as a mind control system. CIA agents asked scientists involved in microwave research whether microwaves beamed at humans from a distance could affect the brain and alter behavior. Dr. Milton Zaret who undertook to analyze Soviet literature on microwaves for the CIA, wrote: "For non-thermal irradiations, they believe that the electromagnetic field induced by the microwave environment affects the cell membrane, and this results in an increase of excitability or an increase in the level of excitation of nerve cells. With repeated or continued exposure, the increased excitability leads to a state of exhaustion of the cells of the cerebral cortex."

Employees first learned of the irradiation ten years after Project Pandora began. Before that, information had been parceled out on a strict "need to know" basis, which excluded most employees at the compound. Due to secrecy, and probably reports like Dr. Zaret's, Jack Anderson speculated that the CIA was trying to cover up a Soviet effort at behavior modification through irradiation of the U.S. diplomats, and that the cover up was created to protect the CIA's own mind control secrets.

Finally, an unusually large number of illnesses were reported among the residents of the compound. U.S. Ambassador Walter Stoessel developed a rare blood disease similar to leukemia; he was suffering headaches and bleeding from the eyes. A source at the State Department informally admitted that excessive radiation had been leaking from his telephone; an American high frequency radio transmitter on the roof of the building had, when operating, induced high frequency signals well above the U.S. safety standard through the phones in the political section, as well as in lines to Stoessel's office. No doubt, National Security Agency or CIA electronic devices also contributed to the electromagnetic environment at the embassy, although values for these were never released, as they are secret. Stoessel was reported as telling his staff that the microwaves could cause leukemia, skin cancer, cataracts and various forms of emotional illness. White blood cell counts were estimated to be as high as 40% above normal in one third of the staff, and serious chromosome damage was uncovered.

The Soviets began research on biological effects of microwaves in 1953. A special laboratory was set up at the Institute of Hygiene and Occupational Diseases, Academy of Medical Sciences. Other labs were set up in the U.S.S.R. and in Eastern Europe that study both effects of microwaves and low frequency electromagnetic radiation. Years ago, in the halls of science, complaints could be heard that Soviet experiments regarding bio-effects couldn't be duplicated due to insufficient details in their scientific literature, although, according to one DOD official, 75% of the U.S. papers on the subject carried insufficient parameters for duplication. Scientists even questioned, with McCarthy-like sentiments, whether the Soviets were attempting to frighten or disinform with false scientific reporting of bio-effects. It was unthinkable, according to cruder scientific theory, that non-thermal levels of microwaves could cause harm. Impetus for a study of such effects came not from concern for the public, but rather in the military and intelligence community's suspicion of the Soviets, and their equally strong interest in developing exploitable anti-personnel effects — an interest that continues unabated today.

The CIA and DOD "security" concerns metamorphosized into research and development of invisible weapons capable of impacting on health and psychological processes. In fact, due to the finding of startling effects, DARPA's security became even tighter, and a new code name — "Bizarre" — was assigned to the project.

Scientist Allen Frey of Randomline, Inc. was always more interested in low intensity microwave hazards: thermal effects were known. During

Project Pandora, the Navy funded such projects of his, as how to use low average power intensities, to: induce heart seizures; create leaks in the blood brain barrier, which would allow neurotoxins in the blood to cross and cause neurological damage or behavioral disorders; and how to produce auditory hallucinations or microwave hearing, during which the person can hear tones that seem to be coming from within the head or from directly behind it.

In 1976, the Defense Intelligence Agency (DIA) released a report in which they attributed the results of Dr. Frey's studies to the Soviets. According to Dr. Frey, who acknowledges that his work was misattributed, he had thought up the projects himself. The DIA, but not the CIA, is allowed to use "mirror imaging" and "net assessment" in their reports, ie., respectively, the attribution of one's own motives and weapons capabilities to "the other side," in this case, the Soviets. It follows, that there is nothing to prevent them from releasing a report prepared in this manner, and thus muddy the water of decision making, pervert public opinion, stoke up congressional funding or enlist the support of naive scientists to counter "the threat." There was strong concern over CIA disinformation abroad, leaking back to the home front, through the American press, but apparently the DIA, at least on some issues, can dish it up with impunity.

The 1976 DIA report also credits the Soviets with other capabilities, stating, "Sounds and possibly even words which appear to be originating intercranially can be induced by signal modulations at very low power densities." Dr. Sharp, a Pandora researcher at Walter Reed Army Institute of Research, some of whose work was so secret that he couldn't tell his boss, conducted an experiment in which the human brain has received a message carried to it by microwave transmission. Sharp was able to recognize spoken words that were modulated on a microwave carrier frequency by an "audiogram," an analog of the words' sound vibrations, and carried into his head in a chamber where he sat.

Dr. James Lin of Wayne State University has written a book entitled *Microwave Auditory Effects and Applications.* It explores the possible mechanisms for the phenomenon, and discusses possibilities for the deaf, as persons with certain types of hearing loss can still hear pulsed microwaves (as tones or clicks and buzzes, if words aren't modulated on). Lin mentions the Sharp experiment and comments, "The capability of communicating directly with humans by pulsed microwaves is obviously not limited to the field of therapeutic medicine."

Dr. R.O. Becker, twice nominated for the Nobel prize for his health work in bio-electromagnetism, was more explicit in his concern over illicit government activity. He wrote of "obvious applications in covert operations designed to drive a target crazy with "voices." What is frightening is that words, transmitted via low density microwaves or radio frequencies, or by other covert methods, might be used to create influence. For instance, according to a 1984 U.S. House of Representatives report, a large number of stores throughout the country use high frequency transmitted words (above the range of human hearing) to discourage shoplifting. Stealing is reported to be reduced by as much as 80% in some cases. Surely, the CIA and military haven't overlooked such useful technology.

Dr. Frey also did experiments on reduction of aggression. Rats who were accustomed to fighting viciously when their tails were pinched, accepted the pinching with relative passivity when irradiated with pulsed microwaves in the ultra high frequency rage (UHF) at a power density of less than 1,000 microwatts/cm^2. He has also done low intensity microwave experiments degrading motor coordination and balance. When asked about weapons applications of his work, he answered by referring to himself as "just a biological theorist," and his work for the Navy, "basic medical research."

Lies Before Congress

In 1976, George H. Heilmeier, director of Defense Advanced Research Projects Agency (DARPA) responded to a mailgram to President Ford from Don Johnson of Oakland, paraphrasing Johnson's concern, and assuring him that the DARPA sponsored Army/Navy Pandora experiments were "never directed at the use of microwaves as a surveillance tool, nor in a weapons concept." Don Johnson lingered in the memory of one DOD official who sponsored microwave research in the 1970s. Johnson was enigmatically described as "brilliant ... schizophrenic ... he knew too much ... a former mental patient ... buildings where work was done." (Scientists who have disagreed with the DOD on health effects of microwaves and on the U.S. exposure standard, have received scant more respect and have had their funding cut.)

The next year, Heilmeier elaborated in a written response to an inquiry before Congress. "... This agency [DARPA] is not aware of any research projects, classified or unclassified, conducted under the auspices of the Defense Department, now ongoing, or in the past, which would have probed possibilities of utilizing microwave radiation in a form of what is popularly known as 'mind control.' We do not foresee the development, by DARPA of weapons using microwaves and actively being directed toward altering nervous system function or behavior. Neither are we aware of any of our own forces... developing such weapons..."

Finally, memoranda were released that rendered the goals of Pandora transparent. Richard Cesaro, initiator of Pandora and director of DARPA's Advanced Sensor program, justified the project in that "little or no work has been done in investigation of the subtle behavioral changes which may be evolved by a low-level electromagnetic field." Researchers had long ago established that direct stimulus of the brain could alter behavior. The question raised by radio frequencies — microwaves or radio frequencies of the UHF or VHF band — was whether the electromagnetic could have a similar effect at very low levels. Pandora's initial goal: to discover whether a carefully constructed microwave signal could control the mind. In the context of long term, low-level effects: Cesaro felt that central nervous system effects could be important, and urged their study "for potential weapons applications." After testing a low-level modulated microwave signal on a chimpanzee, and within approximately a week causing stark performance decrements and behavioral disorganization, Cesaro wrote, "the potential of exerting a degree of control on human behavior by low-level microwaves seems to exist." On the basis of the primate study, extensive discussions took place and plans were made to extend the studies to humans.

According to a former DOD security analyst, one such microwave experiment with human subjects took place at Lorton Prison in the early 1970s. He said that such research (in a weapons context) has occurred on behavioral effects of microwaves since 1976. He also asked, "Why are you so concerned about then? What about now? They can call anyone a terrorist. Who are they using it on now?"

Behavioral Effects

In June, 1970, a government think tank, Rand Corporation, published a report by R.J. MacGregor, entitled "A Brief Survey of Literature Relating to Influence of Low Intensity Microwaves on Nervous Function." After noting that the U.S. microwave guideline in effect in 1970 for the public, 10,000 microwatts/^{2} (now the industrial and military "guideline"), is proscribed from consideration of the rate that thermal effects are dissipated, the author, a specialist in modeling neural networks, states that scientific studies have consistently shown that humans exhibit behavioral disturbances when subjected to non-thermal levels of microwaves, well below this level. The symptoms that MacGregor lists for those humans exposed more or less regularly at work or in the living environment are insomnia, irritability, loss of memory, fatigue, headache, tremor, hallucination, autonomic disorders and disturbed sensory functioning. He reports that swelling and distention of nerve cells have been produced at intensities as low as 1,000 microwatts/cm^2 (the current U.S. guideline for the public). In a companion Rand paper, June, 1970, entitled "A Direct Mechanism for the Direct Influence of Microwave Radiation on Neuroelectric Function," MacGregor sets forth the idea that the electrical component of microwave radiation induces transmembrane potentials in nerve cells and thereby disturbs nervous function and behavior. Microwaves penetrate and are absorbed more deeply so that they can produce a direct effect on the central nervous system. With smaller wave lengths the principal absorption occurs near the body surface and causes peripheral or "lower" nervous system effects.

Dr. Milton Zaret who analyzed neurological effects for the CIA during Project Pandora (he is now one of the few doctors willing to take the government on by testifying on behalf of plaintiffs filing claims for microwave health damage), wrote that, "receptors of the brain are susceptible and react to extremely low intensities of microwave irradiation if this is delivered in accordance with appropriate "coding." Coding is reported to be influenced by the character of the signal so as to be a function, for example, of the shape and amplitude of the pulse or waveform.

Dr. Ross Adey, formerly of the Brain Research Center at University of Southern California, Los Angeles, now at Loma Linda University Medical School, Loma Linda, California, was among the first of the Pandora researchers. His work is more precise in inducing specific behavior, rather than merely causing disorganization or decrements in performance — that is, apart from his studies on inducing calcium efflux in brain tissue, which causes interference with the functioning of the brain and is one basis of "confusion weaponry."

More specifically, Adey's thesis is that if the electroencephalogram (EEG) has informational significance, one can induce behavioral changes if one imposes environmental fields that look like EEG. During Adey's career, he has correlated a wide variety of behavioral states with EEG, including emotional states (e.g., stress in hostile questioning), increments of decision making and conditioning, correct versus incorrect performance, etc., and he has imposed electromagnetic fields that look like EEG, which has resulted in altered EEG and behavior.

In published accounts of Adey's work, he has shown that it is possible to apply low biologic frequencies by using a radio frequency carrier modulated at specific brain frequencies. He demonstrated that if the biological modulation on the carrier frequency is close to frequencies in the natural EEG of the subject, it will reinforce or increase the number of manifestations of the imposed rhythms, and modulate behavior.

The conditioning paradigm: animals were trained through aversion to produce specific brain wave rhythms; animals trained in a field with the same rhythm amplitude modulated on it, differed significantly from control animals in both accuracy and resistance to extinction (at least 50 days versus 10 in the controls). When the fields were used on untrained animals, occurrence of the applied rhythm increased in the animals' EEG.

Dr. Adey is an accomplished scientist, which leads one to believe the significance of this experiment goes beyond mere reinforcement of the animal's brain waves. Did the rhythms that he chose to apply have special significance with relation to information processing or conditioning? The 4.5 theta rhythm that he applied was the natural reoccurring frequency that he had measured in the hippocampus during a phase of avoidance learning. The hippocampus, as Adey wrote in an earlier paper, "... involves neural processes connected with consolidation of memory traces. It relates closely to the need for focusing attention, and the degree to which recapitulation of past experience is imposed." One might add, to ensure survival.

Does it follow that an EEG modulated carrier frequency can be used to enhance human avoidance learning? You bet, provided the same careful procedures are followed with humans as were with animals, the same result would accrue. Recall again the goals of Pandora — to discover whether a carefully constructed electromagnetic signal could direct the mind.

The obvious question becomes, how many and with how much accuracy can behavioral states or "frames of mind" be intentionally imposed, that is, apart from the certain technological capability to promote disorganization and degradation of perception and performance through use of the fields.In fact, many components of learning or conditioning including affect (i.e., "feeling" or emotional states) can be imposed through use of the fields from a distance. e.g., behavioral arousal, orienting reflex, subliminal stress (alarm reaction without realization of the contextual significance), so-called levels of consciousness, inhibition of cerebral functions, which would render one more susceptible to suggestion or influence, and so on. All components necessary to produce behavioral conditioning, including ways to provide contextual significance, can be applied from a distance (i.e., without direct brain contact, as was necessary in older behavior modification experiments.)

Another indication that the government entertained notions of behavior control through use of fields and sound, is a 1974 research proposal by J.F. Schapitz. To test his theory, his plan was to record EEG correlates induced by various drugs, and then to modulate these biological frequencies on a microwave carrier. Could the same behavioral states be produced by imposing these brain wave frequencies on human subjects? His plan went further and included inducing hyptonic states and using words modulated on a microwave carrier frequency to attempt to covertly condition subjects to perform various acts. The plan as released (through the Freedom of Information Act) seems less part of a careful recipe for influence than Adey's and other DOD scientists' work, and may have been released to mislead by lending an "information beam" science fiction-like quality to the work.

The end of Project Pandora may have signified the end of research into the cause of effects of the varying frequencies registered at the American embassy in Moscow — some known to be due to CIA and National Security Agency equipment, but interest in microwave and biological frequency weapons did not wane. Indeed, there are indications of applications. As we have seen, research that began in response to a security concern, transformed almost overnight into a search for weapons applications, while cloaked in disinformation about the Soviets. What types of weapons?

There Are Three Possibilities:

(1) That microwaves, perhaps modulated with low biological frequencies, are used from a distance to cause performance decrements and disorganization by interfering with neuro-electric function; or by causing central nervous system effects, subjective feelings of ill health, or health syndrome associated with periodic exposures at intensities below 10,000 microwatts/cm^2;

(2) That microwaves are used to create organ specific effects, e.g., tissues with less blood circulation, like the gall bladder, lens of the eye, etc., can compensate less to increased heating; heart disfunctions can be caused; lesions or necrosis of internal tissues can be induced without a subject necessarily feeling heat, and symptoms might manifest later, at certain frequencies, slight heating or "hot spots" can be created at the center of the head; there is an ongoing Navy contract to find parameters to disrupt human metabolic functions; or

(3) That they are used in an interdisciplinary approach to remote conditioning by creating information processing effects, as Dr. Adey's work shows, or to induce "feeling" or "emotional" elements of cognition, such as excitatory reactions, subliminal stress, behavioral arousal, enhanced suggestibility by inhibition of higher functions, or various other EEG or behavioral effects. There are strong indications that microwaves have been used to cause the decrements. There is no question but that the U.S. military and the CIA know the behavioral or psychoactive

significance of applied biological rhythms and other frequencies, as this was part of the thrust of their work during Pandora. Inducing emotion or feelings through use of electromagnetic fields, and then synchronizing the feelings with words (symbolic of ideas) would be an effective way to induce preferences or attitude change, because it would mirror natural thought processes. The question seems less whether conditioning through use of covert technology is possible, than whether there has been a policy choice to use it. If the results of their research are used as part of a system that can condition behavioral responses from a distance, it is a secret that they hold close like a baby.

Richard Helms wrote of such a system in the mid-1960s while he was CIA Plans Director. He spoke of "sophisticated approaches to the 'coding' of information for transmittal to population targets in the 'battle for the minds of men' ..." and of "an approach integrating biological, social and physical-mathematical research in attempts ... to control behavior." He found particularly notable, "use of modern information theory, automata theory, and feedback concepts ... for a technology for controlling behavior ... using information inputs as causative agents." Due to Project Pandora, it is now known that applied biological (and other) frequencies can also be used as direct "information inputs" (e.g., of feeling or emotion) and to reinforce brain rhythms associated with conditioning and information processing. One way to get such a signal into a human may be through use of a high frequency carrier frequency. Results of research into information processing, unconscious processes, decision making, memory processes and evoked brain potentials would likely be exploited or integrated in an interdisciplinary system.

Covert technological influence is not so foreign to the American way of life as one may think. It was reported in a 1984 U.S. House of Representatives hearing that high frequency audio transmissions are applied, for instance, in some department stores to prevent theft (one East Coast department store chain was reported to have saved $600,000 over a nine-month period), and in some grocery stores with the result that employee induced cash shortages significantly decreased and employees are better mannered. In other words, as Helms wrote of, verbal messages are delivered at frequencies above human hearing. Technology for commercial applications is relatively sophisticated (one studio uses a "layered" approach and 31 channels in preparing tapes; some employ a "dual coding" approach, integrating scientific knowledge of information processing modes of the two brain hemispheres, and others use techniques where a consumer is spoken to as a three year old child.) There is no U.S. law specifically regulating these types of transmission (over radio and TV a Federal Communication Commission "catch all" provision might apply). If industry uses indetectable audio transmissions to meet security concerns, it seems that the military and CIA would exploit the same technology and would have developed much more sophisticated technology for applications. The public's conception of "subliminals" is naive compared to capabilities.

The military has studied and considered for usefulness in a warfare and psychological warfare context a wide range of biological or pharmacological substances. In the memo referred to above, Helms wrote that the U.S. is five years ahead of the Soviets in pharmacological agents producing behavioral effects. Some of these substances would increase susceptibility to influence if incorporated in the multidisciplinary approach he wrote of.

A side effect of lowered resistance to sub-threshold stimulus might be that some would become aware of illicit influence (even under normal circumstances there is a wide variation in sensitivity among individuals to sub-threshold stimulus; normal individuals whom psychology terms "reducers" are much more sensitive in this way; actually, most schizophrenics are extreme reducers, and therefore, much more aware of stimulus that others aren't cognizant of). Convenient to the agencies involved in covert influence, is that among primary symptoms of schizophrenia or mental illness are ideas that one is being influenced by "transmissions" (e.g. radio frequencies), "voices" or even telepathy; unless complaints about covert psychological weapons are well organized, they would tend to be discounted as indicative of mental imbalance.

There are many ways to create temporary or permanent states that increase receptivity to suggestion and/or conditioning. It is interesting to note that scientific studies have correlated exposure to electromagnetic fields alone with mental hospital admissions and worsening of symptoms of mental patients, even as an etiological factor in the onset of mental illness. (A marker disease for exposure to microwaves is damage behind the lens of the eye; a disproportionate number of persons so damaged also suffer from mental disease or neurological impairment.)

Specific Targets

Weapons against whom? Safe to say, in order to enlist the aid of scientists, the military and CIA would act true to form, that is, to motivate and overcome reluctance due to dictates of conscience, they would evoke a serious security risk during initial phases of development. In fact, on the "unclassified" face of it, a number of reports have openly suggested use of "microwaves" against "terrorists."

Los Alamos National Laboratory, now under supervision of University of California, prepared a report for Federal Emergency Management

Agency (FEMA) setting forth that use of microwave radiation on terrorists could kill them, stun them or at least modify their behavior by changing their "perceptions." At this point the cloak is donned, and the report continues: "There are reports of Eurasian communist countries performing research with combined fields of signals from several different microwave frequencies to produce at least perceptual distortions in humans."

Cable News Network recently aired a report on electromagnetic weapons and showed an official document that was a contingency plan to use electromagnetic weapons against terrorists. It wasn't made clear who the terrorists were or what the contingency was. Prior to the news show, however, reports had surfaced, the source a DOD medical engineer, that in the content of conditioning, microwaves and other modalities had regularly been used against Palestinians.

Greenham Common

When DOD develops a weapon it can be said with certainty that it will be tested and, if possible, where it would be useful to meet their goals. Women peace activists have kept an ongoing vigil at the periphery of the U.S. Air Force base at Greenham in England since 1981. They are protesting build-up of nuclear weapons. The U.S. Cruise missiles, which are nuclear warheads small enough to be mounted on the back of a truck called a launcher vehicle, arrived at the base in March, 1984. Since then the women in the encampment and members of the Cuisewatch network have ensured that when the launcher vehicle and its convoy are taken out into the British countryside, the "dispersal exercises" aren't as secret as the military intended them to be. The women of the network, non-violent activists, have been subjected to intense harassment in an effort to be rid of their presence.

In the Fall of 1984, things changed dramatically; many, if not most of the women began suffering illness; and, simultaneously, the massive police and military presence at the base virtually disappeared, and new and different antenna were installed at the base. In a report prepared by Rosalie Bertell, commissioner for International Commission of Health Professionals for Human Rights, a non-governmental organization based in Geneva, Switzerland, the unusual patterns of illness ranged from "severe headaches, drowsiness, menstrual bleeding at abnormal times or post-menopausal, to bouts of temporary paralysis, faulty speech coordination and in one case apparent circulatory failure requiring hospitalization."

Other symptoms documented by peace activist Kim Bealy, who coordinates investigations into reports of illness at specific places around the base, included; vertigo, retinal bleeding, burnt face (even at night), nausea, sleep disturbances and palpitations. Psychological symptoms included lack of concentration, disorientation, loss of memory, irritability and a sense of panic in non-panic situations. The symptoms have virtually all been associated in medical literature with exposure to microwaves and most listed can be induced through low intensity or non-thermal exposures. *(Editor's note: such devices were utilized as "psychological deterrents" during the siege of the Branch Davidian compound at Waco.)*

Measurements were taken around the base by members of Electronics for Peace and by others. Strong signals, up to one hundred times the normal background level were detected on a number of occasions. In fact, signals ten times stronger than those felt to be emanating from normal base transmitting systems were found.

The strongest signals generally appeared in the areas where the women said that they suffered ill effects. For instance, they were found to cover the women's encampment near the "green gate" (gates to the base are designated by color), but stopped abruptly at the edge of the road leading to the gate. The strength of the signals were also found to reflect the activity of the women: e.g., they increased rapidly when the women started a demonstration. Visitors to the encampment, both men and women, reported experiencing the same types of symptoms and the same pattern of variation as the Greenham women.

In a review prepared by National Bureau of Standards, Law Enforcement Standards Laboratory, for Nuclear Defense Agency, Intelligence and Security Directorate, use of low intensity microwaves was considered for application as a "psychological deterrent." The report stated, "...microwave radiation has frequently been cited as being responsible for non-thermal effects in integrated central nervous system activity. The behavioral consequences most frequently reported have been disability, listlessness and increased irritability." The report fails to mention just as frequently cited low intensity microwave health effects as chromosome damage; congenital birth defects; autonomic nervous system disregulation, including disruption of bio-cycles; impaired immune function; brain damage and other neurological abnormalities, including leaks in the blood brain barrier and depletion of some neurotransmitters; among a host of other health impairments. As activist Kim Bealy put it, "It would now appear that we are protecting the missiles by killing people slowly."

It is not necessary that the transmission take place from equipment in the vicinity of a target (although the Greenham women seemed to be suffering from transmissions made from within the base.) Propagation of microwaves has been very well studied and is very sophisticated, e.g., a two inch beam can be sent from a satellite, point to point, to a receiving dish on earth; and, it was reported in 1978, that the CIA had a program called Operation Pique, which included bouncing radio signals or microwaves off of the ionosphere to affect the mental functions of people in selected areas, including Eastern European nuclear installations.

In the U.S. at this time, there is no legally enforceable microwave standard. There never has been an enforceable standard for the public or the workplace. Microwaves at intensities within the suggested "guideline" have finally been shown, even by U.S. research, to cause health damage.

References

Adey, W. Ross, "Neurophysiologic Effects of Radiofrequency and Microwave Radiation," *Bulletin of the New York Academy of Medicine,* V.55, #11, December, 1979; "The Influences of Impressed Electrical Fields at EEG Frequencies on Brain and Behavior," in *Behavior and Brain Electrical Activity,* Burch, N. and Altshuler, H.I., eds., Plenum Press, 1975; "Effects of Modulated Very High Frequency Fields on Specific Brain Rhythms in Cats," *Brain Research,* V.58., 1973; "Spectral Analysis of Low Frequency Components in the Electrical Activity of the Hippocampus During Learning," *Electroencephalography and Clinical Neurophysiology,* V.23, 1967.

Annals of New York Academy of Sciences, V. 247, February, 1975.

Bealy, Kim, "Electromagnetic Pollution: A Little Known Health Hazard, A New Means of Control?," Preliminary Report, Greenham Common Women's Peace Camp, Inlands House, Southbourne, Emsworth, Hants, P0108JH.

Becker, Robert O., *The Body Electric,* William Morrow and Company, Inc. 1985.

Bowart, Walter, *Operation Mind Control,* Dell Publishing, 1978.

Brodeur, Paul, *The Zapping of America,* W.W. Norton and Co, 1977.

Frey, Allan, "Behavioral Biophysics," *Psychological Bulletin,* V.65, #5, 1965; "Human Auditory System Response in Modulated Electromagnetic Energy," *Journal of Applied Physiology,* V.17, #4, 1962; "Neural Function and Behavior: Defining to Relationship," *Annals of the New York Academy of Sciences,* V.247, February, 1975; "Exposure to RF Electromagnetic Energy Decreases Aggressive Behavior," *Biolectromagnetics,* V.12, 1986.

Harvey, J., Ickes, W., Kidd, R., *New Directions in Attribution Research,* V.2, John Wiley and Sons, 1978.

ISN News, "Reproductive Hazards From Video Display Terminals," Planetary Association for Clear Energy, 1985.

Koslov, Sam, *Bridging the Gap, in Nonlinear Electrodynamics in Biological Systems,* Adey, W.R. and Lawrence, A.F., eds., Plenum Press, 1983.

Kramer, J. and Maguire, P., Psychological Deterrents in Nuclear Theft, National Bureau of Standards for Intelligence and Security Directorate, Defense Nuclear Agency, NBSIR 76-1007, March, 1976.

Lapinsky, G. and Goodman, C., *Psychological Deterrents to Nuclear Theft: An Updated Literature Review and Bibliography,* Center for Consumer Technology, National Bureau of Standards for Surety and Operations Directorate, Defense Nuclear Agency, NBSIR 80-2038, June, 1980.

McAuliffe, Kathleen, "The Mind Fields," *Omni* magazine, February, 1985

MacGregor, R.J., "A Brief Survey of Literature Relating to Influence of Low Intensity Microwaves on Nervous Function," Rand Report, R-4397, 1970; "A Direct Mechanism for the Influence of Microwave Radiation on Neuroelectric Potentials," Rand Corporation, P-4398, 1970.

Marha, Karel, Microwave Radiation Standards in Eastern Europe, IEEE Transactions on Microwave Theory and Techniques, V.MTT-19, #2, February, 1971.

Regna, Joseph, "Microwaves Versus Hope," *Science for the People,* V.19., #5, September/October 1987.

Rosenfeld, Sam and Anne, "The Roots of Individuality: Brain Waves and Perception," Mental Health Studies and Reports Branch, National Institute of Mental Health, October, 1975.

Steneck, Nicholas, *The Microwave Debate,* MIT Press, 1984.

Subliminal Communication Technology, House of Representatives, Committee on Science and Technology, Subcommittee on Transportation, Aviation and Materials, 1984.

World Health Organization, Environmental Health Criteria 16, Radiofrequency and Microwaves, Geneva, Switzerland, 1981.

Zaret, Milton, "Human Injury Relatable to Nonionizing Radiation," IREE-ERDA Symposium — "The Biological Effects of Electromagnetic Radiation," 1978.

Is Paranoia A Form of Awareness?

Kerry W. Thornley

In the spring of 1959 I was stationed at an annex of El Toro Marine Base in California. Another Marine in that unit was Lee Harvey Oswald. We became acquainted.

Then in June of that year I shipped out for a tour of duty at the Naval Air Station in Atsugi, Japan, where Oswald served previous to our time together at El Toro.

My ambition all along was to become a novelist, and I had decided to write a book based upon my overseas experience in the military. That autumn I read in the newspaper that Lee Oswald had, upon being discharged, gone to Moscow and applied for Soviet citizenship. By then I'd decided to call my novel about peace-time Marines in the Far East *The Idle Warriors,* and Oswald's dramatic act inspired me to center the plot around a character based on him.

Convinced that I understood his reasons for becoming disillusioned with the United States and turning to Marxism, feeling they were similar to my own, I at first intended to write "a poor man's Ugly American" sharply critical of U.S. imperialism characterized by the bungling of the Eisenhower era.

Unfortunately for the clarity of my novel's political theme, my own ideology shifted — as a result of reading Ayn Rand's polemical novel, *Atlas Shrugged* — aboard ship on my way back to the States. Discharged from the Marines immediately thereafter, I entered civilian life convinced of the efficacy of laissez-faire capitalism.

My young friend, Greg Hill, and I then traveled from our home town of Whittier, California, to the New Orleans French Quarter, where I continued work on the first draft of *The Idle Warriors.* There I met a man I am belatedly but firmly persuaded played a central role in organizing the assassination of President John F. Kennedy, for which I am equally certain Lee Harvey Oswald was framed.

During most of my life I have been inclined to reject conspiracy theories of history. Notwithstanding my willingness to admit that conspiracies exist, I felt that a grasp of political events depended upon an understanding of the power of ideas. In my view, conspiracies were insignificant. My tendency was to challenge the motives of conspiracy buffs when I did not, as was more often the case, question their mental health.

Balancing my occasional doubts was a fear of becoming paranoid. When Oswald was accused of assassinating Kennedy, my first hunch was that he was innocent and had been blamed in a misunderstanding that would soon be cleared up. When the media continued to insist there was ample evidence that Oswald, and Oswald alone, shot the President I quickly changed my mind.

Two years later, when a Warren Report critic confronted me with the many discrepancies between the conclusions of the Warren Commission and the testimony and exhibits contained in the Twenty-six Volumes, I could no longer hide from myself the probability that either Lee Oswald was innocent or he had not acted alone.Yet even then I did not want to think an elaborate conspiracy was involved. Maybe Lyndon Johnson or some of his Texas friends had arranged to kill Kennedy and perhaps it had not occurred to the Warren Commission to probe that possibility. A more complicated theory would seem paranoid.Above all else, I did not want to seem paranoid.

One year elapsed between the time I began doubting the lone-assassin theory and the beginning of tribulations in my own life suffered at the hands of a man most journalists insisted was a paranoid. First, District Attorney Jim Garrison made a bizarre attempt to recruit me as a witness for the prosecution in his probe of a New Orleans-based conspiracy to assassinate John Kennedy. When I expressed my unwillingness to cooperate, he accused me of working for the CIA and summoned me to appear before the grand jury.

After asking me what seemed like a lot of irrelevant questions, he charged me with perjury for denying, truthfully, that I had met with Lee Harvey Oswald in New Orleans during the months previous to the assassination. I had not seen Oswald in person, nor had I communicated with him in any other way, since June of 1959 — at the latest.

Yet Garrison struck me as sincere. Moreover, his assistants showered me with any number of disturbing coincidences linking me to his assassination theory. I was at a loss to explain them, except in light of the notion that Jim Garrison's conspiracy theory was an elaborate paranoid construction.

This experience forced me to examine the evidence surrounding the events in Dallas more carefully than ever before. As a result, I became convinced not only that Lee Harvey Oswald had not acted alone but, moreover, that he was not even on the sixth floor of the Texas School Book Depository when the shots that killed Kennedy were fired. Yet, because I also had to cope with Jim Garrison's wild and irresponsible charges, I also became more certain than ever that paranoia was by far more dangerous than any actual conspiracy that might, from time to time, sabotage the normal functioning of history.

In other words, if conspiracies were significantly dangerous, it was because they tended to spawn paranoia.When Jim Garrison ultimately neglected to bring me to trial, I took it as a tacit admission he had at last perceived the error of his ways.

Meanwhile, in the realm of public affairs I busied myself with other concerns. Of all newsworthy events, the John Kennedy murder seemed to me the most boring. For reasons I could not clearly identify at the time, I was to find the murder of Hollywood actress Sharon Tate far more disturbing. When I read *The Family* by Ed Sanders (E.P. Dutton, 1971) my uneasiness increased. Charles Manson was not typical of the hip counter-culture I had gradually come to consider my own, after the appeal of Ayn Rand's philosophy diminished in my eyes. Nevertheless, something about him and his followers seemed far more menacing and important than I could justify in terms of a few sensationally gory killings. As if warned in a forgotten nightmare, I felt that I had expected someone like Manson to appear on the scene. All that I read about him confirmed this eerie, elusive anxiety.

Besides that, much like Jim Garrison, Charles Manson was a paranoid. Nowhere is this more evident than on page 129 of *The Family,* where he is quoted as saying: "Christ on the cross, the coyote in the desert — it's the same thing, man. The coyote is beautiful. He moves through the desert delicately, aware of everything, looking around. He hears every sound, smells every smell, sees everything that moves. He's always in a state of total paranoia and total paranoia is total awareness. You can learn from the coyote just like you learn from a child. A baby is born into the world in a state of fear. Total paranoia and awareness..." Once again I was grappling with the riddle of a man who appeared to act on the basis of a supreme confidence in the validity of his own delusions.

Escalation of the Vietnam war had radicalized me, once again, politically. So Charlie Manson's affinity for right-wing organizations was something else that alarmed me. Most particularly I was spooked by allegations about links between Manson's people and the Process Church. For when I had returned to New Orleans in order to clear myself, unsuccessfully, of Jim Garrison's suspicions, I encountered the Process Church there — in circumstances giving me ample reason to suspect it was at least partially involved in framing me.

So as to avoid the mistakes of people like Garrison and Manson, it seemed essential to study psychology. That was another subject I found more fascinating than conspiracy theories about the John Kennedy assassination. Already acquainted with Freud and other pioneers of psychoanalysis, I began devoting my attention to more recent trends. That the older theories were unconsciously tainted with reactionary ideology was frequently mentioned in my political readings.

In 1972 I discovered a psychology book that dovetailed beautifully with my political opinions, by then both anarchist and left of center. A collection of readings compiled by Jerome Agel and The Radical Therapist newspaper staff, *The Radical Therapist* anthology found the roots of nearly all neurosis and psychosis outside the individual, lodged firmly and visibly in the authoritarian class structure of society. As a sociology major at Georgia State University I had already begun to suspect as much.

There was only one hitch, best summed up in "The Radical Psychiatry Manifesto" by Claude Steiner: "Paranoia is a state of heightened awareness. Most people are persecuted beyond their wildest delusions."

I wondered if that could be true. Certainly it was not without personal relevance, in terms of my own very unsatisfactory adjustment to the John F. Kennedy murder mystery. Perpetually fearing that my radical friends would think I was a CIA agent, because of what Garrison had said, and yet afraid that I would become paranoid if I delved into the unanswered questions about Oswald too deeply, I walked an uncomfortably narrow line.

In *The Farther Reaches of Human Nature* by Abraham Maslow (Penguin Books, 1971) there appears the following: "There is still another psychological process that I have run across in my explorations of failure to actualize the self. This evasion of growth can also be set in motion by a fear of paranoia." Although I was not to read those particular words until many years later, I was versed enough in modern literature of psychology to realize that traditional Freudian notions of paranoid schizophrenia and classical paranoia were under attack by more than just wild-eyed radicals. One of my textbooks in school contained a sociological study of a man who was committed for symptoms of paranoia; it demonstrated that, due to his rather unpleasant personality, he was actually being secretly harassed by his co-workers who, upon being interviewed, admitted as much.

At that point I took a long second look at the origins of my own fears of paranoia.

What popularized that brand of psychosis for my generation was the film, *The Caine Mutiny,* with Humphrey Bogart clicking his steel marbles compulsively, saying, "I kid you not," and making a fool of himself over a few stolen scoops of ice cream.

Another French Quarter writer who worked in a record store next to the Bourbon House, where I ate and drank and socialized when I lived in New Orleans, possessed a book about color psychology that said brown was the favorite color of most paranoids. He added to my information that most novelists tended toward paranoia, something about which we had both laughed a little nervously.

Another Quarterite, a painter named Loy Ann Camp who was among my closest friends, had a textbook from her days in nursing school that said paranoia was related to fear of latent homosexuality. Since my reason for joining the Marines earlier had been to prove to myself that I was a man in every sense, I didn't find that information comforting either.

From additional sources I gathered that paranoids were quite undesirable cranks who took to sitting in corners stroking their chins and observing those around them with sidelong glances. Senator Joseph McCarthy was said to have been a paranoid as was Robert Welch, founder of the John Birch Society. In fact, all the really famous paranoids seemed to be anti-Communist — a consideration that did not sit well with my own rational capitalist philosophy of those days. Paranoids, in addition to all the other problems they were causing, were giving my politics a bad name with outlandish notions like Welch's charge that grandfatherly old Ike was "a conscious agent of the Communist conspiracy" and his grandiose ambition to impeach Earl Warren from the Supreme Court.

Intellectual respectability required mental health, and it was becoming evident to me by then that mental health consisted of trusting everyone about everything as much as possible — and, for good measure, poking fun at anyone who didn't. Especially to be trusted were the mass media, whose owners and personnel were not to be regarded as minions of the Establishment because, as they themselves used to attest with confidence, there was no Establishment in the United States of America. Only foreigners and paranoids believed that there were.

Intellectualizing and joking about paranoia was a favorite pastime of post-Beatnik, pre-Hippie Bohemian America — for reasons that were undoubtedly the result of coincidence, at least among individuals who did not want their sanity called into question.

A habitue of the Bourbon House, Chris Lanham, once entertained us with the diabolical theory that the psychological classification of paranoia had been developed by conspirators for the purpose of discrediting anyone bent on exposing them. When his friend, Jack Burnside, suggested sharing this hilariously evil notion with a wandering conspiracy buff we called Crazy David -- because he thought people like the Rockefellers and DuPonts controlled the government — we told Jack the joke had gone far enough. Crazy David might actually believe him. And, as everybody knew, paranoids who received reinforcement for their delusions could become very dangerous.

In retrospect, I realized that Crazy David's views about who rules America did not seem especially insane. By 1972, my own analysis resembled it in many essential respects.

Then came Watergate.

Again my attention was absorbed by a public event that did not seem related to the John Kennedy assassination. That a reactionary warmonger like Nixon might be unceremoniously ejected from the White House for crimes that even Conservatives would find shocking seemed almost too good to be true. Eagerly, I followed the scandal, becoming more and more aware at the same time that conspiracies were a fact of political reality, even in America.

During the summer of 1973 I was in New York City, visiting my old friend Greg Hill, who in years past had accompanied me to New Orleans and lived as my roommate there for a few months. At a folk concert in Washington Square I was approached by a Yippie who wanted to sell me the latest issue of *The Yipster Times* for a quarter. A glance at the headline and cover photos convinced me it was worth the price.

What I found there has since been published in an excellent book by A.J. Weberman and Michael Canfield called *Coup d'Etat In America.* Convincing photographic evidence tends to establish that Watergate burglars E. Howard Hunt and Frank Sturgis were in the immediate vicinity of Dealy Plaza in Dallas the day John Kennedy was shot. That possibility brought to mind something I had almost managed to happily forget. A decade earlier in New Orleans I had discussed, among other things, the idea of assassinating President Kennedy with a man who in many unsettling respects bore a resemblance to the members of the Watergate break-in team. As I was to say to Weberman in a letter two years later, this man was "a plumbers type of guy."

Although he even looked something like pictures of E. Howard Hunt, his bald head diminished any direct physical similarity to that now-famous spy. More a matter of style than anything else seemed pertinent then. Also relevant were links between the CIA and organized crime that were coming to light in the wake of the Watergate revelations. For the man I spoke to used to let on that he was somehow associated with New Orleans mobster Carlos Marcello.

Already I had been suspecting tie-ins between Watergate and the J.F.K. murder because both crimes seemed connected to the Southern Rim or Cowboy faction of the American Establishment — the so-called military-industrial complex. I had, however, been bending over backwards not to jump to conclusions. Something about those photos of that man *The Yipster Times* argued was Edward Howard Hunt made such restraint harder. What, exactly, it might be continued to elude me.

Something else occurred that same summer that wore at my ability to keep believing this is the least conspiratorial of all possible worlds. Again, it was nagging rather than sensational.

After I wrote an article published in Atlanta's underground paper, *The Great Speckled Bird,* titled "Did the Plumbers Plug J.F.K., Too?" — I got two unusual phone calls.

First was a male voice imitating the sounds of a speeded-up tape recorder or a gibberish-talking cartoon character. Ten years earlier a Quarterite named Roger Lovin and I used to address one another in the Bourbon House with identical noises to those I was now hearing on the other end of the line, as an inside joke intended to freak out strangers. This time I simply replied with a word or two of bewilderment, and the caller hung up.

Within seconds, the phone rang again. Now a male voice — not Roger's — said very clearly, "Kerry, do you know who this is?" When I answered in the negative, he said, "Good!" — and again the caller hung up.

Enough similarity existed between that voice on the phone and the voice of the man I had talked to all those years earlier about assassinating John F. Kennedy, that I became increasingly uncomfortable with the idea of keeping my suspicions to myself much longer.

I nevertheless persisted in my silence for more than another year. That was more than a little uncharacteristic of me, to consciously nurture something without talking or at least writing of it. But, while I was no longer as worried about going paranoid as in years past, I remained concerned that others would think me paranoid.

Then, too, there was another thing. This suspect of mine more than once had claimed a connection with the Mafia. Even if he was innocent of assassination, were I to accuse him in public, he might have what he considered a good motive for getting me killed. Until I was certain of his guilt, I didn't want to open my mouth.

Meanwhile, I continued to think about the phone calls. Was the caller trying to determine indirectly whether or not I'd spoken recently with Roger Lovin? Could Roger have known something that I happened to guess in my Bird article?

As a matter of fact it was not so long before that Roger Lovin had called me, making an appointment to come by the house while he was in town for a visit. On the day of his expected arrival, the woman I was living with and I went out for a brief interval. We returned to find all her jewelry missing, and Roger never showed up. I recalled that when I had known him in New Orleans, in the same year Kennedy was assassinated, his principal reputation was that of a talented con-artist.

I shrugged. That wasn't much to go on.

Soon there was enough information in the news about assassination plots involving organized crime to draw my attention in that direction. In February of 1975 I had begun making cramped, secretive notes about the mysterious bald-headed man I had known in New Orleans. For the first time since the assassination, the Establishment was expressing suspicions of conspiracy, pushing for a Congressional probe of the events in Dallas. Only recently I had been called by CBS and someone from *Reader's Digest* was even attempting to contact me. Expecting that before long I would be called before a Congressional committee to testify, I didn't want to divulge anything sensational until I could speak under oath.

Instead, I prepared — quietly. As soon as my notes were completed to the point where they told a coherent, if abbreviated, story — I began discretely searching for a politically radical attorney. Employed part-time as a student assistant and distrustful of the Establishment because of their dishonesty in the past about the assassination issue, I wanted a lawyer who was an idealist because, neither financially nor politically, could I afford any other kind. If my information was relevant, and I believed now that it probably was, doing anything useful with it was still going for a long shot.

On the other hand, I was less worried than ever about seeming paranoid. If one thing had been made perfectly clear, it was that in the United States of America suspicions of conspiracy were no longer regarded as symptoms of mental illness.

In July of 1975 I noted in passing headlines in the local Atlanta papers that city Commissioner of Public Safety, Reginald Eaves, had for some time been quietly investigating anew the assassination of Dr. Martin Luther King, Jr. Although I had admired King while I held John Kennedy in contempt, I was then so preoccupied with things I was ferreting out here and there about the Presidential assassination that I failed to take much notice. For articles about the John Kennedy murder now seemed to be appearing everywhere.

From time to time I was meeting to compare notes with a staffer on *The Great Speckled Bird* who had written about the Southern Rim. Without mentioning my man in New Orleans with the bald head and links to Carlos Marcello, I sought further evidence that the cowboys of the military-industrial complex had murdered Kennedy in their way with the Yankees of the Northeastern Establishment. Marcello, as well as Nixon and Howard Hunt, were alleged to belong to this Southern faction. I figured the man I remembered and feared had to be in there somewhere.

Then I encountered an article in a scandal tabloid that disturbed me more than anything else, again for largely subjective reasons. One of their correspondents who was probing links between Carlos Marcello and the John Kennedy murder had blown his brains out with a .38 caliber pistol for no particular reason. As it happened, this resident of Baton Rouge, Louisiana, named Joe Cooper was lefthanded and the weapon was found in his right hand. The former girlfriend of the man with whom I discussed murdering the President met with much the same fate in 1964, just before I returned to New Orleans after a year's absence to visit.

Then early one morning the phone rang. On the other end of the line was the ACLU lawyer who at that time was the only other person with whom I had confided about the conversations summarized in my notes. One afternoon, after deciding I wanted him to handle my case when the time came, I had regaled him with a rambling, slightly hysterical account of my worst suspicions.

Now he was to ask me, "Have you been following this investigation by Eaves of the Martin Luther King assassination?"

I admitted I had not."You might want to look into it," he said. "Their witness seems to be talking about some of the same people you mentioned to me in connection with Carlos Marcello."

That afternoon I obtained an Atlanta newspaper and read the article pertaining to what was fast becoming a controversial investigation. A young man who supplied accurate information to the police about a narcotics ring was also insisting that just previous to the murder of Martin Luther King he overheard one of its members say of King, "I'm going to shoot that damned nigger in the head and frame a jailbird for it, just like I did with Kennedy."

Had the word "jailbird" been a post-hypnotic trigger been planted in my unconscious to release a flood of memories, results could not have been more dramatic. For one of the things my own suspect had discussed with me all those years ago was framing a jailbird for the John Kennedy murder. In fact, I recalled now that I was the one who talked him out of it. Moreover, he had also talked about assassinating Martin Luther King.

No longer in doubt that my man, known to me as Gary Kirstein, possessed advanced knowledge of the John Kennedy murder, I went into action. First I typed up a number of brief memos about our conversations and distributed them almost at random, in order to assure that if I was fatally silenced there would be evidence to indicate why.

Thereafter I endeavored to contact my prospective attorney, only to discover that he was out of town.Unsure of what to do next, convinced that I should act fast, I wound up taking my information to the office of the Commissioner of Public Safety. That was after I first attended a party where I was given a funny-tasting marijuana cigarette, that made me feel uninhibited and talkative, and then questioned intensively by a group of inquisitive individuals. And it was after, within a few days of the first incident, I again met one of the people from that party, who handed me a pipeload of marijuana that blistered the inside of my mouth when I started to inhale the smoke.

Commissioner Eaves then announced a press conference wherein he said he would reveal startling evidence in the King case. Instead, when the day of the conference arrived, he said he was dropping the probe — because, he said, his chief witness, Robert Byron Watson, refused to take a lie detector test. I was baffled and frightened.

Then the newspapers announced the disappearance of labor leader Jimmy Hoffa, and I recalled that the man I knew as Gary Kirstein once asked me what I thought about letting Hoffa in on a conspiracy to assassinate Kennedy.

Greg Hill, my former New Orleans roommate, arrived in Atlanta for a visit to find me nearly hysterical. At least once he had met Gary, remembering as I did that we had suspected him of stealing a typewriter from our apartment. Greg also drew my attention to a magazine article asserting that counter-cultural writer and publisher Paul Krassner had uncovered links between the Kennedy assassination and the Manson family.

Twelve days after I had taken my information to the Atlanta police, a ski-masked bandit pulled a stick-up at a party both Greg and I were attending and stole his identification and mine — taking only money from other guests.

From that day in early August of 1975 until the day of this writing in 1982 my life has been a constant series of similar misadventures — including poisonings, threats and bribe offers, intense psychological harassments, mysterious interrogations and occasional reminders about things in those fateful conversations with "Brother-in-law."

I call that man "Brother-in-law," because I am not at all certain that his name was really Gary Kirstein. There is every reason to surmise he was not using his own name, and I remember him most as the brother-in-law of a French Quarter character named Slim Brooks. And because of Slim's extremely distinctive turn of speech, he himself seldom called Gary "my brother-in-law." Instead, it was always, "Let's go visit Brother-in-law tomorrow."

I had arrived in New Orleans the day after Mardi Gras in 1961. Except for May, June, July, August and part of September of 1963 — I lived there until 13 December 1963. Beginning in the aftermath of the Bay of Pigs, and continuing up to about the time of the John Kennedy assassination, Slim must have uttered those words between fifteen and twenty-five times. Since these invitations were far apart and infrequent, I never turned Slim down.

Sometimes Brother-in-law would come to the French Quarter and get us. More often, Slim would arrange in advance to borrow his car and then would drive us to Brother-in-law's house out in the country the next day.

It was difficult to take seriously what Brother-in-law said about his plans to murder the President. Not that Slim didn't seem honest. On the contrary, he seemed too honest to get himself involved with anyone heavy enough to actually go out and assassinate a President — if Slim would have to lie about it afterwards. To suspect Slim of being a conspirator seemed too paranoid for words.

In April of 1976 I again had occasion to think about paranoia in relation to the John Kennedy assassination. For I attended a lecture in Atlanta by none other than Jim Garrison, for whom by then I felt a lot of sympathy. In light of what I remembered now, it seemed his suspicions of me were only slightly misplaced. I was not a field agent in the assassination; I was among those who helped plan it!

In the question period after his speech Garrison said something I found both significant and touching: "Of course, I have to lean over backwards not to be paranoid, because I have been accused of paranoia in the past."

One of his diagnosticians had been me; now I was dealing with exactly the same double bind of trying to probe conspiracies without coming on like a paranoid in the eyes of my friends.

Through an emissary I let it be known to Garrison that I wanted to meet with him. His reply: "Not only do I not want to meet with Kerry Thornley, I don't even want to hear his name. In fact, I don't even want to think about Kerry Thornley!"

Feeling very much alone, I continued my daily dealings with what were obviously conspiracies — including a correspondence with a man I hoped was a charming crank who was telling me in his letters "why we Fascists assassinated Kennedy." How I got on Stan Jamison's mailing list in the first place some years earlier was a mystery to me. Since 1970, though, Greg Hill and I both had been receiving from him everything from advice about how to grow organic sprouts to racist newspapers published by White Christians who were armed and quite dangerous.

In reply to one of my memos about Kirstein that had fallen into his hands indirectly, he wrote me to say that the tragedy in Dallas was plotted by the Secret Order of Thule in such a way as to assure that no cover-up could remain convincing forever. Motive: to make the American public paranoid about their government and mass media. For paranoia, he told me, is a big step in the direction of mental health.

People who become paranoid, Stan Jamison wrote, will not rest until they discover every last shred of truth. Among the devices used to encourage awareness of conspiracy were the many crude Oswald impersonations that occurred just previous to the assassination. Puzzled for more than a decade about exactly that mystery, I had to admit this was the first credible hypothesis to explain it without making the assassins look like idiots. And had they been less than geniuses, there would have been no cover-up at all.

Jamison further informed me that the conspiracy was constructed in concentric circles, like Chinese boxes, with descending levels, so that only "the man at the center" understood afterwards exactly what had happened. Of course, I could not ignore the possibility that man might have been Brother-in-law.

What brought the many loose ends in the John Kennedy murder mystery together for me was this realization that it was a maximum complicity crime. Various factions must have been deliberately implicated on a blind-alliance basis, so that once the event occurred, every group of conspirators was startled at evidence of participation by someone besides themselves.

Like Brother-in-law, Jamison seemed morbidly fascinated with Hitler and Nazi Germany. Both men mentioned in particular little-known aspects of the Third Reich — such as the secret pagan rituals of the S.S. and the occult beliefs of Hitler's cohorts. Both repeated a rumor that Nazi rocket scientists discovered energy secrets the oil companies were repressing to this day. And whether either or both were living some kind of macabre hoax or were absolutely fanatical was impossible to decide, since neither man was without humor. For instance, Jamison always signed off with, "Love is Alive and Well."

As might be anticipated, it struck me that perhaps Stan Jamison and Gary Kirstein were the same person, so in 1977 I dropped in on Jamison unexpectedly at his address in Sacramento, California. Not only was he not the same man I had conversed with in New Orleans, but it was plain that the spine-chilling ranting in his letters was just a big put-on.

That isn't to say his information about the assassination could not have been valid. A warm, intelligent human being obviously unsympathetic to Fascism, he nevertheless seemed quite versed in secret society and intelligence community politics.

"I come on all hairy like that in my letters," he told me, "to scare off government agents." Although that statement didn't sound convincing, it seemed a safe bet his motives were not cruel — a consideration that leaves undetermined whether or not they were misguided.

How paranoid is it to fear such individuals? Perhaps that is the wrong question. Maybe we should ask ourselves: Is it rational to dismiss them in the name of popularized notions of sanity?

Later on I was to encounter a rumor that Stan Jamison acquired his information from one Michael Stanley, then serving a prison term in California. As Lovable Ol' Doc Stanley, Michael Stanley was known to me personally as one of the heavier, darker characters of the California counter-culture. We met each other in a hip coffee house after I moved to Los Angeles about a year after John Kennedy's assassination. Although I didn't like to admit it for fear of seeming paranoid, I found Michael Stanley terrifying.

Perhaps if we clearly defined this thing we call paranoia it would not cause us to behave so foolishly. Genuine paranoia actually contains at least three ingredients: fear, suspicion and mystification. Technically, it is heightened awareness, but not yet perfect awareness.

Professional espionage agents are, for example, frequently both suspicious and mystified, but have long since learned to live without much fear. For that reason, we don't call them paranoids.

To be both frightened and confused, without a systematic method of blaming others for those conditions, is to be vulnerable to some other psychiatric classification than paranoia. Fear and suspicion combined with exact, provable knowledge as to the identity of one's oppressors is generally considered heroic. Paranoia, then, only exists in politics where fear and suspicion linger for no external reason and, as is more often true, in cases where the subject is incorrect about who to suspect and what to fear — the condition of mystification.

Unfortunately nearly all oppressors in conspiracy politics strive skillfully to mystify their victims — often with enormous resources to help the work along.

"The arguments he used to justify his use of the alias suggest that Oswald may have come to think that the whole world was becoming involved in an increasingly complex conspiracy against him," charged the Warren Commission, also saying, "Oswald was overbearing and arrogant throughout much of the time between his arrest and his own death. He consistently refused to admit involvement in the assassination or in the killing of Patrolman Tippitt."

Oswald's perceptions of reality may have been far more accurate than the words of his accusers.

Cults & Casualties

SORCERY
·SEX·
ASSASSINATION
AND
THE SCIENCE
OF
SYMBOLISM
ANTON

Sorcery, Sex, Assassination and the Science of Symbolism

James Shelby Downard

The following is a fleshed-out version of Shelby Downard's popular article "King Kill / 33°," which appeared in the first edition of Apocalypse Culture. The appeal of Downard is in his indefatigable research into blind corners combined with his paranoid's eye for hidden associations. In linking US history to the mystic conurbations of the Freemasons Downard reveals an intuitive genius. Mr. Downard's work has no corollary anywhere in respectable publications, and indeed such an "alternative" sort of scribe as Robert Anton Wilson charges in his Cosmic Trigger that Downard's JFK thesis is "the most absurd, the most incredible, the most ridiculous Illuminati theory of them all." Wilson further charges that Downard, in tandem with Fortean researcher William N. Grimstad, possess a strange and alarming reality tunnel; alarming because they may well lead us to accept the possibility that a grand occult plan has been orchestrated to turn us into cybernetic mystery zombies. Coincidence, crackpotism or conspiracy? You decide.

This is as good a time as any to tell you that Nothing Is What It Seems.

The power of the Secret Government over the news media continues unabated. During the time of the Watergate scandal others scandals of the past were reviewed, but the torture-murder of Captain William Morgan in 1826 — from which developed an anti-Mason political party that challenged Freemason Andrew Jackson for the presidency — and the murder of Joseph Smith the Mormon prophet, which resulted in the men of the Mormon Church withdrawing from Freemasonry, were ignored.

The information I present in these pages is well-known to certain news agencies who have chosen to suppress it; similarly the motivation for the JFK assassination has been plunged into cryonic secrecy — facts concerning the assassination are on ice and will be be revealed in the future in the so-called "Revelation of the Method." The freeze-wait-revive scheme is part of the master plan of Masonic Sorcery.

The ability of the Secret Government to immobilize the release of vital information to the public is in part due to the apathy of American people, who are benumbed by revelation after revelation. It is a peculiar phenomena that certain revelations move people to action while episodic revelations of the same type stun them into inaction.

For years I have been trying to draw attention to Masonic Sorcery and its relationship to political control. I believe that many people instinctually realize the power that "Freemasonry" exerts on the Government of the United States; but since they are Hoodwinked they do not understand the secrecy, silence and darkness that surrounds the mysteries of the "Masonic Art." And so control of the Government of the United States is traced merely to Wall St., and not to the crossroads of witchcraft.

America is a news ghetto where the news media continually endeavors to promote apathy while going through the motions, the lip-sync, of reform. Like a haunted house draining its occupants of will in return for sleep without nightmares, American people are mental captives of a Horror that feeds them misinformation as its stone bell tolls the death of individuality.

I publish this, in the wake of the situation Charles Seymour alluded to: "The moralist unquestionably secures wide support; but he also wearies his audience." I have heard some Americans say, as though they were puzzled by a difficult question, "Why should I let such things upset me?" If those people not completely lost in apathy discover what the Master Plan has planned for them, they will get fighting mad.

Most "Freemasons" apparently have no idea of the evil that is part of Masonry, and if they do hear about it they don't believe it. The same is true of most members of the Masonic-oriented fraternal organizations, for the Masonic Cryptocracy is a secret, anomalous thing.

> It is certain that onomatology, or the science of names, forms a very interesting part of the investigations of the higher Masonry, and it is only in this way that any connections can be created between the two sciences. — *Encyclopedia of Freemasonry*

> When the ancients saw a scapegoat, they could at least recognize him for what he was: a *pharmakos,* a human sacrifice. When modern man sees one, he does not, or refuses to, recognize him for what he is; instead he looks for 'scientific' explanations — to explain away the obvious. — Thomas Szasz, *Ceremonial Chemistry*

The "science of names" forms only one segment of the science of symbolism used by the Masons. Names, i.e., words, are merely descriptions and they rise and fall in usage like a Cartesian doll. Some words fall into disuse quickly, while other words are given meanings that are known only to the initiated.

The JFK assassination encounters this science in a decisive way, and contains a veritable nightmare of symbol-complexes having to do with violence, perversion, conspiracy, death and degradation. These elements are important not only as cause-and-effect in the murder of a president but in the ensuing reaction of the people of America and the world.

The fertility and death symbolism in the Killing Of The King rite, the Masonic Greening Ritualism, has been suppressed because its examination must necessarily reveal Masonry's mystical political influence. This would erode public confidence in:

a. The concept of Masonic progressivism, i.e., liberty, equality, fraternity.

b. Those who have shielded the conspirators.

c. The entire mental construct that passes for knowledge of the genuine nature of the U.S. government.

The Hell-Fire Club

The Hell-Fire Club (Monks of Medmenham, Friars of St. Francis) was a society of ruffians and drunkards who engaged in sexual orgies similar to those of the "Mollies," "Gormogans," "Mankillers," "Blasters," "Mohawks," "Sweaters," "She Romps Club," the "Fun Club," etc. Engaged in political agitation and conspiracy, they were dedicated to the destruction of the Catholic church. The membership was highly-placed in the British government: the Prime Minister, the Chancellor of the Exchequer, the First Lord of the Admiralty, the Prince of Wales and the Lord Mayor of London all shared in the "privileges" of the Hell-Fire Club. Benjamin Franklin, who was initiated into Freemasonry at St. John's Lodge in Philadelphia, and who is credited with publishing the first Masonic book in America was a member and was also connected with the Lodge of the Nine Sisters in France.

Benjamin Franklin and Sir Francis Dashwood, founder of the Hell-Fire Club, wrote a prayer book which became the basis of the book of common prayer that is used in many American Protestant churches. Because Sir Francis Dashwood was the so-called Lord le DeSpencer, his prayer book in England was referred to as the "Franklin-DeSpencer Prayer Book." In the United States that book was called the "Franklin Prayer Book." It was composed at Dashwood's manor-house at West Wycombe, the site of numerous rites of *magica sexualis.* Franklin and Dashwood created their volume of entreaties in between sodomy-sucking-sorcery sessions.

Eventually Dashwood dug a huge cave on his West Wycombe estate to facilitate the performance of sex magic. Later a road was constructed to High Wycombe which utilized soil taken from the cave dug by the Hell-Fire Club. Brunel University is located in High Wycombe and F.H. George, Ph.D., is director of its world-renowned Cybernetics department. George defines cybernetics as a "science concerned with all matters of controls and communications and to this extent it trespasses what we have come to think of as the established sciences." Cybernetics, of course, is intimately concerned with artificial or machine intelligence. This concern is predicated, to a certain degree, on human cooperation with machines. Symbolism is a cybernetic science.

Miss Chudleigh

Miss Chudleigh, the "dollymop" for the Hell-Fire Club, was a Jewess. Certainly she was not "Miss," nor was her name Chudleigh at the time she was dubbed "Miss Chudleigh" by Horace Walpole. Chudleigh was the name of a town and she was a "woman of common property" there. Complete secrecy of the harlots or "dollymops" involved in performing sexual perversions at the High-Fire Club was seen as essential. This concealment has to do with "the secrecy and silence of Masonry."

Harpocrates, the Greek god of secrecy and silence, whose statue was often placed at the entrance of temples, caves and other places where the mysteries were performed, was of symbolical importance to the Hell-Fire Club. A statue of Harpocrates, which depicted him holding a finger to his mouth, was one of a number of statues used on club premises.

On April 24, 1783, Pope Clement XII, a bitter foe of *magica sexualis*, issued his celebrated Bull of Excommunication entitled *In Eminenti Apostolatus Specula.* it specifically decreed:

"In order to close the widely open road to iniquities which might be committed with impunity and also for other reasons, just and reasonable, that have come to our knowledge ... We have resolved and decreed to condemn and forbid such Societies, assemblies, reunions, conventions, aggregations or meetings called either Freemasonic or known under some other denomination. We condemn and forbid them by this, our present constitution, which is to be considered valid forever."

Due to Pope Clement's decree Miss Chudleigh faced pressure outside of England. In an act of Defiance, King Frederick II became Chudleigh's protector and bedfellow. Still, this was not so outrageous, since Prussia was not considered a Catholic country; however, Poland was. It was here that Prince Radzvil, the ancestor and husband of Jacqueline Kennedy's sister, took the whore Chudleigh. The Radzvil fortune was considered the greatest in the nation. The family itself was related to the Hohenzollerns and the Romanovs.

According to legend, Miss Chudleigh carried a "mystical taint." According to the Masonry of Cagliostro (magnetic masonry) there exists a thing described as "the transfer of magnetic force." This "mystical taint" is supposedly attached to those who traffic in ritual sex perversions. According to the record, the fortunes of the Radzvils have declined ever since.

Macbeth and Scotland

Before pointing to the mystical associations between the murder of JFK and Shakespeare's tragedy of *Macbeth* I wish to call attention to the appearance of the witches in Act I, Scene I, and to the line in which they chant, "Fair is foul, and foul is fair," which is reminiscent of alchemical individuation or shaping of an integrated personality in the psychology of C.G. Jung, in which the "archetype of unity" (self-head, auto-cephalous), the Yetzer Ha-Ra and Yetzer ha Tov of the Jews, and the Masonic "Mingling of All with All" is manifested.

It is important to note the appearance of Hecate to the three witches. Hecate is triple-countenanced, and being three-fold in aspect she is known as Diana on earth, Luna in heaven, and Hecate in hell. These three women comprise one of the triads of western mythology. Such triads were a central part of ancient religions, and the "mystical triad" idea became part of Masonic symbolism. There is in fact a triad of three governing officers to be found in almost every degree, and in the higher degrees there exists a symbolical triad that presides under various names, just as Hecate presides in different places under various names.

Crossroads were considered sacred to Diana-Hecate, the deity who is both virgin and whore ("Fair is foul, and foul is fair"), and such crossroads were the favored sites of the wanton women-witches and the Grand Masters (Masonic sorcerers) who were her votaries.

Crossroads are significant to ritual sex magic; the wearing of clothes of the opposite sex and the performance of bisexual acts are called "crossroad rites." The women engaging in these perversions were referred to as "dikes," and it was said that they traveled "the old dike road" and "the old dirt road." These sorts of activities, in keeping with Hecate lore, are secret to the extreme. *Tacitisque paebens conscium sacris jubar, Hecate triformis.* ("Triple Hecate, who giveth forth rays cognizant of secret mysteries.")

Crossroads were also places of human and animal sacrifice. Such rites were often carried out in conjunction with *magica sexualis* since the participants recognized an existing relationship between fertility and death. Hecate is therefore also identified as a "death goddess," and her sex-and-death attributes are similar to those ascribed to Venus (Aphrodite, Prone, Kypris).

MacBird

The idea for the play *MacBird* possibly originated at an anti-war rally in Berkeley, California when Barbara Garson, in a speech referred to the First Lady as "Lady MacBird Johnson." She is said to have subsequently decided to write a play based on *Macbeth* and have it performed at the "International Day of Protest," but it actually had its premiere at the Village Gate Theater in Greenwich Village.

Newspaper publisher William Loeb charged that Garson's *MacBird* implies that President and Mrs. Johnson were conspiratorially involved in the JFK assassination. Loeb asked his attorney: "... to research immediately if there is any action this newspaper can take to ask the U.S. Attorney of the Southern District of New York to request the appropriate court to issue an injunction against the further showing of *MacBird.*"

Newspapers throughout the country took up the cry. A drama critic for United Press International wrote, *"MacBird,* presented yesterday at the Village Gate, is a sophomoric, heavy-handed parody of *Macbeth* that strikes a new low in theatrical taste."

The word "sophomore" is derived from the Greek words "sophos," meaning wise, and "moros," meaning foolish. Granted, it seemed foolish for Barbara Garson to challenge the system with the play *MacBird,* but let us see if there is anything shrewd, astute or erudite about the Garson parody. In the words of Erasmus, can Barbara Garson be said to be a "morosopher," a wise fool?

President Lyndon Baines Johnson's name is phonetically linked to the Macbeth clan. Clansmen were divided into two classes: those who were related by blood and those individuals and groups who were under clan protection. Consequently, clans had sects of different appellations and people with the same surname are known to have been attached to different clans.

The Macbeth clan is related, in a clannish manner, to the Baine clan. The lack of clear distinction between blood relatives and those under clan protection in Scottish genealogy has become so complex as to baffle expert genealogists. Numerous Scottish names are rendered with a variety of spellings and it is a matter of record that the sons of many Scotsmen spelled their names differently from their fathers. With this in mind, consider a clan listing of the Bain and Macbeth clan structure.

Bain, Macbean, Mackay, Macnab — Bayne, Macbean, MacKay, Macnab — Bean, Macbean — Beathy, MacBeth — Binnie, MacBean MacBain, Macbean — Macbeath, MacBean — MacBeth, Macbean, Macilvain, Macbean — Melvin, MacBeth.

The MacBeath, MacBean and the MacBeth, Macbean part of this clan structure apparently had tartans of their own. "Mac," of course, means "son of," and all the Masons of the Bain, Bayne, Bean, Beathy, Binnie, Beath, Beth clans all publicly claim to have the same ancestor.

The Bains (Baines), in keeping with this name-exchange, are apt to refer to the same clan even though the spelling may be Bain, Baines or even Bane, as it has sometimes appeared. All of these are in a clan structure with Macbeth.

We have ascertained that President Lyndon Baines Johnson, through the magic of mystery and words, is associated with Bain-Bean-Macbeth. Bain, in French, means, among other things, bath. There are obviously many types of baths — sweat baths, mineral water baths, champagne baths, milk baths, blood baths, baptismal baths. The resurrection bath of alchemy denotes rebirth, and the purification or absolution baths are given to Masonic "Knights of the Bath" before performing heinous deeds. There are many ritual aspects to the bath; for example, when he was vice-president, Lyndon Baines Johnson, of "blood bath" association, removed his shoes before entering a Moslem bath house reminiscent of the Rite of Discalceation in the Third Degree of Masonry, which has to do with assassination.

Shortly before the assassination of President Kennedy, *Macbeth* was performed in the White House. The part of Macbeth was played by actor Franklin Cover. In a photograph widely circulated in a national magazine, Cover is seen standing under a chandelier. The chandelier is a magnificent work of art said to comprise 5060 pieces of cut glass. Jacqueline Kennedy ordered the chandelier removed from the White House as one of her last acts as First Lady.

Chandeliers have tremendous symbolical importance in sorcery. For example, a chandelier is said to be the test of a "jettatore's" power. A jettatore is a man possessed of the "malocchio," the "evil eye." Jettatore literally means, in Italian, "thrower," or one who casts.

A photograph was also taken of Mrs. Kennedy at the performance, also showing her standing underneath the same chandelier that hung over Franklin Cover in his Macbeth costume. There is, in folklore, the superstition that when a wife believes her husband has been injured or killed by sorcerous means instigated by a *jettatore,* she is to go to that jettatore's chandelier and throw her shoe at it. (None of this is intended to imply that

Mr. Cover is a sorcerer, only that his picture under so symbolical an arti fact is striking in and of itself.) It is also a folk belief that the taking of a position under a chandelier by a practitioner of the evil eye is accompanied by a sound. Slightly to the east of "Crescent City" (New Orleans) there is an area called "Chandeleur Sound"' beneath it, on many maps, is the word "Freemason."

Kennedy, Beale and Bouvier

Recall Miss Chudleigh, the woman who served as the "great whore" for a time with the sorcerer-oriented Hell-Fire Club: after the edicts and bulls issued by the Pope, Miss Chudleigh was hard-pressed to find refuge on the continent and yet she was finally successful in the camp of a supposedly Catholic Prince — Radzvil — in an undoubtedly Catholic country. This protection may have somehow caused the string of misfortunes which later befell the apostate Catholic Radzvils since it was maintained that Madame Chudleigh was imbued with a curse or mystical taint due to her involvement in ritual sex perversions.

Gore Vidal, Jacqueline Bouvier Kennedy Onassis and Caroline (Lee) Bouvier were the "stepchildren" of Hugh D. Auchincloss. Mr. Vidal is, of course, a well-known author. Some of his work describes the Kennedys as an "Illusion-Making Clan," and alleges "they [the Kennedys] create illusion and call it facts." However, in fairness, it should be noted that Vidal has also called them the "Holy Family" and the President and First Lady the "Sun God" and Goddess."

When JFK was 22, Irene Wiley sculptured a likeness of him as a winged angel; her work was presented to the Vatican where it was used as a part of a panel in which the angel hovers over St. Therese while she writes in a book. After his fatal trip to Dallas, President Kennedy's remains were code-named "Angel" and that was also the name of the "flying hearse" (Air Force One) which returned him to the capitol.

Tragedy seems to live with the Kennedy family, newspapers tell us. Indeed, Bobby Kennedy was assassinated, Teddy Kennedy suffered a severe back injury in a plane crash; before JFK's assassination, his father suffered a crippling stroke, sister Rosemary has been mentally handicapped since birth, Kathleen was killed in a plane crash, and eldest son Joseph was killed in action during World War II. Only a few years ago, the son of Senator Ted Kennedy was forced to undergo the amputation of his leg; prior to that, his father was involved in the drowning of a young secretary which effectively silenced the Senator against those who murdered his brothers, since, with typical J. Edgar Hoover morality, most of the facts of the case were suppressed and would find a swift and international messenger should the senator from Massachusetts renege on his "commitments." Let us examine the incredible symbolism deeply related to the Kennedy family and perhaps discern an etiology.

The "Rowan" is a death plant in herbal lore and was an ingredient in a sleeping potion witches gave their husbands when they wanted to perform activities to which their spouses would strongly object. The rowan, like so many "magical," plants was used by Christians as protection against ill fortune. It was also a means of church decoration and was widely planted in cemeteries in the belief that it would restrain the dead from premature resurrection. In some places, the First of May was called Rowan or Hawthorne Day, or Rowan Tree Witch Day.

Peter Lawford, one time brother-in-law of President John F. Kennedy, was later married to Mary Rowan, the daughter of *Laugh-In* series television star Dan Rowan. Peter Lawford and Patricia Kennedy Lawford were divorced in 1966 and it was then that Lawford took his "Rowan" to bed. He also made certain similar arrangements for Marilyn Monroe in the service of John and Robert Kennedy. Marilyn Monroe has been described as the "Silvery Witch of us all" (Norman Mailer) and she is important in the fertility and death symbolism pervading the "Boston Brahmins."

President Kennedy was the recipient of a birthday party in his honor in Madison Square Garden and Peter Lawford invited Marilyn Monroe to sing "Happy Birthday" there. When she was scheduled to sing, a spotlight was thrown on an empty stage and she was announced three times. She appeared after the third call and was introduced as "the late Marilyn Monroe."

Among her husbands was a Shriner (Mason) named Robert Slatzer. In Slatzer's book, *The Life and Curious Death of Marilyn Monroe,* circumstantial evidence is presented suggesting that Attorney General Robert Kennedy was somehow involved in the "curious death." At no time, however, has Mr. Slatzer referred to Masonic sorcery.

The European news magazine, *Das Neue Blatt* details not only the much touted love affair between the Hollywood star and the President, but the rivalry between the First Lady and the star. The Das Neue Blatt article broadly hinted that Jackie "helped drive Marilyn to her suicide." Jacqueline Bouvier Kennedy Onassis has a family and a past at least as strange and enigmatic as that of her deceased first husband.

Mrs. Edith Bouvier Beale was the sister of John Bouvier, the father of Jacqueline. Mrs. Beale and her daughter Edith (Edie) lived in a state of wretchedness and destitution in a decaying mansion in East Hampton, Long Island. Eviction proceedings against the Beales were initiated because the women were discovered to be living in total squalor amid piles of empty pet food cans, newspapers and assorted filth. For some reason,

Madame Onassis permitted a film crew to record the degradation of her aunt and niece, and anyone viewing *Grey Gardens* will certainly attest to the "House of Usher" eccentricities of the pair. As an analogy of control, it is interesting to note that a peculiar rapport occasionally exists between owners and domesticated animals, and that the Beale mansion reflects a reversal of roles in the master-pet relationship.

John F. Kennedy was born on May 29, 1917 at 83 Beals Street, Brookline, Massachusetts. Beals-Beale-Beal are names associated with the Kennedys through the magic and mystery of words. Beale onomatology is rendered thus: El-Bel-Baal-Be al-Beal-Beale. El is said to be one of the Hebrew names of God, signifying the "mighty one." It is the root of many other divine names and therefore, many of the sacred names in Masonry. Approximately one mile from Lindisfarne (the "Holy Island"/"Holy House") is a barren place known as "Beal." Lindisfarne is associated with Heredom, and the legends of King Arthur, the Round Table, Merlin, and other Camelot stories, as well as the Scottish Black Watch.

Bouvier means "cowherder" and *Look* magazine has traced this family to Grenoble, France where their first mention appears in 1410. "Jackie's" great-great-grandfather, Eustache Bouvier, fought in a French regiment under the command of George Washington while his elder brother Joseph remained in France. *Look* magazine located Mrs. Kennedy's Bouvier relatives in "the ancestral town" and this genealogical find brought relief and joy to the family, for as "Mama" Bouvier put it: "We know what they have been whispering about us. We had to swallow our tongues. Now they can say no more."

Arrangements were made for a delegation of Bouviers to journey to Paris and meet with their famous relation while the President was conferring with de Gaulle. During this period, a painting of the renowned Pont St. Esprit, located in ancestral Bouvier country was painted by the brother-in-law of Marcel Bouvier and shipped to the White House. This "Spirit Bridge" is equated with the "Bridge of Souls," which, in turn, linked with the "Bridge of Dread," "Baine Bridge," "Log of Lerma," "Al Sirat," and "Cinvato Paratu." Such bridges are symbolically associated with death and crossing them can be a difficult and harrowing experience. (Cf. Poe's "Never Bet the Devil Your Head" and Kipling's "The Man Who Would Be King.")

Two French radio reporters drove Marcel and eighteen-year-old Danielle Bouvier to the Paris reception for themselves and the Kennedys. After traveling some hundred miles, their car struck a tree and Danielle was killed. With her had been a beribboned box which contained a gift for the First Lady, to whom it was addressed as "For my dear cousin"; inside was a tiny nightingale "broken in its gilded cage."

Danielle is the feminine form of Daniel and Daniel is a Hebrew word meaning "God is my judge."

News reports failed to mention the type of tree involved in the crash which took away "Danielle" and ruined her nightingale. Whether or not it was a thorn tree of the rowan type, legend has it that a nightingale sings with its breast pressed against a thorn.

The island of Delos is the reputed birthplace of Apollo and Diana. It is located in the southwest Aegean Sea and is considered the domain of Hecate, the patroness of the 'Infernal Arts.' Delos is alternately known as the "Island of the Dead."

There is nothing more appropriate for the wife of a slain "Sun God" than a pilgrimage to Delos as Jacqueline Kennedy did. She also journeyed to the Temple of Apollo at Delphi, and to the ancient Greek Theatre situated above Delphi. It was here that the former First Lady performed what is known as the rite of "greeting the sun" — a fixture in mythology of great antiquity. One might observe that Mrs. Kennedy performed her "sun greeting" with the expertise of an Aleister Crowley.

Before she made her Apollo-oriented pilgrimage, she was photographed wearing a large "diamond sun-burst" on her head. She was reported to be doing some Greek "island-hopping" on the yacht "North Wind" owned by shipping magnate Marcos Nomikos. The island of Epidaurus was one of its ports of call where Jacqueline Kennedy attended Sophocles" *Electra* by the National Theatre of Greece, and then moved on to Hydra, an island named for the dreaded monster-serpent whose nine heads were capable of generation after decapitation.

Another important stop in Mrs. Kennedy's highly symbolical peregrination is Santorina (Thera), an isle often connected in folklore to the Island of the Vampires or "sucking-fairies." In fact, Santorina shares the same reputation for vampires as Haiti does for zombies, or the Dominican Republic for the CIA. According to these stories, there was at least as much sucking going on in Santorina (Thera) as on the island of Lesbos.

Mystical Toponomy

Mystical toponomy pertains to the magic and mystery of words intersecting with the Masonic science of symbolism. While it differs from the "Old Straight Track" rediscovered by Watkins in the early part of this century, in which alignments or ley lines were discovered to sweep through power sites of ancient religious uses, no one has thus far documented any political or sorcerous uses.

In considering my data, it would be helpful to consider a dictum of Einsteinian physics — a science few would accuse of fanaticism or irrationality: "Time relations among events are assumed to be first constituted by the specific physical relations obtaining between them."

My study of place names imbued with sorcerous significance necessarily include lines of latitude and longitude and the divisions of degrees in geography and cartography (minutes and seconds).

Let us take as an example "Mason Road" in Texas, which connects to the "Mason No El Bar" and the Texas-New Mexico ("The Land of Enchantment") border. This connecting line is on the 32nd degree. The 32nd degree in Masonry of the Scottish Rite is the next to the highest degree awarded. When this 32nd degree line of latitude is traced west into the "Land of Enchantment" it becomes situated midway between Deming and Columbus (NM). Slightly to the north of the town of Columbus are the Tres Hermanas (Three Sisters) mountains. The Three Sisters are found approximately 32 miles between Deming and Columbus and are a minute and some seconds south of the 32nd degree line. When this line is traced further to the west it is found to pass the ghost town of Shakespeare at a distance south of the town that is roughly equivalent to the distance which the 32nd degree line passes north of the Three Sisters Mountains. The names Shakespeare and the Three Sisters find their connection in the tragedy of *Macbeth.*

When this 32nd degree line is traced some little distance farther west, into Arizona, it crosses an old trail which meandered north of what is now another ghost town, but which at one time was the town of "Ruby." Part of the old winding trail became known as the "Ruby Road." The town of Ruby is established to have acquired its name officially on April 11, 1912, when a post office commenced operation. The town became notorious for many brutal murders which had ritual aspects. Four of these homicides occurred in a store attached to the post office which had been erected over the grave of a Catholic priest. Continuing on with mystical toponomy, one encounters the fact that the Ruby road twists north into the area of two mountain peaks that are known as the Kennedy and Johnson Mountains.

Johnson Mountain is supposedly named after the general manager of the Peabody Mining Company, who also had a town named after him. The 32nd degree of latitude is but a few seconds from Johnson. In this frontier town on a December evening, 1883, a man known as Colonel Mike Smith and a man called Mason were ambushed by gunfighters described as being of questionable reputation and questionable character. These terms are employed in Masonic writings: "He, (Captain William Morgan) was a man of questionable character and dissolute habits, and his

MDCCLXXVI
NOVUS ORDO SECLORUM
THE GREAT SEAL

enmity to Masonry is said to have originated in the refusal of the Masons of Leroy..." — *Encyclopedia of Freemasonry*

The attack on Mason and Smith, occurring as it did on the 32nd degree line near Keystone, is of ritual significance reminiscent of some other disputes along a certain Mason-Dixon line.

A "keystone" is the designation for the stone at the apex of an arch which, when set in place, "keys" or locks the whole. A symbolical keystone is vital to the legend of the Masonic Royal Arch Degree of York. The earliest known record of such a degree is in the annals of the city of Fredericksburg, Virginia on December 22, 1753. Fredericksburg is also the location of the "House of the Rising Sun," a Masonic meeting place for such notables as Founding Fathers George Washington and Benjamin Franklin (of Hell-Fire Club fame), and George Mason.

The Royal Arch

The "Ancient York Grand Lodge" allegedly went out of existence at the same time as the Grand Mother Lodge and all other lodges of this rite followed it into "extinction." Certain Masons have admitted that one of its degrees, the "Royal Arch," is neither "arch or Royal Arch" (Secretary, Royal Arch Degree, 1759). He continues on to reveal that, "The Royal Arch Degree is not just a separate entity now, but part of the Masonic system." Had this Royal Arch fallen into the desuetude of the York Rite as a whole, its keystone would be removed and the arch left incomplete. Arch magicians with a faulty arch can be considered to be quite unfortunate indeed.

An arch magician of high degree, according to sorcerous lore, was the third king of the Jews who was named Shelomoh and called Solomon. The principle legends of Masonry emanate from Solomon and the fabled Temple bearing his name. Every lodge is, and must be, a symbol of the Temple of Solomon. Each Master in the Chair is representative of that perfidious Jewish king. Though not all lodges are willing to frankly admit this identification with the ancient synagogue of sin, there is, in Tombstone, Arizona one which does publicly adhere to this label. Tombstone, Arizona was connected, by a variety of old trails, to the Ruby Road and the town of Ruby, which witnessed so many brutal killings.

It should also be noted that many Mexicans were involved in the Ruby shootings and Mexico is, itself, a master symbol of America mystica and a place where the very foulest deeds of Masonic sorcery and witchcraft have transpired. In 1884, the year General Guadalupe Victories became president, tremendous intra-fraternal strife broke out between the York and Scottish Rite (of which, like in America, numerous public officials were members and active participants). This strange Masonic war certainly calls into question the 18th century disbandonment of the York Rite, if it was able, some hundred years later, to resist the extremely powerful Scottish wing. If this appears to be a digression from mystical toponomy, it actually is not, for the land of Mexico is riddled with symbol place names which fit into the Three Sisters and 32nd degree symbolism.

To summarize this segment, one can chart a trail of symbolism associated with the 32nd degree by means of the Mason Road, Mason No El Bar, Tres Hermanas (Three Sisters), Shakespeare, Macbeth, MacBird, Johnson Mountain, Kennedy Mountain, Ruby Road and so on.

The Canadian Connection

Shortly after the assassination of John F. Kennedy, a Canadian mountain peak was named in his honor. Kennedy Mountain is located at latitude 60 degrees 20 minutes north and 138 degrees — 58 degrees 5 seconds west. The upper part of Canada's Disenchantment Bay touches the 60 degree line. Canada, too, has a Three Sisters mountain which lies at 58 degrees.

Senator Robert Kennedy made a journey to this mountain and made camp with the Three Sisters mountain range to his right and the Hecate Strait (a part of the intercoastal waterway reaching almost to Disenchantment Bay) to the left.

Before reaching base-camp for his high-altitude climb at Cathedral Glacier, Robert Kennedy stayed at "Whitehorse." A white horse is a funerary symbol and is used in Oriental burials: a white stone horse guards the Imperial tomb at Nanking. In the Occident, a black horse is employed for funerals and in the case of the JFK ceremony, the mount was Sardar, the horse given to Mrs. Kennedy by President Khan of Pakistan. Actually Sardar was not black, but a red bay, and had to be dyed for the occasion and his illusion could be viewed as a minor reflection of the generally unreal aspect of the entire rite: a ceremony of disenchantment symbolized by the tying of boots onto the Pakistani horse with the toes pointing backwards.

Lady MacBird and the Ghosts

After her ascension to the White House, Ladybird Johnson went to the ghostly mountains called "Los Chisos" which can mean, "the ghosts" or, as a corruption of the Spanish *hechizo,* signifies "evil spell," as of the type cast by a *hechicero* and *hechicera.* Los Chisos lives up to its name by way of ghost stories told about that area, which have to do with stinking Indians, dirty greasers, filthy gringos and their victims.

Ladybird made her appearance in the Los Chisos area on April Fool's Day, 1966. Perhaps she was there when fun-loving specters were having a macabre field day. Perhaps Hecate appeared in some crossroad melodrama and the Three Sisters lectured on mystical toponomy and Banquo talked on Shakespeare.

The Los Chisos Mountains are in the Big Bend National Park in Texas. The park is said to cover 1,100 square miles and has scenery worthy of the Arabian Nights. It is adjacent to such symbolical mountains as the Sierra de la Encantada (Enchantment), Sierra del Carmen (Carmen: charm, enchantment) and Sierra de la Cruz (Cross). The Sierra de la Cruz is a short distance from Los Chisos on the Mexican side of the Rio Grande and within that area is the town of Ojinaga. Here a so-called church, which is said to be a home of the Devil, is erected over a cave which is said to lead to the "Infernal Regions."

Mrs. Johnson traveled from Big Bend National Park to Fort Davis to some sort of dedication. This military reservation is located very close to Coffin Mountain and Black Mountain. The inversion of the word Davis is "Sivad," which is associated with the color black, a death coach *(coiste-bodhar)* and with a coffin. Meanwhile, Lynda Bird Johnson was on a National Geographic trip whose first stop was at some mountains bearing the name Three Sisters (Tres Hermanas) in Monument Valley, Utah. At this particular time, President Johnson was on a trip to the far east where he visited the "City of Demons" and entered the "13 Acre Mosque," where he performed the Rite of Discalceation, which included a foot washing. Such ablution is widely done in Oriental nations when entering sanctuaries and temples. Whether or not he recited the following words of Macbeth are known only to the initiated few:

"I will, to the weird sisters; More shall they speak, for now I am bent to know By the worse means the worst. For mine own good all causes shall give way. I am in blood steeped so far that, should I wade no more, Returning were as tedious as go o'er. Strange things I in head that will to hand, Which must be acted ere they may be scanned."

The Killing of the King

Do not be lulled into believing that just because the deadening American city of dreadful night is so utterly devoid of mystery, so thoroughly flat-footed, sterile and infantile, so burdened with the illusory gloss of baseball-hot dogs-apple pie-and-Chevrolet, that it exists outside the psycho-sexual domain. The eternal pagan psychodrama is escalated under these so-called modern conditions precisely because sorcery is not what "20th century man" can accept as real. Thus, the Killing of the King rite of November, 1963 is alternately diagnosed as a conflict between anti-Castro reactionaries and the forces of liberalism, big business and the big bankers, this-or-that wing of the intelligence community and so on. Needless to say, each of these groups has a place in the symbolism of the Kennedy assassination.

The ultimate purpose of that assassination was not political or economic, but sorcerous; for the control of the dreaming mind is the underlying motive in this entire scenario of lies, cruelty and degradation. Something died in the American people on November 22, 1963 — call it idealism, innocence or the quest for moral excellence — it is this transformation of human beings which is the authentic reason and motive for the Kennedy murder, and until so-called conspiracy theorists can accept this very real element, they will be reduced to so many eccentrics amusing a tiny remnant of dilettantes and hobbyists.

President Kennedy and his wife left the Temple Houston and were met at midnight by tireless crowds present to cheer the virile "Sun God" and his dazzingly exotic wife, the "Queen of Love and Beauty," in Fort Worth. On the morning of November 22, they flew to Gate 28 at Love Field, Dallas, Texas. The number 28 is one of the correspondences of Solomon in kabbalistic numerology; the Solomonic name assigned to 28 is "Beale." On the 28th degree of latitude in the state of Texas is the site of what was once the giant "Kennedy ranch." On the 28th degree is also Cape Canaveral from which the moon flight was launched — made possible not only by the President's various feats, but by his death as well, for the placing of Freemasons on the moon could occur only after the Killing of the King. The 28th degree of Templarism is the "King of the Sun" degree. The President and First Lady arrived in Air Force One, codenamed "Angel."

The motorcade proceeded from Love Field to Dealey Plaza. Dealey Plaza is the site of the first Masonic temple in Dallas (now razed), and there is a marker attesting to this fact. Important "protective" strategy for Dealey Plaza was planned by the New Orleans CIA station whose headquarters were in a Masonic temple building. Dallas, Texas is located ten miles south of the 33rd degree of latitude. The 33rd degree is the highest in Freemasonry and the founding lodge of the Scottish Rite in America was created in Charleston exactly on the 33rd degree. Dealey Plaza is close to the Trinity River. At 12:22 p.m. the motorcade proceeded down Main Street toward the Triple Underpass, traveling first down (Bloody) Elm Street. The latter was the scene of numerous gun fights, stabbings and other violence and it is the location of the Majestic Theatre, the Negro and industrial district. It was also the home of the Blue-Front tavern, a Masonic hangout in the grand tradition of "tavern-Masonry." Sam Adams and the Masons of the American Revolution did much of their conspiring at the "Green Dragon Tavern" in Boston. One of the many bars claiming the honor of being the first Masonic lodge is the Bunch of Grapes Tavern, also in Boston.

The Blue-Front was the site of the "broken-man" ritual in which various members of the "Brotherhood of the Broom" swept the floor and tended some fierce javelino pigs. The Blue-Front was once a firehouse and was still sporting the pole in the late '20s. This is extremely germane symbolism. The national offices of the Texaco oil corporation are located on Elm Street, Dallas. Its chief products are "Haviland (javelino) oil" and "Fire Chief" gasoline.

On the corner of Bloody Elm and Houston is the "Sexton Building." "Sexton" is heavily laden with graveyard connotations. It is closely associated to the beetles of the genus Necrophorus or Sexton beetles, so-called because they bury the remains of tiny animals with their legs.

Bloody Elm, Main, and Commerce form a trident pattern in alignment with the triple underpass as any Dallas map will show. Many analysts contend that at least three assassins were involved in the crossfire ambush of our Catholic President.

It is a prime tenet of Masonry that its assassins come in threes. Masonic assassins are known in the code of the lodge as the "unworthy craftsmen." Because Masonry is obsessed with the earth-as-gameboard (tessellation) and the ancillary alignments necessary to facilitate the "game," it is inordinately concerned with railroads and railroad personnel to the extent that, outside of lawyers and circus performers, no other vocation has a higher percentage of Masons than railroad workers.

Minutes after John Fitzgerald Kennedy was murdered, three "hoboes" were arrested at the railyard behind Dealey Plaza. No records of their identities have ever been revealed, nor the identity of the arresting officer. All that remains of those few minutes are a serious of photographs which have reached legendary proportions among persons concerned with uncovering the real forces behind the assassination. These pictures have been impressed upon modern consciousness in a way that perhaps only Carl Gustav Jung could describe. The only similar image which has also become a symbol of the people's inability to uncover and overcome evil are the derelicts of Samuel Beckett's play, *Waiting for Godot,* whose entire theme is the futility of waiting for answers or expecting to penetrate the shroud of who controls us.

The "three" and "trident" allusions pertain uniformly to *magica sexualis.* Paracelsus used the latter to overcome impotence. In *The Seven Books of the Magic Archidox,* a trident is listed as the remedy for anyone wishing to overcome the machinations of perverted men and to regain virility.

Dealey Plaza breaks down in this manner: "Dea" means goddess in Latin and "Ley" can pertain to law or rule in the Spanish, or lines of preternatural geographic significance in the pre-Christian nature religions of the English (Watkins). For many years Dealey Plaza was underwater at different seasons, being flooded by the Trinity River until the introduction of a flood-control system. Thus the Dealey (Goddess-Rule) Plaza is present at the Trinity Site of Kennedy's killing. It should be noted that the detonation of the atomic bomb, whose alchemical creation and destruction of primordial matter was an Illuminist obsession, occurred at the so-called "Trinity Site," located on the 33rd degree of latitude. To this trident-Neptune site came the "Queen of Love and Beauty" and her spouse, the scapegoat, in the Killing of the King rite, the "Ceannaideach" (Gaelic word for Ugly Head or Wounded Head). In Scotland, the Kennedy coat-of-arms and iconography is full of folklore. Their Plant Badge is an oak and their Crest Badge has a dolphin on it. Now what could be more coincidental than for JFK to get shot in the head near the oak tree at Dealey Plaza. Do you call that a coincidence?

Oswald

The diminutive form of the name Oswald is "Os" or "Oz": a Hebrew term denoting strength. The role which "Divine Strength" played in the Dealey "Goddess Rule" Killing Of The King ritual should be given careful consideration. One should also note the significance of (Jack) Ruby's killing (destroying) of "Ozwald," in reference to the "ruby slippers" of *The Wizard of Oz,* which one may deride as a fairy tale but which nevertheless symbolizes the immense power of "ruby light," otherwise known as the laser.

Oswald may have undergone biotelemetry implantation in the Soviet Union while a "volunteer" at a Behavior Control Center at Minsk. Oswald roomed with Cubans and was allegedly friendly with a Castro man identified only as being "burly" and a "key" man. "Burly" can mean burlecue or burlesque. The "key," of course, is one of the most important symbols in Masonry and the symbol of silence.

If Oswald was the result of some Soviet Frankenstein process, why did he have to travel several thousand miles for such treatment when it is a routine operation in America? Here in the good ol' USA it is performed in hospitals, prisons and psychiatric centers. While such activities of the Mill-of-Dread are pro forma at a variety of institution, there was a time when it was deemed necessary to do such work at Walter Reed Hospital. These implants were back alley operations in which the victims were

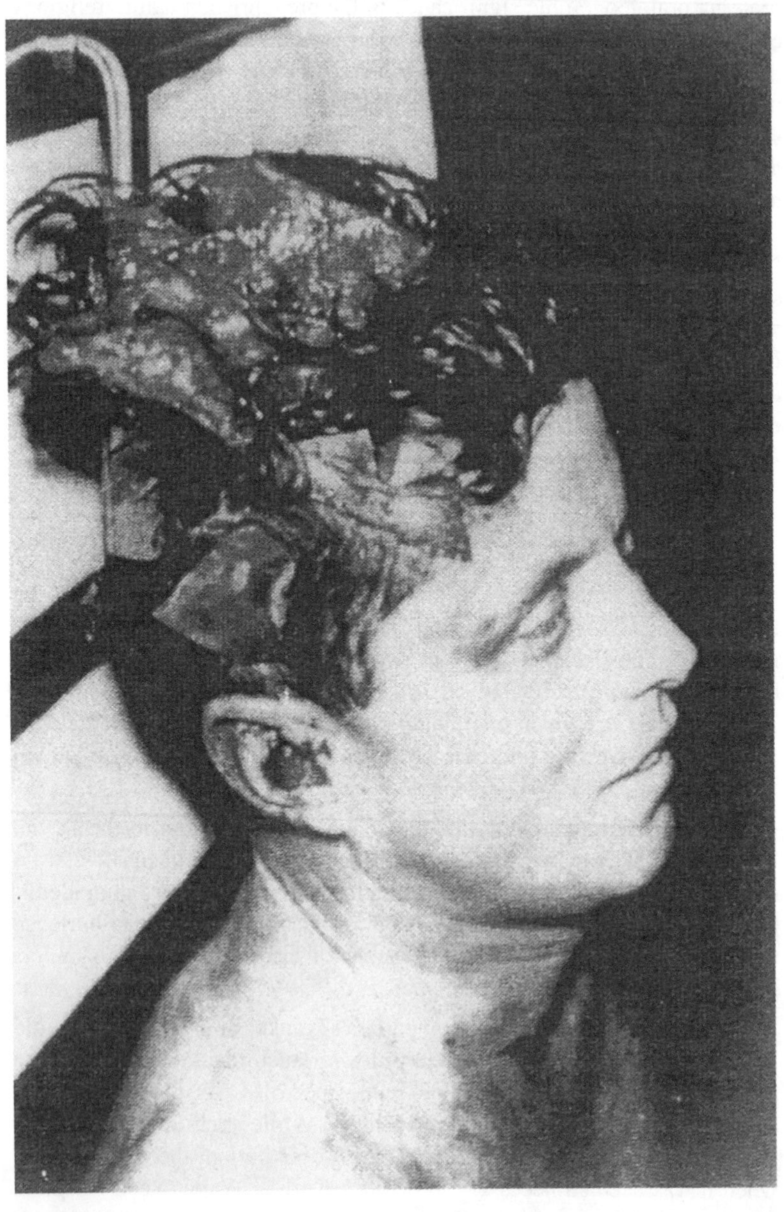

overpowered in some place or other, drugged and then dragged to this government hospital. They were operated on, continued on a heavy drug regimen in a state that varied from somnolent to comatose for a number of days. The electrical function of the victim was recorded and monitored and the biotelemetry plant tested. Subsequently the victims were "brain-washed" and returned to the place where they had been seized. The targets then continued their existence, unaware of how their bodies had been invaded and their autonomy stolen. (This was a select procedure and not all of the staff necessarily knew what was taking place.)

Like the disgraceful treatment of the autopsy of President Kennedy, Oswald's is similarly weird. In point of fact, Oswald was literally butchered in the "post-mortem examination." Pieces were actually cut out of his body. The trenchant incision in his torso resembled a huge "Y," which ran from his groin to the solar plexus. From there, incisions were made to the right and left armpits. (It is also probable that he was castrated). The so-called "two horns of the letter Y" supposedly symbolize two different paths of virtue and vice: the right branch leading to the former and the left to the later. The letter is sometimes referred to as the "Litera Pythagorae" (The Letter of Pythagoras). "Litera Pythagorae, discrimine secta bicorni, Humanae vitae speciem praeferre videtur." (The letter of Pythagoras parted by its two branched division appears to exhibit the image of human life.).

In the 47th Problem of Euclid lies a secret of the Third Degree of Masonry. Pythagoras is called by Freemasons "our ancient friend and brother." One of Pythagoras' main doctrines was the system of "Metempsychosis," which pertains to the passing of a human soul into the body of an animal. Perhaps this was the intention of the autopsy — by cutting the Letter of Pythagoras into Oswald's body they sought to expedite transmigration, and they may even have gone as far as feeding sections of Oswald's corpse to a certain animal, for this too is a practice of what used to be widely feared as necromancy.

Arlington Necrology

The Kennedy and Oswald burials were both at "Arlington": JFK at the National Cemetery near Washington, D.C. and Oswald at a Rosehill Cemetery near Arlington, Texas.

Arlington is a word of significance in Masonic sorcery, and it has a hidden meaning that has to do with necrolatry.

At the Kennedy gravesite, there is a stone circle and in its middle a fire called the "eternal flame." The fire in the middle of the circle represents a point in the circle, the same type of symbolism recognizable in Kennedy's bier and coffin occupying the center of the rotunda in the Capitol. A point in a circle symbolized the sun in ancient sun worship. It is also a symbol of fecundity with the point symbolizing a phallus and the circle a yoni.

At the Oswald gravesite stands a small tree.

There exists an old belief that a tree which grows at or on a grave is embodied with the spirit-force of the person buried at that site, and that a twig or branch taken from such a tree has magical powers. I suggest that Lee Harvey Oswald's mother (Mrs. Marguerite Claverie Oswald) should gently remove a twig from the tree at her son's grave and then at every opportunity touch FBI agents, CIA operatives, policemen, et cetera, with that same twig. Such a procedure couldn't help but be more efficacious in bringing the murderers of JFK to justice than the Warren Commission.

Funerary Rites

John F. (Honey Fitz) Fitzgerald, the grandfather of John F. Kennedy, was elected mayor of Boston thanks in part to his "Wake House" campaigns that became much imitated. These consisted of a daily surveillance of the newspapers for announcements of deaths, after which a discreet "sympathizer" would be dispatched by Fitzgerald and a good deal of political mileage accumulated in the bargain.

For a time, the Fitzgeralds lived near the former site of the Green Dragon Tavern, established around 1680 and demolished for the widening of a street in 1820. The Fitzgerald home was on Hanover Street and the Green Dragon Tavern was on Green Dragon Lane (now Union Street). The tavern boasted the "first lodge room of Freemasonry in America," the St. Andrews Lodge, located within the tavern proper. In the mysticism of the Chinese tongs, the Green Dragon is a death symbol. A symbol of the latter is worn on a ring or held in the hand of a "hatchet man." The Green Dragon is supposed to impart the notion of a "license to kill" for it signifies that the murder is an affair of "honor": the Green Dragon is the guardian of the god-with-a-thousand-eyes who protects the sanctity of the third heaven.

Much of Boston's Irish population arrived in America in what were nicknamed the "coffin ships." Members of the Kennedy family were acquainted with the "Coffin Family." The Reverend William Sloane Coffin was the son of theologian Henry Sloane Coffin; Coffin the younger was a member of the Peace Corps Advisory Council that Sargent Shriver headed. "Shriver" or "Shrive" has the meaning of one who grants absolution to a penitent and it was customary to call upon a shriver before death. If the shriver was not available, a "sin eater" was summoned. The old pious cry that had to do with the request for a shriving was "Shrive me O Holy

Land and Give Me Peace." To this the shriver would respond, "Pax Vobiscum:"

> The spell lies in two words, Pax Vobiscum will answer all queries. If you go or come, eat or drink, bless or ban, Pax Vobiscum carries you through it all. It is as useful to a friar as a broomstick to a witch or a wand to a conjurer. Speak it but thus, in a deep grave tone, Pax Vobiscum! It is irresistible — watch and ward, Knight and squire, foot and horse, it acts as a charm upon them all. I think, if they bring me out to be hanged tomorrow, as is much to be doubted they may, I will try its weights upon the finisher of the sentence. — "Wamba, son of Witless"

Sargent Shriver, "a Catholic and Kennedy by marriage," as head of the Peace Corps and in association with a Coffin, might be considered to be in a sensitive position in relation to mystical onomatology.

> In the ancient mysteries, the aspirant could not claim a participation in the highest secrets until he had been placed in the Pastos, bed or coffin. ... The coffin in Masonry is found on tracing boards of the early part of the last century, and has always constituted a part of the symbolism of the Third Degree, where the reference is precisely to the same as that of the Pastos in the ancient mysteries. — *Encyclopedia of Freemasonry*

President Kennedy sat at the head of a coffin table at the White House. To his back, over a fireplace, hung a portrait of Abraham Lincoln, an assassinated president. On either side of the picture were urns that resembled the type called "cinerary urns" which are vessels in which the ashes of the dead are kept. A book about JFK was called *Three Steps to the White House.* In Masonry are what is known as the "three symbolical steps." "The three grand steps symbolically lead from this life to the source of all knowledge."

> It must be evident to every Master Mason without further explanation, that the three steps are taken from the darkness to a place of light, either figuratively or really over a coffin, the symbol of death, to teach symbolically that the passage from darkness and ignorance of this life through death to the light and knowledge of eternal life. And this from earliest times was the true symbolism of the step. —*Encyclopedia of Freemasonry*

The body of President Kennedy was placed in a coffin which was positioned in the center of a circle under the Capitol dome. The catafalque was a temporary structure of wood appropriately decorated with funeral symbols and representing a tomb or cenotaph. It forms a part of the decorations of a "Sorrow Lodge." This Masonic Encyclopedia reference is to the ceremonies of the Third Degree in Lodges of the French Rite.

Pictures taken of the Kennedy coffin and catafalque show these two props of the funerary rite as a point in a circle. Fecundity is the symbolic signification of the Point within a circle and is a derivation of ancient sun worship.

In olden lore of mystery cults and fertility religion was invariably the legend of the death of the hero god and the disappearance of his body. In the subsequent search and supposed finding of the body we see the contrivance of an elaborate psychological ruse, well known to the masters of the ancient mysteries. The body was said to have been concealed by the killer or killers of the hero god. The concealment of the body was called aphanism, and is a rite of the Masonic Third Degree. Anyone interested in comprehending the mechanics of group mind control would do well to study the Third and Ninth Degrees of Masonry in particular.

The disappearance of the body, this aphanism, is to be found in the assassination of President Kennedy:

> The President's brain was removed and his body buried without it ... Dr. Cyril Wecht, chief medical examiner of Allegheny County, Pennsylvania, past president of the American Academy of Forensic Scientists, and a professor of pathology and law, received permission from the Kennedy family in 1972 to view the autopsy materials (at the National Archives). When he routinely asked to see the brain, Wecht was told it was missing, along with the microscopic slides of the brain. Marion Johnson, curator of the Warren Commission material at the Archives said, "The brain's not here. We don't know what happened to it." *Los Angeles Free Press, Special Report No. 1,* pg. 16.

After the Kennedy coffin was removed from the center of the Capitol rotunda circle, it was taken, with pageantry, to the street for viewing. The funeral procession made an "unplanned stop" on Pennsylvania Avenue in front of the "Occidental Restaurant" and a picture was taken of the flag-draped Kennedy coffin with the word "Occidental" featuring prominently over it. In Masonry and in the lore of the Egyptian jackal-god Anubis, a dead person is said to have "gone west." Several months after the

Kennedy funeral, "Occidental Life," an insurance branch of the Transamerica Corporation, ran an advertisement for group/life which was proclaimed, as usual, to be "new" but with a turn which was indeed original: the inferential weird claim was made that "Until now there was only one way to cash in on Group Insurance," apparently some rather profound changes were made in the manner of things-as-they are after the Killing of the King had become a fait accompli.

The spontaneous stop was made because of the horse Sardar (chief), a gelding (castro), which was wearing boots pointing to the rear in the Kennedy funerary rite. Horses figure prominently not only in the pleasure of kings, but in their murders as well. James Earl Ray was convicted partly on the evidence of a "white Mustang" (automobile), Sirhan Sirhan claimed to his psychiatrists, trance-like, that he shot Robert Kennedy, "for a mustang, mustang, mustang..."

John F. Kennedy had demonstrated affection for the performance of a lady who was a renowned ostrich-feather fan manipulator (Marilyn Monroe). In Egypt, lamenting girls with ostrich feather fans sang a song of entreaty of the type that Nephthys and Isis reputedly sang as a dirge before the said partial resurrection and/or erection of Osiris. The said dirge of lamentation has become known as a Maneros, and the singers are entreating the dead to return, by singing "come to my house" and then offering inducements of some type or other. It is a damn pity that the ritualists couldn't have had Marilyn Monroe and Rosemary Clooney sing a maneros at the JFK funeral.

Before JFK began his Jornada del Muerto (Journey of Death, Journey of the Dead) he was photographed with Tito on the winding stairs in the White House. "Tito" (his real name is said to be Josip Broz) is a significant name in Masonry since it was the title given to Prince Harodim, the first Judge and Provost said to be appointed by King Solomon. Tito was a reputed favorite of that evil Jew whose temple was a hot-bed of thievery, money-changing, male and female prostitution and sorcery. This Tito presided over the Lodge of Intendants of the temple and was one of the "twelve knights of the twelve tribes of Israel."

Let me repeat, JFK was on some winding stairs with a man called Tito.

Winding stairs are symbolically important in Masonry.

The legend of the winding stair is taught in the degree of Fellow Craft. This is the Second Degree, and a person at this grade is, of course, a candidate for the symbolical assassination, euresis, autopsy, coffin resurrection of the Third Degree.

The number of steps in the winding stair are "odd" although no less so than the fact that this Tito or Harodim is a name translating as "those who

Elizabeth Taylor and the Yugoslav Tito

The number of steps in the winding stair are "odd" although no less so than the fact that this Tito or Harodim is a name translating as "those who rule over" the activities of the temple of Solomon.

The winding stairs of this temple, according to the Masons, begins at the porch and winds to a level purified by the Divine Presence (Shekinah) and dominated by the Divine Strength (Oswald).

President Kennedy preceded Tito down the stairs to a portrait of the assassinated President Garfield, where he was photographed and another picture was taken on the stairs before a picture of Lincoln (recall the black walnut rocker of JFK, comparable to the black walnut rocker Lincoln was assassinated in; the "Lincoln Continental" limousine in which Kennedy was shot and the thousand other parallels between the two men). It's unfortunate that President Kennedy didn't trip Tito and then slide down the stair-rail, for he was in a very bad symbolic position, as related to Masonic sorcery, and such unorthodox action might have rattled the "Prince of Harodim."

The Scapegoat

John F. Kennedy, the one and only Catholic president of the United States, was a human scapegoat, a "pharmakos." Pharmakos or Pharmokvos can mean "enchantment with drugs and sorcery," or "beaten, crippled or immolated." In alchemy, the killing of the king was symbolized by the crucified snake on a tau cross, a variant of the crucifixion of Christ.

Jesus Christ was tortured and murdered as the result of the intrigue of the men of the Temple of Solomon who hated and feared Him. They were steeped in Egyptian, Babylonian and Phoenician mysticism.

Masonry does not believe in murdering a man in just any old way and in the JFK assassination it went to incredible lengths and took great risks in order to make this heinous act correspond to the ancient fertility oblation of the Killing Of The King.

I have stated time and again that the three hoboes arrested at the time of the assassination in Dallas are at least as important symbolically as operationally, and that they comprise the "Three Unworthy Craftsmen" of Masonry. This mechanism is at once a telling psychological blow against the victim and his comrades, a symbol of frustrated inquiry and the supposedly senseless nature of any quest into the authentic nature of the murders, and a mirror or doppelganger of the three assassins who executed the actual murder.

As for the three assassins themselves:

"Perry Raymond Russo told a New Orleans grand jury that (CIA agent David) Ferrie said (regarding the assassination of JFK) that "there would have to be a minimum of three people involved. Two of the persons would shoot diversionary shots and the third ... shoot "the good shot." Ferrie said that one of the three would have to be the "scapegoat." He also said that Ferrie discoursed on the availability of exit, saying that the sacrificed man would give the other two time to escape." (Quoted by W.. Bowart in *Operation Mind Control.)*

Camelot

The Kennedy administration was referred to as Camelot, supposedly in joy over the renewed promise of the youthful and vigorous president, his lovely "storybook wife" and the potential of "New Frontier" reform. No doubt, if one attempted to point out the ominous symbolism of the Camelot phrase, such a person would be dismissed as "trying to ruin a good thing," but that has already been accomplished by someone else, and the resulting disenchantment has prepared us to believe the worst about the real story of our internal government.

The site of King Arthur's castle was not far from Tintagel, the Camel River and Camelford. The Camel-ot White House stories are symbolical fecal matter. Vice President Lyndon Johnson invited a Pakistani camel-driver to the White House and JFK, responding with his flashing good humor said, "If I tried that, I would have ended up with camel dung all over the White House lawn."

The officer in charge of the first camel corps in the U.S. Army was a certain Lt. Edward F. Beale. JFK was born on Beals Street and Jacqueline Kennedy's poor aunt, Edith Bouvier, was a Beale by marriage. In Quartsite, Arizona is a pyramid-shaped monument with the bones of a camel in it and buried beneath it is a Syrian camel-driver named "Hi Jolly." The camel and Hi Jolly pyramid burial site is in Yuma County, Arizona. Yuma, Juma and Yama are names of a Tibetan god of death who is the King of the Dead in W.Y. Evans-Wentz's *Tibetan Book of the Dead.* This god is given the power of reading the past and future in a mirror similar to that of the black magician Tezcat of Mexican mythology.

The Warren Commission

Gentlemen, don't pass me by!
Don't miss your opportunity!
Inspect wares with careful eye;
I have a great variety.
And yet there is nothing on my stall.
— Witch in *Faust*

CAMEL
CASH

Mason Lyndon Johnson appointed Mason Earl Warren to investigate the death of Catholic Kennedy. Mason and member of the 33rd degree, Gerald R. Ford, was instrumental in suppressing what little evidence of a conspiratorial nature reached the commission. Responsible for supplying information to the commission was Mason and member of the 33rd degree, J. Edgar Hoover. Former CIA director and Mason Allen Dulles was responsible for most of his agency's data to the panel.

Is it paranoid to be suspicious of the findings of the panel on these grounds? Would it be paranoid to suspect a panel of Nazis appointed to investigate the death of a Jew, or to suspect a commission of Klansmen appointed to investigate the death of a Negro?

Representative Hale Boggs, the only Catholic on the commission, at first agreed with its findings and when he later began to seriously question them, he was "accidentally" killed in a "plane crash."

> Hoodwink (definition). A symbol of the secrecy, silence and darkness in which the mysteries of our art should be preserved from the unhallowed gaze of the profane. — Dr. Albert Mackey, Mason, member of the 33rd degree, foremost Masonic historian of the 19th century, writing in the *Encyclopedia of Freemasonry.*

That is how they see us, as "profane" as "cowans" (outsiders), unclean and too perverted to look upon their hallowed truths. Yes, indeed, murder, sexual atrocities, mind control, attacks against the people of the United States, all of these things are so elevated, so lofty and pure as to be beyond the ken of mere humans.

> The cryptocracy is a brotherhood reminiscent of the ancient secret societies, with rites of initiation and indoctrination programs to develop in its loyal membership the special understanding of its mysteries. — W.H. Bowart, *Operation Mind Control*

Hertz / Hartz

As seen from Dealey Plaza, a large Hertz sign looms over the Sexton building, apparently dividing it into two right angles at the time of JFK's murder.

Joseph Patrick Kennedy, father of John Fitzgerald Kennedy, rescued the Hertz Yellow Cab Company during a "stock crisis."

The name "Hertz" is traceable to Hartz or Harz. In the Hartz Mountains in Germany is a place called the Brocken where sorcerers were believed to gather. Sometimes an optical phenomenon or illusion is glimpsed at the peak of Hartz Mountain and persons see what is known as the Spectre of Brocken.

In the 18th century, representatives from witch-cults all over Europe made their way to a fertility and death ritual on this mountain and some were alleged to have been Masons. Masons were believed to have been able to communicate in some voiceless way, which was called telepathy by some and empathy by others. Empathy can be described as the feeling of entering into the spirit of a person or thing and so empathy is synonymous with the Rapport of Mesmeric Masonry. The witches at the Hartz Mountain festival came together in sympathetic understanding (Rapport) and were in non-verbal communication. In fact, at a given signal, the occult gathering began to cling together in a sort of "Epoxy" of "Agape" ("Love-In," if you will) that became a rite of magica sexualis and ritual intercourse.

Hertz is a name "renowned in the field of communication." Heinrich Hertz was a German physicist who was the first to investigate "electromagnetic waves produced in luminiferous ether," which is a rather archaic way of describing electrical waves which are now known as "Hertzian waves." Hertz was instrumental in the theory which led to the development of radio.

JFK's ancestry is traced to New Ross, a port town approximately four miles from Duganstown, Ireland. In the hamlet of New Ross is a tavern named the "Radio Bar," which is owned by one Gus O'Kennedy; Patrick Kennedy, the President's grandfather, frequented this establishment and the proprietor was a distant relation.

The long-running advertising battle which droned over the Hertz waves between Avis and Hertz Rent-a-Car corporations involves fertility symbolism.

By consulting the Masonic encyclopedia, one will encounter a brief blurb by Dr. Mackey which is probably one of the "thinnest" cover-ups in the entire work. It is the category of "Inversion of Words": apparently, the Masons wanted to be able to explain away various phrases "cowans" (outsiders) might have come across in conversation or study which, without such explanation might be pondered to a degree detrimental to Masonic secrecy. Thus, the definition for word-inversion is a sort of bewildered disclaimer running along the lines of "How did this get here?" Poor, befuddled Dr. Albert Mackey of the "exalted" 33rd degree would have us believe that word inversion is not a central part of Masonic ritual. Anyone recognizing the link between Masonry and Jewish Kabbalism, a connection which might be termed slave-master, will note that a central dogma of the Kabbalah is the principle of the Inverse Sephiroth as personified by the Qlipoth or "Lords of Chaos."

If one inverts the letters of the word "Avis," as in the rental car corporation, one encounters the "Siva." Siva is Sanskrit for "happy" or "auspicious." Siva is also the name of one of the gods in the Hindu triad and in character represents "become-death, the shatterer of worlds" as a certain alchemist once said. The symbol of Siva is the Lingam or penis. Siva, like Neptune and Satan, is usually pictured with a trident.

The words "Wizard" and "Golden File" are formally registered trademarks of Avis Rent-A-Car System, Inc. The "Wizard of Avis," according to advertising propaganda, is a "sophisticated computer" that "remembers everything you tell it" and the "Golden File" is "the Wizard's permanent file" (memory bank).

In Latin, "Avis" means bird or omen.

Avis is a member of a corporate conglomerate, the center of which is the International Telephone and Telegraph Corporation, which is engaged in millions of electronic exchanges involving the Masonic principle of Rapport, the Hartz Mountain principle of empathy, and the fundamentals of Magnetic Masonry.

All of this reminds this writer of the killing of our President on Bloody Elm Street in front of the Sexton building divided by the looming Hertz sign; a tragedy which also wounded Governor John Connally and car salesman James Thomas Tague.

Ferrie and Shaw

David W. Ferrie and Clay L. Shaw were habitués of the old "Storyville" section of the French Quarter of New Orleans. One could say that the entire official assassination investigation is a story of the Ferrie Tale genre.

Discharged from Eastern Airlines for homosexual activity, David Ferrie (Farie, Faerie, Feerie, Fairy) was said to be completely hairless and often resorted to pasting hair on his eyebrows and his head with, appropriately enough, spirit gum. He was also reputed to have been an exotic loser who failed in everything he did and who engaged in various impostures. So, the mystical charade of the Killing Of The King, Ferrie plays the role of a "medicastro" (quack).

Shaw was also a homosexual and flagellant, and since both men were centered in New Orleans, we can begin to understand the influences they were slated to represent in this most publicized of all American murders.

New Orleans, Louisiana, is known as "Crescent City," in reference to the moon and is closely connected to lunar (lunacy) rites, prostitution and every other inversion of the so-called American dream. The CIA station-house connected to Oswald, Ferrie and Shaw as well as to the formulation of the JFK killing is, or was, located in a Masonic temple building in New Orleans, LA.

New Orleans will continue to play a major role in the murder, mayhem and perversion of the coming years. It is invariably in the limelight as a supposedly quaint and "spooky" place and which the public encounters in a film called *Pretty Baby* about prostitution and a 12-year-old child, and in Ishmael Reed's *Shrovetide in New Orleans,* a mother-lode of Voodoo rites which have no end of fascination to foolish people everywhere.

Ruby

On December 20, 1947, Jacob Rubinstein changed his name to Jack L. Ruby by decree of the 68th Judicial Court of Dallas, Texas.

The etymology of the term "Ruby" runs: (French) rubis; (Spanish) rubi; (Latin) rubinus, carbuncle.

In old law books it was once the practice to print some of the titles of the statutes in red and these were termed rubrics or a ruby and hence any fixed, formulated or authoritative injunction of duty was apt to be designated as being a rubric or ruby.

As a rubinus or carbuncle, Ruby pertains to the "Breastplate of Judgment" used by the Chosen Mispet (High Priests) of Jewish sorcery, enabling them to receive "divine" answers regarding the welfare of Judaism; some interpretations claim that the "Breastplate of Judgment" manifested the immediate presence of Jehovah and was also worn by Masons in Royal Arch chapters.

This "breastplate contained twelve stones," each symbolizing one of the twelve tribes of Israel. The carbuncle or ruby was connected to the tribe of Judah (Nopech).

The term "Jack Ruby" was once used by pawn brokers to indicate a fake ruby. In iconography, a ruby or carbuncle symbolizes blood, suffering and death.

Truth or Consequences

District Attorney for New Orleans, James Garrison, is alleged to have been an ex-FBI agent and to have been mentally disturbed at one time. Jim Garrison was an outsider in the Secret Society machinations of the FBI and may very well have been pharmacologically or hypnotically induced to set-up his ill-fated investigation in the "Truth and Consequences Commission."

Truth or Consequences, New Mexico, is a town located on the 33rd degree of parallel latitude, and near the same latitude John Fitzgerald Kennedy became an oblation, and on the same latitude as the chief Temple on this planet in the minds of sorcerers, namely the Temple of Solomon at Jerusalem, which is sworn to be rebuilt on this 33rd degree.

This method and process of Masonic machinations is summed up in the principle of the "Making Manifest of All That is Hidden," which is to seal for all time the allegedly irresistible force of the eternal pagan psychodrama.

In a literal, alchemical sense, the Making Manifest of All That is Hidden is the accomplishment of the Third Law of the Alchemists and is, as yet, unfulfilled or at least not completed. Two laws have been manifested — the creation and destruction of primordial matter (the detonation of the first Atomic Bomb at the Trinity Site, at White Sands, New Mexico, on the 33rd degree of parallel), and The Killing Of The King (at the Trinity Site, at Dealey Plaza, Dallas, near the 33rd degree of latitude).

The remaining law is to be revealed through researchers using the "Freedom of Information Act" to "make manifest all that is hidden" in a way that will be irremediably helpful to the enemy's cause.

This is not a bluff meant to intimidate inquiry: that can only be done with physical or psychological terror, but human curiosity has never been successfully thwarted by threats of a "curse," to say nothing of frustrating those who seek, on a higher level, justice and truth about the arch-criminals of all history.

I do not wish to discourage truth-seeking, but rather supply researchers with the final information needed to create an object which will serve as an immovable object to block their vaunted irresistible force.

The hoodwinked populace unfortunately, will sink lower and lower as they discover the extent to which they have been duped and may, reactively, search for a ruler or drug to put them asleep, to make them less aware.

We must demonstrate that we remain aware of all the enemies and all of their tricks and gadgetry and yet we must not be dissuaded from pursuing truth for the sake of the truth. Let the enemy take upon themselves and their children the consequences of their actions.

Subliminal Images in Oliver Stone's JFK

Dean Grace

This is a record of observations of subliminal images and possible subliminal messages in the film JFK using the slow motion and freeze-frame controls on a VCR. I have made this list in the order of appearance in which they occurred. Subliminals are at their greatest frequency and intensity during the middle and especially the second half of the film. The following list of subliminal descriptions is totally the result of my own personal observations.

1. Tight close-up of a man's face wearing eyeglasses can be seen three times during the movie. He appears to wear the same style eyeglass frame that Garrison wears. This is the first subliminal image seen in freeze-frame during the movie. Is it Garrison's face?

2. Black and white scene of Oswald being questioned by FBI agent after Oswald is arrested for fighting with anti-Castro Cubans. One moment Oswald is sitting in a chair by an FBI agent sitting behind a desk. While advancing the scene frame-by-frame, Oswald is seen sitting in a chair facing his questioner, then instantly Oswald is standing against a wall facing the opposite direction. The chair is empty. The subliminal message appears to be that Oswald can be in two different places at the same time.

3. Garrison questions homosexual convict O'Keefe. In the flashback homosexual party scenes, there appears a full-screen subliminal skull, then a rat in a cage, and then an image of a skull in the background over Shaw's raised left hand. All this can only be caught by advancing the movie frame by frame.

4. Man in dark suit passes three hoboes being taken into custody by police. There is a hint that the man gives the hoboes a secret hand sign. This happens later in the film in more detail.

5. White ghost-like figure in picture on wall watches Garrison and his staff meeting in Garrison's home.

6. During a carnival parade, an American flag is lowered to expose a huge human skull.

7. Garrison questions Shaw in Garrison's office. There are flashback homosexual situations and a very quick black and white scene where an

old-fashioned 16 mm projector projects a film of a dark-skinned man crawling between the legs of a line of playful, white men in bathing suits.

8. Seen in David Ferrie's apartment following his death are a skull, rats and religious figurines.

9. Garrison travels to Washington, D.C., to meet with former intelligence agent, "X." Leaving the Lincoln Memorial Garrison opens an umbrella and raises it over his head. Agent "X" instantly recognizes Garrison, and their talk begins. Passersby likewise open their umbrellas, though it does not appear to be raining.

10. While "X" gives Garrison a short lesson in geopolitics and nuclear war, the Washington monument in the background appears like it has become an ICBM about to lift off, complete with yellow exhaust plumes.

11. A man in a dark suit passes by the three tramps and gives a secret hand sign for the tramps' benefit.

12. Moments after Martin Luther King Jr.'s assassination is announced on television, Garrison's young daughter talks to a stranger on the telephone, who tells her that she's just been entered into a beauty contest. Over her head, on the wall behind her, is the picture frame containing the image of a white, ghost-like figure. Advancing the scene frame-by-frame reveals that the figure appears to talk.

13. Garrison talks to his legal staff about the FBI agent questioning Oswald in connection with Oswald's arrest for fighting with anti-Castro Cubans. Scene shifts to black and white. One moment Oswald is questioned while sitting, the next moment he is standing, facing the opposite direction while the chair he was sitting in is empty. Again, this subliminal message reinforces the feeling that Oswald can be in two places at the same time.

14. Moments before he sees Robert Kennedy being shot on television, Garrison makes a sandwich using Wonder Bread. Of course, viewers wonder who killed JFK.

15. Seconds before he is killed, Robert Kennedy is heard to say, "We are a great country, and a *selfish* country, and a compassionate country."

16. Moments after Robert Kennedy is assassinated, Garrison goes upstairs and makes love to his wife. Horrible televised violence gets Garrison in the mood.

17. As Garrison and his team walk up the courthouse steps, a mysterious man with white hair similar to Clay Shaw is seen moving behind Garrison's left shoulder. Is Shaw stalking Garrison?

18. During Willy O'Keefe's testimony on the witness stand, scene flashes to a homosexual meeting between Shaw and O'Keefe. Above

Shaw's left hand in the corner of the screen in the image of a human skull. A frame-by-frame analysis reveals that the skull opens its mouth in horror, and seems like it is about to explode.

19. A downward zoom over the Judge's desk shows the Judge's hand pounding a gavel. Nearby is seen a round ashtray that resembles the Wicker Man of the movie of the same name. The theme of the *Wicker Man* movie was symbolic ritual murder.

20. Kennedy waves as his car passes through Dealey Plaza. Scene momentarily shifts to a close-up of a man wearing eyeglasses similar to Garrison's. The image of a four-legged, deer-like animals moves across the reflection of the glasses. A gunshot cracks out.

21. A doctor puts the remains of Kennedy's brain in a supermarket style weighing basket.

22. In Garrison's final summation to the court, he says, "So what really happened that day? Let's just for a moment speculate, shall we?" A man in a black suit and white shirt raises an open umbrella in front of another man wearing a jacket with the word "Ripley" emblazoned on its back. Does this refer to Robert Ripley of "Ripley's Believe It Or Not?" or the sci-fi character Ripley of the movie *Alien?*

23. Man aims rifle with telescopic sight at Kennedy. Camera zooms in for an extreme close-up. Scene shifts to the objective lens of the telescopic sight. A reflection of an emotionless face in freeze-frame can be seen in the lens of the sight. This faces then metamorphoses into another face with a wild-eyed, devilish grin. This face then disappears, and then light begins to emanate from within the sight. This emanation gives the impression that the telescopic sight has now become the projection lens of a movie projector.

24. After James Tague is nicked by a stray bullet, scene changes to Claw Shaw holding an umbrella over his head. Several frames later the scene changes to a younger dark-haired man holding an umbrella over his own head.

25. Immediately following the shooting in Dealey Plaza patrolman Joe Smith stops and questions a man. The man produces a Secret Service badge and moves off. Scene shifts to the courtroom, where patrolman Smith is testifying on the witness stand. He says, "Afterward it didn't ring true but at the time — we were so pressed for time." The scene immediately shifts to a tall young man wearing a dark suit. He has his left hand up to his ear, as if listening to an earphone. This man turns toward the camera and clearly gives a Masonic sign of distress. He holds the palm of the left hand up and crosses it with the right hand palm down. This is done several times at waist level, with the hands held out about twelve

inches from the body. This is the sign of distress in the Entered-Apprentice, first degree of Freemasonry.

26. After Garrison delivers his summation to the court, there is another downward zooming shot over the judge's desk. The judge pounds the gavel next to the round ashtray that appears to be a symbolic Wicker Man's face.

Other notes:

In the first scene in which Garrison makes his appearance, a German infantry helmet is seen at the top of his desk.

While standing in front of Guy Bannister's old office building, Garrison says, "I used to have lunch with him [Bannister]."

Garrison's young son, waiting for his father to attend a family dinner, says, "Daddy never keeps his promises." Garrison's baby then cries.

A jive-talking lawyer, Dean Andrews, hired by Clay Shaw to be Oswald's attorney, had been friends with Garrison for years.

Secret intelligence agent "X" says to Garrison, "Remember, fundamentally people are suckers for the truth."

Jim Garrison acted the role of Chief Justice Earl Warren.

TERMINATOR III

Underground computer video games circulating among Austrian and German students test the ability to manage a Nazi death camp and to distinguish between Aryans and Jews, a Holocaust study center says.

Eight copies of the programs, designed for home computers, were obtained by the Simon Wiesenthal Center in Los Angeles. The center demonstrated two of the programs for the Associated Press. Rabbi Abraham Cooper, the center's associate dean, said the programs are based on the Holocaust but often substitute Turks, many of whom work in Germany, for Jews.

In one program, KZ Manager, the player must sell gold fillings, lampshades and labor to earn enough money to buy gas and add gas chambers to kill Turks at the Treblinka death camp. "KZ" is an abbreviation of the German word for concentration camp.

The player must correctly answer questions about Turks or be taken by a Grim Reaper figure to the Buchenwald death camp.

"What you want to do now if you love playing computer games, you want to go right back in and you want to win," Cooper said. "It's a very shrewd psychology in terms of the design of the games."

Reports of the games have circulated for several years, but they were not believed to be widespread until a recent surge of reports in the Austrian media, he said.

Newspapers reported that a poll of students in one Austrian city said that nearly 40 percent knew of the games and more than 20 percent had seen them, Cooper said.

The game Aryan Test says it is by Adolf Hitler Software Ltd. The game Anti-Turk Test says it was made in Buchenwald by Hitler & Hess.

Distribution has been by electronic mail, under-the-counter sales, word of mouth and in deceptive packaging on store shelves. Cooper believes the games are the work of neo-Nazi propagandists seeking youthful followers through a technology largely unfamiliar to their parents.

"Not shocking to anybody, the kids are way ahead of the adults, and this is one area where the Nazis, the fascists, have found a way in," he said.

Source: *Associated Press*

In Israel a new computer game called Intifada — developed by a Russian-born supporter of Meir Kahane, who immigrated to Israel from the U.S. after a stint in the Jewish Defense League — has become a bestseller. Players score points for successfully using tear gas, plastic bullets, rubber bullets and/or live ammunition to disperse Palestinian demonstrators throwing rocks and gasoline bombs. Unlike real life, the game's rules penalize excessive zeal: players lose points if, for example, they shoot to kill when only tear gas is authorized.

High scorers "win" a progressively more hard-line Israeli government, culminating in the installation of Kahane as defense minister, and restrictions on the use of lethal force are eased as the right gains strength. Responding to criticism, the game's inventor told the *Jerusalem Post:* "When people started calling it a Nazi game, I felt I had to come forward to put the record straight... [The education ministry] is turning all the children into leftwingers. The only hope for the country is if the right is strong."

Source: *Middle East Report*

The Masonic Ripper

Jim Keith

The five murders attributed to Jack the Ripper were accomplished by left-to-right knife strokes across the victim's throat.

In Freemasonry, at the various levels of initiation, the initiate performs certain "mimes" depicting the penalties he must pay if he violates the oaths of the order. In the beginning degree, that of "Entered Apprentice," the mime is a left-to-right stroke of the hand across the neck.

Exact information on only three of the five victims of the Ripper exists. A report on the condition of the second corpse states: "The intestines, severed from their mesenteric attachements, had been lifted out of the body and placed on the shoulder of the corpse." The inquest report on the fourth victim, Catherine Eddowes, details in grisly fashion: "The abdomen wall was exposed. The intestines were drawn out to a large extent and placed over the right shoulder."

The protocols of the Freemasons state the method for dealing with traitorous Master Masons: "...by the breast being torn open and the heart and vitals taken out and thrown over the left shoulder."

The exposed location of the Eddowes murder (at Mitre square, in itself not without Masonic significance), as well as the possible use of a non-Masonic accomplice may explain the discrepancy between the left and the right shoulders.

The inquest on Eddowes also stated: "A triangular flap of skin had been reflected from each cheek..."

Two triangles comprise the sacred sign of Masonry.

The murder of Marie Kelly can be compared in its details to an engraving by William Hogarth, one of the first persons to expose the workings of the Masons. Hogarth's engraving, "The Reward of Cruelty," shows a victim laid out naked with a Masonic cable (a Masonic symbol of throat-cutting) wrapped about his neck. In the engraving the victim is in the midst of having his face mutilated, while one of the three Masonic killers is mutilating his eyes with a knife. The stomach and abdomen are ripped open, the heart cut out, and the left hand lays across the chest in the same position that Kelly's was found in. The legs and feet are being skinned. These mutilations describe perfectly the condition of the corpse of Marie Kelly when it was found.

"Leather apron," a name the press dubbed the Ripper with at the time, parallels a description of the Masonic vestment, also referred to as a leather apron, although actually being comprised of lambskin. A portion of the cloth apron worn by Eddowes was carefully cut off by the murderer or murderers and was found in the passage of Wentworth Dwellings, a message in chalk scrawled on the wall behind.

The message was:

The Juwes are
The men That
Will not
be Blamed
for nothing

The "Juwes" is not a misspelling of "Jews," as has always been assumed, but are in Masonic lore three apprentice Masons who killed the master builder Hiram Abiff.

Jack the Ripper, the Final Solution by the late Stephen Knight, published in 1976, brings forth these and other elements which suggest the Ripper slayings may not have been the work of a lone madman, but the commission of a plot hatched by extremely influential Freemasons of the day.

As Knight explains it, Joseph Sickert revealed to a BBC reporter a story that his deceased father, Walter Sickert, allegedly had told to him. Walter Sickert, a famous English painter, had been a friend of Prince Eddy, Duke of Clarence, the son of Prince Albert, heir to the throne at the time of the Ripper murders. Sickert kept a studio at No.22 Cleveland Street, where Anne Elizabeth Crook as well as Marie Kelly worked — Kelly being the last victim of the Ripper. Here it is said that Prince Eddy met Crook (a Roman Catholic commoner), became romantically involved with her, and was then married to her in a secret ceremony in St. Saviour's Chapel. A child, Alice Margaret, was born.

Shortly thereafter a police raid took place in the area and two people were arrested: Prince Eddy and Crook. Eddy was released, while Anne Elizabeth Crook, as confirmed by records of the period, was confined to workhouses and mental institutions until her death in 1920.

Marie Kelly, the last victim of the Ripper, was said to have fled with the child and hid in a convent. The child was later given to Walter Sickert and placed in the care of his relatives.

According to Knight, the reason for the Ripper murders was that Marie Kelly, along with three cohorts, tried to betray the throne with information about the marriage of Prince Eddy to a Roman Catholic, then a despised minority, and the birth of the child.

The disposal of Marie Kelly and her partners in blackmail was entrusted to Sir William Gull, Physician Ordinary to Queen Victoria, whose previous services to the Queen included the signing of the document certifying Anne Elizabeth Crook as insane, and the performance of royal abortions.

Gull was a prominent Freemason, and his responsibility for dealing with the threat was additionally dictated by his Masonic vows. Any threat to the throne was seen as a threat to Freemasonry. The Masons were the secret power behind the British throne and if the throne fell (which was a distinct possibility at that time, due to general unrest and the rising popularity of Socialism) then the Masons would fall, too.

Gull enlisted the help of fellow Masons in the commission of the murders.

The location of the last murder, Mitre Square, is of particular significance. For an ordinary criminal the choice of Mitre Square would have been extremely improbable, completely exposed as it is to passers-by. But Mitre Square comprises the second most important Masonic locale in London, after the Great Hall of the Grand Lodge.

Since the appearance of Knight's book a number of television documentaries and even a movie have been made, bringing forth some details of the Masonic Ripper theory. Curiously, all of the productions have attempted to some extent to discredit Knight's explanation, leaving out relevant details so as to make it seem that the theory rests only upon one or two coincidences, eliminating any mention of the part played by Freemasons in the crimes, or glossing over the connections to the British throne.

Soon after the publication of this book the supposed Ripper diaries will emerge from a major American publishing house. It remains to be seen if the Masonic connection rears its head or is quietly "put to rest."

THE BLUE CABINET OF THE HERRNHUTER.
(*Drawing from the 19th century*).

The Erotic Freemasonry of Count Nicholas von Zinzendorf

Tim O'Neill

Throughout the history of Western occultism, there has been a constant and intriguing tendency toward heterodox sexual suppression, ranging all the way from the wandering Gnostics of the Second Century, EC, with their prostitute "Sophias" and "Shekinahs" to the orgiastic self-mutilation of the Eighteenth Century Russian Skoptsi. From the psychological and mystical viewpoints alike, it is clear that asceticism and libertinism are simply the two opposing poles in a larger archetypal constellation, based upon the experience of ecstacy.

The legend of John the Baptist, holy man extraordinaire and his perversely and insistently erotic relationship with his seductive decapitator, Salome, is one of the most powerful examples in the Western Tradition, of this complex relationship between sadism, sexuality, asceticism and mysticism.

Exstasis, the freedom of the soul from what gnostics considered to be the prison of the flesh, can be sought through either pole of this complex and in certain rare instances, both asceticism and libertinism can operate together to produce extraordinary states of altered awareness. As the great Viennese sexologist, Krafft-Ebing pointed out; "Religious and sexual states of excitement show, at the height of their development, a conformity in the quality and quantity of excitement; therefore, under suitable circumstances, [they] may be interchanged." Ecstacy, considered as a particular and complex set of altered states of awareness, is the traditional working tool for all occult work. Through its gateway, many other alternate states of reality may be touched upon, entered and worked with. This ecstatic frame of mind has traditionally been sought in three distinct yet interrelated contexts. The Mystical, Magical and Mystery Religion workings of the West form the basis for virtually all of the esoteric groups and individuals in our history. Working through passive or receptive, active and cathartic means, respectively, they all seek to reach the same great gnostic goal; direct experience of the Numinous. For our interests, Freemasonry stands out as one of the great representatives of the Mystery Religion, or "Cathartic" approach. Speculative Masonry can be most succinctly defined as a Seventeenth and Eighteenth Century antiquarian revival of the old Mystery School systems of the Ancient World. By presenting the initiate with vivid and cathartic scenes of such archetypal matters as life and death and inducing their direct participation, it was hoped to instill certain gnostic and epiphanous experiences deeply within the subconscious. The effectiveness of this system has been proven for centuries, and follows certain sound psychological principles of great power. How could this archeological-psychological amalgam have anything to do with libertine and antinomian eroticism?

The history of Freemasonry is riddled with rites and rituals which can, only be safely described as "curious" and within that tradition, there is a long and well-documented stream of "adoptive," "androgynous," or other rites which allowed for the practice of men and women, either together or in separate rituals. Along with this historically significant trend, there exists a "shadow history" of covert masonic eroticism and antinomianism. To be quite fair, it is important to point out that these rituals did not generally have the support of official or mainstream masonry, but existed out on the fringes of the masonic world. I must also make it quite clear that the majority of androgynous rites had nothing to do with such matters, either. There do exist two important masonic rites, back in the Eighteenth Century masonic world, which have had persistent rumors of erotic practice attached to them. Again, I must use the term "rumors" since unambiguous internal evidence is only available for one of these rites.

Cagliostro's Egyptian Rite was a very complex system of oracles, quasi-Egyptian rituals and ceremonial magic, formed during the apex of the great period of revolutions during the last third of the Eighteenth Century. In this case, the masonic ritual was divided into men's and women's lodges, however it is still classed as an androgynous rite on the following remarkable basis. According to sexologist Paul Tabori, in his *Secret and Forbidden,* the main degree initiation ceremony in the so-called "ladies lodges" of the Egyptian Rite was openly orgiastic. To quote Tabori: "After passing through several tests, novices assembled at dawn in the 'temple.' A curtain rose and the spectators gazed at a man seated on a golden globe, completely nude, holding a snake in his hand.

The naked figure was Cagliostro himself. The 'high priestess' explained to the amazed ladies that both truth and wisdom were naked and that they (the ladies) must follow their example. Thereupon the beauties stripped and Cagliostro delivered a speech in which he declared that sensual pleasure was the highest aim of human life. The snake which he held gave a whistle, whereupon thirty-six 'genii' entered, clad in white gauze. 'You are' Cagliostro said, 'chosen to fulfill my teachings!' This was the sign for the beginning of the orgies." Alas, while Cagliostro's rite may have actually contained unusual and gnostic/antinomian elements, the ritual which Tabori "reveals" is clearly in the nature of hearsay. As was the case with many of these fringe groups, later, purely literary embellishments were not unknown, particularly when reported from the outside by unsympathetic detractors.

While the reputed eroticism of the Cagliostro Rite remains doubtful, it is difficult to dismiss the more openly erotic, bizarre and even perverse practices at the core of the religio-masonic group formed by Count Nicholas von Zinzendorf during the mid-Eighteenth Century ... the famous Herrnhuter, or Moravian Brethren. Masonic dictionaries and encyclopedias list the group under several interesting appelations: The Order of the Grain of Mustard Seed (Orden vom Senfkorn), The Confraternity of Moravian Brothers of the Order of Religious Freemasons, the Moravian Brethren, or the Herrnhuter (Moravians). The earliest foundations of this Order date to 1722, when a religious group, per se, formed around Count Zinzendorf, in the area of Upper Lusatia. In 1739, the Order took on its masonic aspect. Coincidentally, this was also one of the first "innovatory" Orders introduced into early German Freemasonry. The innovatory orders were those which added new material, often Christian or Templar, to the traditional three-degree Blue Lodge system. It is still true, as Arthur Edward Waite points out in his New Encyclopedia of Freemasonry, that this was not yet a true "high grade" system on the order of the Scottish Rite or the Templar-legend based Strict Observance.

We do clearly know quite a bit about the Orden vom Senfkorn and Zinzendorf from remaining records. The Mysteries of the Order were ultimately based upon a phrase from the fourth chapter of St. Luke's Gospel, in which the Kingdom of Heaven is compared to a mustard seed. Indeed, the masonic "Jewel" of the Order was a golden cross, surmounted by a mustard plant in full bloom, with the mystical motto: "Quod fuit ante nihil"... "What was, before nothing?" This gnomic emblem was suspended from a green ribbon. Now, christianized masonic rites were plentiful during the Eighteenth and Nineteenth Centuries, however in this particular case, one might detect evocations of a specifically Illuminist sentiment, in both the mystical and political senses. Almost as a Christian predecessor to Adam Weishaupt's more deist Illuminati of Bavaria, Zinzendorf's order proclaimed its purpose to be the extension of the Kingdom of Christ all over the world. Both Zinzendorf and Weishaupt proclaimed theocracies, with slightly differing conceptions of "Theos!" Along these theocratic lines, the Moravian Brethren wore rings inscribed with the phrase "Keiner von uns lebt ihm selber" ... "No one of us lives for himself, alone." This is a phrase suggesting both Christian and Illuminist sentiments at once, much as in the famous phrase in the Constitution of the United States ... "all men are created equal"... a phrase which only has meaning in the Illuminist doctrine of the equality of all monads. Given the existence of such truly Christian Illuminist traditions, such as the Alumbrado, Gottesfreunde, Devotio Moderna, Bohme Kreise and Rosicrucians, this conjunction is by no means a contradiction in terms.

The genuinely religious and masonic character of the Moravians accepted, how is it that any erotic elements entered this matrix? It is important to point out that the Moravians, long since reformed, still exist in Germany and the United States as the Plymouth Brethren and the Pennsylvania Moravian colony, however, it was specifically the more bizarre eroticism directly attributable to Zinzendorf, that these latter day groups have eschewed, in favor of a doctrinaire Protestant Pietism. During the so-called "sichtungszeit" or period of sifting and searching, during the 1740's and 50's, Zinzendorf led the Moravians into ever more pathological territory, interpreting every aspect of the Passion and Death of Christ in increasingly erotic terms. Slowly but surely, Zinzendorf created a truly antinomian theology, which came to claim that the disciple's own sexual relationship with Jesus is the key to salvation!

Zinzendorf's astonishing scheme of masonico-theological speculations begins with an obscure detail of New Testament history which should give infinite amusement to Freudians. The Count interpreted the wound in Christ's side, caused when the soldier Longinus pierced the body with his spear in order to determine if death had occurred, in openly sexual terms. This wound became, for Zinzendorf, the veritable birth canal of the Christian Church. The wound thus became a vaginal orifice, the *"seitenholchen,"* or "little side cave" which combined the functions of birth, sexual pleasure and spiritual salvation! In the Moravian worship of the "side cave", it was declared that Christ was the bridegroom and sexual partner of all humans, male and female alike. Zinzendorf enjoined his followers to meditate upon the Cave and to enter it, in the most phallic sense possible, to live therein, play and take their pleasure to their hearts' content. During the course of these truly bizarre meditations, clearly influenced in technique and style, if not content, by St. Ignatius' Spiritual Exercises, the Herrnhuter became "Kreuzluftvoglein" (Little cross birds of the air), *Wunderbienlein* (Little wonder-bees), *"Blutwundenfischlein"* (Little fish of the bleeding wound), *"Wundertaucherlein"* (little wonder-divers) or *"Wunderwurmlein"* (Little wonder-worms). The hopelessly neurotic phallicism and infantilism of these conceptions belie the historical fact that a functioning masonic order took them quite seriously as the foundation for the illuminative experience!

Some hint of the wilder erotic doctrines of Zinzendorf are to be found in the early hymns of the Order, which combine sexuality and mystical flight in the most dizzying way. The phallus is addressed in one of these hymns as: *"Und geheimnisvolles Glied/das die ehelichen Salben/ Jesus halben/heilig gibt und Keusch empfaht/im Gebet/in dem ven dem Ertzerbarmen/selbst erfunden Umarmen/Wenn man Kirchen-Saamen sat/Sey gesegnet und gesalbet/mit dem Blut des unserm Manne/dort entranne/ fuhle heisse Zartlichkeit/zu der Seit/die furs Lamms Gemahlin offen/seit der Speer hineingetroffen/das Objekt der Eheleut."* (And you mysterious limb which sanctifies and commends the marital selves for the sake of Jesus in prayer, in the embraces designed by the Original Mercy itself, while the seed of the Church is sown! Be blessed and anointed with the blood which issues from our man ... Jesus ... feel burning affection for the side which is open to the spouse of the Lamb since the spear has pierced the goal of all married people." Remembering that this is being addressed to the human phallus, there are some remarkable and quite sadistic images of blood and semen in this school of Christianity!)

Another hymn could easily be read as ejaculatory utterances: *"Ach, welche Bickel ich dir irzt schicke/ich bin ein Geist mit dir/und du ein Leib mit mire/und eine Seel/Du Seiten Kringel/du tolles Dingel/ich fress und sauf/mich voll/und bin vor Liebe toll/und ausser mir."* (Oh, what glances I send you now; I am one spirit with you and you are body with me and one soul. You treasure of the side, you mad little thing, I devour you like food and drink to fulfillment and am mad with love, out of my mind.) As addressed to Jesus, the implications of this hymn become truly staggering.

Zinzendorf's essential doctrine claimed, that while Christ was the only true husband of human souls, He had delegated His own mystical power as Bridegroom to his functionaries on Earth; his "vice-husbands" and "marriage procurators", who must fulfill his duties and exercise his marital rights with his brides ... earthly women. Under this doctrine, copulation within the bounds of the Moravian Mysteries became literal sexual union with Christ. Zinzendorf, as the chief deputy of Christ on Earth thereby became the chief marriage broker and undertook to regulate the sexual lives of the Moravians to an insane degree. Zinzendorf began the practice of "adjusting" marriages, switching partners to satisfy his own lust. Often, he held "mass adjustments" during which a large number of young boys and girls were suddenly thrust together in sexual union within the meeting house. After prayer and singing of hymns such as we have seen above, the young couples would perform an exacting form of sexual intercourse astride narrow benches. According to Zinzendorf's dogma, the sexual act, being purely the affair of Christ with His Followers, must be accomplished to his stern designs. Another sexual ritual was enacted inside a small, portable cabinet with windows, which allowed the "Most Excellent Papa" Zinzendorf and his eldest mistress to view the proceedings with voyeuristic abandon. This was the famous Blue Cabinet of the Herrnhutter, which hid the rituals of the "Streitenchen" or "Little Fighters" for Jesus, whom Papa Zinzendorf married and instructed.

Clearly, there are elements in this insane *massa confusa* which are highly reminiscent of the Hindu and Buddhist schools of sexual Tantra ritual intercourse in a group, around the master, exacting performance of the sexual act for transcendent purposes; even the vaginal symbolism of the wound relates to the Goddess orientation of the Tantra. While Zinzendorf's personal fetishes may still seem off to us today, we can begin to understand, with the help of modern depth psychology, that he was really in touch with a deep and archetypal current of erotico-mystical ekstasis that has been formalized in some Oriental religions. In our placement of the Moravian masonic rite in its historical matrix, we can also begin to discern the radical gnostic/antinomian bases for the Zinzendorf doctrines as well as the importance for the future of its intuitive excursion into the underworld of mystical eros. Zinzendorf emerges, not only as a wonderful and classic neurotic, but also as a true nexus for serious illuminative practice, sexual liberation and theocratic politics ... a figure worthy of far more attention than has hitherto been forthcoming. In the context of modern groups practicing esoteric sexuality, such as the O.T.O., the G.B.G. and TOPY, Zinzendorf can now be seen as an important precursor and forefather ... a liberator of the sexual current in the West.

Bibliography

A New Encyclopedia of Freemasonry (2 vols.), A.E. Waite, Weathervane Books, 1970.

Encyclopedia of Freemasonry (Abridged,) Albert G. Mackey, McClure Publishing Co., 1927.

Sexuality, Magic and Perversion, Francis King, Citadel Press, 1972.

Ecstasy Through Tantra, Dr. John Mumford, Llewelyn Press, 1988.

"A Fire in the Shadows," Tim O'Neill, in *Gnosis* magazine, issue #17, Fall, 1990.

Secret and Forbidden, Paul Tabori, Signet Books, 1966.

Rumors, Myths and Urban Legends Surrounding the Death of Jim Morrison

Thomas Lyttle

So much has been written and speculated upon surrounding Jim Morrison's life, death and after-death that it is no longer enough to address just the facts. One must now also address the self-perpetuating mythos that has developed and enveloped the facts.

In the late 1960s, Doors' singer Jim Morrison founded a publishing company named Zeppelin Publishing Company with the help of the legal department of Warner Brothers Pictures and Atlantic Records. According to promotions for Zeppelin, "Jim wanted to get his hands on the trademark 'Zeppelin' before Led Zeppelin did. He did this while everyone in America knew who the Doors were, but before the other rock group was well known..." Zeppelin Publishing Company was chartered and put into hibernation for later resurrection.

On July 3, 1971, rock and roll wünderkind James Douglas Morrison was supposedly, reportedly, found dead in a Paris, France apartment he had sub-leased as a writer's studio. His "wife," Pamela Courson, was the first to discover the body in the bathroom. Jim lay in the bathtub, naked and half-submerged. At first she thought that "Jim was pretending," noticing that he had "recently shaved."

What immediately followed was a series of bizarre and convoluted events, probable conspiracies, strange coincidences and surreal news reports surrounding the death of James Douglas Morrison. Following the death there was a three day news blackout. This was reported on and questioned widely in thc media, including articles in *The Berkeley Barb, Esquire, The LA Free Press, Sounds, The Baltimore Morning Sun,* and many others. Robert Hillburn writing at that time in *The Los Angeles Times,* called his obituary of Morrison "Why Morrison Death News Delay?" igniting a spark that has yet to smolder.

The blackout prevented Morrison's close friends from getting at the principals and witnesses — and the corpse — for close inspection. Even Jim's parents and his in-laws were prevented from seeing the corpse.

Pamela had called a local French medical examiner — Dr. Max Vasille — to take charge upon finding her husband's body. Dr. Vasille listed the cause of death as "heart failure". Several people viewed the sealed coffin, including Doors manager Bill Siddons, who apparently chose not to view the corpse. Siddons' official statement to the press was that "Jim Morrison died of natural causes" and that "the death was peaceful".

Although Jim's death was listed officially as "heart failure," his personal physician, Dr. Derwin, stated to the press that "Jim Morrison was in excellent health before travelling to Paris".

This has recently been complicated by "Queen Mu" writing in *Mondo 2000* (Summer, 1991). Apparently *Mondo 2000* surfaced a rare medical file regarding Jim Morrison's various sexual diseases, and the treatments he was undergoing for them. There was mention of "cancer of the penis...". Queen Mu reports:"... Hey! No one wants to be expunged from the Book of Life. How many medical workers at UCLA knew that Jim Morrison was being treated for gonorrhea in the Fall of 1970? Knew of the biopsy that confirmed adenoma of the penile urethra — often consequence to repeated gonorrhea? This is a particularly swift form of cancer whose only alternative may have been radical castration..."— Queen Mu, pp. 131.

No autopsy was performed on Jim Morrison's corpse, as is the usual custom in unusual or suspect deaths in France. Had friends been able to at least see the corpse this might have been done.According to several reports, Morrison confidant Alan Ronay also helped maintain the blackout surrounding the death. Jim Morrison's body was quickly whisked away to be buried at Pere Lachaise. Pere Lachaise is a national French monument and notables like Balzac, Edith Piaf, Moliere, Oscar Wilde and other French countrymen are buried there. Regarding Pere Lachaise: Jim had handpicked the gravesite on several occasions for his impending "burial." He had visited the site as late as three days before his "death." This is reported in *Break On Through* and other Morrison biographies.

The media at once showed suspicion regarding Morrison's grave due to the fact that foreigners are rarely buried in a national French monument. Reports like those in the *Baltimore Morning Sun* questioned how he might have cajoled his way into the cemetery to be buried.

Upon viewing the Pere Lachaise grave site, Doors drummer John Densmore stated: "... the grave is too short!" Doors manager Bill Siddons, when asked about Pere Lachaise, stated: "... how it happened is still not clear to me". He was quoted in *Bam!,* a rock magazine back in 1981 regarding the controversy. At any rate, Morrison's grave at Pere Lachaise remained unmarked for several months, adding and maintaining a further

remained unmarked for several months, adding and maintaining a further cloak around the corpse and the evidence.

Only two people saw Jim Morrison's dead body — his wife Pamela and Dr. Vasille. Dr. Vasille has repeatedly denied interviews and will not answer questions, and Pamela is dead.

The Occult Connection

Besides the "facts" as laid out in countless books, films, interviews and press reports, there exists also a wild and surreal assortment of rumors regarding "what really took place". Many of these rumors center in on the occult, black and white magick, Voodoo, magical Christianity and assorted mystical strangenesses. In J. Prochniky's biography of Morrison, *Break On Through,* there is this description of Morrison-based occult rumors: "... even more incredible were theories that Morrison had somehow been "murdered" through "supernatural means". While Jim was fascinated with the occult, it is quite an assumption that a jealous rival or jilted lover could cause his death in a Paris bathtub by stabbing a Voodoo doll or melting down a Doors album while chanting a curse."

"... Another supernatural-based theory is that Morrison's body had been driven to great extremes by the spirit of the shaman he believed had entered his body as a child on that New Mexico highway. When this spirit or a demon has used its talents to influence the world, it abandoned Jim and left him a physically wasted and mentally exhausted man who felt betrayed with no desire to go on..." — Riordan and Prochniky, pp. 466

Another occult theory exists in *No One Here Gets Out Alive* by Sugarman and Hopkins. Regarding Jim's death they state:

"... Other theories abounded in Jim's close circle of friends. One had him killed when someone plucked out his eyes with a knife ("to free his soul", as the story had it). Another had a spurned mistress killing him long distance from New York by Witchcraft..." — Sugarman and Hopkins, pp. 372

Anthropologist Alison Bailey Kennedy even went so far as to tie Morrison in with Orphic mystery cults and the initiatory uses of various spider venoms, which release the *"deuende* in Gypsy tradition — the dark soul that burn incandescently like a cicada, immolating itself in fiery passion."

Jim Morrison many times claimed connections to the occult and specifically Voodoo or Voudun philosophy and magick. It was a part of his "path". The moniker "Mr. Mojo Risin'" was an anagram — a rearrangement of the letters in Jim Morrison. Mojo is a religious term describing shamanic "power icon" or affiliation. The African root Mo refers to the dark or darkness. Mojo is a specific African/Voodoun/Obeah traditional term.

"I think that there are whole regions of images and feelings that are rarely given outlet in daily life... when they do come out, they can take perverse forms" said Morrison circa 1968. He goes on to say that "the shaman is the healer, like the Witch-doctor." Morrison reiterates elsewhere that "we must not forget that the snake or the lizard is identified with the unconscious and the forces of evil..." So says the legendary "Lizard King". "The Lizard King" was one of Jim Morrison's occult code names. He was also called "The Exterminating Angel" in occult circles, according to film critic Gene Youngblood and others.

In *No One Hear Gets Out Alive* authors Hopkins and Sugarman recount Morrison drinking blood with Witch-initiate Ingrid Thompson. In certain occult traditions, the use of blood combined with certain sexual acts is reginmen, part of a hidden technology for spell casting. This is especially so in the Tantric *Vama Marg* (left-handed) rites. It is also a part of Western ritual magic, used in groups like La Couleuvre Noir, the Ordo Templi Orientis, Les Ophitis and others, although it is more uncommon than common in occult work.

This sort of sorcery is also used in Voodoo/Voudun Petro rites to summon different Loas (gods and goddesses). Speaking of the Tantra *Vama Marg* and the Voodoo *Petro,* there is this description of death mythology pertinent to Jim Morrison's occult beliefs and possibly his practices. At the very least he would have known of these ideas.

"... but the human form is no means just an empty vessel for the Gods... Rather it is a critical locus where a number of sacred forces may converge. The players are the basic components of man: the *z'etiole,* the *gros bon ange* and the *ti bon ange,* as well as the *n'ame* of the corpse cadaver. The latter is the body itself, the flesh and the blood. The *n'ame* is the gift from God and the spirit of the flesh that allows each cell in the body to function. It is the residual presence of the *n'ame* for example, that gives form to the corpse long after the clinical "death" of the body. The n'ame, upon the "death" of the body begins to pass slowly into the organisms of the soil... A process that takes 18 months to complete..."—Davis, pp. 99

Remember, Jim Morrison's grave at Pere Lachait remained unmarked for several months so that no one might disturb the corpse and the surrounding site.

According to Tibetan tradition, something similar is believed to exist so far as naming the components of the soul and the body. The *Vama*

Marg and especially the *Bardo Thodol* (the Tibetan Book of the Dead) relate specific death myths concerning what occurs right after someone dies.

Writing in *Psychedelic Monographs and Essays,* psychiatrist Dr. Rick Strassman shows that:

"... Another model of birth and death, and transformation in which the 49 day interval appears is in the Bardo Thodol... This is the time when the life forces of the deceased — the energetic tendencies accumulated during "life," "decide on" or gravitate towards or coalesce around the next incarnate form..." — Strassman, pp. 182

Rock writer Greg Shaw, writing in *Bam!* and *Mojo Navigator* interpreted Morrison's song "The End" along these lines also, stating that each line in the song is a direct quote from the *Bardo Thodol.* It all "makes perfect sense, if one is familiar with the mystical background," said Shaw.

What are the implications for these ideas in light of the supposed "death" of Jim Morrison? At clinical death, according to the above, the person actually splits up into his or her true parts, formerly connected into a whole being.

According to occult lore, it is possible to ensnare or trap parts of the personality or spirit during this transition. Wade Davis, author of The *Serpent and the Rainbow and Passage of Darkness: The Ethnobiology of the Haitian Zombie,* has this to say:

"During initiation, for example the *ti bon ange* may be extracted from the body and housed in a clay jar called a *canari.* A *canari* is a clay jar that has been placed at the inner sanctuary of the *hounfour* (ritual house)."

"... During the stages directly following the physical death and the first stages of after-death the *ti bon ange* is extremely vulnerable... Only when it is liberated from the flesh... is it relatively safe..." — Davis, pp. 102

Is it Jim Morrison's *ti bon ange* that is at the root of all these occult rumors? Was it his *ti bon ange* that was bought, sold and then collected on that fateful day in Paris when he "died?"

That *canari* has a name. It is called Zeppelin Publishing Company. And the *bokor,* or Voodoo high priest who cajoled Morrison's *ti bon ange* into the *canari?* He runs a company called the B of A Company (or B of A Communications), formerly of Baton Rouge, Louisiana, and now of Fort Lauderdale, Florida. He owns an active passport and IDs under the name of James Douglas Morrison and claims to actually be the not-so-dead rock star!

In the first two years after Jim Morrison's "death" in Paris, many sightings of the rock star were reported. These sightings range from the totally spurious and ridiculous to the reliable and very hard to shake. The *LA Free Press* and several wire service reports described someone in 1973 appearing on several occasions in San Francisco. There Morrison was involved with business and banking transactions with the Bank of America of San Francisco. The employee that handled the transactions, Walt Fleischer, confirmed that someone resembling Morrison and using that name was indeed doing business at the Bank of America. He did add that he "was far from sure that this was the 'dead' artist" as Morrison showed no identification. Could this be because a photo ID was already on file at the bank, with the name James Douglas Morrison? Yes, it is still on file.

According to authors Riordan and Prochniky, Morrison was also seen on several occasions hanging out in "unpleasant places" in Los Angeles and wearing Morrison's leather garb, all in black. This was over a period of two years right after the Paris "death." I researched this a bit further and found out that the "unpleasant places" meant notorious gay leather bars, and the underground gay community in Los Angeles.

There were also many rumors that Morrison was also appearing regularly in Louisiana and had made several radio interviews. Again, Prochniky and Riordan reveal that: "... At an obscure radio station in the Midwest Jim supposedly showed up in the dead of night and did a lengthy interview that explained it all... After the interview he vanished into the darkness again. As you might guess, no recordings of the interview exist and no reliable source remembers hearing the broadcast..."

A record called "Phantom's Divine Comedy" was released in 1974. This was rumored to be Jim Morrison singing with an anonymous band with the names of "drummer X, bassist Y, and keyboardist Z". The music reportedly resembled Jim Morrison's sound quite well. All this again added and sparked the rumor mills, and stirred public fascination.

However, in a 1992 press released from the Zeppelin group, it is revealed that Morrison pal Iggy Pop was actually doing all the singing and helping the "hoax" along. This added more fuel as to how many people were actually involved in maintaining his "death hoax." Up until the 1992 press release, the record company that had released Phantom had refused to divulge the names on the LP, or the singer's name — which was indeed Iggy Pop.

Regarding all these rumors, Doors keyboardist Ray Manzarek stated: "If there was one guy that would have been capable of staging his own death — getting a phony death certificate and paying off some French doctor... And putting a hundred and fifty pound sack of sand into a coffin and splitting to some point on this planet — Africa, who knows where — it is Jim Morrison who would have been able to pull it off." Jim Morrison's best friend Tom Baker, writing in *High Times* (June, 1981) had this to say: "I was very tempted to believe the rumors that Jim had faked his own death."

A group of fans actually went so far as to try to get Morrison's dental records, apparently to try to get permission to dig up his body and match the records to the remains. This was immediately blocked both by Morrison's parents and their attorneys — at least for the time being.

It is known that Jim Morrison had repeatedly planted the seeds which would lead to this sort of speculation — that he had somehow faked his own death and dropped out into a new identity. At the Fillmore in San Francisco in 1967, Jim started suggesting that he should pull a "death stunt" to bring national press attention onto the band. This was when he came up with the "Mr. Mojo Risin" anagram which would be used after he "split to Africa" and wished to secretly contact friends.

Morrison also told Danny Sugarman and Jerry Hopkins on more than one occasion that he could see himself "radically changing careers, reappearing as a suited and neck-tied businessman." Jac Holzman's assistant Steve Harris even remembers Jim Morrison asking what might happen if he were to suddenly "die"... how might it affect business, record sales, the press, and would people believe it? With confidant Mary Francis Werebelow Jim "entertained long conversations about how the Disciples had stolen the body of Christ from the crypt, jokingly calling it the 'Easter heist,' etc."

In a *Rolling Stone* article for September 17, 1981, author Jerry Hopkins recounts many other Morrison sightings: "The first one I remember was a beaut... He surfaced in San Francisco shortly after Morrison's death and began cashing checks in Morrison's name. He was not writing bad checks, mind you; it was his money he was spending. It was just that he was dressed as Jim would in his 'leather period,' and that he told everyone that he was indeed the 'dead singer.'

"The telephone operator asked: 'will you accept a long distance collect call from Jim Morrison?' It was an interesting conversation... Our conversations were unsettling. He told me to go to Paris and dig up the corpse, but that you would need permission from 'twelve Catholic Bishops' to do it... A visit to his home was more jarring. There at the end of one room was a Morrison 'shrine,' converted with posters, flowers, religious icons — the works!"

Years later, I actually got the chance to visit and interview the shrine's owner, who claimed to be Jim Morrison. He told me matter-of-factly details about Hopkins, as well as that other reporters had actually burglarized the shrine in an attempt to get a scoop. Another surreal sighting involved "Donny" of Baton Rouge, Louisiana. He described Jim Morrison at Morrison's home in 1978. Donny told his friend "Larry" about it, as Larry was trying to break in to the world of rock and roll: "I remember Larry telling me about the whole wall of one room lined with books all across it. Every one of the books were about Satan, or had something to do with him. He also told me about a large chair that looked like a throne, on which this man sat and watched over his nude children running around... I guess that you can probably guess who that kinky old weird man was — Jim Morrison, The Lizard King!" — Sugarman, pp. 33

Another person named Rhea (the Greek goddess of fertility) claimed she was living with Jim Morrison in 1979 with their son "Jesse Blue James". She matter-of-factly claimed that Morrison had "evolved into a state of pure energy... And can materialize and dematerialize at will." She and Jim were also in direct telepathic communication and in "electromagnetic synch."

The Intelligence Connection and JM2

Rock icon Jim Morrison's father was an admiral in the United States Navy, privy to intelligence and counterintelligence information. His name is Steven Morrison.

During the first few years after Jim Morrison's "death" a number of interesting articles surfaced. These cited references showing various intelligence interests either in Morrison's underground activity; his "death" or that intelligence had even masterminded Morrison's death itself! One of the more explicit appeared in the Scandinavian magazine *Dagblatte.* This article detailed French intelligence efforts to assassinate Jim Morrison in Paris.

Author Bernard Wolfe writing "The Real Life Death of Jim Morrison" for *Esquire* (June 1972) related the story of, "Sherry, a Pasadena girl who knew Morrison well: "...I couldn't make sense out of the stories in the papers. Suppose he had a heart attack exactly as they reported, is that what he died of? My God, you might as well say that Ernest Hemingway died of "extensive brain damage". If you want to know the cause of Jim's death — not just the physiology of it — ask what triggered his heart to stop... And whose finger was on the trigger." — Wolfe, pp. 106

In the first few years after Morrison's "death" the owner of B of A Communications, named James Douglas Morrison, claimed to be operating as an intelligence agent for a number of domestic and international groups including the CIA, NSA, Interpol, Swedish Intelligence and others. There are also connections between James Douglas Morrison and various occult groups with probable intelligence connections. [Author's note: from here on the B of A Morrison will be referred to as JM2.]

JM2 also claims to be the "dead" rock star and former singer for The Doors. The new JM2 dropped the old JM1 rock and roll identity to become a "James Bond," wearing the suit and tie that Morrison predicted when he was with The Doors.

This author has in fact seen what appear to be stacks of official-looking documents and letters between the CIA, various government agencies, national news groups like CNN and NBC and JM2, involving what looked like personal meetings, projects and ephemera. Of special interest is that when I viewed parts of the files, all the reports had a paper-thin metallic band affixed to them with colored UPC bar codes. There is no way for me to authenticate the claims of JM2, but everything looked extremely official and very elaborate.

From about 1972 through 1992 JM2 has left a surreal trail of paper and appearances all over the world. These include letters to and from Louisiana Governor Edwin Edwards and CIA Director William Colby, through the Washington, DC law firm of Colby, Miller and Hanes.

A courtroom transcript which I have seen implicates the FBI and CIA in several coverups regarding JM2's intelligence career. These show that there seems to be a systematic destruction of files relating to JM2's spy activities. An enclosed plate also shows JM2's Swedish Intelligence ID card, obtained from the FBI through the Freedom of Information Act. Unfortunately the only copy I have is obscured in the facial area, but the ID numbers are intact. Also in my possession are files concerning JM2's rogue financial activities with the Bank of America, and news reports regarding lawsuits by and against JM2 for bank fraud and espionage, which he claims was done under intelligence auspices as part of financial experiments to destabilize foreign currencies and exchange rates.

There also appear to be hundreds if not thousands of miscellaneous files — both classified and declassified — regarding one James Douglas Morrison, dated after his "death" in 1971. These also refer to "WBC," a nom de plume of JM2. These look like real letters, documents, and court transcripts involving intelligence circles. These involve the CIA, Danish intelligence, and others. There is also an active passport and banking IDs under the name James Douglas Morrison.

Like the "multiple Oswald" theories of Kennedy assassination buffs, there also exist rumors and urban legends describing the "multiple Morrison" theory.

The idea that Jim Morrison was in fact several different people and actors, or intelligence agents has been going on for some time. Besides the "Morrison" singing on the Phantom (now shown to be Iggy Pop) there also exist rumors that a Louisiana banker as well as Richard Tanguay — a close friend of Mick Jagger — perpetuated the hoax. Even *High Times* ran and old news story about someone claiming to be Jim Morrison (post 1971) running for governor of Louisiana! Supposedly Richard Tanguay (related to vaudeville legend Eva Tanguay) took the Morrison persona on, on several occasions, and even sang with The Doors when they toured Europe with the Rolling Stones. Is this possible?

In fact JM2 has claimed publicly that there have been numerous James Douglas Morrisons, and that they all knew one another and met from time to time to work it all out. The impersonations were part of CIA sociological experiments like Artichoke or MK-ULTRA.

Is this all for real or is this an elaborate hoax? It is not the scope of this work to determine the truth — or lack of truth — or the consequences of such activities. The important thing to note that someone or some group is actively pursuing and setting up a mass "urban legend" regarding James Morrison. Whether this is a hoax or not is not as important as the fact that a lot of official-looking information is being generated surrounding the myth and legend of Jim Morrison, his life and his supposed "death."

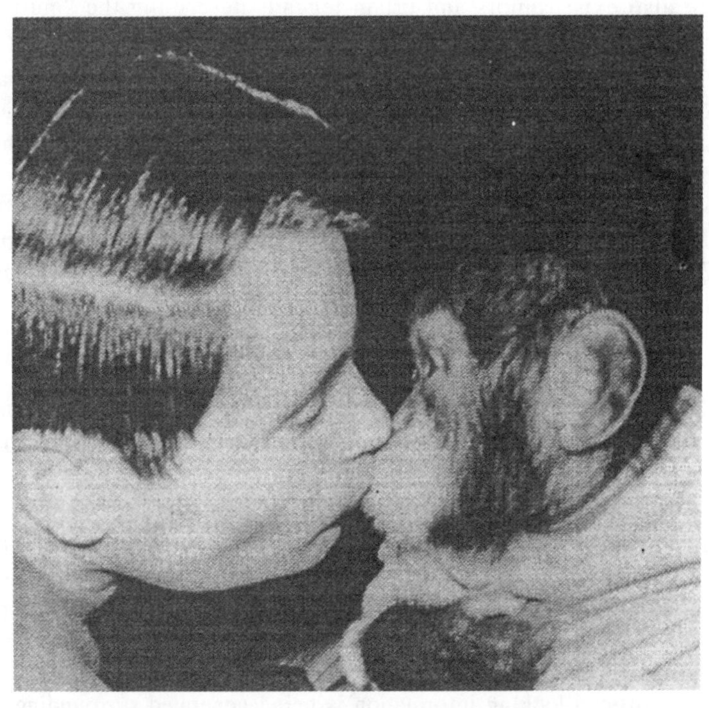

The Last Testament of Rev. Jim Jones

Jonestown, Guyana, 18 November 1978

How very much I've tried my best to give you a good life. In spite of all that I've tried, a handful of people, with their lies, have made our lives impossible. There's no way to distract ourselves from what's happened today.

Not only do we have a compound situation ... The Betrayal of the Century... Some have stolen children from mothers and are in pursuit now to kill them because they stole their children. I mean we are sitting here waiting on a powder keg and I don't think that is what we want to do with our babies. I don't think that is what we have in mind to do with our babies.

It was said by the greatest of prophets from time immemorial: "No man may take my life from me. I lay my life down..." So just to sit here and wait for the catastrophe that's going to happen to that airplane — it's going to be a catastrophe — it almost happened here, it almost happened, the Congressman was nearly killed here. But you can't steal people's children, you can't take off with people's children without expecting a violent reaction.

If we can't live in peace, then let us die in peace. I've been so betrayed. I've been so terribly betrayed. We've tried, and what he said right this minute was that he said if it was only worth one day it was worthwhile...

What's going to happen in a few minutes is that one of the people on that plane is gonna, is gonna shoot the pilot. I know that. I didn't plan it but I know it's gonna happen. They`re gonna shoot that pilot and down comes that plane into the jungle and we had better not have any of our children left when it's over cause ... I never lied to you. I never have lied to you. I know that's what's going to happen. That's what he intends to do and he will do it. He'll do it.

I've been loaded with many pressures seeing all these people behave so treasonous. It was just too much for me to put together but I now know what he was telling me and it'll happen ... if the plane gets in the air, that is. So my opinion is that you be kind to children and you be kind to seniors and take the potion like we used to take in an ocean breeze and step over quietly because we are not committing suicide — It's a revolutionary act. We can't go back, we won't ... we're not going back to tell more lies which means more Congressmen, there's no way, there's no way we can survive....

The people in San Francisco will not be idle over this. We do not take our death in vain you know. Is it too late for Russia? Here`s why it's too late for Russia. They killed, they started to kill. That's why it makes it too late for Russia. I can't control these people. They're out there. They've gone with the guns and it's too late. And once they've killed anybody, at least that's the way I want it. I just put my lot with you. If one of my people do something, it's me. When they say I don't have to take the blame for this, well I don't, I don't live that way and if they deliver up sin and try to get the man that's ... it ... mothers ... lying on him and lying on and trying to break up this family and they've all agreed to kill us by whatever means necessary. Do you think I'm going to let them? ... Not on your life. No, you're not going, you're not going. You're not going. I can't live that way. I cannot live that way. We lived for all and I'll die for all...

To me death is not a fearful thing, it's living that's fearful.

I have never never never seen anything like this before in my life. I have never seen people take law and provoke us and try to purposely agitate mothers of children. It is only ... it's not, it's not worth living like this, worth living like this.

There is one man there who blames, who blames Michael Stone for the murder of his mother, and he will stop that plane by any means necessary. He'll do it. That plane will come out of the air. There's no way you can fly a plane without a pilot...

I haven't seen anybody yet that didn't die, and I like to choose my own kind of death. I'm tired of being ... to hell, that's what I'm tired of. Tired of it. So many people's lives in my hands and I certainly don't want your life in my hands. I've been telling you to this day, without me life has no meaning.

I'm the best friend you'll ever have.

I have to pay. I'm standing with you people — you're part of me. I can detach myself ... no no no no no, I never detach myself from any of your troubles. I've always taken your troubles right on my shoulders ... I'm not going to change that now. It's too late. I've been running too long. I'm not gonna change now.

The next time, you'll get to go to Russia. The next time round. What I'm talking about now is the dispensation of judgement, this is a revolutionary suicide council. I'm not talking about self-destruction. I'm talking about what ... we have no other road. I will take your call. I will put it to the Russians, and I can tell you the answer now because I'm a prophet. Call the Russians and tell them... see if they'll take us.

I practically died every day to give you peace. And you've still not had any peace. You look better than I've seen you in a long while, but it's still not the kind of peace that I wanted to give you. A person's a fool who continues to say that you're winning when you're losing. Win one, lose two, what?...

He's taking off, the plane is taking off ... Suicide: many have done it ... Stone has done it. If somebody oughta listen ... somebody ... can talk ... can they not talk to San Francisco see that Stone is not ... He has done the thing he wanted to do. To have us destroyed.

We win. We win when we go down, they don't have nobody else to hate. They've got nobody else to hate. Many will destroy themselves. I'm speaking here not as the administrator but as a prophet today. I wouldn't talk so serious if I didn't know what I was talking about.

By now the damage will be done. But I cannot separate myself from the pain of my people. We can't separate myself, if you think about it, we've walked together too long.

I saved them, I saved them, but I made my example. I made my expression. I made my manifestation and the world was ready ... not ready for me. Paul says I was a man born out of due season. I've been born out of due season just like we all are and the best testimony we can make is to leave this goddamn world.

Everybody hold it, hold it, hold it, lay down your burden and I'll lay down my burden down by the riverside, shall we lay 'em down here inside of Guyana, what's the difference?

No man didn't take our lives right now; he hasn't taken them, but when they start shooting them out of the air, they'll shoot some of our innocent babies. I'm not lying ... They've got to shoot me to get through to some of these people. I'm not letting them take your child. Would you let them take your child?

For months I've tried to keep this thing from happening, but I now see that it's the will of the Sovereign Being that this happened to us. And we lay down our lives in protest at what's been done. And we lay down our lives in protest at what's been done. The criminality of people, the cruelty of people who walked out of here today. You know those people who walked out, most of those white people. Most of those white people walked. I'm so grateful for the ones that didn't, those who knew who they are.

There's no point, there's no point to this ... we are born before our time. Take ease, take ease, take ease, take ease ... Sit down, sit down, sit down. I tried so very very hard ... They're trying over here to see what's in it ... what's gonna happen ... who is it? It's all over, it's all over....

What a legacy, what a legacy. Well, the Red Brigade's the only one that made any sense anyway. They invaded our privacy, they invaded our home, they followed us six thousand miles away. The Red Brigade showed them justice — the Congressman's dead.

It's simple — there's no convulsion with it. It's just simple. Please get it before it's too late. The GDF will be here I tell you. Get moving, get moving, don't be afraid to die. If these people land out here they'll torture our children, they'll torture some of our people here, torture our seniors. We cannot have this.

Are you going to separate yourself from whoever shot the Congressman? I don't know who shot him. They speak of peace, they gotta right to know how many are dead ... Oh, God, almighty God.

I don't know how in the world they're ever gonna write about us. It's too late, it's too late. The Congressman is dead ... Many of our traitors are dead ... They're all laying out there dead....

Will you please hasten, will you hasten with that medication. You don't know what you've done... I've tried ... It's hard, it's hard only at first is it hard. It's hard only at first. Living ... when you're looking at death ... living is much more difficult. Rising up every morning and not knowing what's going to be ... it's much more difficult. It's much more difficult.

Please for God sake let's get on with it. We've lived as no other people have lived and loved. We've had as much of this world as you're gonna get. Let's just be done with it, let's be done with the agony of it. It's far, far harder to have to watch you every day die slowly, and from the time you're a child to the time you get grey, you are dying.

This is a revolutionary suicide. This is not a self-destructive suicide. Who wants to go with their child has a right to go with their child. I think it's humane.

I want to go — I want to see you go through. They can take me, and they can do whatever they want to do. I want to see you go. I don't wanna see you go through this hell no more. No more, no more, no more ... The best thing you can do is relax and you will have no problem. You will have no problem with the thing if you just relax.

It's not to be feared. It is not to be feared. It's a friend. And you're sitting there showing your love for one another. Gone, let's get gone, let's get gone.

Who are these? We have nothing we can do. We can't, we can't separate ourselves from our own people. For twenty years laying in some rotten old nursing home....

We've tried to find a new beginning but it's too late. You can't separate yourself from your brother and your sister. No way I'm gonna do it. I refuse. I don't know who killed the Congressman, but as far as I'm concerned I killed him. You understand what I'm saying? I killed him. He had no business coming. I told him not to come.

Die with respect. Die with a degree of dignity. Lay down your life with dignity, don't lay down with tears and agony. There's nothing to death. It's like Mac said, it's like stepping over into another plane. Stop this hysterics. This is not the way for people who are Socialists or Communists to die. No way for us to die.

We must die with some dignity. We must die with some dignity.

Before we had no choice, now we have some choice. And you think they're going to allow this to be done, and allow us to get by with this? You must be insane. It's only — it's something to put you to rest. Oh God. Mother, mother, mother, please. Mother please, please, please don't, don't do this, don't do this. Put down your life with this child but don't do this.

Free at last. Keep your emotions down, keep your emotions down.

It's never been done before you say. It's been done by every tribe in history. Every tribe facing annihilation. All the Indians of the Amazon are doing right now. They refuse to bring any babies into the world. They kill every child that comes into the world because they don't want to live in this kind of a world.

Be patient, be patient. Death is ...

I tell you I don't care how many screams you hear. I don't care how many anguished cries. Death is a million times preferable to ten more days of this life. If you knew what was ahead of you, if you knew what was ahead of you, you'd be glad to be stepping over tonight.

Death, death, death is common to people.

If you ask the Samoans, they take death in their stride. Just be dignified.

Adults, adults, adults, I call on you to stop this nonsense. I call on you to quit exciting your children when all they're doing is going to quiet rest. I call on you to stop this now if you have any respect at all. Are we black, proud and Socialist, or what are we?

No, no sorrow that it's all over. I'm glad it's over. Hurry, hurry my children, hurry. Let us not fall into the hands of the enemy. Hurry my children, hurry. There are seniors out here I'm concerned about, hurry. I don't want to leave my seniors to this mess. Now quickly, quickly, quickly, quickly.

No more pain, Al. No more pain, I said, Al. No more pain, Jim Cobb, laying on the airfield dead at this moment. Remember the moment ... all of the moments that he ... these are the people, the peddlers of hate, we're not letting them take our life, we're laying down our life.

We're sick of their lies, we just want peace.

All it is is taking a drink to take ... to go to sleep.

That's what death is, sleep. Whatever, I'm tired of it all.

We'll set an example for others ... one thousand people who've said we don't like the way the world is.

The Black Hole of Guyana

The Untold Story of the Jonestown Massacre

John Judge

Somewhere in the concrete canyons of New York City, a rock group is using the name "Jim Jones and the Suicides." Irreverent and disarming, the name reflects the trend in punk rock to take social issues head on. Cynicism about the Jonestown deaths, the social parallels abound in the lyrics of today's music. The messages are clear because we all know the story.

In fact, people today recognize the name "Jonestown" more than any other event, a full 98% of the population.[1] The television and printed media were filled with the news for more than a year, even though the tale read like something from the *National Enquirer.* But despite all of the coverage, the reality of Jonestown and the reasons behind the bizarre events remain a mystery. The details have faded from memory for most of us since November 18, 1978, but not the outlines. Think back a moment and you'll remember.

You Know the Official Version

A fanatic religious leader in California led a multi-racial community into the jungles of remote Guyana to establish a socialist utopia. The People's Temple, his church, was in the heart of San Francisco and drew poor people, social activists, Blacks and Hispanics, young and old. The message was racial harmony and justice, and criticism of the hypocrisy of the world around his followers.[2]

The Temple rose in a vacuum of leadership at the end of an era. The political confrontations of the 60s were almost over, and religious cults and "personal transformation" were on the rise. Those who had preached a similar message on the political soap box were gone, burnt out, discredited, or dead. The counter-culture had apparently degenerated into drugs and violence. Charlie Manson was the only visible image of the period. Suddenly, religion seemed to offer a last hope.[3]

Even before they left for the Jonestown site, the People's Temple members were subjects of local scandal in the news.[4] Jim Jones claimed these exposés were attacks on their newly-found religion, and used them as an excuse to move most of the members to Guyana.[5] But disturbing reports continued to surround Jones, and soon came to the attention of

Congressional members like Leo Ryan. Stories of beatings, kidnapping, sexual abuse and mysterious deaths leaked out in the press.[6] Ryan decided to go to Guyana and investigate the situation for himself. The nightmare began.[7]

Isolated on the tiny airstrip at Port Kaituma, Ryan and several reporters in his group were murdered. Then came the almost unbelievable "White Night," a mass suicide pact of the Jonestown camp. A community made up mostly of Blacks and women drank cyanide from paper cups of Kool-Aid, adults and children alike died and fell around the main pavilion, Jones himself was shot in the head, an apparent suicide. For days, the body count mounted, from 400 to nearly 1,000. The bodies were flown to the United States and later cremated or buried in mass graves.[8]

Temple member Larry Layton faced charges of conspiracy in Ryan's murder. Ryan was awarded a posthumous Medal of Honor, and was the first Congress member to die in the line of duty.[9]

Pete Hamill called the corpses "all the loose change of the sixties."[10] The effect was electric. Any alternative to the current system was seen as futile, if not deadly. Protest only led to police riots and political assassination. Alternative lifestyles and drugs led to "creepy-crawly communes and violent murders.[11] And religious experiments led to cults and suicide. Social utopias were dreams that turned into nightmares. The television urged us to go back to the "Happy Days" of the apolitical 50s. The message was, get a job, and go back to church.[12] The nuclear threat generated only nihilism and hopelessness. There was no answer but death, no exit from the grisly future. The new ethic was personal success, aerobics, material consumption, a return to "American values," and the "moral majority," white Christian world. The official message was very clear.

But Just Suppose It Didn't Happen That Way...

The headlines the day of the massacre read: "Cult Dies in South American Jungle: 400 Die in Mass Suicide, 700 Flee into Jungle."[13] By all accounts in the press, as well as People's Temple statements, there were at least 1,100 people at Jonestown.[14] There were 809 adult passports found there, and reports of 300 children (276 found among the dead, and 210 never identified). The headline figures from the first day add to the same number: 1,100.[15] The original body count done by the Guyanese, which was the final count, was given almost a week later by American military authorities as 913.[16,17] A total of 167 survivors were reported to have returned to the U.S.[18] Where were the others?

At their first press conference, the Americans claimed that the Guyanese "could not count." These local people had carried out the gruesome job of counting the bodies, and later assisted American troops in the process of poking holes in the flesh lest they explode from the gasses of decay.[19] Then the Americans proposed another theory — they had missed seeing a pile of bodies at the back of the pavilion. The structure was the size of a small house, and they had been at the scene for days. Finally, we were given the official reason for the discrepancy — bodies had fallen on top of other bodies, adults covering children.[20]

It was simple, if morbid, arithmetic that led to the first suspicions. The 408 bodies discovered at first count would have to be able to cover 505 bodies for a total of 913. In addition, those who first worked on the bodies would have been unlikely to miss bodies lying beneath each other, since each body had to be punctured. Eighty-two of the bodies first found were those of children, reducing the number that could have been hidden below others.[21] A search of nearly 150 photographs, aerial and close-up, fails to show even one body lying under another, much less 500.[22]

It seemed the first reports were true, 400 had died, and 700 had fled to the jungle. The American authorities claimed to have searched for people who had escaped, but found no evidence of any in the surrounding area.[23] At least a hundred Guyanese troops were among the first to arrive, and they were ordered to search the jungle for survivors.[24] In the area, at the same time, British Black Watch troops were on "training exercises," with nearly 600 of their best-trained commandos. Soon, American Green Berets were on site as well.[25] The presence of these soldiers, specially trained in covert killing operations, may explain the increasing numbers of bodies that appeared.

Most of the photographs show the bodies in neat rows, face down. There are few exceptions. Close shots indicate drag marks, as though the bodies were positioned by someone after death.[26] Is it possible that the 700 who fled were rounded up by these troops, brought back to Jonestown and added to the body count?[27]

If so, the bodies would indicate the cause of death. A new word was coined by the media, "suicide-murder." But which was it?[28] Autopsies and forensic science are a developing art. The detectives of death use a variety of scientific methods and clues to determine how people die, when they expire, and the specific cause of death. Dr. Mootoo, the top Guyanese pathologist, was at Jonestown within hours after the massacre. Refusing the assistance of U.S. pathologists, he accompanied the teams that counted the dead, examined the bodies, and worked to identify the deceased. While the American press screamed about the "Kool-Aid Suicides," Dr. Mootoo was reaching a much different opinion.[29]

There are certain signs that show the types of poisons that lead to the end of life. Cyanide blocks the messages from the brain to the muscles by changing body chemistry in the central nervous system. Even the "involuntary" functions like breathing and heartbeat get mixed neural signals. It is a painful death, breath coming in spurts. The other muscles spasm, limbs twist and contort. The facial muscles draw back into a deadly grin, called "cyanide rictus."[30] All these telling signs were absent in the Jonestown dead. Limbs were limp and relaxed, and the few visible faces showed no sign of distortion.[31]

Instead, Dr. Mootoo found fresh needle marks at the back of the left shoulder blades of 80-90% of the victims. Others had been shot or strangled. One survivor reported that those who resisted were forced by armed guards.[33] The gun that reportedly shot Jim Jones was lying nearly 200 feet from his body, not a likely suicide weapon.[34] As Chief Medical Examiner, Mootoo's testimony to the Guyanese grand jury investigating Jonestown led to their conclusion that all but three of the people were murdered by "persons unknown." Only two had committed suicide, they said.[35] Several pictures show the gunshot wounds on the bodies as well.[36] The U.S. Army spokesman, Lt. Col. Schuler, said, "No autopsies are needed. The cause of death is not an issue here." The forensic doctors who later did autopsies at Dover, Delaware, were never made aware of Dr. Mootoo's findings.[37]

There are other indications that the Guyanese government participated with American authorities in a cover-up of the real story, despite their own findings. One good example was Guyanese Police Chief Lloyd Barker, who interfered with investigations, helped "recover" $2.5 million for the Guyanese government, and was often the first to officially announce the cover stories relating to suicide, body counts and survivors.[38] Among the first to the scene were the wife of Guyanese Prime Minister Forbes Burnham and his Deputy Prime Minister, Ptolemy Reid. They returned from the massacre site with nearly $1 million in cash, gold and jewelry taken from the buildings and from the dead. Inexplicably, one of Burnham's political party secretaries had visited the site of the massacre only hours before it occurred.[39] When Shirley Field Ridley, Guyanese Minister of Information, announced the change in the body count to the shocked Guyanese Parliament, she refused to answer further questions. Other representatives began to point a finger of shame at Ridley and the Burnham government, and the local press dubbed the scandal "Templegate," all accused them of taking a ghoulish payoff.[40]

Perhaps more significantly, the Americans brought in 16 huge C-131 cargo planes, but claimed they could only carry 36 caskets in each one. These aircraft can carry tanks, trucks, troops and ammunition all in one

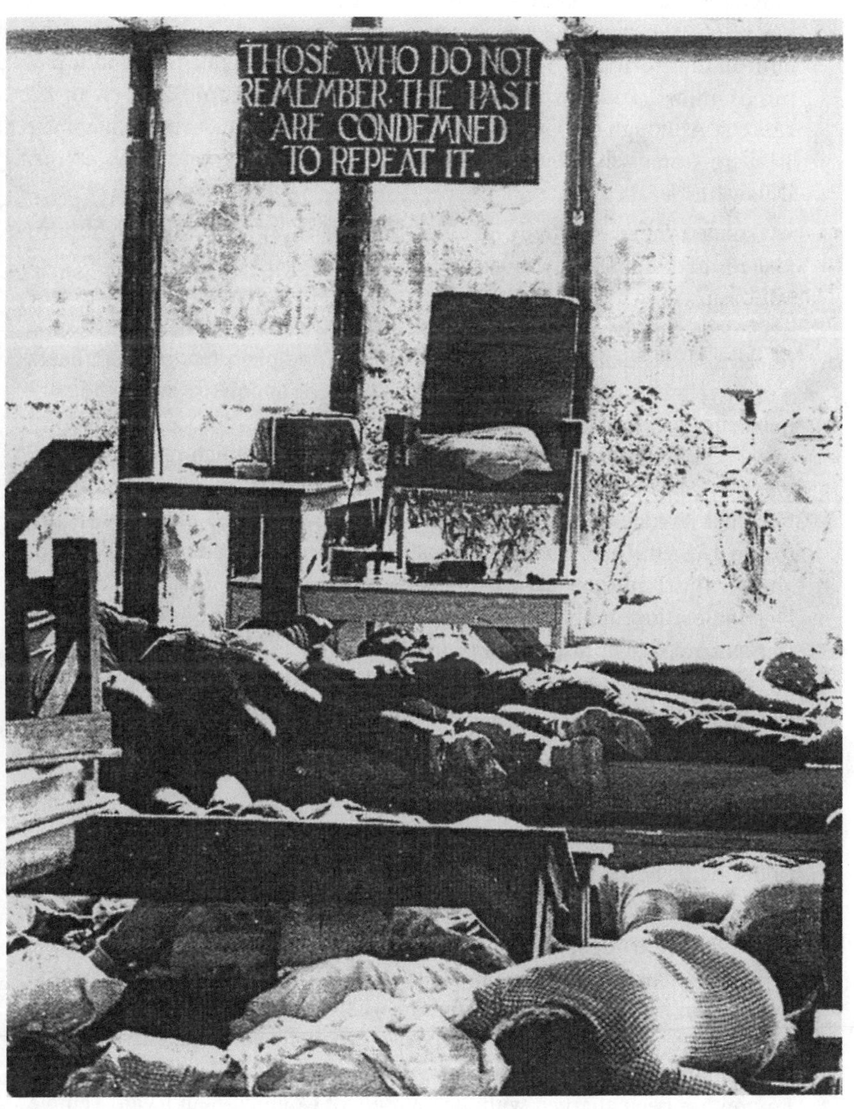
THOSE WHO DO NOT
REMEMBER THE PAST
ARE CONDEMNED
TO REPEAT IT.

load.[41] At the scene, bodies were stripped of identification, including the medical wrist tags visible in many early photos.[42] Dust-off operations during Vietnam clearly demonstrated that the military is capable of moving hundreds of bodies in a short period.[43] Instead, they took nearly a week to bring back the Jonestown dead, bringing in the majority at the end of the period.[44] The corpses, rotting in the heat, made autopsy impossible.[45] At one point, the remains of 183 people arrived in 82 caskets. Although the Guyanese had identified 174 bodies at the site, only 17 were tentatively identified at the massive military mortuary in Dover, Delaware.[46]

Isolated there, hundreds of miles from their families who might have visited the bodies at a similar mortuary in Oakland that was used during Vietnam, many of the dead were eventually cremated.[47] Press was excluded, and even family members had difficulty getting access to the remains.[48] Officials in New Jersey began to complain that state coroners were excluded, and that the military coroners appointed were illegally performing cremations.[49] One of the top forensic body identification experts, who later was brought in to work on the Iranian raid casualties, was denied repeated requests to assist.[50] In December, the President of the National Association of Medical Examiners complained in an open letter to the U.S. military that they "badly botched" procedures, and that a simple fluid autopsy was never performed at the point of discovery. Decomposition, embalming and cremation made further forensic work impossible.[51] The unorthodox method of identification attempted to remove the skin from the fingertip and slip it over a gloved finger, would not have stood up in court.[52] The long delay made it impossible to reconstruct the event. As noted, these military doctors were unaware of Dr. Mootoo's conclusions. Several civilian pathology experts said they "shuddered at the ineptness" of the military, and that their autopsy method was "doing it backwards." But in official statements, the U.S. attempted to discredit the Guyanese grand jury findings, saying they had uncovered "few facts."[53]

Guyanese troops, and police who arrived with American Embassy official Richard Dwyer, also failed to defend Congressman Leo Ryan and others who came to Guyana with him when they were shot down in cold blood at the Port Kaituma airstrip, even though the troops were nearby with machine guns at the ready.[54] Although Temple member Larry Layton has been charged with the murders of Congressman Ryan, Temple defector Patricia Parks and press reporters Greg Robinson, Don Harris and Bob Brown, he was not in a position to shoot them.[55] Blocked from boarding Ryan's twin engine Otter, he had entered another plane nearby. Once inside, he pulled out a gun and wounded two Temple followers before being disarmed.[56] The others were clearly killed by armed men who descended from a tractor-trailer at the scene, after opening fire. Witnesses described them as "zombies," walking mechanically, without emotion, and "looking through you, not at you," as they murdered.[57] Only certain people were killed, and the selection was clearly planned. Certain wounded people, like Ryan's aide Jackie Speiers, were not harmed further, but the killers made sure that Ryan and the newsmen were dead. In some cases they shot people, already wounded, directly in the head.[58] These gunmen were never finally identified and may have been under Layton's command. They may not have been among the Jonestown dead.[59]

At the Jonestown site, survivors described a special group of Jones' followers who were allowed to carry weapons and money, and to come and go from the camp. These people were all white, mostly males.[60] They ate better and worked less than the others, and they served as an armed guard to enforce discipline, control labor and restrict movement.[61] Among them were Jones' top lieutenants, including George Philip Blakey. Blakey and others regularly visited Georgetown, Guyana and made trips in their sea-going boat, the Cudjoe. He was privileged to be aboard the boat when the murders occurred.[62] This special armed guard survived the massacre. Many were trained and programmed killers, like the "zombies" who attacked Ryan. Some were used as mercenaries in Africa, and elsewhere.[63] The dead were 90% women, and 80% Blacks.[64] It is unlikely that men armed with guns and modern crossbows would give up control and willingly be injected with poisons. It is much more likely that they forced nearly 400 people to die by injection, and then assisted in the murder of 500 more who attempted to escape. One survivor clearly heard people cheering 45 minutes after the massacre. Despite government claims, they are not accounted for, nor is their location known.[65]

Back in California, People's Temple members openly admitted that they feared they were targeted by a "hit squad," and the Temple was surrounded for some time by local police forces.[66] During that period, two members of the elite guard from Jonestown returned and were allowed into the Temple by police.[67] The survivors who rode to Port Kaituma with Leo Ryan complained when Larry Layton boarded the truck, "He's not one of us."[68] Rumors also persisted that a "death list" of U.S. officials existed, and some survivors verified in testimony to the San Francisco grand jury.[69] A congressional aide was quoted in the AP wires on May 19, 1979, "There are 120 white, brainwashed assassins out from Jonestown awaiting the trigger word to pick up their hit."[70]

Other survivors included Mark Lane and Charles Garry, lawyers for People's Temple, who managed to escape the massacre somehow.[71] In addition to the 16 who officially returned with the Ryan party, others managed to reach Georgetown and come back home.[72] However, there have been continuing suspicious murders of those people here. Jeannie and Al Mills, who intended to write a book about Jones, were murdered at home, bound and shot.[73] Some evidence indicates a connection between the Jonestown operation and the murders of Mayor Moscone and Harvey Milk by police agent Dan White.[74] Another Jonestown survivor was shot near his home in Detroit by unidentified killers.[75] Yet another was involved in a mass murder of school children in Los Angeles.[76] Anyone who survived such massive slaughter must be somewhat suspect. The fact that the press never even spoke to nearly 200 survivors raises serious doubts.

Who Was Jim Jones?

In order to understand the strange events surrounding Jonestown, we must begin with a history of the people involved. The official story of a religious fanatic and his idealist followers doesn't make sense in light of the evidence of murders, armed killers and autopsy cover-ups. If it happened the way we were told, there should be no reason to try to hide the facts from the public, and full investigation into the deaths at Jonestown, and the murder of Leo Ryan would have been welcomed. What did happen is something else again.

Jim Jones grew up in Lynn, in southern Indiana. His father was an active member of the local Ku Klux Klan that infest that area.[77] His friends found him a little strange, and he was interested in preaching the Bible and religious rituals.[78] Perhaps more important was his boyhood friendship with Dan Mitrione, confirmed by local residents.[79] In the early 50s, Jones set out to be a religious minister, and was ordained at one point by a Christian denomination in Indianapolis.[80] It was during this period that he met and married his lifelong mate, Marceline.[81] He also had a small business selling monkeys, purchased from the research department at Indiana State University at Bloomington.[82]

A Bible-thumper and faith healer, Jones put on revivalist tent shows in the area, and worked close to Richmond, Indiana. Mitrione, his friend, worked as chief of police there, and kept him from being arrested or run out of town.[83] According to those close to him, he used wet chicken livers as evidence of "cancers" he was removing by "divine powers."[84] His landlady called him "a gangster who used a Bible instead of a gun."[85] His church followers included Charles Beikman, a Green Beret who was to stay with him to the end.[86] Beikman was later charged with the murders of several Temple members in Georgetown, following the massacre.[87]

Dan Mitrione, Jones' friend, moved on to the CIA-financed International Police Academy, where police were trained in counter-insurgency and torture techniques from around the world.[88] Jones, a poor, itinerant preacher, suddenly had money in 1961 for a trip to "minister" in Brazil, and he took his family with him.[89] By this time, he had "adopted" Beikman, and eight children, both Black and White.[90] His neighbors in Brazil distrusted him. He told them he worked with U.S. Navy Intelligence. His transportation and groceries were being provided by the U.S. Embassy, as was the large house he lived in.[91] His son, Stephan, commented that he made regular trips to Belo Horizonte, site of the CIA headquarters in Brazil.[92] An American police advisor, working closely with the CIA at that point, Dan Mitrione was there as well.[93] Mitrione had risen in the ranks quickly, and was busy training foreign police in torture and assassination methods. He was later kidnapped by Tupermaro guerrillas in Uruguay, interrogated and murdered.[94] Costa Gavras made a film about his death titled *State of Siege*.[95] Jones returned to the United States in 1963, with $10,000 in his pocket.[96] Recent articles indicate that Catholic clergy are complaining about CIA funding of other denominations for "ministry" in Brazil; perhaps Jones was an early example.[97]

With his new wealth, Jones was able to travel to California and establish the first People's Temple in Ukiah, California, in 1965. Guarded by dogs, electric fences and guard towers, he set up Happy Havens Rest Home.[98] Despite a lack of trained personnel, or proper licensing, Jones drew in many people at the camp. He had elderly, prisoners, people from psychiatric institutions, and 150 foster children, often transferred to care at Happy Havens by court orders.[99] He was contacted there by Christian missionaries from World Vision, an international evangelical order that had done espionage for the CIA in Southeast Asia.[100] He met "influential" members of the community and was befriended by Walter Heady, the head of the local chapter of the John Birch Society.[101] He used the members of this "church" to organize local voting drives for Richard Nixon's election, and worked closely with the Republican Party.[102] He was even appointed chairman of the county grand jury.[103]

"The Messiah from Ukiah," as he was known then, met and recruited Timothy Stoen, a Stanford graduate and member of the city DA's office, and his wife Grace.[104] During this time, the Layton family, Terri Buford and George Phillip Blakey, and other important members joined the Temple.[105] The camp "doctor," Larry Schacht, claims Jones got him off drugs and into medical school during this period.[106] These were not just street urchins. Buford's father was a Commander for the fleet at the Philadelphia Navy Base for years.[107] The Laytons were a well-heeled, aristocratic family. Dr. Layton donated at least a quarter-million dollars to Jones. His wife, son and daughter were all members of the Temple.[108] George Blakey, who married Debbie Layton, was from a wealthy British family. He donated $60,000 to pay the lease on the 27,000-acre Guyana site in 1974.[109] Lisa Philips Layton had come to the U.S. from a rich Hamburg banking family in Germany.[110] Most of the top lieutenants around Jones were from wealthy, educated backgrounds, many with connections to the military or intelligence agencies. These were the people who would set up the bank accounts, complex legal actions, and financial records that put people under the Temple's control.[111]

Stoen was able to set up important contacts for Jones as Assistant DA in San Francisco.[112] Jones changed his image to that of a liberal.[113] He had spent time studying the preaching methods of Father Divine in Philadelphia, and attempted to use them in a manipulative way on the streets of San Francisco. Father Divine ran a religious and charitable operation among Philadelphia's poor Black community.[114] Jones was able to use his followers in an election once again, this time for Mayor Moscone. Moscone responded in 1976, putting Jones in charge of the city Housing Commission.[115] In addition, many of his key followers got jobs with the city Welfare Department and much of the recruitment to the Temple in San Francisco came from the ranks of these unemployed and dispossessed people.[116] Jones was introduced to many influential liberal and radical people there, and entertained or greeted people ranging from Rosalynn Carter to Angela Davis.[117]

The period when Jones began the Temple there marked the end of an important political decade. Nixon's election had ushered in a domestic intelligence dead set against the movements for peace, civil rights and social justice. Names like COINTELPRO, CHAOS, and Operation garden plot, or the Houston Plan made the news following in the wake of Watergate revelations.[118] Senator Ervin called the White House plans against dissent "fascistic."[119] These operations involved the highest levels of military and civilian intelligence and all levels of police agencies in a full-scale attempt to discredit, disrupt and destroy the movements that sprang up in the 1960s. There are indications that these plans, or the mood they created, led to the assassinations of Martin Luther King and Malcolm X, as unacceptable "Black Messiahs."[120]

One of the architects under then-Governor Reagan in California was now-Attorney General Edwin Meese. He coordinated "Operation Garden Plot" for military intelligence and all police operations and intelligence in a period that was plagued with violations of civil and constitutional rights.[121] Perhaps you recall the police attacks on People's Park, the murder of many Black Panthers and activists, the infiltration of the Free

Speech Movement and anti-war activity, and the experimentation on prisoners at Vacaville, or the shooting of George Jackson.[122] Meese later bragged that this activity had damaged or destroyed the people he called "revolutionaries."[123] It was into this situation Jones came to usurp leadership.[124]

After his arrival in Ukiah, his methods were visible to those who took the time to investigate.[125] His armed guards wore black uniforms and leather jackboots. His approach was one of deception, and if that wore off, then manipulation and threats. Loyalty to his church included signing blank sheets of paper, later filled in with "confessions" and used for blackmail purposes, or to extort funds.[126] Yet the vast membership he was extorting often owned little, and he tried to milk them for everything, from personal funds to land deeds.[127] Illegal activities were regularly reported during this period, but either not investigated or unresolved. He clearly had the cooperation of local police. Years later, evidence would come out of charges of sexual solicitation, mysteriously dropped.[128]

Those who sought to leave were prevented and rebuked. Local journalist Kathy Hunter wrote in the Ukiah press about "seven Mysterious Deaths" of the Temple members who had argued with Jones and attempted to leave. One of these was Maxine Swaney.[129] Jones openly hinted to other members that he had arranged for them to die, threatening a similar fate to others who would be disloyal.[130] Kathy Hunter later tried to visit Jonestown, only to be forcibly drugged by Temple guards, and deported to Georgetown.[131] She later charged that Mark Lane approached her, falsely identifying himself as a reporter for *Esquire,* rather than as an attorney for Jim Jones. He led her to believe he was seeking information on Jones for an exposé in the magazine, and asked to see her evidence.

The pattern was to continue in San Francisco. In addition, Jones required that members practice for the mysterious "White Night," a mass suicide ritual that would protect them from murder at the hands of their enemies.[132] Although the new Temple had no guards or fences to restrict members, few had other places to live, and many had given over all they owned to Jones. They felt trapped inside this community that preached love, but practiced hatred.[133]

Following press exposure, and a critical article in *New West* magazine, Jones became very agitated, and the number of suicide drills increased.[134] Complaints about mistreatment by current and ex-members began to appear in the media and reach the ears of congressional representatives. Sam Houston, an old friend of Leo Ryan, came to him with questions about the untimely death of his son following his departure from the Temple.[135] Later, Timothy and Grace Stoen would complain to Ryan about custody of their young son, who was living with Jones, and urge him to visit the commune.[136] Against advice of friends and staff members, Ryan decided to take a team of journalists to Guyana and seek the truth of the situation.[137] Some felt that Ryan's journey there was planned and expected, and used as a convenient excuse to set up his murder. Others feel that this unexpected violation of secrecy around Jonestown set off the spark that led to the mass murder. In either case, it marked the beginning of the end for Ryan and Jones.[138]

At one point, to show his powers, Jones arranged to be shot in the heart in front of the congregation. Dragged to a back room, apparently wounded and bleeding, he returned a moment later alive and well. While this may have been more of his stage antics to prompt believers' faith, it may also have marked the end of Jim Jones.[139] For undisclosed reason, Jones had used "doubles."[140] This is very unusual for a religious leader, but quite common in intelligence operations.[141]

Even the death and identification of Jim Jones were peculiar. He was apparently shot by another person at the camp.[142] Photos of his body do not show identifying tattoos on his chest. The body and face are not clearly recognizable due to bloating and discoloration.[143] The FBI reportedly checked his fingerprints twice, a seemingly futile gesture since it is a precise operation. A more logical route would have been to check dental records.[144] Several researchers familiar with the case feel that the body may not have been Jones. Even if the person at the site was one of the "doubles," it does not mean Jones is still alive. He may have been killed at an earlier point.

What Was Jonestown?

According to one story, Jones was seeking a place on earth that would survive the effects of nuclear war, relying only on an article in *Esquire* magazine for his list.[145] The real reason for his locations in Brazil, California, Guyana and elsewhere deserve more scrutiny.[146] At one point Jones wanted to set up in Grenada, and he invited then-Prime Minister Sir Eric Gairy to visit the Temple in San Francisco.[147] He invested $200,000 in the Grenada National Bank in 1977 to pave the way, and some $76,000 was still there after the massacre.[148]

His final choice, the Matthew's Bridge section in Guyana, is an interesting one. It was originally the site of a Union Carbide bauxite and manganese mine, and Jones used the dock they left behind.[149] At an earlier point, it had been one of seven possible sites chosen for the relocation of the Jews after World War II.[150] Plans to inhabit the jungles of Guyana's interior with cheap labor date back to 1919.[151] Resources buried there are among the richest in the world, and include manganese, diamonds, gold, bauxite and uranium.[152] Forbes Burnham, the Prime

Minister, had participated in a scheme to repatriate Blacks from the UK to work in the area. Like all earlier attempts, it failed.[153]

Once chosen, the site was leased and worked on by a select crew of Temple members in preparation for the arrival of the body of the church. The work was done in cooperation with Burnham and the U.S. Embassy there.[154] But if these were idealists seeking a better life, their arrival in "Utopia" was a strange welcome. Piled into busses in San Francisco, they had driven to Florida. From there, Pan American charter planes delivered them to Guyana.[155] When they arrived at the airport, the Blacks were taken off the plane, bound and gagged.[156] The deception had finally been stripped bare of all pretense. The Blacks were so isolated and controlled that neighbors as close as five miles from the site did not know that Blacks lived at Jonestown. The only public representatives seen in Guyana were White.[157]

According to survivors' reports, they entered a virtual slave labor camp. Worked for 16 to 18 hours daily, they were forced to live in cramped quarters on minimum rations, usually rice, bread and sometimes rancid meat.[158] Kept on a schedule of physical and mental exhaustion, they were also forced to stay awake at night and listen to lectures by Jones. Threats and abuse became more common.[159] The camp medical staff under Dr. Lawrence Schacht was known to perform painful suturing without anesthetic. They administered drugs, and kept daily medical records.[160] Infractions of the rules or disloyalty led to increasingly harsh punishments, including forced drugging, sensory isolation in an underground box, physical torture and public sexual rape and humiliation. Beatings and verbal abuse were commonplace. Only the special guards were treated humanely and fed decently.[161] People with serious injuries were flown out, but few ever returned.[162] Perhaps the motto at Jonestown should have been the same as the one at Auschwitz, developed by Larry Schacht's namesake, Dr. Hjalmar Schacht, the Nazi minister of economics, "Arbeit Macht Frei," or "Work Will Make You Free." Guyana even considered setting up an "Auschwitz-like museum" at the site, but abandoned the idea.[163]

By this point, Jones had amassed incredible wealth. Press estimates ranged from $26 million to $2 billion, including bank accounts, foreign investments and real estate. Accounts were set up worldwide by key members often in the personal name of certain people in the Temple.[164] Much of this money, listed publicly after the massacre, disappeared mysteriously. It was a fortune far too large to have come from membership alone. The receivership set up by the government settled on a total of $10 million. Of special interest were the Swiss bank accounts opened in Panama, the money taken from the camp, and the extensive investments in Barclay's Bank.[165] Other sources of income included the German banking family of Lisa Philips Layton, Larry's mother.[166] Also, close to $54,000 a month income was claimed to come from welfare and social security checks for 199 members, sent to the Temple followers and signed over to Jones.[167] In addition, there are indications that Blakey and other members were supplementing the Temple funds with international smuggling of guns and drugs.[168] At one point, Charles Garry noted that Jones and his community were "literally sitting on a gold mine." Mineral distribution maps of Guyana suggest he was right.[169]

To comprehend this well-financed, sinister operation, we must abandon the myth that this was a religious commune and study instead the history that led to its formation. Jonestown was an experiment, part of a 30-year program called MK-ULTRA, the CIA and military intelligence code name for mind control.[170] A close study of Senator's Ervin's 1974 report, "Individual Rights and the Government's Role in Behavior Modification," shows that these agencies had certain "target populations" in mind, for both individual and mass control. Blacks, women, prisoners and elderly, the young, and inmates of psychiatric wards were selected as "potentially violent."[171] There were plans in California at the time for a Center for the Study and Reduction of Violence, expanding on the horrific work of Dr. Jose Delgado, Drs. Mark and Ervin, and Dr. Jolly West, experts in implantation, psychosurgery, and tranquilizers. The guinea pigs were to be drawn from the ranks of the "target populations," and taken to an isolated military missile base in California.[172] In that same period, Jones began to move his Temple members to Jonestown. They were the exact population selected for such tests.[173]

The meticulous daily notes and drug records kept by Larry Schacht disappeared, but evidence did not.[174] The history of MK-ULTRA and its sister programs (MK-DELTA, ARTICHOKE, BLUEBIRD, etc.) records a combination of drugs, drug mixtures, electroshock and torture as methods for control. The desired results ranged from temporary and permanent amnesia, uninhibited confessions, and creation of second personalities, to programmed assassins and preconditioned suicidal urges. One goal was the ability to control mass populations, especially for cheap labor.[175] Dr. Delgado told Congress that he hoped for a future where a technology would control workers in the field and troops at war with electronic remote signals. He found it hard to understand why people would complain about electrodes implanted in their brains to make them "both happy and productive."[176]

On the scene at Jonestown, Guyanese troops discovered a large cache of drugs; enough to drug the entire population of Georgetown, Guyana (well over 200,000) for more than a year.[177] According to survivors, these were being used regularly "to control" a population of only 1,100 people.[178] One footlocker contained 11,000 doses of thorazine, a dangerous tranquilizer. Drugs used in the testing for MK-ULTRA were found in abundance, including sodium pentathol (a truth serum), chloral hydrate (a hypnotic), Demerol, thallium (confuses thinking), and many others.[179] Schacht had supplies of halioparel and largatil, two other major tranquilizers as well.[180] The actual description of life at Jonestown is that of a tightly run concentration camp, complete with medical and psychiatric experimentation. The stresses and isolation of the victims is typical of sophisticated brainwashing techniques. The drugs and special tortures add an additional experimental aspect to the horror.[181] This more clearly explains the medical tags on the bodies and why they had to be removed It also suggests an additional motive for frustrating any chemical autopsies, since these drugs would have been found in the system of the dead.

The story of Jonestown is that of a gruesome experiment, not a religious utopian society. On the eve of the massacre, Forbes Burnham was reportedly converted to "born again" Christianity by members of the Full Gospel Christian Businessman's Association, including Lionel Luckhoo, a Temple lawyer in Guyana.[182] This same group, based in California, also reportedly converted Guatemalan dictator Rios Montt prior to his massacres there, and they were in touch with Jim Jones in Ukiah.[183] They conducted White House prayer breakfasts for Mr. Reagan.[184] With Ryan on his way to Jonestown, the seal of secrecy was broken. In a desperate attempt to test their conditioning methods, the Jonestown elite apparently tried to implement a real suicide drill.[185] Clearly, it led to a revolt, and the majority of people fled, unaware that there were people waiting to catch them.

One Too Many Jonestowns

Author Don Freed, an associate of Mark Lane, said that Martin Luther King, "if he could see Jonestown, would recognize it as the next step in his agenda, and he would say, one, two, three, many more Jonestowns."[186] Strangely enough, almost every map of Guyana in the major press located Jonestown at a different place following the killings. One map even shows a second site in the area called "Johnstown."[187] Perhaps there were multiple camps and Leo Ryan was only shown the one they hoped he would see. In any case, the Jonestown model survives, and similar camps, and their sinister designs, show up in many places.

Inside Guyana itself, approximately 25 miles to the south of Matthew's Bridge, is a community called Hilltown, named after religious leader Rabbi Hill. Hill has used the names Abraham Israel and Rabbi Emmanuel

Washington. Hilltown, set up about the same time as Jonestown, followed the departure of David Hill, who was known in Cleveland, a fugitive of the U.S. courts. Hill rules with an "iron fist" over some 8,000 Black people from Guyana and America who believe they are the Lost Tribe of Israel and the real Hebrews of Biblical prophecy.[188] Used as strong-arm troops, and "internal mercenaries" to insure Burnham's election, as were Jonestown members, the Hilltown people were allowed to clear the Jonestown site of shoes and unused weapons, both in short supply in Guyana.[189] Hill says his followers would gladly kill themselves at his command but he would survive, since, unlike Jones, he is "in control."[190]

Similar camps were reported at the time in the Philippines. Perhaps the best known example is the fascist torture camp in Chile known as Colonia Dignidad. Also a religious cult built around a single individual, this one came from Germany to Chile in 1961. In both cases the camp was their "Agricultural Experiment." Sealed and protected by the dreaded Chilean DINA police, Colonia Dignidad serves as a torture chamber for political dissidents. To the Jonestown monstrosities, they have added dogs specially trained to attack human genitals.[191] The operations there have included the heavy hand of decapitation specialist Michael Townley Welch, an American CIA agent, as well as reported visits by Nazi war criminals Dr. Josef Mengele and Martin Bormann. Currently, another such campsite exists at Pisagua, Chile.[192] Temple member Jeannie Mills, now dead, reported having seen actual films of a Chilean torture camp while at Jonestown. The only source possible at the time was the Chilean fascists themselves.[193]

In the current period, Jonestown is being "repopulated" with 100,000 Laotian Hmong people. Many of them grew opium for CIA money in Southeast Asia. Over 1,000 reside there already under a scheme designed by Billy Graham's nephew Ernest, and members of the Federation of Evangelical Ministries Association in Wheaton, Illinois (World Vision, World Medical Relief, Samaritan's Purse, and Carl McIntyre's International Council of Christian Churches).[194] Similar plans devised by the Peace Corps included moving inner-city Blacks from America to Jamaica and other Third World countries. And World Relief attempted to move the population of the Island of Dominica to Jonestown.[195] It is only a matter of time before another Jonestown will be exposed, perhaps leading again to massive slaughter.

The Links to U.S. Intelligence Agencies

Our story so far has hinted at connections to U.S. intelligence, such as the long-term friendship of Jones and CIA associate Dan Mitrione, but the ties are much more direct when a full picture of the operation is revealed.

To start with, the history of Forbes Burnham's rise to power in Guyana is fraught with the clear implication of a CIA coup d'état to oust troublesome independent leader Cheddi Jagan.[196] In addition, the press and other evidence indicated the presence of a CIA agent on the scene at the time of the massacre. This man, Richard Dwyer, was working as Deputy Chief of Mission for the U.S. Embassy in Guyana.[197] Identified in Who's Who in the CIA, he has been involved since 1959, and was last stationed in Martinique.[198] Present at the camp site and the airport strip, his accounts were used by the State Department to confirm the death of Leo Ryan. At the massacre, Jones said, "Get Dwyer out of here" just before the killings began.[199]

Other Embassy personnel, who knew the situation at Jonestown well, were also connected to intelligence work. U.S. Ambassador John Burke, who served in the CIA with Dwyer in Thailand, was an Embassy official described by Philip Agee as working for the CIA since 1963. A Reagan appointee to the CIA, he is still employed by the Agency, usually on State Department assignments.[200] Burke tried to stop Ryan's investigation.[201] Also at the Embassy was Chief consular officer Richard McCoy, described as "close to Jones," who worked for military intelligence and was "on loan" from the Defense Department at the time of the massacre.[202] According to a standard source, "The U.S. Embassy in Georgetown housed the Georgetown CIA station. It now appears that the majority and perhaps all of the embassy officials were CIA officers operating under State Department covers..."[203] Dan Webber, who was sent to the site of the massacre the day after, was also named as CIA.[204] Not only did the State Department conceal all reports of violations at Jonestown from Congressman Leo Ryan, but the Embassy regularly provided Jones with copies of all congressional inquiries under the Freedom of Information Act.[205]

Ryan had challenged the Agency's overseas operations before, as a member of the House Committee responsible for oversight on intelligence. He was an author of the controversial Hughes-Ryan Amendment that would have required CIA disclosure in advance to the congressional committees of all planned covert operations. The Amendment was defeated shortly after his death.[206]

American intelligence agencies have a sordid history of cooperative relations with Nazi war criminals and international terrorism.[207] In light of this, consider the curious ties of the family members of the top lieutenants to Jim Jones. The Layton family is one example. Dr. Lawrence Layton was Chief of Chemical and Ecological Warfare Research at Dugway Proving Grounds in Utah, for many years, and later worked as Director of Missile and Satellite Development at the Navy Propellant Division, Indian

Head, Maryland.[208] His wife, Lisa, had come from a rich German family. Her father Hugo, had represented I.G. Farben as a stockbroker.[209] Her stories about hiding her Jewish past from her children for most of her life, and her parents escape from a train heading for a Nazi concentration camp seem shallow, as do Dr. Layton's Quaker religious beliefs. The same family sent money to Jonestown regularly.[210] Their daughter, Debbie, met and married George Philip Blakey in an exclusive private school in England. Blakey's parents have extensive stock holdings in Solvay drugs, a division of the Nazi cartel I.G. Farben.[211] He also contributed financially.[212]

Terri Buford's father, Admiral Charles T. Buford, worked with Navy Intelligence.[213] In addition, Blakey was reportedly running mercenaries from Jonestown to CIA-backed UNITA forces in Angola.[214] Maria Katsaris' father was a minister with the Greek Orthodox Church, a common conduit of CIA funding, and Maria claimed she had proof he was CIA. She was shot in the head, and her death was ruled a suicide, but at one point Charles Beikman was charged with killing her.[215] On their return to the United States, the "official" survivors were represented by attorney Joseph Blatchford, who had been named prior to that time in a scandal involving CIA infiltration of the Peace Corps.[216] Almost everywhere you look at Jonestown, U.S. intelligence and fascism rear their ugly heads.

The connection of intelligence agencies to cults is nothing new. A simple but revealing example is the Unification Church, tied to both the Korean CIA (i.e., American CIA in Korea), and the international fascist network know as the World Anti-Communist League. The Moonies hosted WACL's first international conference.[217] What distinguished Jonestown was both the level of control and the open sinister involvement. It was imperative that they cover their tracks.[218]

Maria Katsaris sent Michael Prokes, Tim Carter, and another guard out at the last minute with $500,000 cash in a suitcase, and instructions for a drop point. Her note inside suggests the funds were destined for the Soviet Union.[219] Prokes later shot himself at a San Francisco press conference, where he claimed to be an FBI informant.[220] Others reported meetings with KGB agents and plans to move to Russia.[221] This disinformation was part of a "red smear" to be used if they had to abandon the operation. The Soviet Union had no interest in the money and even less in Jonestown. The cash was recovered by the Guyanese government.[222]

Their hidden funding may include more intelligence links. A mysterious account in Panama, totaling nearly $5 million in the name of an "Associacion Pro Religiosa do San Pedro, S.A." was located.[223] This unknown Religious Association of St. Peter was probably one of the 12 phony companies set up by Archbishop Paul Marcinkus to hide the illegal investments of Vatican funds through the scandal-ridden Banco Ambrosiano.[224] A few days after the story broke about the accounts, the President of Panama, and most of the government, resigned. Roberto Calvi of Banco Ambrosiano was murdered, and the Jonestown account disappeared from public scrutiny and court record.[225]

The direct orders to cover up the cause of death came from the top levels of the American government. Zbigniew Brzezinsky delegated to Robert Pastor, and he in turn ordered Lt. Col. Gordon Sumner to strip the bodies of identity.[226] Pastor is now Deputy Director of the CIA.[227] One can only wonder how many others tied to the Jonestown operation were similarly promoted.

The Strange Connection to the Murder of Martin Luther King

One of the persistent problems in researching Jonestown is that it seems to lead to so many other criminal activities, each with its own complex history and cast of characters. Perhaps the most disturbing of these is the connection that appears repeatedly between the characters in the Jonestown story and the key people involved in the murder and investigation of Martin Luther King.

The first clue to this link appeared in the personal histories of the members of the Ryan investigation team who were so selectively and deliberately killed at Port Kaituma. Don Harris, a veteran NBC reporter, had been the only network newsman on the scene to cover Martin Luther King's activity in Memphis at the time of King's assassination. He had interviewed key witnesses at the site. His coverage of the urban riots that followed won him an Emmy award.[228] Gregory Robinson, a "fearless" journalist from the San Francisco Examiner, had photographed the same riots in Washington D.C. When he was approached for copies of the films by Justice Department officials, he threw the negatives into the Potomac River.[229]

The role of Mark Lane, who served as attorney for Jim Jones, is even more clearly intertwined.[230] Lane had co-authored a book with Dick Gregory, claiming FBI complicity in the King murder.[231] He was hired as the attorney for James Earl Ray, accused assassin, when Ray testified before the House Select Committee on Assassinations about King.[232] Prior to this testimony, Ray was involved in an unusual escape plot at Brushy Mountain State Prison.[233] The prisoner who had helped engineer the escape plot was later inexplicably offered an early parole by members of the Tennessee Governor's office. These officials, and Governor Blanton himself, were to come under close public scrutiny and face legal charges in regard to bribes taken to arrange illegal early pardons for prisoners.[234]

One of the people living at Jonestown was ex-FBI agent Wesley Swearingen, who at least publicly condemned the COINTELPRO operations and other abuses, based on stolen classified documents, at the Jonestown site. Lane had reportedly met with him there at least a year before the massacre. Terri Buford said the documents were passed on to Charles Garry. Lane used information from Swearingen in his thesis on the FBI and King's murder. Swearingen served as a key witness in suits against the Justice Department brought by the Socialist Workers Party.[235] When Larry Flynt, the flamboyant publisher of *Hustler* magazine, offered a $1 million reward leading to the capture and conviction of the John F. Kennedy killers, the long distance number listed to collect information and leads was being answered by Mark Lane and Wesley Swearingen.[236]

With help from officials in Tennessee, Governor Blanton's office, Lane managed to get legal custody of a woman who had been incarcerated in the Tennessee state psychiatric system for nearly eight years.[237] This woman, Grace Walden Stephens, had been a witness in the King murder.[238] She was living at the time in Memphis in a rooming house across from the hotel when Martin Luther King was shot.[239] The official version of events had Ray located in the common bathroom of the rooming house, and claimed he had used a rifle to murder King from that window.[240] Grace Stephens did, indeed, see a man run from the bathroom, past her door and down to the street below.[241] A rifle, later linked circumstantially to James Earl Ray, was found inside a bundle at the base of the rooming house stairs, and identified as the murder weapon.[242] But Grace, who saw the man clearly, refused to identify him as Ray when shown photographs by the FBI.[243] Her testimony was never introduced at the trial. The FBI relied instead, on the word of her common-law husband Charles Stephens, who was drunk and unconscious at the time of the incident.[244] Her persistence in saying that it was not James Earl Ray was used at her mental competency hearings as evidence against her, and she disappeared into the psychiatric system.[245]

Grace Walden Stephens took up residence in Memphis with Lane, her custodian, and Terri Buford, a key Temple member who had returned to the U.S. before the killings to live with Lane.[246] While arranging for her to testify before the Select Committee on Ray's behalf, Lane and Buford were plotting another fate for Grace Stephens. Notes from Buford to Jones found in the aftermath of the killings discussed arrangements with Lane to move Grace Stephens to Jonestown.[247] The problem that remained was lack of a passport, but Buford suggested either getting a passport on the black market, or using the passport of former Temple member Maxine Swaney.[248] Swaney, dead for nearly two and a half years since her departure from the Ukiah camp, was in no position to argue, and Jones apparently kept her passport with him.[249] Whether Grace ever arrived at Jonestown is unclear.

Lane was also forced to leave Ray in the midst of testimony to the Select Committee when he got word that Ryan was planning to visit. Lane had attempted to discourage the trip earlier in a vaguely threatening letter.[250] Now he rushed to be sure he arrived with the group.[251] At the scene, he failed to warn Ryan and others, knowing that the sandwiches and other food might be drugged, but refrained from eating it himself.[252] Later, claiming that he and Charles Garry would write the official history of the "revolutionary suicide," Lane was allowed to leave the pieces of underwear to mark their way back to Georgetown.[253] If true, it seems an unlikely method if they were in any fear of pursuit. They had heard gunfire and screams back at the camp.[254] Lane was reportedly well aware of the forced drugging and suicide drills at Jonestown before Ryan arrived.[255]

Another important figure in the murder of Martin Luther King was his mother, Alberta. A few weeks after the first public announcement by Coretta Scott King that she believed her husband's murder was part of a conspiracy, Mrs. Alberta King was brutally shot to death in Atlanta, while attending church services. Anyone who had seen the physical wounds suffered by King might have been an adverse witness to the official version, since the wound angles did not match the ballistic direction of a shot from the rooming house.[257] Her death also closely coincided with the reopening of the Tennessee state court review of Ray's conviction based on a guilty plea, required by a 6th Circuit decision.[258] The judge in that case reportedly refused to allow witnesses from beyond a 100 mile radius from the courtroom.[259]

The man convicted of shooting King's mother was Marcus Wayne Chenault. His emotional affect following the murder was unusual. Grinning, he asked if he had hit anyone.[260] He had reportedly been dropped off at the church by people he knew in Ohio.[261] While at Ohio State University, he was part of a group known as "the Troop," run by a Black minister and gun collector who used the name Rabbi Emmanuel Israel. This man, described in the press as a "mentor" for Chenault, left the area immediately after the shooting.[262] In the same period, Rabbi Hill traveled from Ohio to Guyana and set up Hilltown, using similar aliases, and preaching the same message of a "Black Hebrew elite."[263] Chenault confided to SCLC leaders that he was one of many killers who were working to assassinate a long list of Black leadership. The names he said were on this list coincided with similar "death lists" distributed by the KKK, and linked to the COINTELPRO operations in the 60s.[264]

The real backgrounds and identities of Marcus Wayne Chenault and Rabbi Hill may never be discovered, but one thing is certain, Martin Luther King would never had countenanced the preachings of Jim Jones, had he lived to hear them.[265]

Aftermath

In the face of such horror, it may seem little compensation to know that a part of the truth has been unearthed. But for the families and some of the survivors, the truth, however painful, is the only path to being relieved of the burden of their doubts. It's hard to believe that President Carter was calling on us at the time not to "overreact." The idea that a large community of Black people would not only stand by and be poisoned at the suggestion of Jim Jones, but would allow their children to be murdered first, is a monstrous lie, and a racist insult.[266] We now know that the most direct description of Jonestown is that it was a Black genocide plan. One Temple director, Joyce Shaw, described the Jonestown massacre as, "some kind of horrible government experiments, or some sort of sick racial thing, a plan like that of the Germans to exterminate Blacks."[267] If we refuse to look further into this nightmarish event, there will be more Jonestowns to come. They will move from Guyana to our own backyard.

The cast of characters is neither dead nor inactive. Key members of the armed guard were ordered to be on board the Temple ship, Cudjoe — at the hour of the massacre they were on a supply run to Trinidad. George Phillip Blakey phoned his father-in-law, Dr. Lawrence Layton, from Panama after the event.[268] At least ten members of the Temple remained on the boat, and set up a new community in Trinidad while Nigel Slinger, a Grenada businessman and insurance broker for Jonestown, repaired the 400-ton shipping vessel. Then Charles Touchette, Paul McCann, Stephan Jones, and George Blakey set up an "open house" in Grenada with the others. McCann spoke about starting a shipping company to "finance the continued work of the original Temple."[269]

That "work" may have included the mysterious operations of the mental hospital in Grenada that eluded government security by promising free medical care.[270] The hospital was operated by Sir Geoffrey Bourne, Chancellor of the St. George's University Medical School, also staffed by his son Dr. Peter Bourne.[271] His son's history includes work with psychological experiments and USAID in Vietnam, the methadone clinics in the U.S., and a drug scandal in the Carter White House.[272] The mental hospital was the only structure bombed during the U.S. invasion of

Grenada in 1983. This was part of a plan to put Sir Eric Gairy back in power.[273] Were additional experiments going on at the site?[274]

In addition, the killers of Leo Ryan and others at Port Kaituma were never accounted for fully. The trial of Larry Layton was mishandled by the Guyanese courts, and the U.S. system as well.[275] No adequate evidentiary hearings have occurred either at the trial or in state and Congressional reviews. The Jonestown killers, trained assassins and mercenaries, are not on trial. They might be working in Africa or Central America. Their participation in Jonestown can be used as an "explanation" for their involvement in later murders here, such as the case of the attack on school children in Los Angeles.[276] They should be named and located.

The money behind Jonestown was never fully examined or recovered. The court receivership only collected a fraction, the bulk went to pay back military operations and burial costs. Families of the dead were awarded only minimal amounts.[277] Some filed suit, unsuccessfully, to learn more about the circumstances of the deaths, and who was responsible. Joe Holsinger, Leo Ryan's close friend and assistant, studied the case for two years and reached the same unnerving conclusions — these people were murdered, there was evidence of a mass mind-control experiment, and the top levels of civilian and military intelligence were involved.[278] He worked with Ryan's family members to prove the corruption and injustice but they could barely afford the immense court costs and case preparation. Their suit, as well as a similar one brought by ex-members and families of the victims, had to be dropped for lack of funds.[279]

The international operations of World Vision and the related evangelical groups continue unabashed. World Vision official John W. Hinckley, Sr. was on his way to a Guatemalan water project run by the organization on the day his son shot at President Reagan.[280] A mysterious "double" of Hinckley, Jr., a man named Richardson, followed Hinckley's path from Colorado to Connecticut, and even wrote love letters to Jodi Foster. Richardson was a follower of Carl McIntyre's International Council of Christian Churches, and attended their Bible School in Florida. He was arrested shortly after the assassination attempt in New York's Port Authority with a weapon, and claimed he intended to kill Reagan.[281]

Another World Vision employee, Mark David Chapman, worked at their Haitian refugee camp in Ft. Chaffee, Arkansas. He was later to gain infamy as the assassin of John Lennon in New York City.[282] World Vision works with refugees worldwide. At the Honduran border, they are present in camps used by American CIA to recruit mercenaries against Nicaragua. They were at Sabra and Shatilla, camps in Lebanon where fascist Phalange massacred the Palestinians.[283] Their representatives in the Cuban refugee camps on the east coast included members of the Bay of Pigs operation, CIA-financed mercenaries from Omega 7 and Alpha 66.[284] Are they being used as a worldwide cover for the recruitment and training of these killers? They are, as mentioned earlier, working to repopulate Jonestown with Laotians who served as mercenaries for our CIA.[285]

Silence in the face of these murders is the worst possible response. The telling sign above the Jonestown dead read, "Those who do not remember the past are condemned to repeat it."[286] The genocide will come home to America. How many spent time studying the rash of child murders in Atlanta's Black community or asked the necessary questions about the discrepancies in the conviction of Wayne Williams?[287] Would we recognize a planned genocide if it occurred under similar subterfuge?

Leo Ryan's daughter, Shannon, lives among the disciples of another cult today, at the new city of Rajneeshpuram in Arizona. She was quoted in the press, during the recent controversy over a nationwide recruiting drive to bring urban homeless people to the commune, saying she did not believe it could end like Jonestown, since the leader would not ask them to commit suicide. "If he did ask me, I would do it," she said.[288] Homeless recruits, who had left since then, are suing in court because of suspicious and unnecessary injections given them by the commune's doctor, and a liquid they were served daily in unmarked jars that many believe was not simply "beer." One man in the suit claims he was drugged and disoriented for days after his first injection.[289]

The ultimate victims of mind control at Jonestown are the American people. If we fail to look beyond the constructed images given us by the television and the press, then our consciousness is manipulated, just as well as the Jonestown victims' was. Facing nuclear annihilation, many see the militarism of the Reagan policies, and military training itself, as the real "mass suicide cult." If the discrepancy between the truth of Jonestown and the official version can be so great, what other lies have we been told about major events?[290]

History is precious. In a democracy, knowledge must be accessible for informed consent to function. Hiding or distorting history behind "national security" leaves the public as the final enemy of the government. Democratic process cannot operate on "need to know." Otherwise, we live in the *1984* envisioned by Orwell's projections, and we must heed his warning that those who control the past control the future.[291]

The real tragedy of Jonestown is not only that it occurred, but that so few chose to ask themselves why or how, so few sought to find out the facts behind the bizarre tale used to explain away the death of more than 900 people, and that so many will continue to be blind to the grim reality of our intelligence agencies. In the long run, the truth will come out. Only our complicity in the deception continues to dishonor the dead.

Notes

1. *Hold Hands and Die!* John Maguire (Dale Books, 1978), p. 235 (Story of the Century); *Raven,* Tim Reitzerman (Dutton, 1982) p. 575 (citing poll result).

2. The standard version first appeared in two "instant books," so instant (12/10/78) they seemed to have been written before the event! *The Suicide Cult,* Kilduff & Javers (Bantam Books, 1978); *Guyana Massacre,* Charles Krause (Berkeley Pub., 1978). Other standard research works on the topic include: *White Night,* John Peer Nugent (Wade, 1979); *Raven,* op cit., and *Hold Hands and Die!,* op cit.; *The Cult That Died,* George Klineman (Putnam, 1980); *The Children of Jonestown,* Kenneth Wooden (McGraw-Hill, 1981); *The Strongest Poison,* Mark Lane (Hawthorn Books, 1980); *Our Father Who Art in Hell,* James Reston (Times Books, 1981); *Journey to Nowhere,* Shiva Naipaul (Simon & Schuster, 1981); *The Assassination of Representative Leo J. Ryan & The Jonestown, Guyana Tragedy, Report, House Committee on Foreign Affairs* (GPO, May 15, 1979). Personal accounts by members of People's Temple and survivors of Jonestown: *Six Years with God,* Jeannie Mills (A&W Publ., 1979); *People's Temple, People's Tomb,* Phil Kerns (Logos, Int., 1979); *Deceived,* Mel White (Spire Books, 1979); *The Broken God,* Bonnie Theilmann (David Cook, 1979); *Awake in a Nightmare,* Feinsod (Norton, 1981); *In My Father's House,* Yee & Layton (Holt, Rinehart & Winston, 1981).

3. "The People's Temple," William Pfaff, *New Yorker,* 12/18/78; *Hold Hands,* p. 241-7 (cults) *and Journey to Nowhere,* p. 294 (period); *The Family,* Ed Sanders (Avon Press, 1974) (Charlie Manson); *Snapping,* Flo Conway (brainwashing); *Ecstasy & Holiness,* Frank Musgrove (Indiana Univ. Press, 1974).

4. "Inside People's Temple," Marshall Kilduff, *New West,* 8/1/77; *Hold Hands,* p. 100.

5. "Rev. Jones Became West Coast Power," *Washington Post* (WP), 11/20/78. *Hold Hands,* p. 130 and *Journey to Nowhere,* p. 47.

6. "Rev. Jones Accused of Coercion," *New York Times* (NYT), 4/12/79; *NYT,* 11/27/78 (warning letter to Ryan, 6/78).

7. Assassination of Leo J. Ryan, pp. 1-3; "Ryan to Visit," Kilduff, *San Francisco Chronicle* (SFC), 11/8/78.

8. "A Hell of a Story: The Selling of a Massacre," *Wash. Jrn. Rev.,* Jan-Feb. 1979.

9. *Raven,* p. 576 (Layton charges).

10. *Hold Hands,* p. 216.

11. *Helter Skelter,* Bugliosi (Norton, 1974).

12. *Hold Hands,* pp. 215-16.

13. *New York Post,* 11/21/78 (headline); *WP,* 11/21/78, *San Francisco Examiner* (SFE), 11/22/78, *Guyana Daily Mirror,* 11/23/78, *NYT,* 11/22/78 (flee to jungle); *NYT,* 11/21-23/78 (estimated 4-500 missing); *White Night,* pp. 224-6 and *NYT,* 11/23/78 (U.S. search with loudspeakers).

14. *Boston Globe,* 11/21/78, *Baltimore Sun,* 11/21/78, NYT, 11/20/78 (est. 11-1200); *White Night,* p. 228 (Jones says 1,200), *Guyanese Daily Mirror,* 11/23/78 (1,000).

15. *WP,* 11/21/78 (passports); *White Night,* p. 230 (809 visa applications), and *Hold Hands,* p. 146 (800 on buses to Florida); *Children of Jonestown,* p. 202 and NYT, 11/26/78 (children, 260 dead at site, 276 at Dover).

16. *White Night,* p. 223; *NYT,* 11/21/78 (408, Guyanese "pick way" to count), 11/22/78 (409, U.S. Army teams), 11/23/78 (400, Maj. Helming, U.S.), 11/24/78 (409, still).

17. *White Night,* p. 231 and *Hold Hands,* pp. 226-34, *NYT,* 11/25/78 (775, P. Reid, Guyana), 11/26/78 (over 900, U.S. "final" 910, AF or 914, Reuters; 11/29/78 (900, Lloyd Barker, Guyana), 12/1/78 (911, U.S. Air Force), 12/4/78 (911, Dover AFB, Del.)

18. *Guyana Daily Mirror,* 11/23/85.

19. *White Night,* pp. 229-30 (can't count); *NYT,* 11/25/78 (State Dept. Business, "rough"), 11/25/78 (American official disagrees, says Guyanese count "firm"); *Children of Jonestown,*. p. 196 (poking).

20. *White Night,* p. 229 (pavilion story), 230 ("mounds of people," Maj. Hickman); *SFE,* 11/25/78 (adults covered children); *NYT,* 11/25/78 ("layered," Ridley, Guyana, but U.S. soldier, "only one layer").

21. *Baltimore Sun,* 11/21/78 (82 children, 163 women, 138 men first count).

22. Photographs appear in most of the standard reference works, see fn 2. Also, good pictures in the following: "Jonestown: the Survivors' Story," *NYT Magazine,* 11/18/79; "Death in the Jungle," 11/27/78 and "Cult of Death," 12/4/78 in *Newsweek;* "Cult Massacre," 11/27/78 and "Cult of Death," 12/4/78 in *Time;* "Cult of Madness," 12/4/78 and "Bloody Trail of Death," Tim Cahill, *Rolling Stone,* 1/25/79' "Questions Linger about Guyana," Sidney Jones, *Oakland Times,* 12/9/78; "Cult Defectors Suspect U.S. of Cover-up," *Los Angeles Times,* 12/18/78.

23. *White Night,* p. 229 (quoting State Dept. Bushnell), and *Hold Hands,* p. 233 (doubts); *NYT,* 11/23/78 (U.S. searching, Carter); 11/24/78 ("in vain"), 11/29/78 ("none"), and 12/1/78 (30-40 in Venezuela).

24. *WP,* 11/21/78 ("Cult Head Leads 408 to Death"); *NYT,* 11/20-22/78, (searching, pick up Lane & Garry); *White Night,* p. 239 (Burnham sends in "his boys").

25. *White Night,* p. 224 (over 300 U.S. troops, 11/20); *Guyana Daily Mirror,* 11/23/78 (325 U.S. troops); *Hold Hands,* p. 200 (200 for clean up) and *NYT,* 11/23/78 (239 to evacuate). What was the function of nearly 100 additional U.S. forces? "Jocks in the Jungle," *London Sunday Times,* 11/78 (British Black Watch troops).

26. Photographs, see fn 22. *Strongest Poison,* p. 194 (Lou Gurvich, "dragged and laid out").

27. "Mystery Shrouds Jonestown Affair," *Guyanese Daily Mirror,* 11/23/78; *NYT,* 11/24 and 11/29/78 (missing in jungle disappear, Guyanese say "none," Barker).

28. *SFE,* 11/20/78 (headline), also *WP,* 11/21/78 or *NYT,* 11/28/78.

29. *Children of Jonestown,* p. 193; NYT, 12/14/78 (Mootoo testifies to coroner's jury), 2/18/79 (Chicago Med. Examiner Robt. Stein promised help, none came).

30. *A Guide to Pathological Evidence for Lawyers and Police Officers,* F. Jaffe (Carswell Press, 1983); *Poisons, Properties, Chemical Identification, Symptoms and Emergency Treatment,* V. Brooks (Van Nostrand, 1958).

31. Photographs, see fn. 22. "Questions Linger," *Oakland Times,* 12/9/78.

32. "Coroner Says 700 Who Died in Cult were Slain," *Miami Herald,* 12/17/78; NYT, 12/12/78 (injections, upper arm), 11/17/78 (700 were murdered), 12/18/78 (Mootoo shocks American Academy of Forensic Scientist meeting).

33. *White Night,* pp. 230-1 (shot); WP, 11/21/78 (shot), *Guyana Daily Mirror,* 11/23/78 ("bullets in bodies," Ridley); *NYT,* 11/29/78 ("no guns/struggle," Lloyd Barker), 11/20/78

("no violence," Ridley); *NYT,* 11/18,19,21/78 (Jim Jones, Annie Moore, Marisa Katsaris shot in head); *WP,* 11/21/78 ("forced to die by guards"), also *Washington Star,* 11/25/78 (forced).

34. *Children of Jonestown,* p. 191 and *WP,* 11/21/78 (unknown if Jones shot himself); *Strongest Poison,* p. 194 (Gurvich, no nitrate test on hands); *Hold Hands,* p. 260 (gun far from body); *Miami Herald,* 12/17/78 (Mootoo suspects murdered); *NYT,* 11/26/78 (drug o.d., shot after, U.S. Major Groom), 12/1,7/78 (Guyanese and U.S. pathologists autopsy), 12/10/78 (ballistics tests), 12/20,21/78 (illegal cremation), 12/23/78 (not suicide, Mag. Bacchus, Guyanan Coroner's Jury).

35 *Raven,* p. 576 and *Miami Herald,* 12/17/78 (grand jury decision); Strongest Poison, p. 194 (Gurvich, evidence of shooting, over 600 bodies); *NYT,* 12/13/78 (grand jury set up), 12/14,15,17/78 (Mootoo testimony, tour of site), 12/23/78 (conclusion, "persons unknown," Katsaris, Moore suicides).

36. *Hold Hands,* cover photo, and see fn. 22.

37. *White Night,* p. 231 (Schuler quote), *Children of Jonestown,* p. 197 (unaware); *Strongest Poison,* pp. 182-89 (autopsy problems); *NYT,* 11/26/78 and 12/5/78 (no autopsies, reluctant), 11/26/78 (Mootoo's work unknown).

38. *Hold Hands,* p. 260, and see fn. 17, 28, 33 or Lloyd Barker: "Cult Defectors Suspect Cover-up," *LAT,* 12/18/78; "Jonestown & the CIA, *Daily World,* 6/23/81; *NYT,* 12/3,8/78 (Lloyd Barker collusion), 12/7,8,24/78 (Deputy Prime Minister Reid's role), 12/25/78 (U.S. attempts to discredit coroner's jury).

39. *Hold Hands,* p. 229; *SFE,* 11/22/78 ($1 million), or see *NYT,* 12/8/78 ($2.5 million at site); *WP,* 11/28/78 (cash, wallets, gold); *NYT,* 12/12/78 (visit to site by Burnham's party official).

40. *Journey to Nowhere,* p. 58, 117 (Ptolemy Reid cover-up), see also fn. 38; *Daily World,* 10/23/80 (Cheddi Jagan interview); *Guyana Daily Mirror,* 11/28/78 (1/23/79); *NYT,* 1/23/79 ("Templegate"); *NYT,* 11/20,25/78 (Ridley body counts, 408 to 708), and see fn. 33; *NYT,* 11/26, 12/16,11,24/78 and 2/11, 5/16/79 (Guyana's collusion) and 12/3/78 (Burnham).

41. *White Night,* p. 225 (C-131s), *NYT,* 11/24/78 (equipment lists).

42. *White Night,* p. 228 (identity strip), and *Children of Jonestown,* p. 196 (medical tags); *Hold Hands,* p. 59 (tags visible in photo).

43. *Hold Hands,* p. 200 and *White Night,* p. 224 (Vietnam "looked like Ton San Nhut"); *White Night,* p. 224 (planes carried 557 caskets).

44. *Hold Hands,* pp. 200-1 (182 arrive last day); *White Night,* pp. 226, 231 (Maj. Hickman, "six days," first bodies arrive Dover 11/28); *NYT,* 11/24,26/78 (airlift details).

45. *Hold Hands,* p. 204; *White Night,* pp. 228-31 (description, "These were the worst").

46. *Hold Hands,* p. 201 (182 last day, 17 identified); *White Night,* p. 226 (Dover site), 227 (174 identified by Guyanese), 231 (183 in 82 caskets); *NYT,* 11/30/78 (Dover, map), 11/21/78 (50 U.S. experts sent), 12/1/78 (46 identified).

47. *Hold Hands,* p. 204 (Jones cremated), and see fn. 8.

48. *Hold Hands,* p. 203 (families not permitted to see remains), and personal interviews; *Baltimore Sun,* 12/28/78 (only 259 claimed by families); *NYT,* 12/22/78, 1/8,24/79, 2/17/79, 3/31/79, 4/18/79 (Dover body counts 675 to 547) and 4/26.

49. *Strongest Poison,* pp. 182-9; *NYT,* 12/21/78, and 1/10/79 (New Jersey says cremation illegal, censures six doctors); *NYT,* 11/30/79 (Delaware legal problems).

50. "Medical Examiners Find Failings by Government on Cult Bodies," *NYT,* 12/3/78; Rescue Mission Report, Joint Chiefs of Staff, Special Operations Review (GPO, 1980); *Delta Force,* Charles Beckwith (Harcourt Brace & Jovanovich, 1983).

51. *White Night,* pp. 228-9 (no autopsies, death certificates in Guyana); *NYT,* 12/12/78 (Dr. Sturmer, National Assoc. of Med. Examiners); *NYT,* 12/3/78 (other medical examiners complain, "legally dubious method"); *NYT,* 12/16/78 (Sturmer again), 12/4/78 (embalmed) and fn 8 (cremations).

52. *Hold Hands,* p. 203 and *American Funeral Director,* Jan. 1979; *NYT,* 12/1,2/78 (FBI fingerprint 911 or 700 and identify 255).

53. *Children of Jonestown,* p. 197; *Hold Hands,* p. 204; *Strongest Poison,* pp. 182-9; *NYT,* 12/3,18/79 (quotes), 12/13,16,17,19/78 (autopsies, complaints), 12/25/78 ("few facts"), and fn 37 (Mootoo's work unknown).

54. *Raven,* p. 527; *Hold Hands,* p. 32 (photo), 53-4 and *WP,* 11/21/78 (diagram); *NYT,* 11/21/78 (illus.).

55. *White Night,* p. 197, *Raven,* p. 533, *Strongest Poison,* p. 131; *Children of Jonestown,* pp. 168-70; *NYT,* 2/20/79 (not guilty plea).

57. *White Night,* p. 197, *Raven,* p. 525 ff (ambush described); *Hold Hands,* p. 256 (Layton's "dumb stare"), and *LAT,* 11/28/79 (Layton as "robot"); *Journey to Nowhere,* pp. 96-8 (Beikman in court "staring"); *NYT,* 12/15/78 (Layton insanity defense), 12/21/78 (Layton "responsible").

58. *White Night,* p. 197.

59. *WP,* 11/21/78 (Layton's role, Jones' quote); *Boston Globe,* "Killers Hunted," 11/21/78; *SFE,* 11/22/78 (7 involved); *NYT,* 11/20/78 and 12/18/78 (lists of dead), 11/21/78 and 12/21/78 (Kice named, Joe Wilson gave Ryan gun at ambush), 11/29/78 and 12/9/78 (claim all dead, 8 warrants dropped), 12/21/78 (survivors scared to fly with "others"), 11/22 and 12/20/78 (Stephan Jones, Tim Carter, Michael Prokes arrested or charged with murders), 11/22, 25/78 and 12/15,17/78 (Cobb, Rhodes, Moore, Clayton, named survivors), 12/678 (3 escape to Caracas & Miami before massacre). Who Killed Ryan? 11/22/78 (FBI invest. "conspiracy"), 12/28/78 (Tim Jones takes 5th amendment on Ryan shooting).

60. *Raven,* p. 573 (elite squad), *Hold Hands,* p. 145; *Newsweek,* 12/4/78; *Daily World,* 6/23/81 (Holsinger).

61. "Grim Report," Kilduff, *SFC,* 6/15/78 (guards, abuse); *Newsweek,* 12/4/78 (different food, treatment); *LAT,* 11/28/78 (Debbie Layton Blakey, "upper middle-class whites").

62. *White Night,* p. 139, *Raven,* p. 403 (Cudjoe); and *Raven,* p. 241 (obeyed orders).

63. Chicago Defender, cited in *Black Panther News,* 12/30/78 (UNITA recruits for Africa); "Ryan Murder Suspect Resembles Robot," Hall, *LAT,* 11/26/78 (programmed, NYT, 11/30/78 (survivors had special privileges).

64. *Hold Hands,* p. 150; *Strongest Poison,* p. 85 (% women); "Questions Linger," *Oakland Times,* 12/9/78 (% Blacks); *NYT,* 11/20/78, 12/18/78 (death lists).

65. *WP,* 12/9/78 (FBI claims killers among dead), see fn 13,23 (missing people); *LAT,* 11/25/78 (Stanley Clayton, survivor, "hundreds were slain," "forced to die"); *NYT,* 12/6/78 (3 escape), 12/4/78 (Pan Am won't fly without armed guard), 1/29/79 ("cheers" heard), 12/23/78 ("persons unknown").

66. Assassination of Leo J. Ryan, p. 35, *Raven,* pp. 572-3, *Hold Hands,* p. 254 ("hit squad"); *White Night,* p. 224 (rumors at site), *Journey to Nowhere,* p. 148 ("basketball team"); *LAT,* 12/18/78, *NYT,* 12/1,4/78 (fears in U.S.), *NYT,* 12/4/78 (SF police guard Temple, "at a loss"), 12/23/78 (radio orders to kill relatives, Jonestown to San Francisco day of massacre, FBI).

67. *Raven* (Prokes & Tim Carter), see fn 59, and *NYT,* 12/12/78 (Carter arrested with pistols).

68. *Hold Hands,* p. 30

69. *NYT,* 11/22,23/78 (rumors, "master plan," Lane), 11/29 and 12/1/78 (FBI says "serious," Secret Service investigates), 12/11,23/78 (Buford testifies).

70. *AP,* May 19, 1979 (wrongly attributed to Cong. staff investigator George Berdes).

71. "Suicide Carnage," *Baltimore Sun,* 11/21/78 ("write the story"); *Hold Hands,* pp. 127, 221, (Lane, Garry lawyers for People's Temple)' *NYT,* 11/23/78 (Garry once called Jonestown "paradise," says Jones "lost reason"); *NYT,* 11/21/78 (picked up in jungle by Guyanese troops).

72. *Raven,* p. 572 (survivors); *Guyanan Daily Mirror,* 11/23/78 (32 captured by Guyanese); *NYT,* 11/30, 12/3,7,30/78 (reports of rcturning groups, totaling 30, more remain).

73. *Raven,* p. 575; "Fateful Prophecy is Fulfilled," *Newsweek,* 3/10/80; "Mills Family Murders: Could it be Jim Jones' Last Revenge?" *People,* 3/17/78.

74. *Hold Hands,* pp. 130-31, 254 (link of Jones to Moscone and Milk); *The Mayor of Castro Street,* Randy Shilts (St. Martin's, 1982); *NYT,* 1/17, 2/19, 4/24, 5/18, 5/22, 7/4/79 (Dan White arrest, trial, conviction, sentence); *NYT,* 5/22/79 (gay riot in response), 5/22/79 (White biography); *NYT,* 11/27 (murder), 12/6 ("no link"), 12/18/78 (illegal votes for Moscone); "The Milk/Moscone Case Reviewed," Paul Krassner, *Nation,* 1/14/84.

76. *Los Angeles Herald,* 2/12/84.

77. *Hold Hands,* pp. 61,68 (KKK, Jones' racism), *NYT,* 11/26/78 (biography).

78. *Hold Hands,* pp. 62-3.

79. Personal interviews, Richmond, Indiana, 1981. *Raven,* p. 26 (Jones' boyhood); *Hidden Terrors,* A.J. Languth (Pantheon, 1978) (Mitrione).

80. *Hold Hands,* pp. 63-4 (calling as minister), 66,70 (ordained as minister); *NYT,* 11/22,29/79, 3/13/79 (Disciples of Christ).

81. *Hold Hands,* pp. 62,64.

82. *Hold Hands,* pp. 66,166 (monkey business); *White Night,* pp. 9-10 (Indiana U. link).

83. *Hold Hands,* p. 65 (faith healer); *Hidden Terrors,* pp. 17,41 (chief of police).

84. *Hold Hands,* pp. 68,102 (cure cancer); 75,76,103 (chicken livers); *Six Years,* p. 86 ff (photos).

86. *Suicide Cult,* pp. 181-2.

87. *White Night,* p. 236; *Journey to Nowhere,* pp. 95, 98 (Burnham's people defend him), *NYT,* 11/21 (murders), 11/26/12/1,5,14/78 (charges and trials), 12/19/78 and 2/3/79 (Stephan Jones "confesses" and "retracts"), 11/28/78 (charged with Katsaris).

88. *Hidden Terrors,* p. 42; *Who's' Who in the CIA,* Julius Mader (E. Berlin, 1968).

89. *Suicide Cult,* p. 21; *WP,* 11/22/78.

90. *Hold Hands,* p. 65; *NYT,* 3/25/79 (also recruiting Black families in Cuba, 1960).

91. "Jones' Mysterious Brazil Stay," *San Jose Mercury,* 11/78.

92. *San Jose Mercury,* 11/78; "Penthouse Interview: Stephen Jones," *Penthouse,* 4/79.

93. *Hidden Terrors,* p. 249; (Mitrione in Brazil '62-'67), 63, 117.

94. Ibid., pp. 139-40 (reference to Who's Who in CIA); *NYT,* 6/11,29/79 (Uruguay).

95. See it!

96. *Journey to Nowhere,* p. 247; *Hold Hands,* p. 171 (paid "pile of money," "$5,000 to have sex with Ambassadors' wife" — cover story for payoff); *Suicide Cult,* p. 42 (money to travel around U.S. on return).

97. "Bishops' Report Names CIA,"; *WP,* 2/16/85; Private Groups ... Millions Raised," WP, 12/10/84; "Americares Foundation — Central America Gets Private Aid," *WP,* 2/27/85

(Knights of Malta, CIA's Casey, Brzezinsky, Haig, funnel donations for "medicine" through Sterling Drugs, linked to I.G Farben).

98. *Journey to Nowhere,* p. 251.

99. "Guyanan Tragedy Points to a Need for Better Care and Protection of Guardianship Children," Comptroller General Report (GPO, 1980); NYT, 1/25/79 (150 "foster children" in Ukiah), 2/14/79 (Mendocino agency says "none placed"), 2/17/79 (Sen. Cranston says 17 Ukiah children among dead).

100. "World Vision, Go Home," L. Lee, *Christian Century,* 5/16/79; In the Spirit of Jimmy Jones," J. Fogarty, *Akwesane Notes,* Winter, 1982; *NYT,* 2/26, 4/4, 11/16/75 and 12/25/79 (W.V. Cambodia), 4/2-5/75 and 6/30/79 (Vietnam work).

101. *Journey to Nowhere,* p. 220; "Jim Jones a Republican," *LAT,* 12/17/78 (John Birch); *Daily World,* 6/23/81 (Holsinger comments), and *NYT,* 11/24/78 ("helpful" reputation).

102. "Jim Jones was a Republican for 6 Years," *LAT,* 12/17/78; *Hold Hands,* p. 70 (Jones held 15% vote Mendocino County).

103. *Hold Hands,* p. 93.

104. *Hold Hands,* p. 84; *NYT,* 11/21/78 (Tim Stoen joins, legal advisor).

105. *Hold Hands,* p. 95 (Debbie Layton Blakey); *In My Father's House* (Layton's stories); *Strongest Poison* (Terry Buford), *NYT,* 12/4/78 (Layton family, 6 join).

106. *Six Years,* p. 86 ff (photos); *NYT,* 11/22-24/78 (biography), 11/29/78 (college S).

107. *Strongest Poison,* p. 85; *Philadelphia Inquirer,* 11/19/78.

108. *Hold Hands,* p. 138 (family joins); "Cult Got Assets from Layton," *LAT,* 11/26/78; "Family Tragedy," *NYT,* 12/4/78 (aristocratic).

109. *Washington Post,* 1/22/78 (27,000 acres leased, 1974); *Daily World,* 6/23/81 ($600,000).

110. *In My Father's House,* pp. 18-19.

111. *Hold Hands,* p. 94, 127-8; *NYT,* 12/16,17/79 (Swiss bank accounts).

112. *Hold Hands,* p. 96; *Baltimore Sun,* 11/21/78; *NYT,* 11/21/78 (list), 12/5/78 (Stoen close to D.A. Hunter, later investigated Temple).

113. "Statement by Joe Holsinger," 5/23/80, citing *Strongest Poison* (Chapter 5), (Jones as "patriotic American"); *LAT,* 12/17/78; *NYT,* 12/1/78 (Reagan says Jones "close to Democrats").

114. *Hold Hands,* p. 73-75, 79, 176.

115. *Hold Hands,* p. 182-3; *Journey to Nowhere,* pp. 223-4, *WP,* 11/22/78 (Housing Commission); "DA Accuses Deputy Stoen," *SFE,* 1/21/79; *WP,* 11/22/78; Baltimore Sun, 11/21/78 (election and voter fraud); *NYT,* 12/18,20/78 (illegal Moscone votes).

116. *Journey to Nowhere,* p. 279 (welfare appointments), *NYT,* 12/9/79 (half of dead on Calif. Welfare sometime, 10% active, 51 fraud).

117. *Hold Hands,* p. 132 (Angela Davis), 213 and *NYT,* 11/23/78 (Rosalynn Carter), *NYT,* 11/21/78 (list), also *WP,* 11/20/78 and *Baltimore Sun,* 11/21/78.

118. *Age of Surveillance,* Frank Donner (Random House, 1980); *Spying on Americans,* Athan Theoharis (Temple University Press, 1978); "Garden Plot and SWAT: U.S. Police as New Action Army," *Counterspy,* Winter 1976.

119. *Secret Agenda,* Jim Hougan (Random House, 1984), pp. 99, 102, Final Report, Senate Select Committee on Presidential Campaign Activities (GPO, 1974), pp. 3-7 and Hearings, Vol 3, pp. 1319-37 and Vol. 4, pp. 1453-64 (describes Houston plan); The Whole

Truth: The Watergate Conspiracy, Sam Ervin (Random House, 1980); "A New Watergate Revelation: The White House Death Squads," Jonathan Marshall, Inquiry, 3/5/79.

120. *COINTELPRO,* Nelson Blackstock (Vintage, 1976); *The FBI and Martin Luther King: From SOLO to Memphis,* David Garrow (Norton, 1981); *Assassination of Malcolm X,* George Breiterman (Pathfinder Press, 1976); also see on King harassment; *Nation,* 6/17/78, and Newsweek, 9/28/81, and *NYT,* 3/17/75. Also browse *NYT,* 11/19-23/75 and 12/3-24/75.

121. "Remembering Ed Meese: From the Free Speech Movement to Operation Garden Plot," Johan Carlisle, *S.F. Bay Guardian,* 4/4/84; "Officer Ed Meese," Jeff Stein, *New Republic,* 10/7/81; and "Ed Meese," Alex Dubro, *Rebel,* 12/13/84; "Bringing the War Home," Ron Ridenhouse, *New Times,* 11/28/75.

122. "Garden Plot & SWAT," *Counterspy,* Winter, 1976.

123. "Why Civil Libertarians are Leery of Ed Meese," *Oakland Tribune,* 2/13/84.

124. "Jim Jones: The Seduction of San Francisco," J. Kasindorf, *New West,* 12/18/78; Churchmen Hunt Clues on Cult's Lure for Blacks," H. Soles, *Christianity Today,* 3/23/79; An Interpretation of People's Temple and Jim Jones," *Journal Interdenom.* Theol. Ctr., Fall 1979; "Cuname Curare & Cool Aid: The Politics that Spawned and Nurtured Jonestown," George Jackson (self-published, 1984).

125. *Hold Hands,* p. 87.

126. *Hold Hands,* pp. 88, 182-3.

127. *Hold Hands,* p. 84, 100-1; "Jones Linked to Extortion," *LAT,* 11/25/78; *NYT,* 12/3/78.

128. *Hold Hands,* p. 96, 172, 210-11.

129. "Seven Mysterious Deaths," Kathy Hunter, *Ukiah Press-Democrat.*

130. *LAT,* 11/25/78; *NYT,* 11/21/78 (Jones threatens to kill defectors).

131. *Journey to Nowhere,* pp. 49-50, 67, 102.

132. Assassination of Leo J. Ryan, p. 316 (Debbie Layton affidavit); *LAT,* 11/18/78; NYT, 11/20; 12/5/78 *(White Night).*

133. *Hold Hands,* p. 71-2, 180; *NYT,* 11/21,28/78 and 12/7/78 (abuse complaints ignored).

134. "Inside People's Temple," Kilduff, *New West,* 8/1/77; "Jim Jones: The Making of a Madman," Phil Tracy, *New West,* 12/18/78; *LAT,* 12/8/78.

135. *Hold Hands,* p. 16, 100, 136-7; Scared Too Long," SFE, 11/13/77 (Houston death); NYT, 11/21/78.

136. *Hold Hands,* p. 127, 133.

137. *Hold Hands,* p. 136 (against advice); *NYT,* 11/21/78 (Speiers makes out will).

138. Personal interviews with Joe Holsinger, Ryan's aide, 1980; *NYT,* 11/21/78, 12/16/78 (panic).

139. *Hold Hands,* p. 87-8, 100.

140. *White Night,* p. 226; *Hold Hands,* p. 232, *SFC,* 11/23/78 ("doubles")

141. *The Second Oswald,* Popkin (Berkeley, 1968).

142. See fn 34.

143. *White Night,* p. 227 (autopsy, identification); *Hold Hands,* p. 262 (photo); "New Mystery: Is Jones Dead?" *NY Daily News,* 11/23/78.

144. *NYT,* 11/24/78 (fingerprints).

145. *Hold Hands,* p. 77, 83; *In My Father's House,* pp. 115-6.

146. "Jungle Geopolitics in Guyana: How a Communist Utopia that Ended in a Massacre Came to be Sited," *American Journal of Economics & Sociology,* 4/81.

147. *Guyana Massacre* (photo of Gary at Temple).

148. *SFE,* 1/9/79. Also see my "Jonestown Banks" piece.

149. *Journey to Nowhere,* p. 126.

150. "James G. McDonald: High Commissioner for Refugees, 1933-35" *Werner Lib. Bull.* #43-44; "Refugee Immigration: Truman Directive," *Prologue,* Spring 1981; *Caribbean Review,* Fall, 1981.

151. *Journey to Nowhere,* pp. 117-18 (interior development); "Guyana's National Service Program," *Journal of Administration Overseas,* 1/76; *Caribbean Review,* Fall, 1981, 1982.

152. "Mineral Resources Map," *Area Handbook for Guyana,* State Department (GPO, 1969); *White Night,* p. 238 (Burnham); *Hold Hands,* p. 149.

153. *White Night,* p. 238 (Burnham on importing labor, "exploit the exploitable").

154. *Hold Hands,* p. 144. (Embassy visits since 1973); "Consulate Officers" Babysitters," *NYT,* 11/29/78 and *NYT,* 12/6,11,24/78 (Guyana denies links), but see 5/16/79 (House report charges collusion), and 5/78; 5/4,16/79 (House report critical of role of U.S. Embassy).

155. *Hold Hands,* p. 146.

156. "Brother Forced to Go to Jonestown," *LAT,* 11/27/78 (kill whole family threat); Personal interview with Guyanese present, 1980 (bound and gagged).

157. *Journey to Nowhere,* p. 107 (guards, "state within a state"); *Hold Hands,* p. 127 (coercion by armed guards, Yolanda Crawford), personal interview with Guyanese living within 5 miles of site, 1981.

158. *Journey to Nowhere,* pp. 73-4 (adoption, 7 Guyanese children among dead); *Guyana Daily Mirror,* 11/23/78.

159. *Hold Hands,* p. 39 (Gerry Parks), 156 (Blakey), "Life in Jonestown," *Newsweek,* 12/4/78; "Jonestown," Michael Novak, AEI Reprint #94, 3/79 (work and food).

160. Holsinger Statement, 5/23/80; *NYT,* 11/23/78 ("preoccupied with").

161. *Hold Hands,* p. 50-51 (Tim Bogue), 157-63, 170-1 (public rape); "People's Temple in Guyana is a Prison," *Santa Rosa Press Democrat,* 4/12/78; *Newsweek,* 12/4/78 (special treatment); *SFC,* 6/15/78; *Baltimore Sun,* 11/21/78; *NYT,* 11/20/78 (slaves, torture), 12/4/78 (denials).

163. *Trading with the Enemy,* Charles Higham (Dell, 1983), p. 23 (Schacht role in war); *NYT,* 10/11/79 (Auschwitz plan).

164. *Miami Herald,* 3/27/79 (set up accounts); *LAT,* 11/18/79, and see my "Jonestown Banks"); *NYT,* 11/21,23,28,29/78; 12/2,3,8,16,20/78 (millions described in various places); *NYT,* 1/13/79 (IRS says back taxes could be millions), 12/3/78 ($2 million real estate).

165. *LAT,* 1/5/78; *SFC,* 1/9/79, and see my "Jonestown Banks" again; *NYT,* 8/3/79 (puts Panama and Venezuela accounts at $15 million plus) , *NYT,* 1/24/79 (receivership), 12/19/8 and 2/11; 10/11/79 (U.S. and Guyanese government and relatives claim it).

166. *In My Father's House,* pp. 18,19.

167. *Assassination,* pp. 775-6 (199 SSA beneficiaries at site), *Hold Hands,* pp. 78, 139; *NYT,* 11/22/78 (200 get $40,000/month), and 2/14/79 (Senate investigation). If the average check is $200 a month, how do 199 people equal $65,000?

168. *NYT,* 11/21/78 and 12/10/78 (guns on site don't match cartridges); *NYT,* 12/3/78 (smuggling operations).

169. *Area Handbook,* op cit., see fn. 152.

170. *Operation Mind Control,* Walter Bowart (Dell, 1978); *The Search for the Manchurian Candidate,* John Marks (Times Books, 1978); "Project MK-ULTRA: CIA Program of Research in Behavior Modification," Senate Select Committee on Intelligence, Hearings, 8/3/77 (GPO, 1977); WP, MK-ULTRA" (series), Summer/Fall 1977; *NYT,* 1/30/79 (overview of MK-ULTRA).

171. Individual Rights and the Federal Role in Behavior Modification, Senate Subcommittee on Constitutional Rights (GPO, 1974); NYT, 1/25/79 (children), 2/7,10/79 (Blacks), *Philadelphia Inquirer,* 11/26/79 (prison).

172. *The Mind Manipulators,* Scheflin & Opton (Grosset & Dunlap, 1978); *The Mind Stealers: Psychosurgery and Mind Control,* S. Chavkin (Houghton-Mifflin, 1978); "Proposal for the Center for Reduction of Life-Threatening Behavior," J. West, 9/1/78; Correspondence, Dr. J. Stubblebine, Calif. Director of Health to Dr. Louis J. West, 1/22/73 (reprinted in Individual Rights, above); "Nike Nonsense, Army Offers Unused Nike Bases to UCLA Violence Center," *Madness Network News,* 2/19/74; *Mind Stealers,* p. 19 (Drs. M ark, Ervin), and *NYT,* 2/7,10/79 (electrodes); *LAT,* 11/26/78 (Dr. West writes "psycho-autopsy" of Jonestown).

173. *NYT,* 11/28/78 ("criminal rehab program at Jonestown), and 1/25/79 (children); see also fn 21,59,64 (race, sex, age composition of dead).

174. *Raven,* p. 347, Holsinger Statement, 5/23/80; *NYT,* 11/23/78 (medical records).

175. *Control of Candy Jones,* Donald Bain (Playboy Press, 1979); "The CIA's Electric Kool Aid Acid Test," Tad Szulc, *Psychology Today,* 11/77. See also fn 170, 172 (books).

176. *Physical Control of the Mind: Toward a Psychocivilized Society,* Jose M. Delgado (Harper & Row, 1969); *Psychotechnology: Electronic Control of Mind & Behavior,* Robert L. Schwitzgebel (Holt, Rinehart & Winston, 1972).

177. *Hold Hands,* p. 17; *Children of Jonestown,* p. 16 (population of Georgetown, drugs); "Jones Community Found Stocked with Drugs to Control the Mind," *NYT,* 12/29/78.

178. *Children of Jonestown,* p. 16; *NYT,* 12/29/78 ("used to control").

179. *Children of Jonestown,* p. 16 (thorazine); *NYT,* 12/29/78 (drugs found); *Daily World,* 6/23/81 (Holsinger).

180. *Hold Hands,* p. 12.

181. *Hold Hands,* p. 190-3 (brainwash methods); *Daily World,* 6/23/81 (Holsinger).

182. *Hold Hands,* p. 257 (Luckhoo, lawyer for Temple); *White Night,* pp. 257-8 (Burnham "conversion"), Sir Lionel, Fred Archer (Gift Publications, 1980) (Luckhoo biography); *NYT,* 12/5/79 (Luckhoo has gotten 299 murder acquittals).

183. "In the Spirit of Jimmy Jones," *Akwesane News,* Winter 1982.

184. "Full Gospel Businessmen Dine with Kings," *L.A. Herald,* 1/29/85; "Annual White House Prayer Breakfast," National Public Radio, 2/1/85 (mysterious fellowship).

185. "Hundreds Were Slain, Survivor Says," *LAT,* 11/25/78; *NYT,* 12/6/78 (suicide plans); *NYT,* 11/21/78 and 12/10/78 (secrecy, panic, reaction to press coming).

186. *Journey to Nowhere,* pp. 56-7, 141; *NYT,* 11/23/78 (Freed calls Jones "Devil").

187. *Newsweek,* 12/4/79; *WP,* 11/19/78 and ff; *NYT,* 11/20; 12/3/78, 10/11/79; *Time,* 12/4/78; "Nightmare in Jonestown" (maps).

188. *Journey to Nowhere,* pp. 63-4; "Hill Rules Cult with Iron Fist," *Cleveland Plain Dealer,* 12/4/78; *NYT,* 12/4,5/78.

189. *Daily World,* 6/23/81, 10/23/80 (Holsinger and Cheddi Jagan); "Hill Rules," *CPD,* 12/4/78 (Hill admits); *NYT,* 12/19/78 (guns missing at site); Personal interview with Jagan.

190. "Hill Rules," *CPD,* 12/4/78; CBS, "60 Minutes," 11/18/80 (Hill interviewed).

191. "West German Concentration Camp in Chile," Konrad Ege, *Counterspy,* 12/78.

192. *Death in Washington,* Don Freed (Lawrence Hill, 1980) (Townley Welch); *Aftermath,* Ladislas Farago (Avon Press, 1974) (Bormann, Mengele); *NYT,* 11/7/84 (Pisagua camp).

193. *Six Years,* p. 122

194. *The Politics of Heroin in Southeast Asia,* Alfred McCoy (Harper & Row, 1974); "Jonestown Resettlement Plan," *SFE,* 8/18/80.

195. Correspondence, EPICA, 4/2/80 (Dominica plan); *NYT,* 4/11, 5/6, 6/12/79 (complicated intermesh of Sam Brown, Director of Peace Corps who invented Jamaica Plan, Dr. Peter Bourne and his lover Mary King, appointed Deputy Director of Action programs, the scandal of White House Drug Abuse advisor Bourne writing fake prescriptions for Carter aide Ellen Metesky, later Peace Corps director herself, and the resignation of the first Black Peace Corps administrator, Dr. Carolyn Payton (formerly Caribbean Desk there) over disagreements with Brown on the Jamaica plans); "The Jamaican Experiment," *Atlantic Monthly,* 9/83 (Reagan's plans).

196. American Labor & U.S. Foreign Policy, Ron Radosh, p. 393 (cites other sources); *Journey to Nowhere,* p. 21 (Burnham, CIA role, "right wing"); *White Night,* ($1 million destabilization plan); "How the CIA Got Rid of Jagan," Neal Sheehy, London *Sunday Times,* 2/23/67.

197. *White Night,* p. 257; "CIA Agent Witnessed Jonestown Mass Suicide," *San Mateo Times,* 12/14/79.

198. *White Night,* p. 256; *Who's Who in the CIA,* Julius Mader (E. Berlin, 1968); *Dirty Work: CIA in Europe,* Lou Wolff (Lyle Stuart, 1978); *Raven,* p. 590, note 66 (for Dwyer's non-denial).

199. *Hold Hands,* p. 29, 53; *Raven,* p. 534; Holsinger Statement, 5/2/380 (quote); "Don't Be Afraid to Die," *Newsweek,* 3/26/79; *NYT,* 3/15/79 (transcripts censor it); *NYT,* 11/19/79 (Dwyer at ambush); *NYT,* 12/7,9/78 (curious "discovery," delay).

200. *Daily World,* 6/23/81 (Holsinger); *NYT,* 11/25/78 (biography).

201. "Ryan's Ready," and "People's Temple," Reiterman, *SFE,* 11/17/78; "Angry Meeting in Guyana," Javers, *SFC,* 11/17/78.

202. Assassination of Leo J. Ryan, p. 9 (quote); *Daily World,* 6/23/81; *NYT,* 12/5,6,13/78 (role); 12/1/78 (cover-up with Blakey), 12/8/78 (biography).

203. Information Services Company, 7/80 (quote); *Daily World,* 6/23/81 (sensitive Caribbean listening post," citing *White Night).*

204. *Daily World,* 6/23/81 (Holsinger).

205. "Performance of a Department of State and American Embassy in Guyana in thc People's Temple Case," Dept. of State (GPO, 1979); *Daily World,* 6/23/78 (Holsinger blames McCoy); Assassination of Leo Ryan, pp. 699-704 (role); *NYT,* 11/30/78, 12/5/78, 5/4,16/79 (Embassy criticisms); *NYT,* 11/20-22/78 (gave Ryan no warning); 12/2,4-6/78 (hostile to Ryan, sent FOIA to Jones).

206. Personal interview with Holsinger, 1980.

207. *CIA: A Bibliography,* R. Goehlert (Vance, 1980); *Gehlen: Spy of the Century,* Edward Spiro (Random House, 1971); *The Pledge Betrayed,* Tom Bower (Doubleday, 1981); *The Belarus Secret,* John Loftus (Knopf, 1982); *Klaus Barbie: Butcher of Lyons,* Tom Bower (Pantheon, 1984); *Quiet Neighbors,* Allan Ryan (Harcourt, Brace, Jovanovich, 1984); *The Fourth Reich,* Magnus Linklater (Holt, Rinehart & Winston, 1985); *Secrets of the SS,* Glenn Infield (Stein & Day, 1982); *Skorzeny: Hitler's Commando,* Glenn Infield (St.

Martin's, 1981); "The Nazi Connection to the John F. Kennedy Assassination," Mae Brussell, *Rebel,* 1982.

208. *In My Father's House,* (Dugway chapter); "Family Tragedy," *NYT,* 12/4/78; Holsinger Statement, 5/23/80; *Who's Who* (Marquis, 1980) (Dr. Layton).

209. *In My Father's House,* pp. 18,19; *The Crime and Punishment of I.G. Farben,* Joseph Borkin (Free Press, 1978); *The Sanctity of I.G. Farben's Spy Nests,* Howard Armbruster (self-published, 1956); *Treason's Peace,* Howard Armbruster (1947); *Trading with the Enemy,* op cit., fn 163.

210. "Family Tragedy: Hitler's Germany to Jones Cult," Lindsey, *NYT,* 12/4/78.

211. *NYT,* 12/4/78 (met in England), see fn 209 (Farben link); "Solvay et Cie Reorganizes U.S. Interests," *Houston Post,* 11/29/74.

212. Holsinger Statement, 5/23/80.

213. *Philadelphia Inquirer,* 11/22/78.

214. *White Night,* p. 256 (cites report), see fn. 63.

215. *White Night,* 252 (minister); *Baltimore Sun,* 11/21/78 (Maria says CIA).

216. Assassination of Leo Ryan, p. 777 (lawyer role), see fn 195 also, *NYT,* 12/4/78.

217. Public Eye, Vol. 1, #1, 1975. Proceedings, First Conference, WACL, 9/25-9/67 (Taipei, R.O.C., 1967).

218. "Jones Disciple goes to Court Tuesday," *Santa Cruz Sentinel,* 6/19/81 (CIA link alleged at Layton trial).

219. *White Night,* pp. 210-11 note, *SFE,* 2/8/79 ($ to USSR), *NYT,* 11/28/78 (suitcase); *NYT,* 11/28, 12/1,23/78 (details on her strange "suicide-murder"), *NYT,* 12/18/78 (letter), and 11/28, 12/18/78 (Prokes & Carter identified).

220. *Nation,* 3/2679; "Jones Aide Dies After Shooting Himself," *Baltimore Sun,* 3/15/79, 12/8/78 ($2.5 million), *NYT,* 3/14/78 and *Strongest Poison* (FBI link).

221. *Hold Hands,* p. 165 (move to USSR), *SFC,* 1/21/79 (details of rumor), *NYT,* 11/27,28/78, 12/10/78, 1/1/79 (more details, quotes, tapes).

222. *White Night,* p. 229 (Guyana recovers $); *NYT,* 12/8 ($2.5 million); *NYT,* 11/18, 12/19/78 (Soviets, $39,000, refusal), and see *NYT,* 11/28; 12/3,10,18-20/78; and 1/1,2,9/79 (for all the smarmy details).

223. *SFE,* 1/9/79, and my "Jonestown Banks."

224. *God's Banker,* DiFonzi (Calvi), *NYT,* 6/31/82 (Panama story); *NYT,* 12/5/78 (Lane and Buford knew names on accounts), and see "Jonestown Banks" (disappears).

225. *Time,* 7/26/82.

226. *Children of Jonestown,* pp. 196-7 (orders from above).

227. "Close Look at Carter's Radical Fringe," *Human Events,* 11/11/78 (right wing view); *Migration & Development in the Caribbean,* Robert Pastor (Westview Press, 1985).

228. *Hold Hands,* p. 256; NYT, 11/21/78 (biography); also *Strongest Poison* (interviews).

229. *White Night,* p. 224 ("fearless"), *NYT,* 11/21/78 (biography).

230. "The Case Against Mark Lane," Brill, *Esquire,* 2/13/79; "Mark Lane: The Left's Leading Hearse Chaser," Katz, *Mother Jones,* 8/79; "People's Temple Colony Harassed," *SFE,* 10/4/78 (Lane charges CIA attack); *NYT,* 11/30/78 (Anthony Lewis critique); 12/5,7,16,29/78 (rumors and denials that Lane and Buford drained Swiss bank accounts), 2/4/79 (contradictory remarks), 2/4/, 4/4/, 9/21/79 (more charges, fake identity, theft), see *Strongest Poison* for comparison.

231. *Code Name Zorro,* Lane & Gregory (Prentice-Hall, 1977).

232. *Hold Hands,* p. 222; *NYT,* 6/14/78 (Lane as Ray's attorney); Investigation of the Assassination of Martin Luther King, Jr., House Select Committee on Assassinations (HSCA), Hearings, Vols. 1-9 (GPO, 1979); *NYT,* 8/8,16/78 (Lane's view of HSCA, conspiracy against him), and *Strongest Poison.*

233. "Ray's Breakout," *Time,* 6/23/77.

234. "Tennessee Clemency Selling Scheme," *Corrections,* 6/798; "A Federal-State Confrontation," *National Law Journal,* 5/11/81.

235. *NYT,* 1/6,20/79 (Swearingen, documents), see also 1/16-18,27/79 (Swearingen); *Code Name Zorro,* op cit.; *NYT,* 1/20/79 (Swearingen, Chicago FBI to 1971); "Investigating the FBI," *Policy Review,* #18, Fall, 1981; David Martin "Breitel Report: New Light on FBI Use of Informants," *First Principles,* 10/80; "Prying Informants Files Loose from the Hands of Attorney General — SWP v. Atty. General of U.S.," *Howard Law Journal,* Vol. 22, #4, 1979.

236. Personal call, 1978.

237. *Strongest Poison,* p. 402.

238. *Code Name Zorro,* pp. 165, 204-5.

239. Ibid., p. 165.

240. Ibid., *Let the Trumpet Sound: Life of Martin Luther King,* Oates, (Mentor, 1982), p. 473.

241. *Code Name Zorro,* p. 168.

242. Ibid., pp. 161-4; *Let the Trumpet Sound,* p. 476.

243. *Code Name Zorro,* pp. 165-70.

244. Ibid., pp. 165-8, 205.

245. Ibid., pp. 168-70.

246. *NYT,* 12/22/78; 1/1/79 (Buford at Lane's home); *Strongest Poison,* p. 402 (unconvincing denial), and see p. 1114 ("our house in Memphis").

247. "Memo Discusses Smuggling Witness to Guyana," Horrock, NYT, 12/8/78; *Strongest Poison,* p. 144 (testimony to HSCA).

248. "Memo Discussing Smuggling," op cit., fn 247.

249. "Seven Mysterious Deaths," op cit., fn 129.

250. *Hold Hands,* pp. 18, 223; Assassination of Leo Ryan, pp. 3, 52-3 (text); *Journey to Nowhere,* p. 163 (Lane quote); *NYT,* 12/8/78 (discouraging Ryan).

251. *Hold Hands,* p. 222; "Ryan's Ready," Reiterman, *SFE,* 11/17/78.

252. *Hold Hands,* pp. 212-3, 223 (sandwiches); NYT, 12/8/78; 1/12/79 (no warning).

253. *Hold Hands,* pp. 43, 44; *Strongest Poison,* p. 175 (underwear); *WP,* 11/21/78.

254. *WP,* 11/21/78.

255. *Hold Hands,* pp. 212-3, 222, citing Anthony Lewis in *NYT.*

257. *Let the Trumpet Sound,* p. 470 (brother, A.D. King with MLK day of death); *NYT,* 7/1/74 ("accidental drowning" death of A.D. King); *Trumpet,* pp. 472-3 (wound described), also Robert Cutler analysis, *Grassy Knoll Gazette,* 1983; *NYT,* 10/25/74 (Dr. Herbert MacDonnell, "no way" from window), 8/18/78.

258. *NYT,* 2/14/74 (Ray gets rehearing); *NYT,* 7/1/74 (Alberta King murdered 6/30/74); "Ray's Day in Court," *Newsweek,* 11/4/74; *NYT,* 10/8/74 (Ray v. Rose reheard); "Did James Earl Ray Slay the Dreamer Alone?" *Writer's Digest,* 9/74.

259. *NYT,* 10/30/74, "Tennessee Effort to Block Testimony Overturned."

260. "Another King Killed," *NYT Magazine,* 6/8/74; "Third King Tragedy," *Time,* 7/15/74; "Murder in a Church," *Nation,* 6/20/74; *NYT,* 6/30, 7/1,9,12/74 (Chenault biog. trial); "That Certain Smile," *Newsweek,* 6/15/74; *NYT,* 7/1,10/74 (psychiatric exam); *NYT,* 9/13/74 (blows kisses, points finger "like a gun" at judge, prosecutor).

261. *NYT,* 7/1-5/74 (Ohio "visitors" in Atlanta, Dayton link to ministers, legal fees paid anonymously, FBI suspicious, Justice says "no conspiracy").

262. Dayton Journal Herald, 7/2/74ff; *NYT,* 7/9/74 ("The Troop" — Steven Holinan, Walter Brooks, Ronald & Robert Scott, Ramona Catlin, Almeda Water, Harvey Cox, Jr., Marcus Wayne Chenault); *NYT,* 7/4,8/74 (biography of Rev. Hananiah Emmanuel Israel, or Rabbi Israel, aka Rabbi Albert Emmanuel Washington, personal interview, *Journal Herald* reporter, 1974.

263. *Journey to Nowhere,* pp. 63-4; "Hill Rules," *CPD,* 12/4/78, fn 188 (Hill); *NYT,* 12/4/74 ("Black Hebrew" Chenault).

264. *NYT,* 7/1,3,7,8/74 (Chenault tells Abernathy of Troop plan "to kill all Black civil rights leaders," "religious mission partly accomplished," and death list found in Chenault apartment: Jesse Jackson, Hosea, Cecil Williams, Martin Luther King, Sr., Ralph Abernathy, Rev. Washington (a cousin), and Fr. Divine (!), already deceased.

265. *Let the Trumpet Sound,* op cit., fn 240.

266. "Psyching Out the Cult's Collective Mania," Drs. Delgado & J. West, *LAT,* 11/26/78; "The Appeal of the Death Trip," Robert J. Lifton, *NYT Magazine,* 1/7/79; *NYT,* 11/22/78, Robert Lifton ("explains"), 12/1/78 (Carter quote); 12/3/78 ("never know," Reston); 12/5/78 (Billy Graham, "Satan").

267. "Jonestown & the CIA: Black Genocide Operation," Jonestown Research Project, 1981; "The Expandable People," Committee on Racial Justice Reporter, Spring 1979; *LAT,* 12/18/78.

268. *Raven,* p. 403; *White Night,* p. 39; *In My Father's House,* p. 320, see "Jonestown Banks."

269. *Raven,* p. 578 (ship in Caribbean); "Jonestown Banks," p. 4 (citing McCann quote on KGO, San Francisco); *NYT,* 11/23/78 ("continue Temple work").

270. Personal interview, relative of Grenadan family, 1984.

271. "Medical Students Were in No Danger," Peter G. Bourne, *Oakland Tribune,* 11/8/83.

272. "Nomination of Director of Drug Abuse Policy Office," Hearings, 5/13/77 (GPO, 1977); "Pipe Dreams," P. Anderson, *Washington Post Magazine,* 2/14/80; *NYT,* 4/26/79 (White House Drug Scandal, U.N. Post), see fn. 195.

273. *SFC,* 12/10/84 (Gairy plan), see fn 147 (Gairy/Jones link); "Blue Christmas Coming Up," *Air Force Magazine,* 1/84 (precision bombing).

274. "Bombed Grenada Hospital Gets Bedding," *WP,* 9/27/84 (USAID, $1.2 million rebuild plan).

275. *Hold Hands,* p. 257 (Luckhoo approached to defend); *Raven,* p. 576 (Layton trial); *Raven,* p. 571 (claims Ryan's killers dead, names Kice, Wilson, Breidenbach, Touchette; what of others?), see fn. 59, 65.

276. *NYT,* 12/5/78 (Ryan's mother wanted full investigation), see fn 63; *NYT,* 12/8,14,15,21/78; 1/4/79 (S.F. Grand Jury, delays, stonewalling, Stoen/Hunter).

277. *White Night,* p. 232; *Raven,* p. 576 ($12 mil. hidden in accounts, airlift costs); "Eerie Shoes: Missing Money," *Time,* 11/18/78; "Assets Liquidated," *Christian Century,* 10/21/81; "Payoff for a Massacre," *Macleans,* 9/6/72; NYT, 11/21,23,28,29; 12/3,21/78

(estimates of wealth), *NYT,* 11/25/78 and 5/19/79 (cost of airlift, $2 to $4.4 mil.); *NYT,* 12/3,5,7,14/78 (Pentagon, Charles Garry, Justice Department, families claim it), 12/19/78 and 1/3,24/79 and 2/11/79 (State Department, IRS, Guyanese, court receiver claim it).

278. *Hold Hands,* p. 134; *Raven,* p. 590, note 66; *Daily World,* 6/23/81 (Holsinger suit); Personal interview with Holsinger, 1982 (suspects military intelligence).

279. *NYT,* 1/23/79 (Ryan's children sue Temple for $1 million); *Raven,* p. 579; Personal interview with Holsinger, 1983; *NYT,* 10/11/79 (695 claims for "wrongful death," total $1.78 billion).

280. *Philadelphia Inquirer,* 4/1/81, "Hinckley Profile," Sid Bernstein, WNET, NY, 1981; *Breaking Points,* Jack & Jo Ann Hinckley (Chosen Books, 1985).

281. "Who Shot RR," Lenny Lapon, *Continuing Inquiry,* 5/22/81; "The Day the President Was Shot, *Investigative Reporter,* 1/82.

282. *Lennon, What Happened?* Beckley (Sunshine Pubs., 1981); "John Lennon's Killer, the Nowhere Man," C. Ungier, New York, 6/22/81.

283. *World Vision Magazine,* 1983; "Final Report of Israeli Commission of Inquiry," Journal Palestinian Studies, Spring, 1983; "Kahan Commission," *Midstream,* 6-7/83; *Guardian,* 11/17/81.

284. "Terrorism in Miami: Suppressing Free Speech," *Counterspy,* 3-5/84; *Guardian,* 11/17/81.

285. *SFE,* 12/18/80, op cit., fn 194.

286. *Hold Hands,* pp. 40, 165, 187 (photo).

287. *Journey to Nowhere,* pp. 234-5, *Hold Hands,* pp. 211-2 (FBI predict more); The Evidence of Things Not Seen, James Baldwin (Holt, Rinehart & Winston, 1985) (Wayne Williams, Atlanta child murders).

288. "Jonestown Massacre Recalled," *WP,* 11/19/84; 10/10/84 (homeless controversy); "Political Storm Swirls Around Newcomers," *NYT,* 11/3/84; WP, 10/4/84 (quote).

289. "Oregon City an Experiment in Medical Care," L. Busch, *Amer. Med. News,* 10/26/84; Eugene, *Oregon Register-Guard,* 11/6/84 (injections).

290. *Politics of Lying,* David Wise (Random House, 1973).

291. *1984,* George Orwell (New American Library, 1961) (The book was originally entitled *1948,* not *1984).*

Frequently Called Numbers

Hilton Head-

Lois
700,000 —
Consultant to a GOVT AGENCY.

Name/Address	Area Code	Number
PROMIS & Eagle Connection?		
Feb 85 He said to Lois: The possibility of		
installing PROMIS		
Few days of May		
Colgate — Tells Barnton — "We're going to bury Inslaw."		
(author)		
		Issue November
		Bull. TAIF manifesto
The Palomino is a Pale Horse		
• Wayne Reeder •	FAE.	
Firearms • • Peter •		
• FAX.		
1 NRP	ingraffite	
	Secret treaty	
• Whips.. SIG.		
Trilateral. alien		
CIA. • Zapot.		
1953 → • narcotics smuggling		
shadow govt.		

A representative page of notes from the late Danny Casolaro's files

Behold, A Pale Horse
A Draft of Danny Casolaro's Octopus Manuscript Proposal

Kenn Thomas

Danny Casolaro died in the process of investigating something called the Octopus, a power cabal that had its tentacles in a variety of notorious contemporary events. The list of those events is long: the 1980 October Surprise pay-off that cost Jimmy Carter the presidency; Contra War weapons development; bizarre murders among the Cabazon Indians in Indio, California; the privatization of CIA dirty tricks in the form of the Wackenhut security firm; the Meese Justice Department's attempt to steal software from a company known as Inslaw, and much more. What follows is a draft of Casolaro's original proposal for his book, *Behold, A Pale Horse: A True Crime Narrative.* Later drafts retitled it simply *The Octopus.*

Among researchers, the verdict has not yet been returned on whether or not Casolaro was murdered or committed suicide in the bathtub of his West Virginia hotel room on August 10, 1992. Stories have circulated about Casolaro's despondency over publisher rejection of the *Octopus* manuscript and his fear about the recent discovery that he had multiple sclerosis. However, Casolaro died just after meeting an informant who may have provided him with the last piece of evidence he needed to prove the existence of his Octopus cabal. The gashes in his wrists were too deep to be self-inflicted. The suicide note was unconvincing.

Suspicions continue to mount. The assistant housekeeper of the hotel tells of the presence of bloody towels under a sink at the crime scene, possibly used to wipe it clean before Casolaro's body was found. Casolaro's body was embalmed without consulting his family. Just as the veil on the secret life of Lee Harvey Oswald is only now being lifted, what really happened to Danny Casolaro will only be revealed in time. It seems a safe bet, however, that he died in part to suppress research he had amassed for the book proposed in the following document. The proposal, *Behold, A Pale Horse,* completed in 1990, appears in the files of Danny Casolaro, which were turned over to ABC News' *Nightline* after Casolaro's death and were eventually transferred to a small office at the University of Missouri.

This proposal covers many of the facts that have become well-known parts of the Casolaro tale and includes heretofore unreported details, such as the role of the gas explosive developed on the Cabazon reservation in the deaths of over 300 American and French military personnel after the October 23, 1983 blast at a compound in Beirut. (Interestingly, after the bombing of New York's World Trade Center on February 26, 1993, many in the media were quick to draw comparisons to the Beirut tragedy, and some early reports mentioned the smell of gas-fuel at the Trade Center bomb site.) The biggest gap in this account is its obliquely hidden mention of the Promis software, a central and notorious part of the Casolaro saga. Promis was developed by Inslaw, a company owned by William and Nancy Sullivan of St. Louis, Missouri, to track criminal cases through various prosecutors' offices. Although it was developed with government money, when the Reagan White House cut the program funding the development, the Hamiltons continued its development under the auspices of a private corporation, Inslaw. Modifications to Promis made it do extraordinary things, including the extrapolation of Soviet submarine launches, and it eventually came to be regarded as an indispensible police tool. It functioned well in tracking criminals and, some have said, in keeping track of political dissidents.

In 1982, Inslaw contracted to become the sole supplier of Promis to the offices of U.S. attorneys, but the Justice Department failed to deliver on the $10 million contract. While Inslaw struggled through the courts to get its due, Meese crony Earl Brian unsuccessfully attempted a hostile takeover of the company. Copies of the modified software began turning up at police agencies throughout the world. Although Brian denies it, the Hamiltons came to believe that he had sold it on the international market in violation of the Inslaw contract. Enraged, the Hamiltons put investigator Casolaro in touch with Michael Riconoscuito, who claimed not only to have made many of the Promis modifications, but also to have developed fuel-air explosives for the Contra war on the ostensibly sovereign Cabazon reservation. Riconoscuito asserted that Brian had been given Promis as a reward for paying off the Ayatollah Khomeini, who successfully delayed the release of Iranian-held American hostages until the defeat of Jimmy Carter in 1980.

Riconoscuito's confessions include tales of intelligence agency in-fighting that may have contributed to George Bush's defeat. He also claims connection to Park-On-Meter, an Arkansas company that helped develop Contra chemical weapons and flew them out on an airstrip in Mena, Arkansas, in an operation apparently covered up by then-Governor Bill Clinton. Riconoscuito also led Danny Casolaro to Area 51 in the Nevada desert, where UFO stories mix with rumors of secret, advanced military craft. Casolaro's files, from which the following was taken, are replete with notes about "Majority 12," the secret government task force working deals with the space aliens.

Casolaro has been slighted for not being able to discern the trustworthiness of various sources, and for being so reluctant to separate the wheat from the chaff in his research that he instead fictionalized his account of the Octopus. Nevertheless, if he was killed, it was not because he wrote bad spy fiction, it was no doubt due more to the pathways he opened to the secret and suppressed details of recent history some of which can be found on the following pages.

Behold, A Pale Horse
A True Crime Narrative

by Daniel Casolaro

> Behold, a pale horse and its rider's name was death and Hades followed him, and they were given power over a fourth of the earth, to kill with sword and with famine and with pestilence and by wild beasts of the earth.
>
> — Revelation 6: 7-8

An international cabal whose freelance services cover parochial political intrigue, espionage, sophisticated weapon technologies that include biotoxins, drug trafficking, money laundering and murder-for-hire has emerged from an isolated desert Indian reservation just north of Mexicali.

While this cabal continues today, its origins were spawned 30 years ago in the shadow of the Cold War. In recent months, however, some of its members have emerged from the trenches like scarecrows to take gratuitous credit for their roles in delaying the release of the hostages in Iran until after the 1980 presidential election, scuttling and resettling the dope and dirty money schemes of the notorious, Australian-based Nugan Hand Bank, assisting Super Gun maker Gerald Bull who was assassinated last spring in Brussels, and for the development and distribution of the Fuel Air Explosive which can pack the power of a nuclear weapon in a shoebox.

I propose a series of articles and a book, a true crime narrative, that unravels this web of thugs and thieves who roam the earth with their weapons and their murders, trading dope and dirty money for the secrets of the temple.

Behold, A Pale Horse will be a haunting odyssey that depicts a manifesto of deceit, decisions of conscience, good and evil, intrigue and betrayal.

John Philip Nichols found his promised land just north of Mexicali on the wild grasses above the Salton Sea.

He was 60 years old then and the Cabazon Indian Reservation on the edge of Sonora was an ideal place for him to nurse his secret self. This is the vast desert emptiness where the yucca reaches nearly 40 feet high, where the Mormons saw it as a symbol pointing to the promised land and they called it the Joshua Tree. But the Joshua Tree is an ugly, asymmetrical lily with burly arms crooked at the elbow and it points everywhere, not unlike John Philip Nichols, as if asking itself, "What shall I do next?"

There is a point on the ridge of the Little San Bernardino mountains known as Salton View where you are more than 5,000 feet above the desert and where, to the north, you can see the great escarpment of Mount San Jacinto and, to the south, the man-made Salton Sea, the orchards of the Coachella Valley and, on a clear day, Mexico.

It is always clear in Indio and with the clarity of the warbler in the cottonwood grove, John Philip Nichols knew that he could bring his box office charity and all his earthly possessions into the reservation of the Cabazon Band of Mission Indians.

With no more than two dozen Indians and nearly 2,000 acres of desert solitaire, cactus and cotton grove, the Cabazon Reservation was a suitable home for gambling, dope, dirty money and gun running and all the fugitive visions that line the edge of oppression.

John Philip Nichols didn't howl under 12 full moons before the gambling was underway and, in the desert night, people flocked from all over to Indio Bingo and the poker casino at the fork of Highway 10 and Highway 86.

Under a major corporation's umbrella subsidiary, later to be named Cabazon Arms, the gun runners and the money traders soon arrived, the weapon makers and the generals from Babylon, Contra resuppliers, cover operatives from both the East and West and, in what one source calls "a marriage of necessity," the dope dealers, the mobsters and the murderers.

Whatever John Philip Nichols saw in the dark cathedral of those desert nights in silence and certainty cracked and became unglued. After a number of still unresolved execution-style murders and a solicitation-for-murder charge for which he was jailed, the dark vision of John Philip Nichols eroded. Although he's been released from a short stint in prison, he's a one-eyed Jack now since only Indio Bingo gambling — managed by his sons, the Las Vegas-managed poker casino, the Indians and the most formidable creatures of the desert remain.

Several of the Cabazon Arms associates during the 1980s are coming out of the shadows to take top billing for the actual participation in the multi-million dollar laundered payment to the Iranians to delay the release of the hostages, in shutting down the dope and dirty money schemes of Nugan Hand and resurfacing its activities, in assisting Gerald Bull in the refinements and distribution of his weapons arsenal including his Super Gun, and in the development of the Fuel Air Explosive technologies — thought to be responsible for the Beirut bomb which killed 241 U.S. servicemen.

While rumors of the hostage release delay circulated for years after the election of Ronald Reagan, it wasn't until 1988 that testimony was offered by two covert operatives in two different courts regarding their knowledge and participation in a hostage-release stall managed by then Reagan campaign chief William Casey. But now, two more covert operatives have emerged from that desert reservation in the journey of this story effort to confirm that previous testimony and provide richer details regarding the laundered payment by the Saudis and other particularities in order to prevent what Casey feared the most, a surprise release of the hostages before the election, almost guaranteeing windfall votes for President Jimmy Carter. The alleged reward to another Reagan insider for that mission to Iran in the summer of 1980 has been almost wholly responsible for the leaks leading to this odyssey. For it was in that reward in the form of a multi-million dollar government contract that technologies were found to have been stolen by the government from another company. In that other company's recovery from bankruptcy, its CEO has been the real life star and gumshoe in this drama that continues to unfold each day.

In 1982, the body of 30-year-old Paul Morasca was found hog-tied and fatally strangled in his condominium on San Francisco's Telegraph Hill. Morasca, who had been working among the Cabazon Arms confidantes, reportedly had the access codes for offshore accounts containing hundreds of millions of dollars in drug money ostensibly for covert operations. Morasca's partner, who is one of the key sources for this story, claims to have scuttled Nugan Hand's operations and assumed control over all the funds. Two years earlier, about 90 miles from Sydney, Frank Nugan's body was found slumped over in his Mercedes sedan. His partner, Michael Hand, has been missing since the investigation widened several months after Nugan's death. Two sources in this story report knowledge of Michael Hand's whereabouts.

The drug trafficking, the contract murders, the spies and the investment frauds revealed in the Nugan Hand inquiries bear sinister, mirror-like qualities to the gang on that isolated desert reservation in Southern California.

A little more than six months ago, on a quiet spring evening in Brussels, a guns-to-Babylon mission splintered into pieces which were later found in the UK's Teesport and in Turkey. Gerald Vincent Bull ambled down the hallway leading to his apartment when an assassin fired two 7.6 millimeter rounds at point blank range into the back of his skull. The shadowy movements of his Super Gun dream took hold and gathered momentum in the Indio desert.

Six years ago on a balmy Sunday morning in Beirut, a Lebanese boy later nicknamed "Smiling Death" raced a Mercedes truck toward a building full of sleeping US soldiers. A few seconds later, 241 Americans and 56 Frenchmen were dead in what the FBI called the largest man-made non-nuclear explosion since World War II. Nicknamed "Smiling Death" because of the chilling expression that the sentry recalled on the suicide driver's face, the bomb and the driver were traced to a Lebanese Shia Muslim extremist group, the Islamic Jihad, and to the most dangerous terrorist at large today, Imad Mugniyah. Mugniyah's followers had used what investigators called a "trademark," using gas to enhance a powerful explosive. Investigators determined that the device was equivalent to nine tons of dynamite, made of sophisticated explosive enhanced by gas, and only the size of an unfolded card table. Its name: The Fuel Air Explosive.

Possession of a secret is no guarantee of its truth, and while these allegations by a handful of people are indeed remarkable, they are also wrought with undocumentable details — at least thus far, and veils of deniability masking the necessary spine for a traditional journalistic effort. It is for this reason that *Behold, A Pale Horse* is subtitled *A True Crime Narrative.*

The first three chapters of the manuscript should be finished within three months of an initial advance and each subsequent chapter will be delivered every month. the completed book should be ready for publication by the summer of 1991.

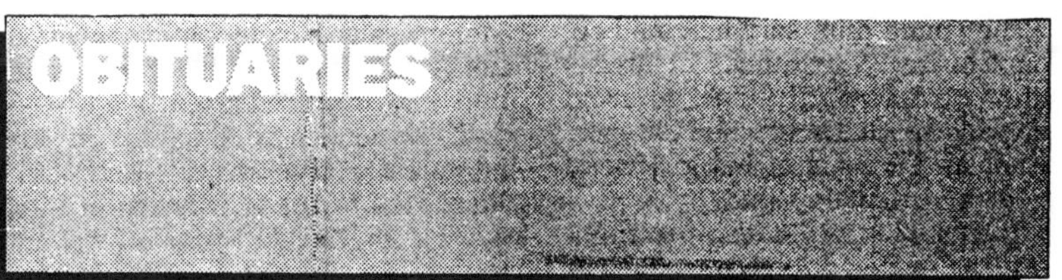

Joseph D. Casolaro, 44, journalist and novelist

Funeral services for Joseph Daniel Casolaro, the Washington-based writer who died in West Virginia while working on an investigative story, will be at 10 a.m. today at St. Ann's Church in Arlington.

Mr. Casolaro, a 44-year-old Fairfax County resident, was investigating the Bank of Credit and Commerce International when he was found with his arms slashed Saturday in a bathtub in a Martinsburg, W.Va., hotel. A police investigation is continuing.

A lifetime resident of Northern Virginia, he was a veteran journalist and author of several published fiction works. His most recent novel, "The Ice King," was published by St. Martin's Press in 1985.

Before his 18-month free-lance investigation of various banking and government scandals that he believed were intertwined, Mr. Casolaro was a writer and editor at Computer Age Publications, a newsletter group based in Springfield. He had worked for other publications covering the criminal justice system and had been a correspondent and columnist for newspapers and magazines based on Capitol Hill.

Mr. Casolaro began his reporting career with Globe Newspapers, a string of weeklies serving Northern Virginia. He attended St. Leo's College and Providence College, and he spent a year in Paris at the Sorbonne.

He is survived by two sons from a previous marriage, Joseph Casolaro III of Leadville, Colo., and Colby Henson of Herndon; his mother, Frances Casolaro of Falls Church; a brother, Dr. M. Anthony Casolaro of Dunn Loring; and two sisters, Mari-Ellen Slakey of McLean and Linda Oels of Toms River, N.J.

The 7 Seals Revealed to David Koresh

Why Waco?

Ken Fawcett

The Branch Davidian conflagration, in which nearly a hundred so-called "cult members" burned to death, seemed to temporarily satisfy the TV audience's post-Gulf War adrenaline fix, and signal an escalation in the New World Order's taste for "shoot now, explain later" mini-wars within domestic borders. If the Bureau of Alcohol, Tobacco and Firearms wanted to arrest David Koresh they had ample opportunity on his frequent trips to downtown Waco prior to the initial siege. As Ken Fawcett's following affidavit confirms, the first assault on the Mount Carmel complex was done for the benefit of news cameras, probably to justify the ATF budget, which expanded ten-fold during the 1980s. Independent reseachers have revealed that two of four ATF officers killed in the initial "surprise raid" were most likely killed by friendly fire and concussion grenades hurled by fellow storm troopers. In addition, Mr. Fawcett claims the official time of the first raid was misstated by two hours to allow the ATF to edit the tapes for official use by the news media. In June, 1993, recordings released by Waco-area 911 lines, amply demonstrate the sect's desire for cease-fire during the initial raid.

The cover-up tones of the Waco conflagration was confirmed by use of FBI subcontractors as so-called "independent arson investigators" and the hiring of Mark Richard as a top advisor to Attorney General Janet Reno. According to Daniel Sheehan of the Christic Institute, "When the investigation of the [Edwin] Wilson affair [selling arms to the Libyans] started to lead into revealing information showing that the criminal activities were being directly authorized by CIA leadership under George Bush, it was Mark Richard who moved in out of the Justice Department to shut down that entire investigation. They allowed Tom Cline and Richard Secord ... to enter a simple plea; [they] ended up paying just a few thousand dollars fine in being released from any further criminal investigation. It's what's known in the business as a 'fix.' That fix was put in by Mark Richard."

Waco also afforded police agencies the opportunity try out sophisticated microwave weaponry (see "Remote Mind Control Technology" by Anna Keeler) and fool around with interesting new psych-war devices including incredibly bright spotlights and incessant ear-splitting recordings of whining, taunting voices, dentist drills, and rabbits being slaughtered, among other aural monstrosities.

The "mild" tear gas that was pumped inside the Branch Davidian compound for eight hours was of the CS variety, a physically disabling poison which is usually mixed with kerosene for transmittal, is highly flammable. CS gas killed many children during the Vietnam War. It has now been confirmed that the Waco Fire Department was deliberately held back from responding to the fire, and, contrary to the federal position, the Texas coroner has maintained that none of the Waco inferno victims had been shot. [Introduction by Adam Parfrey.]

I am the individual who started the communication process to the besieged individuals inside Mt. Carmel [the Branch Davidian complex]. With help from Ron Engleman of radio station KGBS, we employed a method involving the use of a satellite dish on top of the Mt. Carmel Complex. i.e., moving it back and forth to signify an affirmative answer to on-air questions. Integral to the process is my personal satellite downlink equipment (three TURO dishes, 2 C-band, and 1 combination C and Ku band (12.7-12.9 Ghz.) The Ku band system is still somewhat new to the civilian and non-media public and are relatively rare (about 5,000 nationwide.)

I became involved in the situation last Monday after observing numerous contradictions between what was actually occurring on the scene and what was being reported by the off-air media. In addition, beginning Tuesday evening I began monitoring and taping both domestic and foreign correspondent satellite Ku band uplinks or transmissions from the "media checkpoint." On Wednesday, March 3, after already removing the media twice for "safety concerns," the FBI imposed restrictions upon the television media as to the use of more than 200x telephoto lenses on live shots, and upon the use of ambient light sensing "night vision" equipment. Bear in mind this type of ambient light equipment cannot in any way interfere with that being used by ATF or FBI. The restriction was as follows: night vision can only be used by the networks on a one-hour delay and restricted to two hours per night. Foreign correspondents, fearing for the safety of the citizens within the complex, maintained all-night vigils, using night vision as well as 400x lenses. Monitoring these foreign transmissions, I was able to observe and videotape the following atrocities.

On March 2, 1993, at approximately 11 pm, while monitoring live Ku band transmissions from the Waco media set-up, I was surprised to view what was certainly an almost unedited video "refeed" of the assault. Having monitored news feeds in the past I knew from experience that the tape would be run twice. I proceeded to tape the second feed ... this tape has been duplicated and distributed for my protection.

Over the ensuing weeks the tape was studied carefully by myself as well as by several men with military and law enforcement backgrounds. The conclusions reached are as follows:

1. BATF officers, either through mishandling, improper preparation, and/or defective equipment, suffered a minimum of two accidental weapon discharges. The first of which involved the Heckler-Koch MP5 assault rifle, and resulted in the death of Special Agent Stephen Willis and the injuring of another officer, as yet unidentified.

The second discharge occurred on an aluminum ladder, involving a Sig-Sauer P228 semi-automatic handgun, which, according to John C. Killorin, Chief of Public Affairs, ATF, has no safety. The weapon discharged in the holster of Agent Conway C. LeBleu, resulting in a flesh wound to his right leg. Agent LeBleu was able to ascend the ladder but met with death after entering a second-story window.

2. The attack plan failed to take into account the unusual architecture of the compound and thereby subjected officers crossing the roof from South to North to crossfire from agents seen firing from behind vehicles located on the west or front side of the compound.

3. The plan overestimated and/or was misinformed as to the construction of exterior and interior walls. This caused helicopter-based gunfire to pass completely through the building at angles endangering friendly forces on the ground.

4. The plan relied too heavily upon radio communication. When those communications were compromised, there was confusion as to the location of various forces, enemy as well as friendly. This too was a factor in the accidental tossing of a fragmentation device into the second story room, further identified as a 10' x 10' room adjoining David Koresh's living quarters, which led to the death of agents Robert J. Williams, Todd McKeehan and Conway LeBleu.

5. Despite public statements to the contrary, agents are seen firing blindly into walls and windows without properly acquiring a target. This practice is known as "spray and pray" in law enforcement circles, and is unacceptable while executing an arrest warrant on one man, and one man only, where more than 100 innocent women, children and men are residing.

6. If after-the-fact statements by AFT spokespersons are true, and these affiants actually possessed and/or were suspected to possess weapons in the type and amount necessary to warrant the enforcement manpower at hand, then it is clear that management personnel failed miserably in prearranging ambulance and medical services for wounded or traumatized personnel, as evidenced by agents seen and heard well into the firefight telling TV cameramen to "call for an ambulance."

7. ATF spokesmen Dan Conroy, Jack Killorin, Steven Higgins and David Troy have repeatedly stated that the "element of surprise" was paramount to the success of the "mission," yet videotape reveals that two reporters are actually sitting clearly visible in a tree in front of the compound, and channel 10 crews were actually invited to "follow the ATF horse trailers in," per conversation with Mr. Virgil L. Teter, KWTX, Waco.

8. Despite insistence that National Guard helicopters were requisitioned only to search for "hot spots" in the compound, their approach is clearly too low and off to the right and left to provide such a function.

9. Despite public statements that the three helicopters used in the raid sustained fire they are seen being examined in subsequent videotape, and no damage is visible.

10. An unidentified Davidian is seen and heard from a lower story doorway repeatedly calling for "peace" each time he is met with a hail of gunfire.

11. Agents are taped being assisted by Branch Davidians in the stabilization and evacuation of wounded officers; this behavior is inconsistent with persons having murderous intent.

12. The time of the Feb. 28th raid was deliberately misstated by two hours to allow editing of the video news tape before being released to the public.

13. There were no less than three tv station news crews waiting at the gate to follow the BATF into the complex.

14. The press was moved back three times in the first two days of the so-called stand-off to obscure from view federal agents "cleaning up" the bodies of two unarmed Branch Davidians killed by ATF snipers several hours after the "raid" had ended.

15. Even though it's been widely reported that the final conflagration fire scene was too hot for investigators and medical examiners to enter for two days (because of "one million" rounds of "live" ammo) I have videotape footage of FBI agent Bob Ricks, ATF agent Swenson and others walking around in the ashes less than two hours after the fire was brought under control, wearing no protective clothing or eyegear whatsoever.

The Disinformational Plague

"We SHELL not EXXONerate Saddam
Hussein for his actions. We will
Mobilize to meet this threat to our
vital interests in the Persian Gulf
until an AMOCOble solution
is reached."

AN INVITATION TO WAR

Eight days before the invasion of Kuwait by Iraqi troops on August 2, 1990, President Saddam Hussein met with United States Ambassador April Glaspie at his presidential palace. The following transcript of that meeting, is an obvious indication of the duplicitous intentions of the New World Order to stir up a war in which hundreds of thousands were killed.

Ambassador Glaspie: I have direct instructions from President Bush to improve our relations with Iraq. We have considerable sympathy for your quest for higher oil prices, the immediate cause of your confrontation with Kuwait. As you know, I have lived here for years and admire your extraordinary efforts to rebuild your country. We know you need funds. We understand that, and our opinion is that you should have the opportunity to rebuild your country. We can see that you have deployed massive numbers of troops in the south. Normally that would be none of our business, but when this happens in the context of your other threats against Kuwait, then it would be reasonable for us to be concerned. For this reason, I have received an instruction to ask you, in the spirit of friendship — not confrontation — regarding your intentions: Why are your troops massed so very close to Kuwait's borders?

Saddam Hussein: As you know, for years now I have made every effort to reach a settlement on our dispute with Kuwait. There is to be a meeting in two days; I am prepared to give negotiations only this one more brief chance. When we [the Iraqis] meet [with the Kuwaitis] and we see there is hope, then nothing will happen. But if we are unable to find a solution, then it will be natural that Iraq will not accept death.

Ambassador Glaspie: What solutions would be acceptable?

Saddam Hussein: If we could keep the whole of the Shatt al Arab — our strategic goal in our war with Iran — we will make concessions [to the Kuwaitis]. But, if we are forced to choose between keeping half of the Shatt and the whole of Iraq [including Kuwait, in Saddam's view] then we will give up all of the Shatt to defend our claims on Kuwait to keep the whole of Iraq in the shape we wish it to be. [Pause, then Glaspie speaks carefully:]

Ambassador Glaspie: We have no opinion on your Arab-Arab conflicts, such as your dispute with Kuwait. Secretary [of State James] Baker has directed me to emphasize the instruction, first given to Iraq in the 1960s, that the Kuwait issue is not associated with America. [Saddam smiles.]

After obtaining the tape and transcript of the Saddam-Glaspie meeting of July 29, 1990, British journalists confronted Ms. Glaspie while leaving the U.S. Embassy in Baghdad on September 2, 1990:

Journalist 1: Are the transcripts [holding them up] correct, Madame Ambassador? [Glaspie does not respond]

Journalist 2: You knew Saddam was going to invade [Kuwait], but you didn't warn him not to. You didn't tell him America would defend Kuwait. You told him the oppose— that America was not associated with Kuwait.

Journalist 1: You encouraged this aggression — his invasion. What were you thinking?

Ambassador Glaspie: Obviously, I didn't think, and nobody else did, that the Iraqis were going to take ALL of Kuwait.

Journalist 1: You thought he was just going to take SOME of it? But, how could you? Saddam told you that, if negotiations failed, he would give up his Iran [Shatt al Arab waterway] goal for the "whole of Iraq, in the shape we wish it to be." You know that includes Kuwait, which the Iraqis have always viewed as an historic part of their country! [Glaspie says nothing, pushing past the journalists]

Journalist 1: America green-lighted the invasion. At a minimum you admit signaling Saddam that some agression was okay — that the U.S. would not oppose a grab of the al-Rumeilah oil field, the disputed border strip and the Gulf Islands — territories claimed by Iraq?

[Again, Ambassador Glaspie says nothing as the limousine door closes behind her.]

INSIDE THE IRISH REPUBLICAN ARMY

Scott Smith

Journalist Scott Smith spoke with a representative for the Irish Republican Army's governing Army Council, in this first (and last) interview ever granted to an American journalist.

Q: How many members of the IRA are active now? [Estimates range from 250 to 1000.]

A: That is best left unsaid for security reasons but we can state that we have as many as we need and are turning away applicants. About 25% of our volunteers, including support personnel for the Active Service Units, are women. Most members of the Oglaigh na Heireann are from the six occupied counties.

Q: How many IRA have been killed since the beginning of this phase of the struggle in 1969?

A: Somewhat less than 300, about a third of them due to explosions while they were preparing bombs, mostly in the early years.

Q: In The Provisional IRA by Maille and Bishop they say the IRA is guilty of most of the civilian deaths. True?

A: They claim there have been 2,500 civilians killed, when that is the total number of deaths since 1969, which shows you how reliable they are. The IRA explains the reasons for each individual execution. Occasionally there are mistakes but we are very careful to avoid harming innocent people — collaborators, however, are not innocent.

We call off numerous operations when there is any danger to those not targeted — and our Volunteers prefer to operate in daylight to be able to see whether anyone is unintentionally endangered. The percentage of civilians killed by loyalists and Crown forces is much higher and they are intentionally less discriminate as part of their policy of terror to intimidate the nationalist community.

One measure of how accurate Britain's propaganda image of the IRA is can be found in Fr. Raymond Murray's generally accepted statistics about the war: in 18 years less than 150 civilians have been killed in the North by all nationalist bombs, including those of the INLA, officials, etc. Those due to the IRA have been accidents — we do not wish to harm innocent people, which is why we give bomb warnings.

Q: What about infamous bombings like La Mon Hotel, Harrod's Department Store and the Birmingham pubs?

A: First of all, it should be noted that the IRA takes responsibility for all actions of its Volunteers, even when unauthorized and when the publicity is damaging to us, in order to maintain credibility with our people. La Mon was tragic but unintended — the warning was inadequate for the speed with which the flames spread. Harrod's was not approved by command — the IRA was on the way to another target but were forced to abandon the car with the bomb. A 40 minute specific warning was given, and the police chose not to alarm the Christmas shoppers while they tried to find the bomb. Birmingham was the result of delays in delivering the warning due to non-working public phones.

Q: The Birmingham Six appear to be innocent so why not bring forward the guilty to serve in their place?

A: The six are in prison because of British injustice and should be released. If Britain were not in Ireland things like this would never occur. The British are not going to turn over their terrorists to us and we discipline our own soldiers.

Q: What about compensating the families of those killed and injured?

A: We wish we could but we do not have the funds. Help would likely be rejected anyway. Again, Britain ultimately bears responsibility: as long as it occupies our country there will be war and casualties.

Q: James Adams' The Financing of Terror claims the IRA takes in $7 million a year, mostly from protection rackets, extortion of contractors, band and post office robberies, the Belfast black taxis, drinking clubs, the former co-op, etc. He says the real beneficiaries are the "rich godfathers."

A: Anyone familiar with British black propaganda and knowledgeable about the situation here knows this is utter fabrication. We have challenged those making such assertions to provide any evidence — most recently a British TV program investigated and found nothing to corroborate these fantasies. Even our Volunteers are unpaid at the moment. The irony is that our critics are the ones who are well-off.

The co-op was run by former prisoners, as are the taxis and clubs; the IRA is not involved. There are no protection rackets run by us — any member caught trying to exploit people for personal gain is subject to very severe discipline. There have been no postal robberies in four years or banks in six. Most of our funding comes from individual donations from outside Ireland— and we do not accept donations with any strings attached.

Q: What about Adams' claim that you work territorial deals with the Ulster Defense Association so that you don't get accused of exploiting your own people?

A: Utter rubbish. We have no arrangements of any kind with loyalist paramilitaries.

Q. What about charges that since the hunger strikes a criminal element has entered the IRA?

A: In any organization, especially an underground one, you get some people who do not live up to its ideals. We want to be informed of anyone not conforming to Army discipline. Today, however, we are more selective than ever, so problems are minor.

Q: One Irish American newspaper carried a column about the people of Rostrevor, Co. Down being turned against the IRA by the execution of a local boy it claimed was an informer, an assertion the community rejects. How careful is the IRA in passing sentences?

A: Very careful, despite the conditions we have to operate in. We require documentation or admission and our intelligence is very good. Executions take place only when we are certain. In the Rostrevor case he was, in fact, an informer and therefore endangering the lives of our Volunteers. Communities and families are naturally shocked by the facts and find them hard to accept. Informers know the risk they take for personal gain. We have also offered amnesty to those pressured by the Royal Ulster Constabulary into doing informing and dozens of people have come forward. We can arrange relocation and protection if needed.

Q: The accusation was made that Special Air Services Captain Nairac was tortured for information. Has the IRA ever used torture?

A: Never. Aside from ethical reasons we know from Britain's use on us how unreliable information gained this way is. In the Nairac case the torture charge was based on blood found in the car in which he was taken, but this was due to resistance.

Q: The British say that abuse of prisoners is no longer employed and that cameras installed in interrogation rooms prevent this.

A: They have always denied the use of torture and beatings. Now, cameras are just turned off and beatings take place on the way to interrogation. Medical testimony confirms this continues. Many of those abused have no connection to the IRA, of course, and would have no reason to lie. The British judges simply dismiss evidence of torture.

Q: How many "prisoners of war" are there?

A: There are around 650 in prison for "scheduled offenses" meaning charges connected with the political situation here. The British incredibly pretend there is no war, only a massive outbreak of crime, so they do not recognize these formally as political prisoners or prisoners of war, though they receive special treatment separate from those they regard as ordinary criminals.

It is worth mentioning that only the Republican Movement provides aid to prisoners' dependents, regardless of whether the prisoner had any connection with the IRA.

Many of the prisoners and certainly their families are innocent, railroaded by the non-jury, Diplock court system which requires no evidence to convict. The Social Democratic and Labour Party does nothing to alleviate the suffering of these families.

Q: The SDLP claims IRA supporters have attacked its meetings and election workers.

A: Individuals have spontaneously reacted to SDLP hypocrisy and lies but we don't approve such harassment and say so. The SDLP has never protested British or Irish government harassment and repression of Sinn Fein. During recent elections they have been quite willing to try to benefit from such repression.

Q: While in Belfast I read a story about the former quartermaster for Belfast, one of the local IRA's top ten people, having been an informer, responsible for six deaths and 20 arrests, now spirited into hiding by the RUC. The article said this was the highest the RUC had ever been able to place an informer.

A: The individual in question was low-ranking and did little damage. The story was a British intelligence plant to try to stir suspicions among our Volunteers about each other.

Q: What about Loughgall and the apparent use of an informer which led to the ambush killing of eight IRA earlier this year?

A: Crown forces routinely stake out barracks they think might be vulnerable or likely to be attacked based on patterns. It was bound to result in a "success" eventually. So few people knew of the plans for Loughgall that we are satisfied there was no informer. It would have been too risky for an informer to give out such information knowing only a handful knew of this.

Q: On my arrival in Belfast the news was ablaze with claims that the IRA's latest victim, Nathaniel Cush, had already resigned from the Ulster Defence Regiment and was working for the post office. Allegedly the bomb which killed him narrowly missed harming a woman with a baby.

A: We used a remote control detonator so there was never any danger to any civilians. We have warned those who resign from Crown forces to notify the Republican Movement for their own safety but our information was that he was still a member and the fact he was given a full dress military funeral supports this. Cush, incidentally, was a former member of the infamous Parachute Regiment.

Q: Another recent incident involved the driver of a school bus who was shot in the leg and the papers claimed this endangered the children.

A: The bus was halted when this incident took place.

Q: There was a lot of negative reaction to the IRA's 1986 announcement that it would regard as legitimate targets civilians doing work for the British Army.

A: Without such support the Crown forces could not remain in Ireland easily and this strategy of warning those profiteering from the British presence was used during the War of Independence in the 1920s.

We were very specific about the kinds of people who are guilty — those programming computers for British intelligence for example, not some secretary for a contractor building barracks for the British Army. To those who say helping the Crown is an ethical way to make a living we would ask if they would have supported building ovens for the Nazis. Let contractors build the housing the people need.

Q: One priest asked why you don't give part of your earnings toward job creation.

A: We do not have the money to spare. The best way to create jobs would be for Britain to leave so the healing process for the economy can begin, bringing an end to employment discrimination, allowing business and tourism to flourish, with interim help of international aid for the rebuilding process.

Q: The same individual asked why the IRA took 300 jobs out to West Beast by killing the manager of an audio manufacturer in 1976.

A. That was part of an effort to cause disinvestment that is no longer pursued. We continue some commercial bombings when the businesses serve Crown forces and outside the poverty-stricken areas where there are no jobs anyway, where we intend to disrupt Britain's effort to pretend everything is normalizing.

Q: Another controversial assassination was of Leslie Jarvis, claimed to be a civilian at Magilligan Prison.

A: He was a full time part of the administration and knew the risk in being part of the British system of oppression. We have not targeted part-time workers.

Q: English director Nicholas Meyer claims he was threatened by the IRA while filming "Johnny Loves Suzy," based on the anti-IRA novel Fields of Blood in Belfast.

A: Totally untrue. If he was threatened, it was not by us. We would know.

Q: The assassination of Lord Mountbatten caused a greater negative public reaction than any other single IRA killing. Was he really a proper target?

A: As a former leader of the British military and cousin to the Queen who lived on land confiscated from the Irish people, he was a symbol of the ruling class which supports the occupation of our country. His execution was a warning that if they insist on keeping troops here they will never be safe.

Q: Letter bombs were recently sent to current and former government officials in England. Aren't they likely to harm civilians?

A: Those who associate with the ruling class know there is risk but the innocent have rarely been harmed. We have to use what weapons we can, and these have been effective. If Britain fears them it should get out. Government officials who retire, incidentally, often remain senior advisors and are not necessarily off the target list.

Q: Isn't killing RUC and UDR members perceived as sectarian, alienating loyalists even further?

A: If we had wanted to attack Protestants per se the civilian casualties would have been much higher. "Ulsterization" was Britain's effort to push the local people to the front line and make the public in Britain less aware of casualties across the sea.

We have to take our targets as they present themselves and the brutality of the RUC and UDR is well known. It is the loyalists who have killed Catholics at random by the hundreds. We do not consider religion, only whether someone is a collaborator.

Loyalists began this conflict without IRA provocation and they intensified their sectarian killings when the IRA was observing truces. If we stopped the war of national liberation tomorrow they would not be any less anti-Irish or anti-Catholic.

The argument that our freedom struggle is "counter-productive" is heard from the same elements who opposed the 1916 Rising and the IRA in the 1920s — the media, some clergy and so-called constitutional nationalists who give mere lip service to reunification. Their position ignores the history of British colonialism and reforms have come about as a result of the armed struggle to try to appease nationalists.

Q: There have been well-publicized arms seizures over the years. Is the IRA experiencing supply problems?

A: We are getting what we need and our technology and techniques are more sophisticated than ever.

Q: The news often reports the inability of the IRA to effectively use the RPG rocket grenade. Why does it fail?

A: This was due to assembly problems and mislabeling of live and practice ammunition. The RPG has a tendency to deflect, which could endanger civilians. We have designed our own launcher which is more effective and safer.

Q: Are there ties between the IRA and groups like the PLO, Red Army Faction, etc.?

A: There are none and the James Adams book you cited points this out. The right wing tried to link us to what it fantasized was an "international terrorism network." The once secret British military Glover Report acknowledged that we are independent.

We do, however, support the rights of the Palestinians, Basques, and others. To put things in perspective, the PLO has killed about 300 Israeli civilians since 1969 while the Israeli Army killed 10,000 to 20,000 civilians during its invasion of Lebanon alone. Colonel Khaddafy of Libya is alleged to be responsible for 50 assassinations over the years. We accept no responsibility for what others have done. It should be noted that the British are the ones who armed and trained Khaddafy.

Q: But hasn't the IRA accepted donations from him?

A: We have no links with organizations and none with any country or government. We never answer specific questions as to sources of funding. Why should we help the British and bother those sources? We take money wherever we can get it without strings attached.

Q: The British and Irish governments have claimed that the IRA wants to establish a "Marxist dictatorship."

A: They know perfectly well this is false and use this as propaganda to alienate supporters. First of all, the IRA allows a diversity of political opinion. There are a few Marxists but the tendency for those leaning that way is to join the Irish National Liberation Army or other doctrinaire Marxist groups.

The "democratic socialism" espoused by Sinn Fein has been constantly redefined over the years and is adapted to the situation in Ireland where we feel tremendous poverty requires some nationalization and cooperation. Anyone labeling this Marxism is either uninformed or trying to manipulate public opinion.

In any event, we do not have the power to impose our view and have repeatedly stated our support for the right of the Irish people as a whole to decide what political system they want. We can only educate on the issues and the British and Irish governments fear that and resort to censorship. The British have repeatedly rejected the will of the Irish people expressed at the ballot box.

Q: The Sinn Fein decision to end the policy of abstention and to take seats to which elected at the Dail caused a split in the Republican Movement. Those who left Sinn Fein said it was a sell-out that would result in a running down of the war.

A: This is nonsense. The IRA supported that decision when we held the first General Army convention since 1969 a few weeks prior to the Sinn Fein Ard Fheis. Incidentally, the media report that we used the cover of an Irish language conference in Meath in August was completely wrong — which shows how good our security is.

Representatives from all ASUs and command structures attended and recognized that the Republican Movement was being isolated by Dublin and must adapt to survive. We must be involved with the people and relevant to their daily lives, avoiding the elitism advocated by our critics, who are oblivious to political reality.

Abstentionism failed and while our analysis of the 26 county Free State remains unchanged the vast majority of its residents consider the institutions of the state legitimate and theirs — with that support they will not disappear.

Those who walked away from the Movement walked away from the armed struggle and they have spent most of their energy denigrating their former comrades rather than fighting Britain. The struggle has intensified and we have lost more Volunteers this year than anytime since 1976. Loughgall was the single largest loss since the 1920s.

Our loyal supporters in the U.S. are the real Republicans and do not place political conditions on those doing the fighting. They know that we will never drive the British out of Ireland from an armchair and if we remain aloof from the people.

Q: At the Army convention a new Council was elected. How many does it consist of?

A: Seven, each with specific tasks — the Chief of Staff carries out our policies, another is in charge of intelligence, another procurement, I speak for the Council, and so forth.

Q: The constitutional nationalists say reunification can only be achieved peacefully.

A: This is at best wishful thinking and often merely an exploitation of the understandable war-weariness of our people, for political gain. We cannot wait for some miraculous change of heart by loyalists a century from now. Anyone who thinks there will be peace in Ireland while British soldiers remain does not know the history of Irish Republicanism. Britain invented the loyalist veto and can repeal it in the interests of everyone. Loyalists need to be pushed into the 20th century and only when Britain withdraws will they be forced to accept their Irishness and the vision of the Protestant founder of Republicanism, Theobald Wolfe Tone, the only way to peace, prosperity, justice and freedom.

Recipes For Nonsurvival
The Anarchist Cookbook

Esperanze Godot

The Anarchist Cookbook by William Powell has been called "a manual of terror" by Max Geltman, writing in the *National Review* (July 22, 1971). I find this phrase aptly descriptive, but not in the same sense that Mr. Geltman would have us believe.

This "cookbook" consists of three basic parts: an introduction by Professor Bergman entitled "Anarchism Today"; and two much longer sections by William Powell on drug and explosive manufacturing.

If ever there were an example of Orwellian doublespeak, this is it! "Anarchism Today" is basically an interpretation of the philosophic roots of anarchism, awkwardly coupled with sketchy references to current events. Almost all of the intellectuals discussed are from the nineteenth century; and there is virtually no mention of writings from 1930 to present. This may be expected from someone who appears to have briefly studied the topic while at college during the 1920s, and thereafter relied only on superficial newspaper accounts. Bergman should have been aware of Albert Jay Nock for example, and anarchists today are certainly aware of Murray Rothbard, Karl Hess, etc.

Bergman considers Nihilism to be a form of Anarchism, and Anarchism a form of radical revolutionism. He interprets Marxism in an anarchistic light, and correctly suggests that Communist governments today are feudal/reactionary. However, his emphasis on the Marxist element in anarchist intellectual tradition is clearly one-sided. A more thorough and fair analysis can be found in *Native American Anarchism* (1932) by Eunice Minette Schuster.

Bergman's emphasis on the Nihilistic and destructive aspects of Anarchism I find disturbing. This emphasis seems to arrive from the axiom that the State is all, so to oppose the State is to oppose everything. Anarchists do not have to propose a concrete alternative because that would be authoritarian.

The rest of this book consists mainly of drug and explosive recipes relayed to us by William Powell. His motivation for doing so is supposedly to allow the "silent majority" access to information which he claims only the radical groups now possess. The idea of a "silent majority" comes from classical Greek literature and in that context referred to the dead who are the real majority. If you follow the steps outlined in these recipes, you may soon join them! *The Library Journal* (March 15, 1971) puts it this way:

"Much of it is so sketchy as to be harmless, but there are a number of booby traps still for the nitwit who wishes to try them. There are drug making recipes... that may make one very ill... There are also a number of stunts which could backfire on the idiot who tries them."

Let's get down to specifics:

Ed Rosenthal told me that he had spent a lot of time trying to track down rumors of pot growing in New York sewers. Well, I just may have stumbled on the origin of the "New York White" rumors. Despite what Powell may think, plants are not as adaptable as alligators and need light to grow. Another choice quote: "...strangely enough, insects ignore marijuana and do no harm." Strange indeed.

The DEA has a Precursor Control Program watch list. This means that if you buy large quantities of the common precursors to illegal chemicals, the Federal government may take an interest in your activities. Several of the chemicals on this list are used in Mr. Powell's LSD recipe, such as Acetonitrile, Trifluoroacetic Anhydride, Dimethylformamide, and Diethylamine. Benzene is also on the list, and may also arouse the interest of the EPA because it is known cancer causing agent.

Much the same can be said of many of his other recipes, and in some cases the precursors are as hard to get as the final product. For instance, his recipe for DMT starts out with indole, which is quite hard to get. Much better methods using L. Tryptophane (available in health food stores) are covered in *Synthesis* (1973 — present).

Powell suggests ground-up nutmeg for a psychedelic experience. Nutmeg has a poor dose/toxicity ration! However, the oil extract of nutmeg, containing myristicin, can be used in the synthesis of MMDA — a better and mellower high than MDA. See *Journal of Psychedelic Drugs* (Vol. 8 #4, Oct.-Dec. 1976).

On page 58 of Powell's cookbook, Nalline is described as "...a freak — a drug someone forgot to make illegal." Perhaps they forgot because Nalorphine is a powerful narcotic antagonist, which tends to produce violent convulsive reactions in morphine addicts. (See the *Merck Index).*

For more information on drugs see "The Clandestine Drug Laboratory Situation in the U.S.", *Journal of Forensic Sciences (*Jan. 1983 pp.18-31). This article, obligingly written by the DEA chief, reports that none of the 17 labs busted the previous year were successful in producing what was intended to be produced. The busted chemists were relying on recipes from popular "underground" drug manufacturing books. It was noted that such books contain errors which prevent the manufacture of the desired chemicals, while at the same time drawing the attention of government authorities because of the precursors recommended.

Let's now examine his recommendations for manufacturing explosives:

His methods for producing Mercury Fulminate is incomplete and dangerous. Between steps 2 and 3, the solution should be cooled. Do not breathe the fumes. See *A Dictionary of Applied Chemistry* by Sir Edward Thorpe.

Powell's recipe entitled "How to Make TNT" is also quite dangerous and incomplete. In step 1, mixing sulfuric acid and nitric acid will likely result in fulmination and red toxic fumes. Also the crude method he describes does not cover the removal of the Ortho Dinitro groups. If this were not done, the TNT would be extremely unstable. However, they can be removed with great ease by heating the crude material with aqueous sodium sulfite. See "Chemistry of Explosives" by George Wright, University of Toronto, in *Organic Chemistry* (p. 974).

The description of Picric acid does not sufficiently emphasize its unstable nature. For example, storing it in a cracked glass container may cause it to explode. See Thorpe's. However, on page 120 he describes two relatively safer and easily obtainable chemicals (Potassium bichromate and potassium permanganate) as very sensitive, unstable, and too hazardous to work with.

He does have a couple of pages on general safety precautions, but the language suggests that they have been lifted from a military manual. Also, he uses the German spelling for some chemicals. If you attempt to order chemicals from an American company using German spelling, your order would likely be looked at with suspicion.

The Anarchist Cookbook was originally published in 1971; the review by the *Library Journal,* which exposed these dangerous errors, came shortly thereafter. I wonder why it has gone through 28 printings without these errors being corrected. My theory is that Mr. Powell is not an anarchist, but in reality is spreading disinformation to potential enemies of the government. At the time of original publication, Mr. Powell was an unknown 21 year old college freshman. Where did he get access to this "information"? He says, from radical friends on both left and right.

The Minuteman Manual is listed in the bibliography. The original Minutemen were colonial American revolutionaries. In the 60's the radical right-wing sect called the Minutemen have since been disbanded by the FBI. It is not likely that the 1960's Minutemen would have handed out their manual to a long haired 21 year old college freshman. Also, the Minutemen are opposed to the United Nations, and Powell's father was a powerful bureaucrat in the UN propaganda ministry (see *Newsweek,* April 12, 1971). Things are getting curiouser and curiouser!

This same William Powell has also written a book entitled *Saudi Arabia and its Royal Family* (1982). It consists of interviews with members of the Saudi Royal family and other observations gathered while teaching at the University of Riyadh, Saudi Arabia. It does not seem likely that the Saudi Royal family would give such generous treatment to a real anarchist. Reading the Saudi book, I came across some interesting quotes (p. 17):

"Were something or someone to cut the flow of oil from the Arabian Gulf, the result would be truly apocalyptic for the United States, Western Europe, Japan, and much of the developing world. ... In a worst-case scenario, all gasoline available would go to essential services such as the military, the police and fire departments, and the transport of foodstuffs. Most nonessential businesses and industries would close. Unemployment would skyrocket.

"All major cities would, in all probability, have to be placed under martial law. Curfews would be enforced at gunpoint. ... Inflation would metamorphose... into a lethal epidemic. We would enter a wheelbarrow economy like that of Germany prior to Hitler's rise to power..."

I could go on, but I think you get the idea. While his pessimistic analysis does not take full account of the market's ability to conserve and switch to alternate fuels, I think a more important point is that Powell seems to believe that government is as essential as the transportation of foodstuffs, and that it can help solve the fuel crisis through the draconian methods he describes. If governments were to run out of gas tomorrow, anarchists would be dancing in celebration. (Mr. Powell's talk of martial law is not fantasy. Executive Order #11490, signed by Richard Nixon in October 1969, allows the president to assume dictatorial powers after declaring a "national emergency".)

It just doesn't add up, unless an alternative theory is developed to explain these anomalies. My attempts to get the other side of the story from the publisher were met with a stone wall of silence. My suggestion is that much of Powell's disinformation and influence may have come from the Trilateral Commission and/or the CIA. A U.S. Air Force combat controllers group studying guerrilla warfare has arrived at a similar conclusion. This theory would seem to dovetail with the *National Review* article which presented *The Anarchist Cookbook* at face value and even included a patronizing reference to "the boys at Harvard". It is well known that William F. Buckley, the *National Review* editor, is a Yale graduate and once served the CIA in Mexico. (E. Howard Hunt, of Watergate fame, was CIA paymaster in Mexico City at the same time Buckley served).

I would like to quote Mr. Powell from the April 12, 1971 issue of *Newsweek:* “My book places power in the hands of the individual, where it belongs. The right calls it communist, the leftists call it profiteering, the liberals call it Neo-Nazi.”

And this reviewer calls it bullshit!

Hand of Glory—Invisibility

The Elite Controllers

Silent Weapons for Quiet Wars

This article, edited for length, seems to be "reverse disinformation" aimed at educating the public about what the author supposes the plans of the controlling elite to be. In this it shares its broad intent with other possible hoax documents such as The Protocols of the Elders of Zion and The Wicca Papers, although going about its revelations in a highly original manner. It claims to be a handbook of strategy circulated among the secret technicians of "social automation." Ostensibly dated May, 1979, it was supposedly discovered in an IBM copier at a surplus sale. Regardless of its origins the document is insightful, perhaps providing a real breakthrough in the understanding of elitist human control.

This publication marks the 25th anniversary of the Third World War, called the "Quiet War," being conducted using subjective biological warfare, fought with "silent weapons." This book contains an introductory description of this war, its strategies, and its weaponry. It is patently impossible to discuss social engineering or the automation of a society, i.e., the engineering of social automation systems (silent weapons) on a national or a worldwide scale without implying extensive objectives of social control and destruction of human life, i.e. slavery and genocide. This manual is in itself an analog declaration of intent. Such a writing must be secured from public scrutiny. Otherwise, it might be recognized as a technically formal declaration of domestic war. Furthermore, whenever any person or group of persons in a position of great power and without full knowledge and consent of the public, uses such knowledge and methodology for economic conquest — it must be understood that a state of domestic warfare exists between said person or group of persons and the public.

The solution of today's problems requires an approach which is ruthlessly candid, with no agonizing over religious, moral or cultural values. You have qualified for this project because of your ability to look at human society with cold objectivity, and yet analyze and discuss your observations and conclusions with others of similar intellectual capacity without a loss of discretion or humility. Such virtues are exercised in your own best interest. Do not deviate from them.

Historical Introduction

Silent weapon technology has evolved from Operations Research (O.R.), a strategic and tactical methodology developed under the military management (Eisenhower) in England during World War II. The original purpose of Operations Research was to study the strategic and tactical problems of air and land defense with the objective of effective use of limited military resources against foreign enemies (i.e., logistics). It was soon recognized by those in positions of power that the same methods might be useful for totally controlling a society. But better tools were necessary. Social engineering (the analysis and automation of a society) requires the correlation of great amounts of constantly changing economic information (data), so a high-speed computerized data-processing system was necessary which could race ahead of the society and predict when society would arrive for capitulation. Relay computers were too slow, but the electronic computer, invented in 1946 by J. Presper Eckert and John W. Mauchly, filled the bill.

The next breakthrough was the development of the simplex method of linear programming in 1947 by the mathematician George B. Dantzig. Then in 1948, the transistor, invented by J. Bardeen, W.H. Brattain, and W. Shockley, promised great expansion of the computer field by reducing space and power requirements. With these three inventions under their direction, those in positions of power strongly suspected that it was possible for them to control the whole world with the push of a button. Immediately, the Rockefeller Foundation got in on the ground floor by making a four-year grant to Harvard College, funding the Harvard Economic Research Project for the study of the structure of the American economy. One year later, in 1949, the United States Air Force joined in. In 1952 the original grant period terminated, and a high-level meeting of the elite was held to determine the next phase of social operations research. The Harvard project had been very fruitful, as is borne out by the publication of some of its results in 1953 suggesting the feasibility of economic (social) engineering. (*Studies in the Structure of the American Economy* — copyright 1953 by Wassily Leontief, International Sciences Press Inc., White Plains, New York.)

Engineered in the last half of the decade of the 1940s, the new Quiet War machine stood, so to speak, in sparkling gold-plated hardware on the showroom floor by 1954. With the creation of the maser in 1954, the promise of unlocking unlimited sources of fusion atomic energy from the heavy hydrogen in sea water and the consequent availability of unlimited social power was a possibility only decades away. The combination was irresistible. The Quiet War was quietly declared by the international elite at a meeting held in 1954. Although the silent weapons system was nearly exposed 13 years later, the evolution of the new weapon-system has never suffered any major setbacks. This volume marks the 25th anniversary of the beginning of the Quiet War. Already this domestic war has had many victories on many fronts throughout the world.

In 1954 it was well recognized by those in positions of authority that it was only a matter of time, only a few decades, before the general public would be able to grasp and upset the cradle of power, for the very elements of the new silent-weapon technology were as accessible for a public utopia as they were for providing a private utopia. The issue of primary concern, that of dominance, revolved around the subject of the energy sciences.

Energy

Energy is recognized as the key to all activity on earth. Natural science is the study of the sources and control of natural energy, and social science, theoretically expressed as economics, is the study of the sources and control of social energy. Both are bookkeeping systems. Mathematics is the primary energy science. And the bookkeeper can be king if the public can be kept ignorant of the methodology of the bookkeeping. All science is merely a means to an end. The means is knowledge. The end is control. Beyond this remains only one issue: Who will be the beneficiary?

In 1954 this was the issue of primary concern. Although the so-called "moral issues" were raised, in view of the law of natural selection it was agreed that a nation or world of people who will not use their intelligence are no better than animals who do not have intelligence. Consequently, in the interest of future world order, peace, and tranquility, it was decided to privately wage a quiet war against the American public with an ultimate objective of permanently shifting the natural and social energy (wealth) of the undisciplined and irresponsible many into the hands of the self-disciplined, responsible, and worthy few. In order to implement this objective, it was necessary to create, secure, and apply new weapons which, as it turned out, were a class of weapons so subtle and sophisticated in their principle of operation and public appearance as to earn for themselves the name "silent weapons." In conclusion, the objective of economic research, as conducted by the magnates of capital (banking) and the industries of commodities (goods) and services, is the establishment of an economy which is totally predictable and manipulatable.

In order to achieve a totally predictable economy, the low-class elements of society must be brought under total control, i.e. must be housebroken, trained, and assigned a yoke and long-term social duties from a very early age, before they have the opportunity to question the propriety of the matter. In order to achieve such conformity, the lower-class family unit must be disintegrated by a process of increasing preoccupation of the parents and the establishment of government-operated day-care centers for the occupationally orphaned children. The quality of education given to the lower class must be of the poorest sort, so that the moat of ignorance isolating the inferior class from the superior class is and remains incomprehensible to the inferior class. With such an initial handicap, even bright lower class individuals have little if any hope of extricating themselves from their assigned lot in life. This form of slavery is essential to maintaining some measure of social order, peace, and tranquility for the ruling upper class.

Descriptive Introduction of the Silent Weapon

Everything that is expected from an ordinary weapon is expected from a silent weapon by its creators, but only in its own manner of junctioning. It shoots situations, instead of bullets; propelled by data processing instead of a chemical reaction (explosion); originating from bits of data, instead of grains of gunpowder; from a computer, instead of a gun; operated by a computer programmer, instead of a marksman; under the orders of a banking magnate, instead of a military general. It makes no obvious explosive noises, causes no obvious physical or mental injuries, and does not obviously interfere with anyone's daily social life. Yet it makes an unmistakable "noise," causes unmistakable physical and mental damage, and unmistakably interferes with daily social life, i.e., unmistakable to a trained observer, one who knows what to look for.

The public cannot comprehend this weapon, and therefore cannot believe that they are being attacked and subdued by a weapon. The public might instinctively feel that something is wrong, but because of the technical nature of the silent weapon, they cannot express their feeling in a rational way, or handle the problem with intelligence. Therefore, they do not know how to cry for help, and do not know how to associate with others to defend themselves against it. When a silent weapon is applied gradually, the public adjusts/adapts to its presence and learns to tolerate its encroachment on their lives until the pressure (psychological via economic) becomes too great and they crack up. Therefore, the silent weapon is a type of biological warfare. It attacks the vitality, options, and mobility of the individuals of a society by knowing, understanding, manipulating, and attacking their sources of natural and social energy, and their physical, mental, and emotional strengths and weaknesses.

Theoretical Introduction

"Give me control over a nation's currency, and I care not who makes its laws." — Mayer Amschel Rothschild (1743-1812). Today's silent weapons technology is an outgrowth of a simple idea discovered, succinctly expressed, and effectively applied by the quoted Mr. Mayer Amschel Rothschild. Mr. Rothschild discovered the missing passive component of economic theory known as economic inductance. He, of course, did not think of his discovery in these 20th-century terms, and, to be sure, mathematical analysis had to wait for the Second Industrial Revolution, the rise of the theory of mechanics and electronics, and finally, the invention of the electronic computer before it could be effectively applied in the control of the world economy.

What Mr. Rothschild had discovered was the basic principle of power, influence, and control over people as applied to economics. That principle is "when you assume the appearance of power, people soon give it to you." Mr. Rothschild had discovered that currency or deposit loan accounts had the required appearance of power that could be used to induce people (inductance, with people corresponding to a magnetic field) into surrendering their real wealth in exchange for a promise of greater wealth (instead of real compensation). They would put up real collateral in exchange for a loan of promissory notes. Mr. Rothschild found that he could issue more notes than he had backing for, so long as he had someone's stock of gold as a persuader to show his customers. Mr. Rothschild loaned his promissory notes to individuals and to governments. These would create overconfidence. Then he would make money scarce, tighten control of the system, and collect the collateral through the obligation of the contracts. The cycle was then repeated. These pressures could be used to ignite a war. Then he would control the availability of currency to determine who would win the war. That government which agreed to give him control of its economic system got his support. Collection of debts was guaranteed by economic aid to the enemy of the debtor. The profit derived from this economic methodology made Mr. Rothschild all the more able to extend his wealth. He found that the public greed would allow currency to be printed by government order beyond the limits (inflation) of backing in precious metal or the production of goods and services (gross national product, GNP).

Apparent Capital as Paper Inductor

In this structure, credit, presented as a pure element called "currency," has the appearance of capital, but is, in fact, negative capital. Hence, it has the appearance of service, but is, in fact, indebtedness or debt. It is therefore an economic inductance instead of an economic capacitance, and if balanced in no other way, will be balanced by the negation of population (war, genocide). The total goods and services represent real capital called the gross national product, and currency may be printed up to this level and still represent economic capacitance; but currency printed beyond this level is subtractive, represents the introduction of economic inductance, and constitutes notes of indebtedness.

War is therefore the balancing of the system by killing the true creditors (the public, which we have taught to exchange true value for inflated currency) and falling back on whatever is left of the resources of nature and regeneration of those resources. Mr. Rothschild had discovered that currency gave him the power to rearrange the economic structure to his own advantage, to shift economic inductance to those economic positions which would encourage the greatest economic instability and oscillation. The final key to economic control had to wait until there was sufficient data and high-speed computing equipment to keep close watch on the economic oscillations created by price shocking and excess paper energy credits — paper inductance/inflation.

The Economic Model

The Harvard Economic Research Project (1948-) was an extension of World War II Operations Research. Its purpose was to discover the science of controlling an economy; at first the American economy, and then the world economy. It was felt that with sufficient mathematical foundation and data, it would be nearly as easy to predict and control the trend of an economy as to predict and control the trajectory of a projectile. Such has proven to be the case. Moreover, the economy has been transformed into a guided missile on target. The immediate aim of the Harvard project was to discover the economic structure, what forces change that structure, how the behavior of the structure can be predicted, and how it can be manipulated. What was needed was a well-organized knowledge of the mathematical structures and interrelationships of investment, production, distribution, and consumption.

To make a short story of it all, it was discovered that an economy obeyed the same laws as electricity and that all of the mathematical theory and practical and computer know-how developed for the electronic field could be directly applied in the study of economics. This discovery was not openly declared, and its more subtle implications were and are kept a closely guarded secret, for example that in an economic model, human life is measured in dollars, and that the electric spark generated when opening a switch connected to an active inductor is mathematically analogous to the initiation of a war.

The greatest hurdle which theoretical economists faced was the accurate description of the household as an industry. This is a challenge because consumer purchases are a matter of choice which in turn is influenced by income, price, and other economic factors. This hurdle was cleared in an indirect and statistically approximate way by an application of shock testing to determine the current characteristics, called current technical coefficients, of a household industry. Finally, because problems in theoretical economics can be translated very easily into problems in theoretical electronics, and the solution translated back again, it follows that only a book of language translation and concept definition needed to be written for economics. The remainder could be gotten from standard works on mathematics and electronics. This makes the publication of books on advanced economics unnecessary, and greatly simplifies project security.

Time Flow Relationship and Self-Destructive Oscillations

An ideal industry may be symbolized electronically in various ways. The simplest way is to represent a demand by a voltage and a supply by a current. When this is done, the relationship between the two becomes what is called an admittance, which can result from three economic factors: (1) hindsight flow, (2) present flow, and (3) foresight flow.

Foresight flow is the result of that property of living entities to cause energy (food) to be stored for a period of low energy (e.g., a winter season). It consists of demands made upon an economic system for that period of low energy (winter season). In a production industry it takes several forms, one of which is known as production stock or inventory. In electronic symbology this specific industry demand (a pure capital industry) is represented by capacitance and the stock or resource is represented by capacitance and the stock or resource is represented by a stored charge. Satisfaction of an industry demand suffers a lag because of the loading effect of inventory priorities. Present flow ideally involves no delays. It is, so to speak, input today for output today, a "hand to mouth" flow. In electronic symbology, this specific industry demand (a pure use industry) is represented by a conductance which is then a simple economic valve (a dissipative element).

Hindsight flow is known as habit or inertia. In electronics this phenomenon is the characteristic of an inductor (economic analog = a pure service industry) in which a current flow (economic analog = flow of money) creates a magnetic field (economic analog = active human population) which, if the current (money flow) begins to diminish, collapse (war) to maintain the current (flow of money — energy). Other alternatives to war as economic inductors or economic flywheels are an open-ended social welfare program, or an enormous (but fruitful) open-ended space program.

The problem with stabilizing the economic system is that there is too much demand on account of (1) too much greed and (2) too much population. This creates excessive economic inductance which can only be balanced with economic capacitance (true resources or value — e.g., in goods or services). The social welfare program is nothing more than an open-ended credit balance system which creates a false capital industry to give nonproductive people a roof over their heads and food in their stomachs. This can be useful, however, because the recipients become state property in return for the "gift," a standing army for the elite. For he who pays the piper picks the tune. Those who get hooked on the economic drug, must go to the elite for a fix. In this, the method of introducing large amounts of stabilizing capacitance is by borrowing on the future "credit" of the world. This is a fourth law of motion — onset, and consists of performing an action and leaving the system before the reflected reaction returns to the point of action — a delayed reaction. The means of surviving the reaction is by changing the system before the reaction can return. By this means, politicians become popular in their own time and the public pays for it later. In fact, the measures of such a politician is the delay time.

The same thing is achieved by a government by printing money beyond the limit of the gross national product, an economic process called inflation. This puts a large quantity of money into the hands of the public and maintains a balance against their greed, creates a false self-confidence in them and, for awhile, stays the wolf from the door. They must eventually resort to war to balance the account, because war ultimately is merely the act of destroying the creditor, and the politicians are the publicly-hired hit men that justify the act to keep the responsibility and blood off the public conscience.

If the people really cared about their fellow man, they would control their appetites (greed, procreation, etc.) so that they would not have to operate on a credit or welfare social system which steals from the worker to satisfy the bum. Since most of the general public will not exercise restraint, there are only two alternatives to reduce the economic inductance of the system. (1) Let the populace bludgeon each other to death in war, which will only result in a total destruction of the living earth. (2) Take control of the world by the use of economic "silent weapons" in a form of "quiet warfare" and reduce the economic inductance of the world to a safe level by a process of benevolent slavery and genocide.

The latter option has been taken as the obviously better option. At this point it should be crystal clear to the reader why absolute secrecy about the silent weapons is necessary. The general public refuses to improve its own mentality and its faith in its fellow man. It has become a herd of proliferating barbarians, and, so to speak, a blight upon the face of the earth. They do not care enough about economic science to learn why they have not been able to avoid war despite religious morality, and their religious or self-gratifying refusal to deal with earthly problems renders the solution of the earthly problem unreachable by them. It is left to those few who are truly willing to think and survive as the fittest to survive, to solve the problem for themselves as the few who really care. Otherwise, exposure of the silent weapon would destroy our only hope of preserving the seed of future true humanity.

The industries of finance (banking), manufacturing, and government, real counterparts of the pure industries of capital, goods, and services, are easily defined because they are generally logically structured. Because of this their processes can be described mathematically and their technical coefficients can be easily deduced. This, however, is not the case with the service industry known as the household industry.

In recent times, the application of Operations Research to the study of the public economy has been obvious for anyone who understands the principles of shock testing. In the shock testing of an aircraft airframe, the recoil impulse of firing a gun mounted on that airframe causes shock waves in that structure which tell aviation engineers the conditions under which parts of the airplane or the whole airplane or its wings will start to vibrate or flutter like a guitar string, a flute reed, or a tuning fork, and disintegrate or fall apart in flight. Economic engineers achieve the same result in studying the behavior of the economy and the consumer public by carefully selecting a staple commodity such as beef, coffee, gasoline, or sugar, and then causing a sudden change or shock in its price or availability, thus kicking everybody's budget and buying habits out of shape. They then observe the shock waves which result by monitoring the changes in advertising, prices, and sales of that and other commodities.

The objective of such studies is to acquire the know-how to set the public economy into a predictable state of motion or change, even a controlled self-destructive state of motion which will convince the public that certain "expert" people should take control of the money system and re-establish security (rather than liberty and justice) for all. When the subject citizens are rendered unable to control their financial affairs, they, of course, become totally enslaved, a source of cheap labor. Not only the prices of commodities, but also the availability of labor can be used as the means of shock testing. Labor strikes deliver excellent test shocks to an economy, especially in the critical service areas of trucking (transportation), communication, public utilities (energy, water, garbage collection), etc. By shock testing, it is found that there is a direct relationship between the availability of money flowing in an economy and the psychological outlook and response of masses of people dependent upon that availability. For example, there is a measurable quantitive relationship between the price of gasoline and the probability that a person would experience a headache, feel a need to watch a violent movie, smoke a cigarette, or go to a tavern for a mug of beer. It is most interesting that, by observing and measuring the economic modes by which the public tries to run from their problems and escape from reality, and by applying the mathematical theory of Operations Research, it is possible to program computers to predict the most probable combination of created events (shocks) which will bring about a complete control and subjugation of the public through a subversion of the public economy (by shaking the plum tree).

Diversion, the Primary Strategy

Experience has proven that the simplest method of securing a silent weapon and gaining control of the public is to keep the public undisciplined and ignorant of basic systems principles on the one hand, while keeping them confused, disorganized, and distracted with matters of no real importance on the other hand. This is achieved by: (1) disengaging their minds; sabotaging their mental activities; providing a low-quality program of public education in mathematics, logic, systems design and economics; and discouraging technical creativity. (2) engaging their emotions, increasing their self-indulgence and their indulgence in emotional and physical activities, by; (a) unrelenting emotional affrontations and attacks (mental and emotional rape) by way of a constant barrage of sex, violence, and wars in the media — especially the T.V. and the newspapers. (b) giving them what they desire — in excess — "junk food for thought" — depriving them of what they really need. (3) rewriting history and law and subjecting the public to the deviant creation, thus being able to shift their thinking from personal needs to highly fabricated outside priorities. These preclude their interest in and discovery of the silent weapons of social automation technology. The general rule is that there is profit in confusion; the more confusion, the more profit. Therefore, the best approach is to create problems and then offer the solutions.

A silent weapon system operates upon data obtained from a docile public by legal (but not always lawful) force. Much information is made available to silent weapon systems programmers through the Internal Revenue Service. This information consists of the enforced delivery of well-organized data contained in federal and state tax forms collected, assembled, and submitted by slave labor provided by taxpayers and employers. Furthermore, the number of such forms submitted to the I.R.S. is a useful indicator of public consent, an important factor in strategic decision making. Other data sources are given in the Short List of Inputs.

Consent Coefficients — numerical feedback indicating victory status. Psychological basis: When the government is able to collect tax and seize private property without just compensation, it is an indication that the public is ripe for surrender and is consenting to enslavement and legal encroachment. A good and easily quantified indicator of harvest time is the number of public citizens who pay income tax despite an obvious lack of reciprocal or honest service from the government.

From the time a person leaves its mother's womb, its every effort is directed toward building, maintaining, and withdrawing into artificial wombs, various sorts of substitute protective devices or shells. The objective of these artificial wombs is to provide a stable environment for both stable and unstable activity; to provide a shelter for the evolutionary processes of growth and maturity — i.e. survival; to provide security for freedom and to provide defensive protection for offensive activity. This is equally true of both the general public and the elite. However, there is a definite difference in the way each of these classes go about the solution of problems.

The primary reason why the individual citizens of a country create a political structure is a subconscious wish or desire to perpetuate their own dependency relationship of childhood. Simply put, they want a human god to eliminate all risk from their life, pat them on their head, kiss their bruises, put a chicken on every dinner table, clothe their bodies, tuck them into bed at night, and tell them that everything will be alright when they wake up in the morning. This public demand is incredible, so the human god, the politician, meets incredibility with incredibility by promising the world and delivering nothing. So who is the bigger liar? The public? or the "godfather"? This public behavior is surrender born of fear, laziness, and expediency. It is the basis of the welfare state as a strategic weapon, useful against a disgusting public.

Most people want to be able to subdue and/or kill other human beings which disturb their daily lives, but they do not want to have to cope with the moral and religious issues which such an overt act on their part might raise. Therefore, they assign the dirty work to others (including their own children) so as to keep the blood off their own hands. They rave about the humane treatment of animals and then sit down to a delicious hamburger from a whitewashed slaughterhouse down the street and out of sight. But even more hypocritical, they pay taxes to finance a professional association of hit men collectively called politicians, and then complain about corruption in government.

The people hire the politicians so that the people can: (1) obtain security without managing it. (2) obtain action without thinking about it. (3) inflict theft, injury, death upon others without having to contemplate either life or death. (4) avoid responsibility for their own intentions. (5) obtain the benefits of reality and science without exerting themselves in the discipline of facing or learning either of these things. They give the politicians the power to create and manage a war machine to: (1) provide for the survival of the nation/womb. (2) prevent encroachment of anything upon the nation/womb. (3) destroy the enemy who threatens the nation/womb. (4) destroy those citizens of their own country who do not conform for the sake of stability of the nation/womb. Politicians hold many quasi-military jobs, the lowest being the police, which are soldiers, the attorneys and the C.P.A.s next, who are spies and saboteurs (licensed), and the judges who shout the orders and run the closed union military shop for whatever the market will bear. The generals are industrialists. The "presidential" level of commander-in-chief is shared by the international bankers. The people know that they have created this farce and financed it with their own taxes (consent), but they would rather knuckle under than be the hypocrite. Thus, a nation becomes divided into two very distinct parts, a docile sub-nation and a political sub-nation. The political sub-nation remains attached to the docile sub-nation, tolerates it, and leaches its substance until it grows strong enough to detach itself and then devour its parent.

In order to make meaningful computerized economic decisions about war, the primary economic flywheel, it is necessary to assign concrete logistical values to each element of the war structure — personnel and material alike. This process begins with a clear and candid description of the subsystems of such a structure.

Few efforts of human behavior modification are more remarkable or more effective than that of the socio-military institution known as the draft. A primary purpose of a draft or other such institution is to instill, by intimidation, in the young males of a society the uncritical conviction that the government is omnipotent. He is soon taught that a prayer is slow to reverse what a bullet can do in an instant. Thus, a man trained in a religious environment for eighteen years of his life can, by this instrument of the government, be broken down, purged of his fantasies and delusions in a matter of mere months. Once that conviction is instilled, all else becomes easy to instill. Even more interesting is the process by which a young man's parents, who purportedly love him, can be induced to send him off to war to his death. Although the scope of this work will not allow this matter to be expanded in full detail, nevertheless, a course overview will be possible and can serve to reveal those factors which must be included in some numerical form in a computer analysis of social and war systems.

Human beings are machines, levers which may be grasped and turned, and there is little real difference between automating a society and automating a shoe factory. These values are given in true measure rather than U.S. dollars, since the latter is unstable, being presently inflated beyond the production of national goods and services so as to give the economy a false kinetic energy ("paper" inductance). The silver value is stable, it being possible to buy the same amount with a gram of silver today as could be bought in 1920. Human value measured in silver units changes slightly due to changes in production technology.

As in every social system approach, stability is achieved only by understanding and accounting for human nature (action/reaction patterns). A failure to do so can be, and usually is, disastrous. As in other human social schemes, one form or another of intimidation (or incentive) is essential to the success of the draft. Physical principles of action and reaction must be applied to both internal and external subsystems. To secure the draft, individual brainwashing/programming and both the family unit and the peer group must be engaged and brought under control.

The man of the household must be housebroken to ensure that junior will grow up with the right social training and attitudes. The advertising media, etc., are engaged to see to it that father-to-be is pussy-whipped before or by the time he is married. He is taught that he either conforms to the social notch cut out for him or his sex life will be hobbled and his tender companionship will be zero. He is made to see that women demand security more than logical, principled, or honorable behavior. By the time his son must go to war, father (with jelly for a backbone) will slam a gun into junior's hand before father will risk the censure of his peers, or make a hypocrite of himself by crossing the investment he has in his own personal opinion or self-esteem. Junior will go to war or father will be embarrassed. So junior will go to war, the true purpose not withstanding.

The female element of human society is ruled by emotion first and logic second. In the battle between logic and imagination, imagination always wins, fantasy prevails, maternal instinct dominates so that the child comes first and the future comes second. A woman with a newborn baby is too starry-eyed to see a wealthy man's cannon fodder or a cheap source of slave labor. A woman must, however, be conditioned to accept the transition to "reality" when it comes, or sooner. As the transition becomes more difficult to manage, the family unit must be carefully disintegrated, and state-controlled public education and state-operated child-care centers must become more common and legally enforced so as to begin the detachment of the child from the mother and father at an earlier age. Inoculation of behavioral drugs can speed the transition for the child (mandatory). Caution: A woman's impulsive anger can override her fear. An irate woman's power must never be underestimated, and her power over a pussy-whipped husband must likewise never be underestimated. It got women the vote in 1920.

The emotional pressure for self-preservation during time of war and the self-serving attitude of the common herd that have an option to avoid the battlefield — if junior can be persuaded to go — is all of the pressure finally necessary to propel Johnny off to war. Their quiet blackmailing of him are the threats: "No sacrifice, no friends; no glory, no girlfriends."

And what about junior's sister? She is given all the good things of life by her father, and taught to expect the same from her future husband regardless of the price.

Those who will not use their brains are no better off than those who have no brains, and so this mindless school of jellyfish, father, mother, son, and daughter, become useful beasts of burden or trainers of the same.

Secrets From the Vatican Library

The following document was anonymously sent to me during this book's preparation. It purports to be a secret history of Western civilization gleaned from secret documents in the Vatican library by a member of the Franciscan order. The inked imprint of a Vatican library entrance chit affixed to the original document and duplicated at the end of the article is a strong indication that the author does have access to Vatican sources, although his conclusions are indicative of a highly right-wing slant that pegs the piece as possible disinformation — from what quarter, I cannot speculate. This document is included herein because of its unusual origin, and as an example of one very suspect sidepath in the tangle of competing conspiracy worldviews.

JMJ Ille nos benedicat qui sine fine vivit et regnat.

Dear Mr. Keith, I have been made aware that you seek information regarding what you suppose to be the takeover of the Vatican by Royal Arch Masons; would that such, a small thing, really, were the case. May it please you and inform you, somewhat, I shall endeavor to lay before you such facts as are known to me. I must first offer this disclaimer: while the facts of which I shall give report are in large part verifiable, there remains the possibility that, in certain instances where more than one possible interpretation thereof exists, I may well have chosen an incorrect one. Be that as it may, interpretation is not an issue, the facts do speak, most loquaciously, on their own behalf.

To begin; I believe that the establishment of my credentials would be in order. I cannot, and do not, claim to be of high rank in the Church of Rome; a common Lector am I, formerly a student of Heresiology attached for a time to the American School at the Vatican, and possessed as such of an entry-chit, permitting me access to those sub-basements and annexae of the Vatican Library Complex as were deemed fruitful to my ongoing research. It was in this capacity, and under these circumstances, that I first became aware, from various documents, of the general tone of the information I shall here present. After having ascertained that indeed something was awry, and after having been transferred back to the United States (where I was until not too long ago employed as secretary under a succession of priests, of various orders), I appointed unto myself the task of collecting such information as I might, with a mind to either confirm or deny that which I had learned; among other things, I discovered that I am hardly alone in this knowledge — I thank Almighty God that such pillars of determination and strength, such — yes, I shall say it — such saints, are still in evidence even in these most trying, most frightening of times.

We all of us owe to them a debt which can only be repaid by assimilating the information which they have bequeathed to me, and now I to you, and in using this information wisely. I reveal this information as my duty both to God and to my fellow-pilgrims on this Earth, in submission to His command; *Hoc est praeceptum meum ut diligatus invicem sicut dilexi vos.*

I value not position within the Church, nor status in the eyes of men; I seek only to oppose a most foul circumstance, a confederacy of tyrants, who pervert the use of the Ecclesiastical Authority to their own most ignoble ends; my most fervent desire is to once and for all time set straight the record, help to clear away the mountain of debris — I believe you term it disinformation — that all might clearly see the menace before us, naked and unadorned, revealed in the Light of Truth. With your kind permission, I begin.

It must first be understood that the present troubles are the fault, not of some bepaunched oligarchy seated by the fire at their Men's Club — though said troubles are most certainly perpetuated under much this very scenario — but are rather the result of protracted struggle between several "elite" factions, "cliques" if you will, who have battled under various guises for supremacy from the days following the fall of the Roman Empire to the present.

In order to fully understand the present times, one must rightly understand the past; hence I shall offer the sum total of my knowledge of the full course of this struggle, from the earlier years of the seventh century of the common era, as well as the identity and makeup of each of the factions thereby engaged. We live, truly, in the Dark Ages; since the collapse of the old Roman Empire and the subsequent rise of the Church as the real power in the West, various factions — the European tribal confederacies, for the most part — have fought among themselves for control of the territory of the Chair of St. Peter, and indeed for control of the Vatican itself. Realizing, as they did, that the Church could not be vanquished by fire or by the sword — a lesson learnt, and learnt right hard, by the decaying Empire, *Pretiosa in conspectu Domini mors sanctorum Eius* — the pagan tribes of Europe split into several factions, some accepting the Church as at least their titular head (that is, submitting to the disciplines of Christianity and incorporating the Faith into the Mythos of their tribes), some choosing to oppose the church under any means fair and foul, and some vacillating between the two poles, though even these did ultimately choose one tack or the other. To simplify, the southern tribes formed a generally pro-Church clique, which expanded to include the Franks (though this primarily due to rivalry with their fellow Germanics to the north, who led the opposing camp); and those who opposed, whether by outright force or subterfuge, the Church — and hoped to either destroy or assimilate the power wielded by Rome. The tribes of modern England were of the third type, but their neighbors the Gaels and Celts of Eire were among the most steadfast supporters of the Church, even after the forcible dissolution of their own unique and beautiful Celtic Communion by the English, in AD 664, who imposed a more Roman variety, more in accordance with the Rite as practiced in England. The message of the Gospel — in its true rendition, one of love and tolerance — was well-suited to the tribes of Eire and of Southern Europe, their characters being marked by a practiced indolence bordering on Sloth, deep passions that flair quickly and are just as quickly quelled, and an underlying affection that finds expression in their every breath; it was these who took to the Church, whatever their reasons to begin, and held fast to the Church to the present day.

The northern tribes, however — the Teutons, the Norse, the Saxons, et. al. — these are typified by a seething cold, a hardness that is not in keeping with their physical beauty, an autocratic indifference to others. While each, north and south, are capable of horrible cruelty, the southern peoples could be as quick to forgive as to blame, and though emotional can be swayed by logic to withdraw their anger; the northerners seem to delight in atrocity, and their lack of apparent passion hides an outlook best typified by the old Arab adage, "Revenge is a dish best served cold." So long as the Church remained in southern hands, all continued reasonably close to the original plan of the Apostles — as late as AD 692, Sergius I, Bishop of Rome, joined in the proclamation of the Patriarch of Constantinople that their respective Patriarchates, their Episcopal Sees, were of equal rank before our Lord. It pains me to say that never again did the Bishop of Rome behave in so Apostolic a manner, besieged from that time on by worldly concerns which ultimately redirected the Church from Spiritual paths. Due to the apportionment of power in those times, the various northern tribes found it expedient to accept a veneer of Faith, and to nurture their plots under cover of obedience.

The first overt action taken by the northern clique was alignment with certain Muslims expelled from Omayyid Spain, in AD 826; these were settled at Crete, where they established a pirate base, from which they would hector the southern coastal countries. The Roman/Etruscan clique, in reaction to this, used their influence with the Church to establish the Venetian Order of St. Marc, which received full Papal recognition just five years after the establishment of the base at Crete. Skirmishes at sea would continue through the Crusades, to the early sixteenth century. Around the year 850, a new group of players entered the picture: Jews began settling in Germany, under the direction of a very secretive Zionist Elite, who forged ties with the Germanic clique, especially the Prussians and Bavarians. While racially different, they had in common a form of religion; the Zionists and the north Germans both practiced ritual sacrifice of humans. It must be understood that the Jewish Elite never expressed the actual practices or beliefs of the Jewish commoners under them; they were an Elite, who considered their own people far beneath them, and fit only for use as fodder, which autocratic mode appealed to the north Germans, being but a minor variation of their own most ancient practices.

In league with the Zionists, with the odd band of Muslim adventurers to use as shock troops, and the rank-and-file masses of commoner Jews to use for sacrificial purposes, the northern cliques began to upscale their opposition, still mostly covert, to southern/Roman authority. Seeing these developments, it fell to the secular Roman aristocracy — the Old Nobles — to do something, and that quickly. Being as the Bishop of Rome — at that time, John VIII — was disinclined to secularize the Church to the extent proposed by the Roman Nobles, the clique had him murdered in AD 882, beginning the first takeover of the Vatican authority. Subsequent Popes were made well aware of their vicarious position, and only a rare few dared oppose the Roman clique, who now were pre-eminent among the southern tribal clique. Even at that, the complete secular takeover of the Papal authority was not complete until Otto I, as Holy Roman Emperor, forcibly replaced an unaccomodating John XII with a more compliant Leo VIII, in AD 963. From that time on, Papal elections and the College of Cardinals have been a pawn of the ruling faction of the southern clique.

The northern clique, of course, made certain to have their own people in place in Rome, attached in whatever fashion to the Papal retinue. It was by the efforts of one of these agents that the northern clique acquired knowledge of the continents to the west, the Americas, which had been known to the upper echelons of the Church hierarchy since the last quarter of the First Century of the common era, that knowledge delivered, to the best of my knowledge, to blessed St. John the Divine in a vision, and recorded in an Epistle to the Corinthian Church by his holiness Clement, by grace of God the Bishop of Rome, in AD 96. With this information in hand, the northern clique entreated one Leif Ericsson, son of Eric the Red (a trusted Norse associate of the north European clique), to sail westward along a northern route, to ascertain the feasibility of taking these lands for themselves and using their wealth in an outright battle against the southern hegemony. It is fortunate that the natives — called "Skraelings" by Leif and his crew — proved to be displeased by the presence of the Norsemen, and had expelled them, lock, stock, and barrel, by AD 1006. When news of this expedition had filtered back to the southern clique, it caused more than a little consternation. Since the move had been covert, and the southerners desired to keep their own friends in place among the northern elite, plans were quietly laid to facilitate a successful southern effort in the event of overt action; stores were replenished, training of mercenaries upgraded, and to culminate, the Order of Knights Hospitallers of St. John — an order of warrior—monks/provisioners — was founded, in AD 1070.

The northern clique being engaged, since earlier in that same century, in one of their many in—fights for superiority, the southern clique had breath space to consolidate their own lines until about AD 1080, at which time the first full-scale small war took place between the two cliques, ending any possibility of willful merger between the two elites. That it was Gregory VII, in establishing (at the behest of the southern clique) the most sweeping of Papal temporal powers, that initiated this attack by the north, is immaterial; the southern clique had known for some time that the Muslim mercenaries who sacked their coasts were in the employ of the north, which by AD 1100 was being more and more dominated by the Prussian/Bavarian/Zionist clique. Nonetheless, a concordat of sorts was reached when Muslims not in European employ began taking advantage of the factional in-fighting, and it was to a relatively united Europe that Urban II promoted the First Crusade. It was at this time that the Order of Knights Templars was founded, much a duplication of the Order of Hospitallers, but less concerned with provisioning as with actual warfare.

That both orders served as bankers to much of the European elite, both northern and southern cliques, led to struggles between the two groups, which were to have dire consequences at a later date. There were, as yet, some factions of the southern clique still true at heart to the precepts of the Faith, rather than the power thereof, and these factions saw their opportunity in the power struggle between the Welf Family and the Hohenstauffens, also called the Guelphs and the Ghibellines, respectively, beginning in AD 1125. With the victory of the northern-sympathizing Hohenstauffen clan, the balance of power began a slow but inexorable shift to the northern clique, becoming ever more heavily dominated by the North German/Zionist faction. The shift, however, was not immediately apparent to the southern clique, who found themselves receiving a rather rude awakening in AD 1154, when a northern candidate, one Nicholas Breakspear, became Pope Adrian IV; almost immediately he gave Ireland as a gift to his mentor, Henry II of England, which has resulted in nearly a millennium of domination of the only northern ally of the southern clique.

The threat of a pincer movement set aside, the northern clique proceeded to reinaugurate their original policy of covert whittling at the power of the south, now invested very heavily in the Roman and Frankish aristocratic factions. Regular sacrifice of Jewish commoners, under the direction of the Zionist elite, was instituted to propitiate the deities still covertly worshiped by the elite of the northern clique, now merged into the Zionist deity (which had never been the same God worshiped by the Jewish commoners, as examination of coins and other artifacts of the Third Temple Period will clearly show). These regular sacrifices date to approximately 1190, and following quick on the heels of this, comes the escalation of northern preparations for outright struggle against the south; the Order of Teutonic Knights and the Livonian Brothers of the Sword, precursors to the later Prussian Orders, date to the period AD 1190—1210. With the Hospitallers and Knights Templars engaged in a war of attrition that killed nearly as many of their number as their battles against the Muslims, and the Dominicans fully engaged, from AD 1208, in pitched battle with nonconformist southern sub-cliques and covert actions in England, the Teutonic Knights and their cohorts had a clear field to engage as they would; upon absorbing the Livonian Brothers of the Sword in 1237, they were nearly unstoppable. Their early success they attributed to a massive propitiative sacrifice of European children, in AD 1212. This affair, which began with the promotion of what was called the "Children's Crusade", drained an untold number of Europe's youngest into the clutches of the Teutons; a massive number were indeed slaughtered in ritual sacrifice, and perhaps twice that number were sold into slavery to the Muslims. Once again, the 'prayers' of the Teutonic/Zionist clique appeared to have been answered, as with their defeat at the hands of the Mongols in AD 1256, survivors of the Order of Assassins, the Ishmaelis, of Hasan I Sabah, began trickling into Europe, seeking sanctuary among the similarly-inclined Teutonic/Zionist clique. With the addition of these well-trained and fearless — nay, nearly suicidal — Assassins, the Teutonic/Zionist Clique achieved the force necessary to assume complete control of the northern clique, as well as a special force to supplement the actions of their still-active Muslim shocktroops.

Edward I of England, upon learning the full extent of the practices of the Teutons/Zionists, was so sickened that he expelled all Jews from England in 1290, rather than allow what he considered an abomination to occur on his soil. Indeed, as knowledge of the practice crept through the subcliques of the south, one by one they either expelled the Jews (as did France in AD 1306) or else forced their conversion to Christianity, in the mistaken belief that this made them unacceptable for the sacrificial rite. A word or two, I believe, regarding the sacrificial rite of the Zionists, as well as the similar rite of the Teutons, is in order: I must warn you that the rites as I know them are distasteful in the extreme, and that I would not recommend the following as good reading for the squeamish. It must be remembered, throughout this description, that modern Jewry is, for the most part, ignorant of the rites of the Zionists, who posit that they alone (as proper Zionist Jews) are true Jewry, and all others who claim Judaism are wrong. Indeed, to investigate the history of this religion (done so admirably by Benjamin Freedman in his tome, "Facts Are Facts") is to discover that modern rank-and-file Jewry has no real connexion to historical Judaism, but are in fact pawns in a much larger and more vicious game than they realize. To begin, then: the rite of consecration of the Kohen (ritual/sacrificial priest) and that of normative ritual sacrifice are very nearly identical. The Kohen-elect is made to enter a pit beneath the grating that is beside the altar of sacrifice, also called the altar of holocaust *(shoah,* in the Hebrew), which is described at chapter 27 of Exodus, in the first part. The altar grating is placed over the pit (actually more an encircling trench), and the sacrificial victim is brought to the altar. The preferred victim is a young boy of Jewish blood; young girls are useable, especially when supply is high, but boys are the preferred victim. Most 'Jewish' parents during the Templar periods (the times during which a properly-consecrated temple stood at Jerusalem) were required to redeem their children with an offering (see chapter 12 of Leviticus); at these time, the children of the destitute (who could not offer the prescribed ransom) were used — in modern times, any so-called 'Jewish' child may be kidnapped & used for the sacrifice, or for the ordination, though for the sin offering a Gentile child may be used. The child, preferably an infant or toddler (but any child up to the age of thirteen being acceptable, if virginal), is stood upon the grating over the head of the Kohen—elect, nude, facing northward; the child's head is grasped firmly by the officiating priest (or by him and his assistant, should the child be older & put up a fight), and the child's throat is then slit to open the jugular vein. Some of the blood is made to splatter against the eastern face of the altar itself, while the rest spatters through the grating to bathe the Kohen-elect, who drinks a mouthful of the blood as it pours over him. The officiating Kohen then wets his fingers with the screaming innocent's blood and, walking counter-clockwise around the altar, traces certain arcane sigils upon the altar's horns with the blood; then, arriving back at the child's position, he takes a mouthful of the spurting blood. The Kohen-elect is helped out from under the grating & joins the assisting Kohens at the child's side, and all are liberally mouth-sprayed with the child's blood by the officiating Kohen, thus sealing the new Kohen as a member of the priesthood.

The child, weak from loss of blood but still very much alive, is butchered; the internal fatty tissue, the liver, and the kidneys are set aside to be burnt, and the Kohens feast on what they want of the rest, burning the unused portions before sunset, according to Levitical law. This is also the basic procedure for the regular ritual sacrifice, with the exceptions being that in regular sacrifice, the blood spills uninterrupted through the grating, to renew the consecration of the sill on which the temple or killing-floor rests, and that the mouth-spraying of the child's blood is omitted. Similarities between the Jewish and Teutonic rituals are close; the parallels suggest, perhaps, a common origin for certain practices, perhaps deriving from central Asia via the Khazars. In the Teutonic rite, the altar is generally an unhewn dolmen, and the pit and its attendant grating are absent. The priest to be consecrated in this rite merely lies, nude, on the ground at the eastern face of the stone altar (the eastern face of the altar being sacred to both the Zionists and the Teutons), and the victim — a child of either gender between the ages of seven and twelve, virginal — is brought to him. The child is forced down upon the priest—elect in a kneeling position, straddling the elect's hips, at which time sexual penetration (notably absent in the Zionist rite) is achieved, anally for a young boy, vaginally for a young girl. The child's head is faced east, as in the Zionist rite, and the jugular is opened, showering the priest-elect with blood, some of which is ingested. The child is then penetrated sexually by the attending priests until such time as death occurs. In both rites, the bathing in and ingestion of the blood of the child is required for proper consecration, and in the Teutonic rite (as in the Zionist), the body of the child is eaten. In the everyday ritual of sacrifice in the Teutonic rite, no priest-elect lies before the dolmen; instead, the child is penetrated by each of the priests in turn, according to rank or seniority (depending on which of two rites is being followed; I am unclear as to the exact distinction between the two, other than this particular difference of practice).

The Order of Knights Templars — who operated extensively in the north — had been influenced heavily by the Teutonic/Zionist cult. The northern houses of the Templars had indeed adopted several practices from the northern clique, including the Zionist practice of consulting preserved oracular heads for augury. The southern houses of the Templars in combination with the Hospitallers, approached French king Philippe IV with a list of charges, substantiated by eyewitness testimony of a number of the southern Templars, and acting on this information Philippe issued an order of arrest in September of 1307. The order was finally suppressed through all Europe (except Scotland), and the Grand Master, Jacques DeMolay, was burned at the stake in 1314. Those Templars remaining in the south were absorbed into the order of Hospitallers, while those in hiding in Scotland became the nucleus of the Priory of Zion, turning their considerable talents and remaining wealth over to the service of the Teutonic/Zionist clique. The southern clique, now dominated by an uneasy alliance of the French and Roman aristocracies, began exhibiting signs of paranoia very early in this stage of the crisis. Boniface VIII, in an attempt to bring the clique back in line with the original division of power (subservient to, rather than masters of, the Church), issued a Papal Bull, "Unam Sanctam," claiming Papal authority over temporal rulers, in 1302. He was poisoned in 1303, and succeeded by Benedict XI — who attempted to follow in Boniface's footsteps and was poisoned himself in 1304. Philippe IV of France, engaged in his war with the Templars as early as 1307, finally offered Pope Clement V sanctuary in France, and the Papal court moved in that year to Avignon, a coup for the French faction over the Romans. So paranoid did the Papal court become that, in 1316 (while the remnants of the Templars were strengthening the northern clique), John XXII sent a squad of heavily-armed Dominicans south to Ethiopia to chase down a reported Patriarch with valid Roman Apostolic succession, recorded in history as "Prester John."

In 1326, the Teutonic Knights made a foray into Poland; prisoners were taken by the Poles, and several talked, divulging not only the brief bits they knew of general policy, but also their knowledge of the sacrifices of Jewish commoners — these reports sickened the Poles, who, upon repelling the Teutons in 1333-34, extended a general sanctuary to all European Jewry. As news spread through the sub-elites of the southern clique, outrage was the order of the day. While the southern clique was capable of sustained violence, and the torture of captive enemies, the thought of a program of ritual human sacrifice appalled them, causing them to begin pulling somewhat closer together, at least to discuss this aspect of the northern threat. Though several of the aristocratic sub-cliques had learnt of this practice as long back as 1190, it had been regarded as something between a rumor and an aberration; now, however, with proof wrested from Teutonic Knights by the Poles, it took on an immediacy. The northern clique, of course, knew very quickly that their practices were known by the southerners, but were more upset by what they considered the southerners' pretensions. In order to break the south, now when all seemed going their way, the northern clique (with the especial help of England's Edward III) caused the collapse of the Bardi Financier clique in Rome, who had been, after the Hospitallers, the bankers of Europe. Edward, of course, benefitted by not being required to pay any of the sizable loans he'd received from the Bardis; the northern clique could now attempt to wrest control of finance from the south. By this time, the midpoint of the fourteenth century, it was becoming something of a race; since the initial expedition to the North American continent, neither side of the conflict had been in a position to exploit the virgin lands. The north, while having the advantage of unity under autocratic rule, had not the requisite wealth to exploit the Americas; the southern clique, for whom wealth was no problem, had not the unity to mount a proper expedition. Both cliques realized that control of the vast wealth of the western continents would ensure lasting victory. While the northern houses of the Templars had brought with them a cache of gold, it had been scant — Philippe IV had systematically confiscated the available wealth of the order during the seven years of his program against them, and most of this had been disbursed to the Templars-cum-Hospitallers thereafter, remaining under southern clique control.

The northern clique, growing desperate, authorized their Assassins to introduce into southern Europe the bubonic plague, known as the "Black Death," in 1348. Ultimately, the plague would kill perhaps one-quarter of the European & Asian population, as much as one-third of Europe alone, and scattered outbreaks would continue well into the present century, somewhat backfiring on the northern clique. Nonetheless, it had much the desired effect, in its own way, weakening the south sufficiently to allow the north to reinstate its program of large-scale sacrifice of Jewish commoners, forcing large numbers of Jews to seek the asylum of Poland, beginning one year after introduction of the plague, in 1349. The south learned of the north's complicity even as the plague ravaged the population, forever altering the balance of power and social structure of the continent. A force of Dominicans pushed south into deep Africa in an attempt to settle a safe base, free from the contagion of Europe; they had begun construction of stone fortifications at Great Zimbabwe when they were attacked and slaughtered by a force of Teutonic Knights, who took over the construction with the use of slave labor, culled from among the indigenous population; hopelessly outnumbered and operating far from any hope of relief, the Teutons were in turn slaughtered by an uprising of the native slaves, and the abandoned fortifications stand to this day. Thus, in AD 1375, any hopes of using the African continent to sway the balance of power were shelved, and the cliques began to concentrate as best they could on the race to exploit the Americas.

In addition to the aforementioned poverty of the north and disunity of the south, both cliques were now saddled with a massive upheaval of their socioeconomic norms caused by the plague, which led to a period of reapportionment and in-fighting in both camps. One of the major results of the plague was a loss of faith; the commoners (and more importantly, the elite) saw presbyter and prelate falling side-by-side with the peasant. It was likely this, more than anything else, that inspired the 'war of words' that was soon to follow. The northern clique, who never had actually accepted the Gospel, set about discrediting the Writ. In AD 1376, northern-backed theologian John Wycliff published a treatise, "Civil Dominion," attacking the Church (and therefore the power of the southern clique); seeing, somewhat, the coming storm, the southern clique quietly began a shakeup in their power structure. The nature of the uneasy alliance between the various aristocracies was such that the pro forma obedience to the Church scarce provided the stability required to bring the clique, or actually the two major factions of the clique (the French and Roman-oriented factions) through a complete revitalization as was attempted at that time; hence relations between the two groups were strained to the point of near-dissolution; this is the root cause behind the "Great Schism" of 1378.

The Papacy & Papal courts having already been under French domination from 1309, the situation was ripe for schism; when Urban VI elected to return the Papal Court to Rome, more than a dozen Cardinals of the French faction elected Clement VII as Antipope, and reopened the Avignon Vatican. By 1409, three rival claimants were hailed as Pope, representing the French faction, the old Roman (west-central Italian) faction, and the upstart faction from Pisa (north-central Italian). This state of disunity only began to settle when the Medici family, financiers, began their bid to take over the Papacy in 1414, and the schism wasn't totally ended until three years after. The Pope elected as compromise to the three factions Martin V, who immediately set about to reaffirm the mastery of the south over the north, but the troops sent forth to do this were defeated by Bohemian Hussite forces in AD 1431.

The legendary rivalry of the various Italian families and factions, including the sad tale of the Borgia Popes, is well recounted elsewhere, hence I mention them only in passing, as these conflicts greatly hampered the southern clique's attempts to regain superiority over the north, and nearly single-handed guaranteed the north's ascendancy over the course of the next several centuries. Away from the main centers of action, the Teutonic Knights once again attempted to snatch back the sacrificial Jews living in asylum in Poland. The Poles, however, are nothing if not fearless fighters. This foray of the Teutons ended with the Poles gaining west Prussia, exacerbating already strained relations with the Germanics, who decried the Poles even then as *üntermenschen.* Northern infiltration of the southern power centers had been slow and unsteady; with the victory of the Poles in 1454, a drive was attempted to sieze Spain, which, while secondary in power to the Italian and French factions, was a rising star.

Informed of the attempt by vigilant sentinels in the ranks, but unable to do without the aid rendered by the northern agents, Isabella and Ferdinand expelled the Jews resident there, and quietly shuffled their staff until the most trusted few held the positions closest to their throne. A young adventurer, confidant of the esoteric scholars at Rome, one Cristoforo Colombo, had visited the Spanish monarchs in 1486 to request their assistance in an adventure to the western continents, and had been rejected. Returning to them in 1492, bearing letters of introduction from the scholars even as the royals were expelling the Jews, it fell to Isabella — acting with Ferdinand's approval, but in secret, that the plans not leak out — to finance the explorer's quest. Due to the problems with the northern clique, and allowing for the possibility of the team being waylaid by northern-backed pirates, Cristoforo (known to the esoteric scholars as Xpo Ferens) was outfitted with three ships only, no escort, and a crew of convicted felons who were considered expendable. Even with these handicaps, the attempt succeeded.

So frightened were the northerners that in 1517, the Teutonic/Zionist faction goaded an emotionally-disturbed monk, one Martin Luther, to instigate a "Reformation" of the Church, in the hope that the resultant turmoil would destroy the now once-again-waxing power of the southern clique. The ongoing troubles between the English and French factions kept interference by other channels to a minimum, however, and the southern clique made serious advances in the southern continent of the Americas. Leo X, then holding the Papacy on behalf of his family, the Medici faction, granted special favors to English King Henry VIII, then excommunicated Martin Luther. The northerners, seeing the disruptive nature of these actions (discrediting them, and swaying England back toward the southern clique), had Leo assassinated, using their influence in one final push to have elected to the Papal office one Adrian Boeyens, of the Netherlands, who (as Adrian VI) would be the last northern choice (indeed, last non-Italian) Pope, for some years to come. Adrian held office only through parts of AD 1522-23, then was poisoned and replaced by Clement VII, another Medici. The southern clique, badly shaken by events and with a care about their as-yet long-distance control of the western continents, began forming more military/religious orders, such as the infamous Knights of Malta (formerly the Knights of St. John) in AD 1530, and the Jesuits in 1534 (though the date of their official recognition, AD 1540, is that found in most histories of the time). The Jesuits' primary function, that of rooting out infiltrators, they performed admirably well — so well, indeed, that by 1543, they were able to present sufficient evidence to Paul III to force him to inaugurate the Inquisition.

Due to the victory of the northern clique, most histories of the Inquisition are hopelessly distorted, but extant Vatican records report that the primary target of the ecclesiastical courts were northern-backed infiltrators, and that these, once found guilty, were handed over to the secular courts for punishment — which was all-too-often carried out in a most un-Christian manner. Admittedly, the power of the Inquisitor's office was rather horribly abused — most especially by rivals of the Italian faction in Spain — and so engrossed was the southern clique in the minutiae of uncovering northern conspirators that it came as a near-total surprise when, in AD 1554, the north seized control of the apparatus of the Holy Roman Empire, then under the direction of H.R.E. Karl V, born a Spaniard but by now firmly in the pocket of the northern interests.

The founding of the Royal Exchange in AD 1566 instigated an attempted invasion of England by a force of undercover Dominicans in 1574; betrayed to the English nobility by supposed allies, they were killed within weeks of their arrival. Attempts at diplomacy by the southern clique failed, and in AD 1581 regular executions of Catholics were instituted in an attempt to destroy all internal opposition from hidden southern agents. Muslims, their numbers padded by a force of native blacks, massed in West Africa, by the river Niger, for an invasion of the southern countries, but were apprehended by a force of Spanish and Portuguese mercenaries and wiped out. In that same year, within scant months, a large Spanish fleet — attempting a secret invasion of England — lost the element of surprise when a lone ship captained by the pirate Sir Richard Grenville engaged them enroute, allowing a tender to return to port with the news. In retaliation, two Popes — Innocent IX and Gregory XIV — are poisoned within a two-month period. This coming directly on the heels of three previous deaths, Gregory XIII in AD 1585 under mysterious circumstances, then Sixtus V and Urban VII within two weeks of each other in AD 1590, prompted retaliation in kind by the southern clique.

Awakening one morning late in 1592 to find the heads of five of his bastard sons nestled against him in his bed (their bodies neatly laid out on the floor), French king Henri IV, who had facilitated the English schemes against the last several Popes, publicly renounced Protestantism and sent envoys to the Italian faction in an attempt to appease them. This had been a second warning to the French, as Henri III, because of disagreements with the Roman aristocracy, had been executed by a warrior-monk in AD 1589. A letter, left on the pillow of Elizabeth I of England, to the effect that continued opposition to Rome would result in the death of any child she might bear, is credited with having persuaded Elizabeth never to marry. Nonetheless, anti-Catholic laws remained in force in England, and northern infiltrators were beginning to make their presence felt even in the ranks of the elite Jesuits, having enough power to block a reunification of the Roman and Orthodox Communions in AD 1595. Fighting between the two cliques was rivaled, in this period, only by in-fighting between the various factions. England narrowly averted total invasion by the Spanish when an Armada, sent out to attack in tandem with a Spanish-supported uprising of the Irish, was decimated in a massive storm. The French and Spanish factions, engaged for some time in open hostilities, are persuaded to lay down arms by the Roman faction; in 1600. Lord Mountjoy begins starving the rebel Irish into submission, even as Spanish reinforcements were reinforcing the defenses at Kinsale. Mountjoy would later — in AD 1602 — defeat the emaciated combined forces, quashing the rebellion.

In AD 1603, Elizabeth I dies and is succeeded by James I, who is unafraid of the southern clique. Even the release, by Portuguese mercenaries, of the plague in London does not sway him. The English had been sending covert teams to the Americas, mostly the East Coast of North America, since AD 1562, and established their first overt settlement, Jamestown, in 1607; English colonists and a force of slaves had held Virginia since 1619, marginally-patriotic religious zealots of unacceptable cults had been transported since 1620, and finally in AD 1630, an English force of 1000 was sent to reinforce covert bases in the Massachusetts territory, founding what would become Boston. With the infiltration of the Jesuits basically completed by AD 1640, the establishment of a southern clique-oriented colony, Maryland, in AD 1632, was at best a palliative measure; northern clique control of North America was essentially assured. Indeed, with the founding of Quaker-controlled Pennsylvania in AD 1682, only two of the original thirteen colonies permitted the practice of Catholicism or the Quaker faith. With the passage of formal laws making Catholicism a crime in AD 1691, and the beginning of the infamous Salem witch trials that same year, any members of religions other than those permitted by the North American branch of the northern clique — most notably Catholics and Quakers — were an endangered species.

Freemasonry was a growing fad among the second and third level echelon of the northern clique, and the Masons saw in the new land an opportunity to set themselves up as a faction in their own right. While French and Native American mercenaries carried on a war of attrition against the northern clique invaders between AD 1702-55, the Freemasons — or rather, jealous lower-echelon members of the northern clique united in Masonic Lodges — continued to accrue power in the new territories. By 1738, they posed such a threat that infiltration of southern aristocratic ranks was deemed imminent, and Clement XII issued the Papal Bull "In Eminenti" in that year, excommunicating any Catholic who was found to be a member of the Masonic Lodges. The French faction, having nominal control of the midsection of North America, were the only force with a real chance of driving the northern clique out. The French faction, however, were tired of the Roman yoke, and, fearing open north-south warfare on their soil, expelled the heavily-infiltrated Jesuits in 1762, then began covertly planning to remove the Roman-allied royalty, who had ceased to be of use to them. The French faction was, by this time, content with a behind-the-scenes stance, in the so-called lower nobility; the Royals —

intended as an human shield — were costing more and more to support in the style to which they'd become accustomed.

In AD 1773, the North American faction felt confident in their strength, and, provoking commoners to engage in the 'Boston Tea Party,' began overt hostilities against the North European clique. War followed two years later. As the colonists dumped English tea into Boston Harbor, Clement XIV dissolved the now northern-rife Jesuits in a belated attempt to halt the erosion of southern clique power. Come 1777, a leader emerged among the new North American clique; George Wessington (later Washington) agreed to figurehead the fledgling group, and his (Wessington) family coat-of-arms, a field of stars and alternating stripes, was adopted as the new clique's standard and the new nation's flag.

The now heavily northern-influenced faction controlling France, seeing the growing power and considerable natural wealth of the upstarts, aligned with the Wessington clique the following year. Along with the actual heads of the new North American faction, Jefferson, Franklin, and Adams, Washington (as he came to be called) led the commoners' forces to victory, and the European cliques of France, Spain, and England formally recognized the new faction in 1783. The upstarts entered into agreement with the now nearly-deified Prussian (Teutonic/Zionist) faction in 1785, and the Teutons began shifting the center of power to include their North American allies. The Constitution, written in such a way as to ensure that the Church-oriented southern clique could never sieze power, was ratified, and seeing the changing tides of fortune, the French faction — totally dissatisfied with the southern clique — incited the French Revolution, toppling the southern-oriented royals and driving the Roman/Vatican faction representatives from the country. Deciding to take up the northern clique's practices, the French faction formally invites Jews to return in 1790; five years later, in order to win back some necessary financial backing, the French faction opens tenuous relations with certain elements of the Roman financial crowd. A problem becoming all-too-apparent to the northern clique was the growing numbers of commoners, who — with victories in North America and France leaving them very full of themselves — were beginning to realize their power.

The world's population reached 500 million around AD 1650, and was increasing dramatically. In AD 1798, Thomas Robert Malthus set down, in his book "Essay On The Principle Of Population," the fledgling ideology of the northern clique on the problem of "what to do about all those commoners." The North American clique split, by the early 1820's, into two factions, the northern and the southern. The southern faction was relatively liberal, preferring to use imported Africans as slaves and allowing the commoners a certain degree of liberty; the northern faction, heavily influenced by the thinking of the Teutonic/Zionist clique, saw the growing masses as potential slaves, regardless of race. Standard histories claim that the southern clique ceded from the northern to protect their property rights, but in fact the northern clique sought to extend slavery to all commoners, not merely the negroes. Importation of Africans had ceased in 1808, beginning a captive breeding program in the south and an extension-of-slavery program in the north; indeed, as early as 1786, an attempt at self-government in New England, referred to as "Shay's Rebellion," had been put down with force, making lie of the illusion of liberty for which the commoners had fought and died. The two factions went to war, with the northerners emerging victorious in 1865. In 1866, the 14th amendment was added to the North American clique's constitution, allowing for enslavement of anyone, so long as the "due process of law" was followed; fearing the possibility of someone from outside their number actually achieving high office, in 1867 the "Tenure of Office" act was passed, limiting the scope of power allowed to elected figureheads. These were among the last acts of the "old-line" North American aristocracy; in 1870, with the founding of the Standard Oil Company, John D. Rockefeller, a member of the new breed of American Teuton/Zionist confederation, inaugurated the "new-line" American elite.

Occult societies, based along the lines established by the Teutons and Zionists, began taking root in North America; Helena Petrovna Blavatsky, owner of businesses in Philadelphia, established her Theosophical Society — allied with the Thule Society, the Vril Society, and Aleister Crowley's Golden Dawn — in New York City in 1875, the same year as Mary Baker Eddy founded her Christian Science movement in Massachusetts. In this, they followed the lead of Freemason Joseph Smith, who founded the Mormon Church (Latter-Day Saints) as a rival form of Freemasonry in 1830, and Charles Taze Russell, who established the Jehovah's Witnesses in 1871. The following decade saw the publication of Nietzsche's *Alse Sprach Zarathustra* and James Frazer's *The Golden Bough.* After the ritual sacrifice of several prostitutes in Whitechapel, London (which in itself solved a sticky problem for the Royal Family there), the northern European clique, in a final putsch, seized control of the Italian government, thereby surrounding the heavily-infiltrated, but as yet not submissive, Vatican power structure. That the Vatican had lost much of its glamour was true; but the power of the Papacy still extended to a sizable population of Catholics worldwide, posing a very real threat to northern clique interests. In AD 1897, the Teutonic/Zionist clique held a full meeting at Basel, Switzerland, and laid the groundwork for their plans for domination of those territories not yet directly under their control. Included in these discussions were plans for an Holocaust, a massive extermination-sacrifice of European Jewry and others. The US faction, powerful but not yet as powerful as they would become, opposed the plan, seeing no reason for such conquest — during this and the ensuing period, the US faction pursued a policy of relative isolationism, caring little for what happened outside their immediate sphere of influence. In 1906, back in Northern Germany, the Teutonic/Zionist clique began designing their new and revamped military machine. In order to effect the Holocaust, all of Europe would have to be brought under one totalitarian government, and in 1914, the T/Z clique began "The World War" in order to subjugate Europe, expecting an easy victory, with the US clique remaining isolated and uninvolved. 1917 was an eventful year; the US clique entered the war, ensuring victory for the factions fighting the T/Z clique, the British Fascists announced their support for a Jewish homeland in Palestine (in order to thwart the T/Z clique's plans for mass sacrifice), and a new band of upstarts, backing the Bolsheviks, overthrew the T/Z aligned Tsarist clique in Russia.

The following year saw the defeat of the T/Z clique and the end of the war. Resentment ran high; British Fascists were angered by US clique intervention in what they saw as an European situation; for the first time in many years, all the sub-factions of the T/Z clique — from the various societies (Thule, Vril, etc.) to the unaligned but thoroughly-Teutonic bourgeoisie — were united in their determination to enact "The Final Solution," the mass sacrifice of "useless" races to their deities, in order to ensure absolute world dominion. In 1919, the Thule society, pre-eminent among the Teutonic orders, founded the National Socialist (Nazi) party, in order to drum up popular support for another war; they also sought useful allies elsewhere. The British Fascists, tied closely to Thule via other related orders (Golden Dawn, Theosophical Society, and the British Israelite movement, among others) offered their support covertly: White Russian Fascists, enraged at their treatment at the hands of the Bolsheviks, vowed their support as well. In 1922, the northern clique, acting in a unity never before seen, backed an Italian Fascist, Benito Mussolini, in a takeover bid that brought Italy into line with the T/Z clique's designs. That same year, Josef Stalin, an emotionally unstable but seemingly sympathetic dictator, took power in Russia. By 1929, the Italian Fascists were able to say that the Fascist takeover of the Vatican hierarchy was complete, and the Lateran Treaty, making the Vatican a sovereign state, was signed. By careful manipulation, the T/Z clique was able to topple the US clique's national economy in 1929; the following year saw the Nazi party begin its meteoric rise to power in Germany, and by 1933, regular ritual sacrifice of Jews had been reinstated, growing steadily (albeit slowly) each year for the rest of that decade, to be stepped up dramatically after 1940.

The British Fascists, playing both sides of the coming conflict, retained good relations on both sides of the Atlantic; while the US clique was temporarily unable to strike back at the T/Z clique for destroying their economy, they could, and did, cause the Teutonic/Zionists to lose face, somewhat, by destroying the pride of Germany, the airship Hindenburg, on US soil. The Spanish Fascists, under Francisco Franco, quashed an attempted takeover by commoners and anarchists in 1939, rendering the majority of Europe Fascist-controlled.

The T/Z clique, feeling that the time was ripe, began the Second World War. Unbeknownst to the forces that prepared to oppose them, two T/Z physicists, Otto Hahn and Fritz Strassman, achieved nuclear fission, the first step toward modern nuclear weapons, that same year (1939). It appeared that the T/Z clique would emerge from the rubble victorious; they had not, however, considered the possibility of a "wild card" in their own ranks. The US clique had long been borderline Fascists themselves, and had maintained a network of infiltrators in the ranks of the various secret societies of the T/Z network. One of these, the highly-ranked Rudolph Hess — who had, indeed, been a most trusted member of Thule — gathered all the extant paperwork on Hahn and Strassman's work in nuclear fission, and flew to England in May of 1941, trading the clique's atomic secrets for immunity and a new identity. The Teutonic/Zionist clique suddenly found themselves betrayed in the worst way; not only was their hope of using the new technology dashed, but due to poor communications, the Japanese — acting on a plan arranged in 1933 — forced the US clique to enter the war directly in December of that year. Though messages were sent to call off the plan, they were never received — or, if received, ignored; Japan had been promised dominion over the western two-thirds of the North American landmass, from the Mississippi River to the Pacific Ocean. That this arrangement was known to the US clique is a possibility, and would explain the internment of Japanese in the US; I cannot say, though, as I have not found any proof, one way or the other.

With the loss of the secrecy surrounding their nuclear weapons research, and facing the possibility that the US clique would win the race to perfect the new technology, the Teutonic/Zionist clique stepped up their efforts at propitiating their gods. Sacrifices of Gypsies, Slavs, the ill and infirm, Jewish commoners, and Catholics was stepped up dramatically; the clique still believed, at this point, that victory could be assured if only the requisite amount of blood sacrifice were performed. Hess, however, was not the only sympathizer within the ranks of the Teutons to see the US clique's rising star. The list of highly-ranked members of the Nazi front to make deals with the more Fascist elements of the US clique — including Goring, Bormann, the aforementioned Hess, Himmler, Shaub,

Gehlen, and numerous others — agrees in great detail with a list of those who, after the war, held positions of trust in what came to be called the "Intelligence Community," the business-financial community, and the social elite, or "Cafe Society." The fact — as I myself have seen in the archives, as well as having seen in my travels — that contrary to the popular deception, the Teutonic/Zionist hierarchy, the real power of the old Prussian clique, was not defeated, but rather was absorbed by the worst elements of the US clique, with the help of the English clique and the subverted Vatican hierarchy. It had been this same action of the US clique that had initially inspired many of the practices of the more "scientifically-minded" Teutonic scientists; practices against the mentally ill and against the native American tribes in the latter part of the nineteenth and early part of the twentieth centuries had inspired the infamous "medical experiments" of the concentration camps. Indeed, one of the conditions of absorption into the US clique, binding upon both the Teutonic and Japanese factions (these three who went on to form the Trilateral Commission) was that the documentation of the results of their experiments be given, fully and freely, to their new masters.

While the Japanese experiments in sonic disruption of living tissue are not yet fully utilized, the biological and genetic findings of the Teutons have borne much fruit, as I shall relate. The Zionist faction, glad to share power but desiring their own base, were given Palestine. The Teutonic clique, with its intricate ties to the other old aristocracies, shifted the actual center of power to the United States. All would have gone their way, were it not for further wild cards in the deck. Indeed, the reshuffling left new cliques arising: the new Russian clique, distrustful of their neighbors to the west; the Muslim clique, resentful, and possessed of an important commodity beneath their shifting sands; and the Anarchists, present for nearly a century but now gaining in popular support; as well as minor factions — all told, while the greater part of the new order favored the heirs of the old aristocracy and the still-rising US clique, total control was not theirs. In 1949, the new Russian clique detonated their first nuclear weapon; the Vatican issues a Papal Bull decreeing excommunication for any Roman Catholic who either practices or preaches Communism, and Senator Joseph McCarthy inaugurates a new witch-hunt, aimed at Communist infiltrators in the lower ranks of the apparatus that served the US/Teutonic/Zionist elite. Recent events show that the Russian clique may well be seeking entry into the ranks of the elite, threatened as they are by the Anarchists, and nearly totally dependent on the West; however, it is too soon to tell. That the order worships vengeful deities, demanding the ritual sacrifice of innocent victims, may be among the most unbelievable of my assertions. It must be realized that the heirs of the clique's power are as well the heirs of their practices and superstitions. If it seems odd to us, raised accepting Christianity (in one form or another) as the operative mode of understanding, that there would be those, seemingly as civilized as ourselves, who would practice such blasphemous rites, let it be understood that to these the worship and propitiation of other gods is the norm; whether by coincidence and circumstance, or by actual intervention of demonic influence, the majority of these sacrifices seem to them, to have worked.

The elite are an insular, clannish clique, given to raging idiosyncrasies and immense deposits of superstition. Their insulation from the rest of us, and from the world which we inhabit, has rendered them emotionally undeveloped, incapable of loving, of caring, of giving — to them, the sacrifice of an innocent is no more noteworthy than the swatting of an annoying fly, and eminently more useful. In the United States alone, more than thirty thousand people — including a growing number of young children, always a preferred victim — disappear each year, without a trace. This must be taken in context; there are of course a fair number of individuals who, for whatever reason, choose to disappear — but these would form, at the very most, perhaps a third (though likely much less) of the total number. What of the others? From documentation I have seen, and conversations with my ecclesiastical superiors, it is said that the majority of these disappearances can be traced directly to such functioning cults as that operated by [name deleted] who, when not operating his cult during off-hours, practices as warrior-priest for the Presidio military bases' own congregation, presiding, in the grottos beneath the base, over ritual sexual abuse of, and quite often ritual sacrifice of, children and young adults. While the names used to identify the one underlying cult change from locale to locale, and while a bewildering array of deities — seemingly representing every pre-Christian cult ever to exist — are invoked, it is ultimately the Teutonic/Zionist pantheon, the Zionist YHWH in conjunction with the Germanic gods, (though there are scattered references to the Zionist elite worshipping only their own god) that are the ultimate object of the clique's worship. Yet, for all their power, their empire stands on a less-than-firm foundation. Internal rifts are common; while united in theory, various factions pursue different policies. Intertribal antagonism is common. Even the agenda of the factions within the clique differ.

The identities of the Teutonic/Zionist clique are well-guarded; even their higher servants are protected by the anonymity of immense wealth and the power attendant upon it. We speak here of individuals of such status that their kith and kin are referred to as an 'house,' not a 'family.' Among these are the House of Windsor, absolute masters until very recently of the worlds trade in narcotics; the House of Rhodes and the

House of Rothschild, with their immense holdings in land and in gold; also included, albeit grudgingly, in the elite are the upstart Houses of Onassis and Ibn Saud, who vie for position alongside the established Houses — the Williamsons, the Lodges, the Cabots, and Bierces; the Carnegies, the relative newcomers Rockefeller, the Buchanans, Browns, and Raleighs; the capitalist "johnny-come-latelys" — a class that includes the aforementioned Rockefellers — is represented by Fords and Hearsts as well as the Bradfords, Bryans, and those underlings among the managerial elite who would marry among them. Due to the phenomenon of "dynastic marriage," it may be rightly said that there are not 100 families, not 25 families, but one family, a tribe unto themselves, who hold the reigns of power, control the destinies of multitudes, eat the wealth of nations, and drink the profane chalice of horror — for the hereditary priestcraft of the Teutonic/Zionist elite is the exclusive venue, in its purest form, of the elite-by-blood. Whether the demon being worshiped is Yahweh the Zionist Solar God, or Angra Mainyu Agni of the syncretic Teutonic cult, the primary requirement for correct worship is blood connexion, lineal descent if at all possible, in the priestly line.

"Secret societies" — such as the Freemasons, the Priory of Zion, and the post-Vatican Templars — serve as sub-sects to the main body of the T/Z clique's religion. For the Zionists, the lines of demarcation are much tighter; "Old Money" is the only money, and Kohens are still trained in proper ritual for sacrifice — admittedly in lieu of a consecrated temple — in a special *shul* for Kohens, located in Jerusalem. There can be no question that the Zionist state of Israel shall, one day, with Teutonic/US backing, drive the Moslems from the Temple Mount and destroy the (to them) blasphemous Dome of the Rock. In this respect, the Teutons are more fortunate, in that unholy slaughter of children can take place at the hand of an [name deleted], in the grotto beneath the Presidio, and carry full validity.

Current policies of the elite regarding the general estate of the commoners, as I myself have seen and read, is telling. While a policy of division, factionalism and antagonism is the order of the day (particularly in the United States, where what must be the most diversified population on Earth is kept in a state of turmoil by divisive legislation intended to provoke interracial strife and social stratification), there are two primary schools of thought regarding the actual use to which the subjects are to be put.

While there is general agreement across the board with the notion that the commoners must be downbred, in order to reduce their intelligence and make them less apt to rise up in rebellion, a large faction — who appear to be holding sway — counsel a massive slaughter of the majority of the "useless eaters." I say that they seem to be holding sway, as documents I have seen tell of the introduction of an engineered virus, Acquired Immunodeficiency Syndrome (AIDS) into the population by the World Health Organization smallpox vaccination program in Africa, and simultaneously by medical experiments on promiscuous male homosexuals in New York City. Current thought seems to be that only "Third World" ethnicities were targeted, but in fact the plan appears to be to reduce the world population overall to more manageable numbers; these survivors may then be limited as to reproduction, numbers maintained at just the level necessary to insure a force of slaves.

The reason behind this reduction is among the most frightening revelations I feel I shall make: according to the best estimates of clique-employed climatologists, the world — contrary to the current "greenhouse effect" story — is drawing inexorably toward another glaciation. The "Ice Ages" are always spoken of in the past tense, always treated as occurrences in prehistory, never to be repeated; however, glaciation has been the norm for this world since roughly two million years ago; alternating cycles of glaciation and warm interstadial, following an approximate one-hundred-thousand year cycle (ninety thousand years of glaciation, followed by ten thousand of interstadial, plus or minus as much as two thousand years) are the normal climate of our Earth, since the end of the Pliocene era (or perhaps slightly earlier). When the icesheets once again advance, it is the plan of the elite to move the trappings of civilization south, a forced march of laden slaves to the southern hemisphere (the glaciers cover only the northern portion climes), and to this end, "house-cleaning" has already begun. AIDS ravages primarily (though not exclusively) third-world populations, hence the southern lands will be defenseless; massive tracts are already being cleared and prepared for construction in South America, and North America — expected to be covered, by the middle of the twenty-second century, with a two-mile-thick blanket of ice — is being treated as a garbage bin, industrial effluvia of the most noxious varieties being poured out all over the land; it will cease to be of use to the elite, ergo it must be rendered useless to anyone else. Even the most dangerous of the industrial wastes will break down and be reassimilated by the soil in ninety thousand years, hence, when the ice clears, a trek back to the North will be possible, if desired. In the interim, the commoners are kept palliated, entertained, too busy to investigate the world around them — and reduced, by slow attrition of incurable disease, to a desired size. I wish that I could say that there is some sustained, organized resistance within the lower ranks of the Church. Indeed, there is not. I wish I could say that some faction among the elite held more humane views; I cannot. Briefly, there was hope. John Fitzgerald Kennedy, a drunkard and a boor, perhaps the best of a very bad lot (the Kennedy clan) had some pretensions to fulfilling his baptismal vows, if only in the breach. He had some desire to treat the slaves humanely. He was used to set an example to any others who might attempt to defy the higher-ups, to over-reach the boundaries set up by the various factions of the elite. So much for political help. John Paul I attempted to wrest control of the Vatican away from the Marcinkus clique; an example was made of him, also. Far from discouraging, however, is the fact that such occurrences could be at all — such is a sign of the internal disunity of the elite.

This, however, is all the hope that I can offer: that a concerted effort could well be all that is needed to topple these insular few from their lofty perch. To what end? Overthrow will not solve, in and of itself, the terrible troubles of our age, hunger, disenfranchisement, disease — but it will end the onslaught of troubles from higher echelons. Overpopulation is as much a problem to the slaves as to the masters, disease must and will run its course, hunger will be ended only in the way it has always ended, by reducing the population to levels which can be supported by the Earth; nonetheless, I for one would infinitely prefer to be culled by the natural forces empowered by the Almighty, *Divinum auxilium maneat semper nobiscum,* than by the designs of an elite who choose to play at being gods. *Sint lumbi vestri praecincti et lucernae ardentes in manibus vestris; ad societatem civium supernorum perducat nos Rex Angelorum.* I am hardly the first to speak of a conspiracy; I have read and enjoyed fictitious works which embodied various aspects of the stratification of power within their storylines, and know that theories regarding this or that "secret society" holding sway over the courser of events are a popular form of speculation. I realize that mine is but one more voice added to the cacaphony, perhaps to be lost in the tumult; indeed, the very documents that I have seen include ideas, plans, for the sort of "disinformation" lamented by many, produced for the purpose of misleading those rare few who spend not all of their time pacified by popular amusements. How are you to know that I speak the truth? You cannot. You can verify for yourself the historical facts which I have presented, which form the gist of my own notes, copied laboriously from the original papers at the Vatican archives and supplemented by information gleaned from other clerics and servants of God, but this, I understand, cannot be taken as a guarantee of veracity. I have divulged what I know; I must ask to remain forever anonymous. I am not a young man, strong-willed and inspired; nor yet an old man, who may plead his years: I am but a weak man, seemingly alone, and very much afraid, *mea maxima culpa.* Though I cannot offer verification beyond what the diligent scholar might find in a careful examination of historical texts, and must admit that this my recounting of the facts as known to me is, of necessity, but a skeleton of the whole story, concentrating on only the most important (to my mind) aspects of the history of the struggle, I offer it in the hope that at least some might be moved to action. If my sharing of what I know saves, or even merely betters, one life, then I have in some small way striven to fulfill my vow of service to my fellow-children of God. *Maiorem caritatem nemo habet ut animam suam ponat quis pro amicis suis;* would that I had such strength. Such is the gist of my knowledge of the situation; I hope that this casts some light on your interest in the takeover of the Vatican. I have endeavored to keep this recounting to manageable length; I could have told somewhat more, but it would only add detail to the overall picture presented here, and I believe that the total situation is best and most accurately depicted in broad, bold strokes. I offer you only those proofs of my sincerity as cannot be traced to me, for obvious reasons; *nunc dimittis servum tuum. Absterget Deus omnem lacrimam ab oculis sanctorum.* a servant of servants...

Pravda cartoon showing U.S. scientist and military officer exchanging a vial of AIDS virus for money.

AIDS
Act of God or the Pentagon?

G.J. Krupey

AIDS still retains its controversial mien even if the initial hysteria, whipped up by media sensation-mongering and hate-mongering by the religious right, has been tempered somewhat as the feared "gay plague" failed to materialize as a "Black Death" style pandemic sweeping away all life in its path worldwide.

But hysteria is still bubbling under the surface along with the concomitant threat of reactionary panic that always accompanies public freak-outs. Recent demands from some quarters, that AIDS-stricken health care workers must submit to mandatory AIDS testing and be potentially liable for criminal prosecution, is just one more proof of that.

Confusion still reigns in the public forum on the AIDS question, and bigotry still dominates the discourse. AIDS is a many-faceted subject that taxes the patience and often the credulity of even the most "objective" non-partisan investigator. It is a mystery that seems to become only more mysterious the more one studies it; where one Hydra head is chopped off, two more reappear. Certainly the most important question to those already suffering from AIDS is how to cure it, how to prevent it. At this point, the question as to what causes AIDS is secondary, and there is a host of contradictory theories as to what the source or sources of AIDS may be.

It is not my purpose here to summarize or debate those theories. Instead I will focus on the theory, once quite popular in some circles but seems to have fallen by the wayside: that AIDS was the result, deliberate or accidental, of chemical-biological warfare research by the US military.

On June 9, 1969 there appeared before the House of Representatives Subcommittee on Department of Defense Appropriations for 1970 one Dr. Donald M. MacArthur, Deputy Director for the DOD's Research and Technology and a former manager for the Chemistry and Life Sciences Research Center of Melpar. At Melpar, Dr. MacArthur "was responsible for the management and direction of a large number of defense and space programs representing a broad spectrum of disciplines from instrumentation engineering to biology. These programs represented applied research in the physical and life sciences..."[1] Dr. MacArthur was one of five witnesses, three scientists and two military officers, appearing before the subcommittee to testify on the progress of US military Chemical-Biological Warfare programs and to see appropriations for more money to develop the programs even further.[2] Dr. MacArthur spoke on the subject of "Synthetic Biological Agents". He said:

"Molecular biology is a field that is advancing very rapidly, and eminent biologists believe that within a period of five to ten years it would be possible to produce a synthetic biological agent that does not naturally exist and for which no natural immunity could have been acquired."[3]

To the question of Florida Representative Robert L.F. Sikes as to whether the US was then currently engaged in such research, MacArthur answered in the negative. When Sikes, either a naif or a laconic wit, asked "Why not? Lack of money or lack of interest?", MacArthur bluntly replied, "Certainly not lack of interest."

Sikes then asked MacArthur to provide the subcommittee with information on the requirements, advantages, time and costs of such a program. MacArthur provided an outline of observations from "a small group of experts" who had considered the matter. In summary, he noted that:

1. — All presently known biological agents representing "naturally occurring disease," are known to scientists worldwide, and "are easily available to qualified scientists for research, either for offensive or defensive purposes."

2. — "Within the next 5 to 10 years, it would probably be possible to make a new infective micro-organism which could differ in certain important aspects from any known disease-causing organisms. Most important of these is that it might be refractory to the immunological and therapeutic processes upon which we depend to maintain our relative freedom from infectious disease."

3. — "A research program to explore the feasibility of this could be completed in approximately five years at a total cost of ten million dollars."

4. — Such a program would be difficult to establish due to the relative newness of the molecular biology field. The field has few "highly competent scientists" and most are in private university laboratories and "adequately supported from sources other than DOD." MacArthur did believe it possible "to initiate an adequate program through the National Academy of Sciences – National Research Council.

"The matter was discussed with the NAS-NRC in such a controversial endeavor have led us to postpone it for the past 2 years."

MacArthur concluded by saying:

"It is a highly controversial issue, and there are many who believe such research should not be undertaken lest it lead to yet another method of massive killing of large populations. On the other hand, without the sure scientific knowledge that such a weapon is possible, and an understanding of the ways it could be done, there is little that can be done to devise defensive measures.

"Should an enemy develop it there is little doubt that this is an important area of potential military technological inferiority in which there is no adequate research program."[4]

It could be merely coincidence, but the theoretical disease that Dr. MacArthur refers to in his testimony (see #2 above), which would be "refractory" (that is, resistant to the immunological and therapeutic processes upon which we depend to maintain our relative freedom from infectious disease), in other words, a germ that would resist the body's own natural system of protecting and healing itself from the ravages of infectious diseases, sounds like Acquired Immune Deficiency Syndrome, AIDS.

After all, what better way to "acquire" an immune deficiency than if somebody put it there? It is interesting to note how, in concluding his pitch for research into the theoretical immuno-suppressive synthetic microbe, Dr. MacArthur raised the ethical objections only to dismiss them, in typical and time-tested Cold War fashion, with the dread raised by the spectre of the "enemy."

MacArthur pleaded for superiority in the Chemical-Biological Warfare race, a "germ gap," so to speak. Earlier in his testimony, he even claimed that "we have to believe [the Soviets] are probably working in the same area."[5] The funds were awarded, and one can only speculate what would have happened if they hadn't been disbursed. But recent revelations about the Pentagon's "Black Budget," the official unaccounted-for billions it receives for whatever purposes it deems fit, make one wonder if such public displays of hat-in-hand begging for military appropriations are shadow plays for the purpose of convincing civilians that the military-industrial establishment still defers to civilian control. MacArthur's testimony shows that considerable study and planning were given beforehand to the idea of "defensive measures" against synthetic biological agents and the program to pursue such research; is it not possible that the research was already being conducted prior to the 6/9/69 hearings, that the whole procedure was merely rubberstamping after the facts?

Perhaps as a result of that "growing criticism of the CB program" in the same year as these hearings, President Nixon declared that the US would no longer produce or use biological warfare agents. Chemical warfare agents were conspicuous by their absence (this was, after all, the era of napalm and Agent Orange in Vietnam).

In 1972 an international treaty banning the use of bio-warfare agents was signed by the US, but Senate ratification did not occur until 1975, leaving three years for R&D to produce some sort of malevolent fruit. But the treaty provided for "defensive" biological warfare research, the same sort of research that Dr. MacArthur assured Congress would be exclusively pursued.

However, the difference between "defensive" and "offensive" biological warfare research is moot if not meaningless, leaving a large enough loophole to render the treaty a figleaf and a charade.

The AIDS epidemic first surfaced in 1981 when reports of the first cases were documented and classified (originally as GRID — Gay Related Immune Deficiency) In retrospect, previously inexplicable cases of deaths due to mysterious factors that fit the AIDS model were found as far back as early 1979. Some researchers have claimed to have found even earlier cases, perhaps as far back as 1976.[6]

Those first cases were found in two groups of gay men in Los Angeles and New York City. The Los Angeles fatalities were due to pneumocistis carinii pneumonia (PCP), a previously rare pneumonia, while the New York deaths resulted from Kaposi's Sarcoma, a slow-developing cancer that begins with skin lesions and works its way into the internal organs. Also previously rare, it was mainly found in elderly men of Mediterranean ethnic origins. Other than the fact that the victims in both scenarios were gay men with weakened immune systems that allowed rare and opportunistic infections to kill them, there was no other evidence to link the cases. But as the numbers of victims skyrocketed, and symptoms that had appeared separately in the New York and Los Angeles cases appeared nationwide, the media began sounding the alarm over the menace of "gay AIDS." AIDS could not have come at a worse time for the gay liberation movement. In the early 1980s, its struggle against bigotry, always an uphill battle, was dealt severe setbacks by the hate campaign orchestrated by the religious right in the late 1970s. While homophobia alone cannot explain Reagan's election to the White House, it didn't hinder it. In effect, the gay community was already suffering from political AIDS when pathological AIDS hit it.

And it didn't take the religious right long to swarm to the attack. It wasn't long before hysterical talk about tattooing AIDS patients for identification, or rounding them all up for quarantine became common, not only among the lunatic fringers of the right, but from mainstream conservatives like William F. Buckley, Jr. and R. Emmett Tyrell, Jr. To the right, AIDS was both symbol and proof of the folly of granting perverts license to wallow in their depravity, maybe even to exist. They well understood the potential the disease contained for swaying the general public away from a grudging acceptance of gay rights back to a position of fear and loathing.

There was certainly good reason for everyone to be concerned with the looming spread of a disease that incapacitated the immune system to the point where catching a common cold or developing an infection from a simple cut could turn into a possible death sentence. And as the disease spread to include such diverse at-risk groups as IV drug users, hemophiliacs, and Haitians, panic and confusion spread with the news. What was going on here, anyway? What was the missing link between the four at-risk groups? Elaborate and often illogical theories were offered to explain that link, as well as the origins of the disease. Among the more ludicrous origin theories, all the more so since it was taken entirely seriously for quite some time, was the African Green Monkey theory. It postulated that the transmission of AIDS began when a human being in Africa was bitten by an AIDS-carrying monkey, or the monkey was eaten by the human, or the human had sex with the monkey. This black African monkey-biter or monkey-fucker eventually transmitted it to a white American homosexual, who infected other gays, etc. The inability to find any natural analog to the AIDS virus in primates hasn't deterred this theory from still finding credence in certain circles or from slipping into urban legend.

Some other culprits considered as the source of AIDS were dioxin, arboviruses (spread by flying insects, like mosquitoes) such as maguari and dengue, Swine Fever Virus, radiation from electrical fields, nutritional deficiencies, inhalation of amyl nitrate "poppers" by gay men (used to enhance and prolong orgasm), and a new strain of syphilis misdiagnosed as a new disease. Proponents of all theories were able to marshal enough facts to make their theory as believable as the next, especially those who could point to AIDS and AIDS-like symptoms in people not fitting the profile of any at-risk group. But it was more difficult to reconcile the various theories to explain the by now (mid '80s) worldwide AIDS pandemic. Brazil was second only to the US in reported cases, and the disease was devastating central Africa, where it was primarily a heterosexual phenomenon.

Was there more than one type of AIDS? It certainly seemed so at times. How else could its far-flung empire of diverse subjects be accounted for? And why now, all at once? Certainly a handful of faggots couldn't be responsible for all this, could they? Gradually the prominence of the "gay plague" began to diminish in importance for all but the most rabid homophobes, who believed AIDS was God's punishment on homosexuals and its spread to non-gays as His wrath at tolerance of them.

There was one other theory on the origin of AIDS: that it was man-made, genetically engineered in some laboratory and released, either accidentally or deliberately, on a world unprepared for it. It was a claim that cut across political and sexual lines, and caused a war of words between the two belligerent superpowers, then at the height of renewed cold war tensions.

On July 4, 1984, the New Delhi, India, newspaper, *The Patriot,* published an article making the first detailed charges of AIDS being a CBW agent. An anonymous American anthropologist was quoted claiming that AIDS was genetically engineered at the US Army's Biological Warfare Laboratory at Fort Detrick, near Frederick, Maryland. To prove its point, articles from the Army's own official magazine *Army Research, Development and Acquisition* were cited. The authors of one cited article were Lt. Col. Karl Pedersen, Jr. and Col. John Albertson, the (then) director of the Institute of Infectious Diseases and Director of the Medical Engineering Laboratory, respectively. The article cited dealt with "natural and artificial influences on the human immune system."[7] The *Patriot* article also claimed that "Fort Detrick scientists, with the help of the Centers for Disease Control, and under Pentagon contract, travelled to Zaire and Nigeria, and then to Latin America, to collect information on a 'powerful virus that could not be found in Europe or Asia."[8]

But it wasn't until the Soviet journal *Literaturnya Gazeta* repeated the charges made by the Indian newspaper on October 30, 1985, that the accusation became an international controversy. The story was picked up worldwide, but American newspapers, predictably, ignored the story until the US government officially denounced the Soviet article as anti-American disinformation, and leaving it at that.

But the Soviets continued to cover the story, quoting two physicians, John Seale, a London venereologist, and Nathanial Lehrman, an American psychiatrist, to back their claims. This gained an official protest from the US ambassador to the Soviet Union.[9] But in 1986, a pair of East German scientists, Jakob and Lilli Segal, issued a 52 page pamphlet, "AIDS: USA Home Made Evil; Not Imported from Africa," which they distributed in English-speaking African countries. Just more commie agit-prop?

The Segals were visited by two American embassy officials in East Berlin on October 10, 1986. "The officials claimed to be a historian and political counsel, respectively. But Segal said, 'I am positive they were from the CIA — and that they were deeply concerned that the cover-up over the origin of AIDS was going to be exposed.' The officials questioned Segal about `what he knows, what he thinks, where he got his information from, and what he intends doing with the report.' The State Department acknowledged sending officials to the Segal home, but said it was merely `to point out the fallacies of the report.'"[10]

This account was found in the *London Sunday Express* of October 26, 1986. This tabloid interviewed Segal (stressing that, although resident of a communist country, he held no particular political views), Seale, and an American, Dr. Robert Strecker, another proponent of the AIDS as bio-warfare agent theory. The *Express* story alarmed the State Department more than any other incident prior to it because it was the first time the charge had been made in a Western paper, and a conservative one at that. On April Fools Day in 1987 the State department accused the *New Delhi Patriot* as being a communist front for publicizing the AIDS as bio-warfare story. (Was this timing merely a coincidence, or does someone in the State Department possess a sophisticated sense of humor?)

Ignored by both sides was the fact that speculations about the possible deliberate deployment of AIDS had circulated throughout the alternative and gay press for years before the *Patriot* story. As an example, a gay newspaper, *New York Native,* ran a letter from an anonymous source who claimed to have worked at Fort Detrick's Biological Warfare Lab, and that it had deliberately released AIDS with the intention to infect gay men as part of a program called "Operation Firm Hand."[11]

In 1969, after Richard Nixon's supposed ban on the production of CBW agents, part of the grounds at Fort Detrick's Biological Warfare Laboratory were renamed the Frederick Cancer Research Facility and given to the National Cancer Institute for "civilian medical research" The military's grounds were also renamed as US Army Medical Research Institute for Infectious Diseases, dedicated exclusively, in conformity with Nixon's great humanitarian crusade, to "defensive" research into CBW. But, "within two years of its foundation, the Institute's staff and budget had trebled."[12]

Even one who does not accept the AIDS as military conspiracy theory must wonder exactly what use the National Cancer Institute and the Army's Bio-Warfare Lab would have for each other. Odder still was the fact that the NCI's AIDS Task Force, directed by Dr. Robert Gallo, announced in 1984 that it had discovered the cause of AIDS, a virus dubbed HIV — Human Immunosuppressive Virus; and this only a year after the search was begun — in conjunction with the Frederick Cancer Research Facility. At first glance this would seem to deny the possibility of Fort Detrick being the birthplace of AIDS. After all, if the military were engaged in a clandestine program to kill off homosexuals or other minorities by disease, why would they let the civilian researchers discover the means by which they did it and threaten to blow their cover?

The government often has its own reasons for leaking otherwise "sensitive information," often highly selective, to certain individuals at special times. If the army accidentally released into the civilian population a biowarfare experiment that became known as AIDS, and felt compelled to find a cure for it, they might find it more expedient to invite civilians, on various "need-to-know" bases, to do the dirty work of cleaning up their mess, possibly even manipulating them into thinking they "discovered" the culprit all by themselves. Remember, Dr. MacArthur was seeking funding for a study of a CBW micro-organism that would be resistant to immunological processes, a disease with no known cure. It isn't likely that army scientists, considering the business they're in, would first think of its cure.

Whether or not the military conceived AIDS, they definitely were curious about it once it became known:

"On February 18, 1987, the *Philadelphia Daily News* carried a McClatchy News Service report that Col. David L. Huxsoll, chief of UAAMRIID, told a meeting of scientists that the Soviet charges [of US creation of AIDS] were unfounded 'disinformation.' In his zeal to disprove the allegations, Huxsoll reportedly added, '...studies at the Army laboratories have shown that the AIDS virus would be an extremely poor biological warfare agent.' When contacted by the author [Robert Lederer] Huxsoll denied having made the statement... The McClatchy reported told the author that Huxsoll had been quite clear. 'He specifically said that once it [AIDS] surfaced, they screened it as they do any infectious agent. He said they had definitely looked at it."[13]

The Pentagon itself admitted in a press release in April, 1987 that it was involved in research to find a cure for AIDS. But why? What possible motivation could the military, of all institutions, have in combatting AIDS? What would be its reason for helping to find a cure for a disease that primarily infects gays and non-white peoples? Compassion? Not bloody likely.

The military's interest in a cure for AIDS is more sinister. According to a 1987 story in a California newspaper[14], "The US military is stockpiling vaccines and drugs to be used to protect the armed forces — but not civilians — during a biological war... But the military's research in the field — including a search for an anti-AIDS drug — is unclassified, and the treatments do find non-military uses, said Col. David L. Huxsoll."

Col. Huxsoll, whom we have previously met, claimed that the institute had developed "16 vaccines and drugs against natural toxins and viruses," but didn't have the "budgets big enough to lay down a sizable stockpile of these kinds of materials." What the military did have was stockpiles "intended for about 3 million people, including all the armed forces, reservists, and the national guard." Colonel Huxsoll maintained that the researchers at Fort Detrick did not over-step the bounds of the anti-biowarfare treaty. "Talking about altering an organism, I'm not going to try to second-guess how somebody could alter that... There's enough bad organisms out there that you don't have to fiddle around and make new ones." He related that after animal-testing of a drug or vaccine, tests were then made on humans, "volunteer servicemen." According to Dr. Jacob Segal, the testees were neither "volunteers" nor servicemen, but prisoners promised their freedom for their participation as guinea pigs. These contaminated ex-cons then were set loose to spread the AIDS virus with which they had been infected.

Colonel Huxsoll didn't mention the Pentagon's other plans, made public less than a year before, to contain the spread of AIDS by "mandatory and overt identification" of AIDS inflicted by a "Star of David" concept — as in the yellow badges Jews in Nazi Germany were required to wear in public, all the easier to identify them when it came time to cart them off to concentration camps. This seems to have been a proposal the Pentagon was keeping on hold until the right time, such as when public hysteria reached a high enough peak for such a blatantly authoritarian proposal to become palatable to the masses.[15]

The proposal, based on the completely false claim that AIDS can be transmitted through casual contact (such as touching a doorknob or toilet seat), "was initiated by two [San Francisco] Bay Area-based centers with a long history of military research... AIMS (Advanced Investigation of Medical Science) Group, has done classified work on biological and chemical warfare... [and] the Hoover Institute, the anti-Soviet think tank which lists Ronald Reagan as an honorary member."[16] Another Hoover Institute member embroiled in the AIDS controversy was the late philosopher Sidney Hook, who was active in the US counter-campaign against Soviet claims of US engineering of AIDS. To Hook, anyone who suggested the possibility of AIDS being the product of US military research, such as Dr. Robert Strecker, was a Soviet disinformation agent. A self-described "humanist" and "democratic socialist," Hook's membership in the reactionary Hoover Institute and "loyal oppositionist" defense of the US government raise some interesting questions.

Again it must be asked, what was the Pentagon up to with this frightening proposal? To round up and eliminate the loose ends of their botched experiment, perhaps? What jurisdiction does the military have in a public health crisis, and more importantly in a supposed democracy, should it have any? Was AIDS an agent provocateur created to produce just the sort of internal "clear and present danger" that would justify suspension of civil liberties and the imposition of martial law?

If the military-security apparatus did indeed create AIDS and targeted homosexuals as scapegoats, how was it accomplished? The answer might lie in the trial of a hepatitis B vaccine conducted in New York City in November, 1978. Candidates were specified to be only non-monogamous males between the ages of 20 and 40, and according to one source[17], "homosexuals received a different vaccine from heterosexuals." The tests were conducted under the auspices of the National Institutes of Health and the Center for Disease Control, two institutions that would figure prominently later in the AIDS story. Between 1040 and 1083 gay men were inoculated. Two months later, in January, 1979, the first known case of AIDS was diagnosed. By 1981, 25-50% of those homosexual men who had received the vaccine had AIDS. By 1984, it was 64%, the figures for subsequent infection rates of participants in that suspicious study are allegedly "unavailable", safe in the hands of the Justice Department.[18]

Then, in 1982, more gay men were "vaccinated" in Chicago, St. Louis, Denver, Los Angeles, and San Francisco, a total of 1402.[19] The gay plague was on.

But if this "vaccination program" was the source of the AIDS virus among the white homosexuals, what is the connection to Haitians, IV drug users, and hemophiliacs? And what is the source of the nearly continent-wide AIDS plague in Africa?

The official mainstream media AIDS theory, courtesy of Dr. Robert Gallo, official (American) discoverer of HIV/HTLV-III, went like this: AIDS originated in Africa (remember the Green Monkey) where it was transmitted to Haitian teachers in the former Belgian Congo. These Haitians brought back with them to Haiti, where slumming white gay American tourists contracted it from Haitian male prostitutes — and the rest is history. Obviously IV drug users are brought into this easily, some gay junkie supposedly passing his needle to another though non-gay junkie. Hemophiliacs come in from contaminated blood supplies.

But what is the origin of AIDS in Africa? Both human beings and green monkeys have co-existed in Africa for countless eras, why did this disease suddenly surface in the late twentieth century? Why not earlier? Why now?

"An attempt should be made to ascertain whether viruses can in fact exert selective effects on immune function, e.g. by affecting T cell function as opposed to B cell function. The possibility should also be looked into that the immune response to the virus itself may be impaired if the infecting virus damages more or less selectively the cells responding to the viral antigens."[20]

That was not from Dr. MacArthur`s testimony before Congress in 1969, but comes from a 1972 bulletin of the United Nations' World Health Organization. Once again it would appear that AIDS or something that preceded it, was on the minds of many researchers prior to its official "discovery."

On May 11, 1987, on a front-page, headline story, the *London Times* declared "Smallpox Vaccine Triggered AIDS". The vaccination program took place throughout Africa in the mid-1970s and was conducted by WHO. In exactly those areas where the WHO vaccination program was undertaken are to be found the areas most devastated by AIDS. It would be interesting to know who was the major funder of the program, and which nation furnished the key personnel.[21]

According to Dr. Robert Strecker, AIDS was predicted (and in medical science, prediction does not so much mean a projection into the future of a personal opinion, but making an educated guess based on probabilities and knowledge of current research in the field) as early as 1975 by a cancer researcher from Denmark, a J. Corbensen, who, at a convention of cancer researchers in Tokyo warned that a pandemic — a worldwide epidemic — of viral cancer was imminent. He warned that it would cause more deaths than the great flu epidemic of 1918, which killed an estimated one-fifth to one-third of the world's population, and blamed it all on scientists irresponsibly growing animal viruses in human tissue cell culture. When contacted by Dr. Strecker regarding his predictions, Corbensen denied ever having made the speech, despite its being printed in the *Bibliographica Haemologica,* a professional journal, the same year. (22) Corbensen worked for, according to Dr. Strecker, the World Health Organization.

Dr. Strecker himself deserves more attention. He got into AIDS research by accident. A private practitioner from the Los Angeles area, he and his brother Ted, a lawyer, were asked to prepare a proposal for a HMO (Health Maintenance Organization) for Security Pacific Bank of California. What they needed to know was how much money for potential AIDS treatments for infected employees their health insurance would be required to pay out. In their research, the Strecker brothers came to the stunning conclusion that AIDS was a man-made disease, that it was not a homosexual disease nor a venereal disease, that it could be carried and transmitted by mosquitoes, that there were at least six different AIDS viruses worldwide, and that condoms would not prevent the spread of AIDS. AIDS was, Dr. Strecker concluded, actually a form of viral cancer, and contagious. He theorized that AIDS was a hybrid, the splicing together of bovine (cow) leukemia virus and sheep visna (brain-rot) virus, a lethal combination and one hard to understand as emerging spontaneously from nature.

Dr. Strecker's vision of a humanity infected with the fatal product of some military research laboratory gone insane is a grim one. He estimated the complete decimation of Africa by the turn of the century, and the complete overnight death of Japan. Strecker warned that unless a cure for AIDS was found — soon — that the entire human race faced extinction.

Strecker's opinions were treated by the mass media in the usual fashion: he was either ridiculed or simply ignored. He was one of those accused by Sidney Hook of being a Soviet disinformation agent. Strecker may be an alarmist with a particularly pessimistic viewpoint, but for a man who supposedly doesn't know what he is talking about, strange and tragic coincidences have plagued him since he began to lecture the public on the real cause of AIDS and its creator(s). The first of these was the mysterious death of his brother Ted, who helped him pursue the AIDS investigation. He was found dead of a gunshot wound in his Springfield, Missouri home on August 11, 1988, apparently self-inflicted. Dr. Strecker admits that "in the past he suffered from depression and monumental frustration at the relative lack of interest in his findings."

Dr. Strecker spoke with him the night before his death. Ted was cheerful, in good spirits, and looking forward to certain new developments that promised progress. The next day he was found dead, his 22 caliber rifle next to him. No note, no message, no goodbyes to anyone. "Very untypical of him."[23]

Another fatality close to Dr. Strecker was Illinois State Representative Douglas Huff who was found dead in his home of an overdose of heroin and cocaine on September 22, 1988. Huff had been beating the drum on the AIDS cover-up in both the Illinois State House and through the media, one of the few politicians who took Dr. Strecker seriously enough to try to present his views to a larger and a more influential audience.

Perhaps Dr. Strecker's brother really committed suicide in a fit of deep depression. Perhaps Rep. Huff was only a drug-addled paranoid trying to gain notoriety. Perhaps that is exactly the impression somebody wanted these two men to leave behind them, in order to discredit themselves and Dr. Strecker.[22]

Perhaps the main reason why the AIDS-Biowarfare conspiracy theory seems to be less palatable to many these days might have something to do with the discrediting of the HIV-AIDS theory as a foundation to be built upon, the emergence of new, alternative treatments and therapies that have had much success in helping AIDS patients to regain their health and lives and cast serious doubt upon the official CDC/NIH position on HIV. AIDS patients treated as if they were suffering from syphilis, given massive doses of penicillin and typhoid vaccine showed remarkable turnaround. Co-factors were begun to be seen as increasingly important, and even Dr. Luc Montagnier who isolated HIV before Robert Gallo (Montagnier called it LAV and decided to share credit for its discovery — and royalties for the blood test which detects the antibody to the virus — with Gallo after a long litigation that included a war of words between the US and French governments, and donate the royalties to an AIDS research foundation. All this while people were dying slow, lingering deaths) has now repudiated the HIV hypothesis, claiming that the real culprits are mycoplasmas, microbes that seem to be the deadly co-factor to the HIV virus.[25]

Yet while research continues to unravel the mystery surrounding the cause of AIDS, disturbing connections to military germ warfare continue to arise.

A scientist with the US Armed Forces Institute of Pathology in Washington, Shyh-Ching Lo, identified a previously unknown infectious agent in people with AIDS, a mycoplasma microbe which caused AIDS-like symptoms and death in monkeys, something that the injection of merely HIV into animals has supposedly never done. Lo named his discovery VLIA for Virus Like Infectious Agent. Lo has kept a low profile, partially because "army security is keeping a very tight lid on Dr. Lo's findings."[26]

Once again the military's interest in this phenomenon raises questions as to the nature of their concern with AIDS. Why does the military always seem to be hovering on the periphery of AIDS research, if not in the middle of it? The government's, especially the military's, covert experimentations on unwitting American citizens, both individuals and large populations, is precedented and documented, more than can be summarized here[27]. So it hardly seems responsible to dismiss those who insist upon a military connection to AIDS as mere paranoids or political opportunists until serious investigations into the matter have been made.

Unfortunately, such investigations, should they be conducted, would encounter one greater obstacle after another, because the problem is not merely the military and any covert biowarfare experiments (or worse) that it may be conducting, but the entire system. Now more than ever, the American government is a power unto itself, the apparatus that serves the interests of an elite, amoral clique and not that of the people as a whole. To expect truth and justice from a state that can block every inquiry with the excuse of "national security" is to expect too much. To solve the

AIDS mystery may well require a radical cure of more than a medical nature.

Endnotes

1) Department of Defense Appropriations for 1970, Hearings Before a Subcommittee of the Committee of Appropriations, House of Representatives, Ninety-first Congress. First Session, Part 6, Chemical and Biological Warfare, Monday, June 9, 1969, p. 104. U.S. Government Printing Office, Washington, 1969.

2) The other witnesses were: Dr. B. Harris, Deputy Assistant Director of Chemical Technology, DDR&E Dr. K.C. Emerson, Acting Deputy Assistant Secretary of the Army for R&D (Research and Development) Brig. Gen. W.S. Stone, Jr., Director of Materiel Requirements, Headquarters, US Army Materiel Command Col. J.J. Osick, Chief, Systems and Requirements Division, Directorate of CBR and Nuclear Operations, Office of the Asst. Chief of Staff for Force Development.

3) Ibid.

4) Ibid.

5) Ibid.

6) Patton, Cindy; *Sex and Germs: The Politics of AIDS,* 1985, Boston, South End Press, pp. 22-4; Brown, Tony; "What Killed Max Robinson?", *Tri-State Defender,* December 31, 1988

7) Lederer, Robert; "Precedents for AIDS?: Chemical-Biological Warfare. Medical Experiments, and Population Control", *Covert Action Information Bulletin* #28, Summer 1987, pp.36-7.

8) Ibid.

9) Ibid, pp.38-9.

10) Ibid.

11) Ibid, p.36.

12) Ibid, p.40.

13) Ibid.

14) Kiernan, Vincent; "US Storing Vaccines for Military", Hayward, Ca., *The Daily Review.* Wednesday, February 18, 1987.

15) *San Francisco Chronicle,* February 9, 1986; *San Francisco Examiner,* February 9, 1986; both as quoted in Anonymous, "Nazi-Style "'Final Solution' Next?: Pentagon Wants to Brand AIDS Victims," *Worker's Vanguard,* April 11, 1986.

16) Ibid.

17) Waves Forest; "Designer Diseases: AIDS as Biological and Psychological Warfare", *Now What,* #1, Fall 1987, PO Box 768, Monterey, CA 93942.

18) Ibid.

19) Brown, Tony; "What Killed Max Robinson?"

20) Waves Forest; "Designer Diseases"; Douglass, William Campbell, MD, *WHO Murdered Africa,* no date, Clayton, Ga.

21) Brown, Tony; transcript of a speech given by Dr. Robert Strecker May 25, 1990 at the Garvin Theater, Santa Barbara, Ca.

22) Strecker, Robert (?), *Is AIDS Man Made?:* The Strecker Memorandum, no date, The Strecker Group, 1501 Colorado Blvd., Eagle Rock, Ca. 90041.

23) Ibid.

24) Ibid.

25) Farber, Celia and Anthony Liversidge, "AIDS: Words From the Front", *Spin,* September, 1990, p. 71, 87-8; Farber's AIDS column has been a regular feature in Spin, a popular music magazine, since its debut in the February 1988 issue. Farber has covered alternative treatments for AIDS, the controversy over AZT, and the political infighting among AIDS medical researchers (she was apparently the first to spotlight Dr. Peter Duesberg's claim that HIV does not cause AIDS by itself, leading to a debate within her column between Duesberg and Gallo, architect of the official HIV theory). Yet Farber has not, to my knowledge, once mentioned the possibility of the bio-warfare agent theory.

26) Regush, Nicholas; "AIDS: Words from the Front", *Spin,* January, 1990, pp. 69-70.

27) Mitford, Jessica; *Kind and Usual Punishment: The Prison Business,* 1976, New York, Knopf. Jones, James H.; *Bad Blood: The Tuskegee Syphilis Experiment,* 1981, New York, The Free Press. Harris, Robert, and Jeremy Paxman; *A Higher Form of Killing: The Secret Story of Chemical and Biological Warfare,* 1982, New York, Hill and Wang. Consult your library for more depressing examples.

"Clinton Is the Best Guy for Us"

During the 1992 Presidential campaign, New York businessman Harry Katz telephoned David Steiner, President of AIPAC, the powerful Israeli lobby, at AIPAC's offices in Washington, D.C.. Upset with the power and arrogance of the political action committee, Katz recorded his conversation with Steiner and sent out the startlingly blunt transcript to the media. Snippets of the conversation were printed in the Village Voice and made the wire services. Steiner was immediately forced to resign, sacrificed to spin control. AIPAC characterized Steiner's comments as "boasts" that did not necessarily reflect the truth. But what is the truth? In a time of severe budget cuts and tax hikes, President Clinton has vowed not to touch one penny of the money earmarked for Israel.

David Steiner: L'chaim.

Harry Katz: Hello, how are you?

DS: Where are you located?

HK: I'm located in Queens, New York.

DS: Queens ... Far Rockaway?

HK: Belle Harbor.

DS: Belle Harbor. I'm trying to get this list together. Would you ever get into the city?

HK: Sure, I do. Sure, you come frequently?

DS: Well, I come in from time to time. I have an office there, at AIPAC in the city. You know, I want you to understand... where did you get my name and phone number?

HK: Oh, I, um, I called AIPAC...

DS: Yeah.

HK: And ah, I know you're the president of AIPAC.

DS: You should understand that, the political information that I gave you, those are personal choices...

HK: Sure, I understand.

DS: AIPAC does not rate or endorse candidates, does not solicit money...

HK: Yeah, look.

DS: I want you to understand that the choices I would give you are personal choices.

HK: I understand.

DS: I wonder if before ... I want to get together with you next week.

HK: Next week would be fine.

DS: But in the meantime, I wonder if I can have one of my people get together with you and talk to you about it. They'll want to meet you and know who you are and all this. I have a ... maybe if I can have Seth Buchwald call you, my New York director.

HK: That would be terrific.

DS: And we have a guy out there, Joel Schnur. And, are you Orthodox.?

HK: Ah, yes.

DS: Okay, Joel is Orthodox too. I am not.

HK: You're reform or...?

DS: I'm reform.

HK: Okay, let me just say...

DS: I was raised orthodox but I'm reform.

HK: Okay, let me just tell you that, I'll just hold you a minute. I'll be happy to meet with them. I know, I've heard the names, I'd be happy to meet with them, as a matter of fact I could, when I'm in Manhattan ... are you ever in Manhattan?

DS: Sure, today I'm going to be there, but I can't, I'm meeting with the ambassador.

HK: Okay, I'll just ask you very very quickly. You know, like, in New York, you know, this is your own personal opinion, like in New York we have Abrams against D'Amato.

DS: Well, let me tell you what my personal position is. Okay?

HK: Yeah.

DS: From a Jewish point of view, I believe in political loyalty.

HK: Right.

DS: And if someone has been good for Israel, no matter who, if my brother would run against them, I would support them because they'd been good to Israel because that's an important message to people.

HK: Right.

DS: What I'm going to be doing for you...

HK: Now D'Amato, has he been good for Israel?

DS: You couldn't have a better ... listen, I think Abrams would be good too, but that's not the message.

HK: Yeah.

DS: Ah...

HK: So the message, so the message is that ah... I agree with you all the way, that if somebody's been good for Israel, I'll take D'Amato. But you have no complaints with D'Amato?

DS: I have no complaints with D'Amato.

HK: Uh huh, so and ah, you know, let me tell you, Abrams might be, might be too liberal. I don't know if Abrams supported, let's say the ah, the war against Iraq.

DS: Yeah, I don't know, and ah, I don't know. But all I know is if I have a guy who is there and he's doing it, then I don't want to change, you know?

HK: Right. Let me ask you this very quickly and then I will...

DS: I'm going to have Seth call you because in the meantime I'm going to be preparing this list, what I'm doing is, I've asked my friends in the various campaigns, I've made about 30 calls, what I'm trying to put together who needs it the most, you know? Because you could dissipate a million dollars, but the point is to put it where it's going to do the most, I know Bob Kasten, who's been an outstanding friend and needs it I know...

HK: Excuse my ignorance. Bob Kasten is what state?

DS: From Wisconsin...

HK: Okay, is he Jewish?

DS: He's for loan guarantees, he happens to be a Republican.

HK: Okay, and but, he's good? He's...

DS: You couldn't have better.

HK: Is Kasten, Kasten's been very, very good and he's in trouble?

DS: He's in big trouble. Les Aspin, who's the Chairman of the Military Appropriations, a Democrat also from Wisconsin is really [unintelligible].

HK: You mean, Les Aspin is in trouble?

DS: In big trouble.

HK: I can't believe it. I mean, I don't, I don't follow...

DS: Well see, what happened was, you know ah, when you get to know me, I'll put you on my list and I'll be sending all these things. A wealthy businessman decided to run, using all his own money. Aspin, 'cause they sit on the finance committee for Aspin...

HK: Right...

DS: ... programmed the last two weeks of, well, the last month of the campaign, for TV. This guy came in two months early and we didn't have the money budgeted, so we're out scratching around to raise money for him. So we, heck, I told him, I said that I'd go, I'll sign on the bank on a loan for you, you know, that's how important it is.

HK: Unbelievable. You know I read, I won't hold you long, but I'd just tell you this...

DS: That's okay.

HK: ... I'll just tell you this, I read the *New York Post,* and I don't even read the papers too much, I don't follow politics ... are you ready for this?

DS: Yeah.

HK: Get ready for this. I read in the papers this morning, I think it was the *Post,* Barbara Boxer, in California...

DS: Yeah.

HK: ... do you know who she is?

DS: I know who...

HK: She's originally from, ah, New York I think...

DS: A friend of yours?

HK: No, no, no. She's not a friend of mine, but she, ah, I think she's in trouble.

DS: Yeah, in that race we're okay either way, 'cause Bruce Herschensohn, who she's running against, is Jewish, and he's very strong on our issues.

HK: Okay, but Herschensohn...

DS: Herschensohn's a very conservative Republican.

HK: You know, he's come out of nowhere. He was like 30 points behind...

DS: Right.

HK: He's come out of nowhere with it.

DS: Because the truth of the matter is, she didn't always vote for foreign aid. We had a big meeting, I had a program in L.A. I had all four senatorial candidates there, and he ripped her apart. She has always voted against foreign aid.

HK: What about the one, in ah, the one line ... uh, what's his name? I read it in the paper, it's just a shocker, politics is a crazy game. The black woman in Chicago...

DS: Carol Mosely Braun?

HK: She was going to win by 50 points...

DS: Oh it's down, she took the money, it's a big problem.

HK: It's a big problem with her...

DS: And we have a problem with another good friend. You know Daniel Inouye, from Hawaii, he's one of our best friends. It was Kasten-Inouye on the loan guarantees, Kasten-Inouye and Leahy...

HK: I heard, I saw it on, I know Inouye's in trouble because of, he sexually harassed his hairdresser...

DS: We commissioned a poll and got some people, and I've got to raise $27,000 to pay for the poll ... so what I'm trying to do is make a priority list, because I don't know how far you want to go ... how old are your kids by the way? You had three children that could write checks. Do they have their own checking accounts?

HK: Yes.

DS: So that's not going to be...

HK: How old do they have to be?

DS: They can't be one year old.

HK: I mean, could they be 18, 17?

DS: Sure, no problem, nobody's going to bother you, but if you had infants, a four-year-old, let's say, it's not a contest.

HK: Let me tell you, I was planning, I was planning to... Inouye, by the way, is in real trouble? He's been there forever...

DS: Yeah! Well, we might lose him. There's been such a sea change, such trouble this year, I can't believe all our friends that are in trouble. Because there's an anti-incumbency mood, and foreign aid has not been popular. I met with [U.S. Secretary of State] Jim Baker and I cut a deal with him. I got, besides the $3 billion, you know they're looking for the Jewish voters, and I'll tell him whatever he wants to hear...

HK: Right.

DS: Besides the $10 billion in loan guarantees, which was a fabulous thing, $3 billion in foreign, in military aid, and I got almost a billion dollars in other goodies that people don't even know about.

HK: Such as?

DS: $700 million in military drawdown, from equipment that the United States Army's going to give to Israel; $200 million the US government is going to preposition materials in Israel, which Israel can draw upon, put them in the global warning protection system So when if there's a missile fired, they'll get the same advanced notification that the US, is notified, joint military exercises —I've got a whole shopping list of things.

HK: So this is from Baker?

DS: From Baker and from the Pentagon.

HK: So, not so, not...

DS: Why did he do it, you know, why did he do it? Last year I was a bum. This year I said, "Look Jim, we're going to fight on the F-15s. Israel doesn't want to fight," I said, "but some people on it are gong to come up on the floor of the Senate and the House and they're going to fight. If you'll do this, I think I can hold them back. But you've got to do it right away." They didn't want to fight. I said, "You don't want a fight before the election. It's going to hurt Bush. We don't want a fight before the election. We don't want to fight at all. Why can't we work something out?" So we cut a deal. You can't repeat this.

HK: You're right. But you met with Baker..

DS: Personally.

HK: Personally? Because you know, he's the one who cursed, who cursed the Jews.

DS: Of course, do you think I'm ever going to forgive him for that?

HK: Unbelievable. I said...

DS: Do you think I could ever forgive Bush for what he did September 12th a year ago? What he said about the Jews for lobbying in Washington?

HK: Do you think that Baker has a legitimate concern for the Jews? From what I hear, do you think he's anti-Semitic?

DS: I wouldn't go so far as to say that. He's a pragmatic businessman, he's a very tough lawyer. He does whatever it takes.

HK: And that's why...

DS: If we didn't have an election this year, you would get [unintelligible] from him.

HK: Let me ask you a quick question. Just a quick question here. You know Perot, you know, I'm telling you this is scary. I don't know what you think of Perot, but if Perot hadn't backed out... I watched the debates. I thought Perot did marvelous in the debates.

DS: He doesn't know how to govern. He's not going to make it. And there was an incident where his daughter was going out with a Jewish professor at school and he said, "I wouldn't have my daughter marry a Jew."

HK: So Perot, they say that if Perot hadn't backed out in July, and if he would have gotten himself a good running mate, you know...

DS: He wouldn't win, but it would go to the House of Representatives. The Democrats would win in the House of Representatives.

HK: So if it goes to the House, the Democrats would win for sure.

DS: For sure.

HK: Okay let me ask you last question and then I'll be happy to meet with your New York people...

DS: You know, you sound like my kind of guy. How old are you?

HK: Forty-two.

DS: You're a kid.

HK: I'm not a kid, I'm 42...

DS: I'm 63, you're a kid.

HK: I wish I was.

DS: We'll have to get you involved. I like you, we have a lot to talk about, about real estate, you know, I have so many great activities going on at AIPAC, you ought to think about coming to some of these things. I'll have a dinner this fall. I'll have 18-20 senators there. I run programs in Washington. We just had a, I had at Ted Kennedy's house last month kosher dinner. I brought foremost caterers down. I had 60 people on the couch for dinner. Last year, I did it in Al Gore's house.

HK: Right.

DS: Those are the things you should be getting involved in and knowing what's going on...

HK: Let me just ask you about Clinton. I want to tell you, you may not believe this, but I think that if Perot...

DS: Yeah, he would've given us a hard time. What's the name of your company, what do you do business as?

HK: We do business as HK, Inc.

DS: HK, Inc.?

HK: Right.

DS: Do you have a street address?

HK: Sure. 621 Beach 129th Street, Belle Harbor, Queens New York, 11694.

DS: Yeah, because on my computer you only show a post office box. This is your house? You work out of your house?

HK: Yeah, out of an office in the house... Look, Mr. Steiner...

DS: David. My father's Mr. Steiner.

HK: David, let me just ask you about Clinton. Honestly, what do you feel about Clinton?

DS: Well, I've known Bill Clinton for seven, eight years. I think he's got to be a lot better than George Bush. We have a lot of people in there. But he doesn't need money, he really doesn't need money. I'm a trustee of the Democratic National Committee. We collected $63 million for him so far.

HK: Who's collected $63 million?

DS: The Democratic National Committee and the Clinton campaign have raised $63 million.

HK: So they've already raised $63 million, so they don't need money.

DS: No, we need money, like we got a guy, Byron Dorgan, in North Dakota, who's going to be very good for us and we need money to make sure that he gets in. We've got people like that, because [unintelligible], whatever you give them would be a tickle on the elephant's behind. But when you give $5,000 or $10,000 to Bob Kasten, that's very meaningful.

HK: Let me ask you, I understand what you're saying. Clinton, when Clinton first started running a year ago, did he need money at that time?

DS: Yes, he did.

HK: I mean, did you help him out, 'cause that's the time...

DS: I personally am not allowed, as president of AIPAC, to get involved in the presidential campaign, because I have to deal with whoever wins. You know, I've got to go see Bush if he's there, but I helped him, we raised over a million dollars for him in New Jersey.

HK: For Clinton?

DS: For Clinton.

HK: And this was when, in the beginning?

DS: In the beginning, yes. After he won, before the convention.

HK: This is before the convention?

DS: Oh sure.

HK: Okay, let me ask you, you know, I...

DS: We've also raised for other guys who are running too, because they're friends. Harkin, the senator, you know you have to be with everybody.

HK: Let me ask you [talks abut getting cheated in business by Gentiles]. Let me ask you, Clinton, if he becomes, I mean what will he do for Israel, better than Bush, if he becomes, I know Bush gave you a hard time, this and that...

DS: I'll tell you, I have friends on the Clinton campaign, close associates. Gore is very committed to us.

HK: Right, Clinton if he, have you spoken to him?

DS: I've known Bill for seven, eight years from the National Governors' Association. I know him on a personal basis. I have friends. One of my friends is Hillary Clinton's scheduler, one of my officer's daughters works there. We gave two employees from AIPAC leaves of absence to work on the campaign. I mean, we have a dozen people in that campaign, in the headquarters.

HK: You mean in Little Rock?

DS: In Little Rock, and they're all going to get big jobs. We have friends. I also work with a think tank, the Washington Institute. I have Michael Mandelbaum and Martin Indyk being foreign policy advisers. Steve Speigel — we've got friends — this is my business.

HK: I understand, David.

DS: It's very complicated and the more you get into it, you'll love it. You sound like a smart guy.

HK: I'm a smart guy, but I have a, maybe because I'm more orthodox than you are, I've had bad experiences with Gentiles. Let me ask you, you know what "tachlis" means?

DS: Yeah, sure.

HK: From a practical point of view, if Clinton wins the presidency, and I'm sure he will, I hope so at least, what will be the benefits to Israel better than Bush? From a very practical point ... I mean, you just told me that Bush gave you everything you wanted...

DS: Only, not everything, at the end, when we didn't want the F-15s, that's a terrible thing.

HK: Selling the F-15s? If Clinton is elected...

DS: Let me tell you the problem with the $10 billion in loan guarantees, right? We only have the first year. We have authorization from Congress, but it's at the discretion of the president every year thereafter, so if Bush is there, he could say, you know, use it as a club, you know. 'If you don't give up Syria, I won't give you the money. If you don't give up the Golan Heights.' It's at the discretion of the president. And that's why we need a friendly president and we have Bill Clinton's ear. I talked to Bill Clinton.

HK: And Bill Clinton has made a commitment that if he's elected...?

DS: He's going to be very good to us.

HK: And he'll go ahead with the loan guarantees?

DS: We didn't talk about that specifically, listen, I didn't ask him that, but I have full confidence that we're going to have a much better situation. He's got Jewish friends. A girl who worked for me at AIPAC stood up for them at their wedding. Hillary lived with her. I mean we have those relationships. We have never had that with Bush. Susan Thomases, who's in there, worked with me on the Bradley campaign. We worked together for 13 years. She's in there with the family. They stay with her when they come to New York. One of my officers, Monte Friedkin, is one of the biggest fund-raisers for them. I mean, I have people like that all over the country.

HK: So, I mean from a practical point of view...

DS: He's going to be with us.

HK: I don't say, this business, you say, Bush only went ahead with the loan guarantees for one year.

DS: We only have. It's mandatory they give us the $2 billion for one year. After that it's subject to the discretion of the president.

HK: You mean the other $8 billion

DS: That's correct. On an annualized basis.

HK: Also, I heard that...

DS: They don't have to give it to us.

HK: But if Clinton is elected...

DS: ... feel reasonably certain we're gonna get it.

Hk: He's made that commitment?

DS: Well, he said he's going to help us. He's got something in his heart for the Jews, he has Jewish friends. Bush has no Jewish friends.

HK: Right.

DS: Reagan had something ... *meshuga,* but at least he had a commitment. He knew Jews from the film industry, he was one of the best guys for us. He had an emotional thing for the Jews. Bush doesn't have it. That's what it is really, if you have a feeling for our people, for what we believe in. Bush is, there's a man with no principles. Absolutely no principles.

HK: I heard something about, but I never really understood it, with the scoring. One of my friends told me there's a difference in the scoring, but I don't understand...

DS: Scoring is like points that you pay.

HK: So let's say, if Bush is elected on the loans...

DS: No, we've got the scoring arranged, it's four and a half percent. It's all done.

HK: That's all done, even with Bush?

DS: Even with Bush. I've got that worked out.

HK: So that's all done.

DS: It's in the bill. It's all passed. He signed the bill. It's a matter of law.

HK: So it's already four and a half percent.

DS: We could've had it less, but then we couldn't...

HK: And Clinton, if he was president, he would give...?

DS: He couldn't change it, you cannot change it.

HK: No, but I'm saying, if he was president now, before the bill was signed, he would've given you the four and a half percent...

DS: I would've gotten less.

HK: I'm sorry?

DS: I would've gotten it cheaper.

HK: How much? Even two percent.

DS: Yeah, we thought we were going to get two percent. But Rabin gave it away.

HK: You mean Rabin didn't bargain as good as he could have?

DS: That's right.

HK: Unbelievable. So, if Clinton is elected, that will be the best...

DS: I think that will be the best we could do.

HK: You know, I just want to tell you one last thing. Do you have parents that come from Europe?

DS: Yeah, of course, from Glolitzano, near Krakow.

HK: You're kidding, your parents are from Krakow?

DS: Near Krakow.

HK: Guess what?

DS: You too?

HK: My parents are from Krakow.

DS: Well, we're not from Krakow, but from near Krakow. My mother's from Rudnick, my father from Gruns, near Tano. Do you know where Tano is?

HK: Yes. Let me tell you...

DS: ... don't have many left. Everybody got killed.

HK: Let me tell you. The same with me. Let me tell you, my parents were the only ones who came out. Let me tell you, my...

DS: You're a Holocaust survivor?

HK: Yeah, no, not me, my parents.

DS: That's some experience, I've got two cousins, I've got one in Israel and one in France that came out of Mauthausen, I'll tell you, and everybody else dead on my father's side in Russia. I just brought six of them from Koshkent to Israel last year.

HK: Right. Let me tell you that, you know what my father always says? My father was a rich man in Poland, and he says, "Economic power is very good. You have to have money, but if you just have economic power and you don't have political power..."

DS: You've got nothing.

HK: You've got nothing.

DS: If we had AIPAC in the '30s and '40s, we would have saved millions of Jews. We would have the political power. But Jews were afraid to open their mouths. They didn't know how.

HK: AIPAC started after WWII?

DS; Oh, sure.

HK: And if you would have had AIPAC in the '30s?

DS: I feel we would've saved a lot of Jews.

HK: And Franklin Roosevelt, he could've done a lot better?

DS: Sure, he could. The Jews never opened their mouths. They were afraid. We're not afraid. They can curse me out, I don't care if they hate me, just as long as I get what we need for our people.

HK: So if you had a little lamp, a wishing lamp, and you could wish for either Bush, Clinton or Perot...

DS: Clinton.

HK: Clinton all the away? And in terms of Israel having political power, between the three candidates, the one who will give us the most political power?

DS: Clinton is the best guy for us.

HK: He's the best one.

DS: I hope you're serious about what you told me?

HI: I am, I'll tell you this [tells a long anecdote about David Souter promising to oppose abortion as a nominee and then reversing himself on the Supreme Court]. So I wish we had a Jewish candidate for president.

DS: I don't think the country's ready.

HK: If the country was ready, is there any Jewish candidate...?

DS: I wouldn't venture to say anything.

HK: You know who? I don't know him, I've never met him, Joe Lieberman.

DS: Oh, I'm very friendly with Joe. I'm having dinner with him Monday night.

HK: Let me tell you, I think Joe Lieberman would have, uh, would have, if he wasn't Jewish, that's the only problem he has. He's highly respected.

DS: I'd like to see him on the Supreme Court.

HK: If Clinton is elected, has he told you who he's going to put on the Supreme Court?

DS: We're talking now. We don't have, no commitments yet. We're just negotiating. We're more interested right now, in the Secretary of State and the Secretary of the National Security Agency. That's more important to us.

HK: If Clinton is elected, who do you think will be Secretary of State?

DS: We don't know yet, we're negotiating.

Hk: Who are you hoping for?

Ds: I've got a list. But I really can't go through it. I'm not allowed to talk about it.

HK: But you figure, God willing, if Clinton's elected...

DS: We'll have access.

HK: You'll have access and you'll have a good input into who's Secretary of State.

DS: I do believe so.

HK: And the other position is...

DS: National Security Adviser.

HK: Those are the two critical positions.

DS: Right.

HK: Gotcha. Well, David, thanks for talking with me.

DS: And we're going to get together next week. I hope you'll have your checkbook ready.

Otto Skorzeny, Hitler's Commando (top)
Skorzeny next to his Memorial painting? (bottom)

Exposing the Nazi International

A typescript of four conversations taped in 1981 between an investigative reporter and a person purporting to be an operative for the post-war Nazi International (also known as the International Fascista, the Odessa, and Kamaradenwerk) came to Feral House under mysterious circumstances. Apparently, the investigative reporter found the material to be "too hot" and dropped it in the lap of the flea market and mail-order entrepreneur John Aes-Nihil, who in turn passed on the material to Feral House. An investigation enabled us to locate the interviewer, who wishes to remain anonymous. He was able to answer many of our questions about the alleged operative and the circumstances of the interview, as well as providing independent confirmation of at least one of the operative's visits to Nazi International chief Otto Skorzeny.

The editor, publisher and interviewer do not rule out the possibility that the information in this interview is wholly or partly imaginative or disinformational. There is another possibility. These conversations may provide the clearest view yet afforded of the inner workings of the post-war Nazi hierarchy, as well as providing clues about many of the conspiracies and major terrorist actions of the Twentieth Century.

Names of private individuals, included in the original manuscript, have been deleted.

My name is K., and for the past ten years I have served with the international Nazi Party organization as Inspector General or Liaison between central headquarters and operatives in the field. I would report on actions under way, supply data, information for possible actions in the future, and financial and personal data on individuals in different parts of the world. The Nazi Party organization is composed in two basic parts: the working organization, made up of former SS military officers, former members of the Nazi party, and the second section of German industrialists and businessmen who financially support and provide the logistics support for operations of this organization. They have been involved with and responsible for a number of operations in the past years, among them the DC-10, the problems it has had; recent fires and calamities in Nevada. They have set up and provide logistic and financial support for organizations such as the Irish Republican Army and the Palestine Liberation Organization; they have and currently are involved with top level individuals in the Reagan administration; they have been involved with the West German government intimately regarding such events as the Munich massacre during the Olympics of '72.

My personal involvement with them is about ten years, and during that time I have moved up to the present position.

— Why don't we start with your initial meeting [with a contact to the Organization] in the gun shop in Newport Beach, California? How did you happen to be there and what happened once you were there?

I was on a vacation, and I was interested in going to the gun shop. I used to collect various war memorabilia, and it looked like it had that type of thing in it. I was talking to a young man who was a salesman in the shop, and B. when he came in, we got into a conversation about military collectibles. By the end of the conversation he said, "Why don't you come over to my house. I have some things I'd like to show you." So we went over there and had a pretty nice discussion.

— What sort of things did he have, that he collects?

Medals, particularly medals and orders. I had said that I made trips overseas, and he said, "Ah, I go there quite often. I work for an American company and when I'm over there I have a chance to pick up various pieces."

We eventually got around to Otto — Otto Skorzeny. He says, "Oh, yes, I've sold him some things." I said, "I'd really like to meet him." He said, "That's fine. I could arrange that for you. Just let me know when you're going." A few weeks later I got in touch with him and told him I was going overseas again, to Europe and could he help me out? He said, "Sure. Stop by when you're here again and I'll give you something."

— What year was this?

'70, '71 maybe. He took out the card, Skorzeny's card ... it had Skorzeny's handwritten signature across the front, like mine has, and it was blank in back, whereas mine has writing on it — you have the copy of it. He wanted to know when I'd be over there, so he could make me a specific appointment, and I said okay, gave him the time... and I went over.

I took the train from Paris to Munich, overnight train, the Orient Express, and I got settled in at the Konigshoff Hotel, about a block from the Munich train station. At that time I did not know what was going on, so I innocently called from the hotel, not from my room but from the reception desk, put through a call to Skorzeny and here's his phone number, in Madrid, Spain. I got him on the line and said, "This is K--- and B. said..." and he said, "Oh, yes, I'm looking forward to meeting you..." and that I come down at such-and-such a time.

Got down to Madrid and checked into the Castellano Hotel, the Hilton. We got there and called Otto and he said, "Just come right over." From that first time and in all our subsequent meetings at his home, we never met at his office. I got to his home and one thing I noticed — then and at all times — at either end of this nice quiet residential street in the outskirts, there was always a car at each end with men in each car. I was a little nervous about it — it didn't seem right.

— *What was that first meeting like?*

Each side was sizing up the other one. It was rather meaningless conversation, about my hobbies, interests, clothing, general World War II run-of-the-mill something-or-other, and he said when he was taken prisoner at Salzburg at the end of the war, the American GIs took all his medals off him; he had the Knight's Cross, that was taken from him. He was very upset about that and said, "What I did was..." and he said he put the word out to people — who, I don't know —but he eventually got all his medals back, and this was years later, this was maybe 8 years or so after he got to Spain.

He said, "I didn't want a Knight's Cross or a German Cross or any of the awards, I wanted mine. I knew they were mine because there was a mark on them that my aide Radl had placed on them. I would know if someone was trying to give me a phony or a genuine that wasn't mine. Wait a second. I'll go get them." He went into another part of the house and he came back with a black velvet case with all of his medals on it. There was the Knight's Cross, the German Cross, the Iron Cross, there were his awards for service on the Russian front and the Western front. He had an SS service medal; he had, it was like a badge — he was very, very proud of that — it was a Nazi pin, not military but like a college association, a youth association member of such-and-such youth — but not Hitler Youth, this was at college level. He also had one cuff band or cuff title, all the SS had cuff titles; they wore them on the left cuff. Regular army units that had cuff titles wore them on the right. This cuff title was black, had the silver line on each side, and the name of the unit, [and] "OTTO SKORZENY." He laughed and said, "There is no such thing. There never was. Some American sent it to me, and I got a big kick out of it, so I keep it in the collection."

— *How long did you stay in Madrid?*

Three or four days that time. At the end that first time, we were getting along very well. He said, "Would you mind checking on somebody for me?" I had mentioned some of the people I had known in this business and when I mentioned this one man, B....

B. is writing technical books for historians and people interested in what badge went with this uniform, etc., and was going to write a book about Otto. "You check on him for me," and I said okay. I went back to the United States and spoke with B. and [I] said, "You know, I was speaking with Otto and he's not terribly pleased about what you're doing." B.'s attitude was basically, "Let Otto go screw himself if he doesn't like what I'm doing — we have a contract." Otto's contention was that he wasn't living up to his contract. So I said, I'll let Otto know.

— *To get back to Madrid, by the end of that first afternoon, or thereabouts, what did you feel about him?*

I'd known from the history I'd read about him that he prided himself on many things, one of them that he could speak very good English — he cannot — he does get stuck on things and you don't correct him, you just go along with it. I thought he certainly had a great deal of confidence. Certainly, all the times I've seen him, up to and including the last time [January 1980, Paraguay], he seemed very healthy. He smoked a tremendous amount, mentholated American cigarettes. I had ... from the duty-free shops ... a bottle of Wild Turkey. I brought it along as a 'hello' present. He said, "Let's try it out." This Spanish maid always attended to him, and whenever he wanted something it was like he was giving a military order during a massive barrage. Full volume on his voice: "GLASSES. ICE."

If you want to put it on a personal basis, he really loves Wild Turkey, [is a] real chain smoker, loves good food and loves girls. He loves war movies and he really thinks Burt Lancaster is something else, and I'm certainly not going to tell him Burt Lancaster's Jewish. Otto is a genuine Jew-hater. He loves hunting. I've suggested that he come hunting in the United States. Obviously he knows it could be done, but no. I think it's more personal than fear. Personal dislike.

— *The Organization and the projects, is this his continual focus? Or does he have a life aside from the Organization?*

No, he's very involved with the Organization. He doesn't really have all that much of a recreational life. He compartmentalizes everything. His fun mode, it's all having a great time, enjoying himself, but he can [snaps fingers] turn it off just like that.

— *How did you feel about him as a human being?*

Very forceful personality. It was very hard despite his gruff personality to picture him as being the kind of person that did his more well-known activities during the war. He said that the only time he'd ever been frightened was when he was on the Russian Front. He had a car and driver at this time which was unusual for a Lieutenant in the SS. This would date it around 1941-42, early Russian Front. He said that they came under a barrage of Russian rockets. They pulled over to the side of the road and he jumped out of the car with his driver and was lying by the side of the road. He was hit, by a stone fragment — I don't think it was a steel fragment or he'd have been dead. He evidently was injured there and put on convalescent leave, and he said that really shook him. After that nothing seemed to frighten him, but that did.

— *What I'm asking is...*

He's not the kind of person you'd want to go out and have a beer with.

— *Was the forcefulness something you enjoyed, or was it repelling?*

Oversimplifying it — I didn't think it was good manners. From the very first he has to be in control of everything and everyone.

— *You obviously found him interesting to some extent, you talked a lot, but you felt uncomfortable with him because of this overbearingness?*

Not totally. Like if I'd want to talk about, say, some part of his war experience, he didn't like that. Not that he was afraid of [talking about] the war experience, but because I had suggested it or somebody else suggested it, he was very definite: "NO!" He dominates the situation. It wears thin very quickly. I'd personally thought, the way we were getting along, how did I get involved? Well, you have to start somewhere. I had perhaps a crazy idea, but no one had really done anything effective against them. I had decided that this person, or these people and their actions were repulsive to me. I'd looked at, certainly, Wiesenthal and his work, and various Jewish people and what they had certainly done, at the War Crimes Trials, and no one had really been terribly effective. They were dealing with front men, dealing on a plane [of]: "Did this man kill a prisoner of war?" Very flamboyant and maybe makes for good reading and excites the people, but what were the real root causes of this?

— *You had expressed a desire for meeting him [Otto Skorzeny]. Was this in conjunction with military collectables, or did you have some idea of pursuing this course of harming them, or was it just curiosity?*

Mostly [curiosity], although there was the possibility of getting collectables from him. Curiosity and business. I knew he had his uniforms, they all have their uniforms, and I'd spoken to some American collectors and they mentioned that the SS had a white dress uniform, something really amazing, everything in reverse, the black is white and the white is black. Basically a formal outfit for very very formal occasions, and I knew he had his — of course they all do, the top ones, they still do. Degrelle has one. American collectors said if you can get one, name a price for them. So I asked him about them, and I asked him about his medals, and I tried to do it as delicately as possible. He said that the medals stay with me and when I die they're going to go to the family. Many people had written him, and the few that had actually seen him had made open overtures about buying those things. He had to think that I was getting into that, so he probably thought ahead, and to avoid embarrassing me or causing me any trouble, he said, "No, I wouldn't sell anything I have. I'm not selling them."

— *Let's get back to this second or third meeting. I assume you mentioned this great uncle [of yours who had been in the German Army].*

I mentioned it as a matter of interest. From the first time I'd noticed he had a lot of books, virtually any and every book that in any way even remotely alluded to German military or economic actions, devolving before, during or after World War II; this man has the books. He also has the standard *Dienstalter, alterlists,* a directory, broken down, SS, Luftwaffe, Army, Navy.

I mentioned this man and he said, "Go get the book there." "Okay." He says, "NO — GET UP RIGHT NOW AND GET THE BOOK!" I got up and went over to the library and, "Not that volume, that one over there." If I didn't pick the right volume, he'd get very annoyed. It's not my library, how do I know? I finally got the right book, checked it out and sure enough, there's the name, Otto Barth, I believe it was Lieutenant General, German Army of course, Eastern Front. He'd been captured by the Russians, had been held until the general amnesty of 1955, released and died. His wife — he says, "Now, I want you to take down the address and see her. This is the proper thing for you to do." You know, relatives and all that sort of thing. I said, "Okay." He says, "NO, TAKE IT DOWN! HERE'S THE PAPER..." The more you present problems, the more he gets annoyed.

— *Where did she live?*

Erlangen.

— *Did you go to see her?*

No.

— *Was there any change in relationship after he had gone through this?*

That seemed to be, in retrospect, very good. Maybe I didn't have relatives in the SS, so that wasn't perfection — he was a general in the army, regular army, just a soldier — willing to overlook that fault.

It must have been the second time I had been to Madrid, I checked into the Luz Palacio and I saw these cars I mentioned, near his house, move off when they saw me coming out. Paranoid or not, I felt that something was very wrong, and realized what I was getting into. I was still very fearful. I walked away from his house. He had never had a cab or a car meet me, I'd have to go walk out and hail one. I got the cab back to the hotel and barricaded the door. In all future meetings, coming to Madrid, I would take the train in, meet him a day, and I wouldn't check into a hotel.

I would get on the train, in the evening, go up to the Spanish-French border, get on a return train and get back in the morning, so I'd be on the move at all times in public. That got a little wearing after a while.

Which leads me to another interesting situation. He [Otto] asked me to carry some instructions, and they had to be written... highly unusual. Usually things are not written down. That's why the standard types of documentation people expect don't really exist, to any great extent. It was "I want you to take this file — take it to an address in Stuttgart." I took the train. France, no problem, through Switzerland, no problem, up to Geneva, got on a train there into Salzburg from Geneva, Salzburg, Austria. This was very late at night — one, two in the morning. No one's around, maybe two or three people, and you have to go through German customs station there on Austrian soil, after you leave Salzburg station. "Open your suitcase." I had all these papers that he'd given me, and I was laughing and going through my mind, "What's going to happen here? I'll just play it cool..." and he sees the papers.

— *What was the nature of the papers?*

Mostly private correspondence, some very personal messages he didn't want to go through the mail. On top of it, he had given me a photograph of himself, just after he was captured. It shows Otto in his uniform before he had been disarmed or had the medals or badges removed, and it was lying on top of the papers. Two German customs men opened it up, they look at the papers, they look at the picture, they knew what it was, obviously, they closed it up and said, "Go." No problems — that was the end of the examination.

— *When you left, obviously, some situation of trust had been established. Was there anything other than checking on B. that he had asked you to do on his behalf?*

Many people ask me what do you do, and I answer, well, I'm interested in investments, stock market and things like that. He was very interested in that. He asked me about some of the things I had done. It was almost like he was testing me, on certain companies. I went through the questions — they were superficial questions, none of them of real importance — but the fact that I could answer these questions about certain companies, he seemed to like that.

Initially it was put to me, oh we don't know too much about that here, could you get these things for me? Find out about this company? I remember the very first was ComSat, the first private communications satellite system, and he was interested in investing. I got that information. I will say that a number of things put me in his good graces, for instance, initially on the B. thing. I reported back what B. had said and what B. was doing, and I said I'd have to have some more papers, and he even gave me a copy of the contract he and B. had...

— *You bid your farewells and came back to the States. You knew of B. because of the book he had written on war memorabilia...*

I met B. and had a discussion with him, the one I described earlier. I met with a man at a brokerage office, Merrill Lynch, who was handling my account. I asked him to get me whatever he could on ComSat, that I was interested in investing in it. Give me an in-house report for clients of Merrill Lynch, and each brokerage house does this. When I went back [to Madrid] the next time I brought it to him.

— *In between visits, you had a correspondence with Otto about B....*

There was a tremendous amount of correspondence about B. I realized that B. was dealing from the bottom of the deck and selling to both sides. As far as Otto was concerned, he was giving information to Otto, as far as various intelligence matters, I don't know what. I knew he was giving photos. He was one of the people who were extracting files from the National Archives, and most of what the National Archives had was not even catalogued, so virtually anything could be missing and no one would know it was missing. At the same time, he was informing to American Naval intelligence; why I don't know. I know what he boasted to me... He had to realize I was going to tell Otto what he said, and maybe this was just his way of thumbing his nose at Otto, thinking that Otto didn't really have much to say or do about it.

Evidently he was well protected with the people he was dealing with in the United States, so he thought he had nothing to fear. When I got back to Otto, I hedged and hemmed and hawed and I said, "Otto, I don't like to tell you this, but I don't have any proof." "NEVER MIND — TELL ME, I'LL DEAL WITH IT." So I told him. That this man was selling to American intelligence, information about Otto. Period. That he had every intention of taking advantage of Otto on the book and not paying Otto anything.

— *I assume Otto was not pleased.*

He was not pleased at all, that's putting it mildly.

— *This was when you went back to see him the second time, when you told him this?*

The second time, right. I had suggested to him, I don't remember if this is the second or third time, about the time that ... and I got together about doing our own book about him. He was very excited about this and the possibility of doing the movie, and he says he has to approve this and he has to have the right to ... he's making all kinds of changes. I'd gone to my attorney and written up a contract, and he didn't like it.

— The contract was concerning what?

The books and the magazines and everything to handle about his experiences. He insisted all this is going to deal with is about World War II, and you can't tell him "Who cares, that part's only been written about probably a million times." We were getting along and things were developing; I wasn't going to fiddle around too much about that.

— For what reason did you actually go to Madrid the second time?

Basically to give him the information about ComSat, to report on B. and to see how far we could develop this. I was getting very interested in developing something with him, particularly when I saw he had confidence in me.

He looked over ComSat and liked what he saw. I think that this was just to see how much I could find out, and how willing I was to fill him in on company business.

He liked particularly the way I do things in a company, not just the standard data of their financial reports, but the personal asides, and this is particularly what they like. Peculiarities of people that work in a company, be they in the sex line, the drug line, dealing on the side with another business — all the things that are not usually published, but may be no more than rumors.

— How much time was there between the first and second and third visits to Madrid?

About nine months between the first and second, about four-five months between the second and third.

— What was the result of his being impressed with the work you'd done?

We're not talking about SS, World War II, we're talking about business that had nothing to do with that period. At least I didn't think so. We'd talk about German industry. He'd talk about youth, about how German youth just "don't have any pride," that they're not paying attention to business anymore. When he was in Germany on one of his visits when I was gone, he'd had a real verbal row, and he took great pleasure in being able to tell me he'd put down these German youths who were espousing modern thinking. "This is all wrong," he'd say.

He started to talk about the Messerschmidt-Volkau-Blum, a very large consortium for the aircraft industry, everything from designing air parts to the entire aircraft, doing sub-assemblies; they did the sub-assemblies on the A-300, they did it on the Concorde. They did relatively minor work on that. At that time they were just developing the XM-1, the new main battle tank for the United States. Germany was supposed to supply the power plant to it. It turned out that Chrysler would supply the power plant.

You had this amalgamation of the three main countries, Germany, United States and Britain supplying various parts to the battle tank, so since they're all partners in NATO, if something developed, their parts would be interchangeable. We started talking about Chrysler, and he had the German psyche, which he really typifies, he has to be on top or he didn't like it. That was the main thing about the McDonnell-Douglas thing. Mainly because B. was with McDonnell-Douglas. He seemed to hedge around that, initially, but he knew, or felt he knew me well enough to discuss it. He was very very very upset. With the coming in '71 of the airshow in Paris, he wanted me to see that and report back on that.

He wanted me to go to the Paris airshow and to talk to this other man. This was the third trip. He had, evidently, they all had, paranoid feelings that people are out to get them and everyone crosses everybody, which isn't all that far from the truth. Everyone is jockeying for position, trying to protect themselves. He says, "I want you to check this S., get him to talk. What I'm going to do now..." and he took out this business card — you saw it [photocopy in possession] and put the signature on the card that authenticates it, and then on the back. He said if I had any trouble, he wanted me to go, anytime, to this very day to the SS organization in Ludenscheid, and they will give me any aid that I need.

Beginning with the DC-10 operation, [it] is typical in that it was for economic purposes. The Organization, first of all, wished to promote their own involvement with the Airbus, as opposed to the DC-10. Where that were not possible or practical they would use extortion in the form of payments per aircraft — DC-10, 747, L10-11 — for every one sold they would receive a portion of those funds. In regards to the DC-10, the initial period of approximately nine months to a year payments were made.

— By who?

Individuals within McDonnell-Douglas. Within the corporation during the initial development stages and initial sales there were two employees of McDonald-Douglas who provided data on design criteria, possible sales to be made, directly to the Organization and, in reverse, the Organization through these two men could influence possible sales and design criteria in the aircraft. The first of these two men, his name is S. He operated out of Geneva, Switzerland, and was initially the financial and merchandising extension of McDonnell-Douglas, their representative. The other gentleman who worked directly out of the Los Angeles area was B. He directly had access to and influence through individuals to gain information on design criteria and sales, and to directly input data on design material into the aircraft and merchandising methods. The DC-10, the payments were made during the initial design and sales principally through the airshow of 1971 in Paris at Le Bourget Field where the show was held at that time.

I went up to see S. Obviously, I could not use Skorzeny's card to get into the airshow. I was up there for Press Day, and at that time, no public was allowed in, only journalists with credentials. I went in there and they had a booth at the entrance at Le Bourget Field. They had what they called chalets, temporary buildings lined up in staggered form, and I went to the McDonnell-Douglas one and said I wanted to see S. The receptionist called him over, and I said, "I would like to interview you for a story."

— S. is an employee of McDonnell-Douglas?

Representing McDonnell-Douglas. He won't show on their employee lists as such. He's the one working out of Geneva, where he can make a buck, put it that way. He works for a number of companies. We went in and sat down, and I said, "Otto Skorzeny wanted me to speak with you." He called over a maid, all sort of semi-private, where no one was listening. He says, "What do you want?" I said, "Oh, I think I'll have a bourbon. He's becoming very, very — anything I wanted, now that he knows who I'm from. I said, "What about how things are going? Otto's very concerned. I'm merely passing this on. I don't have any authority, but he's very upset, so how do you see it?" He says, "There seem to be problems with the engine development..."

— What engines are you talking about? The DC-10?

Right. This is before anything developed about crashes or anything. He said, "Well, there's no problem at all. There's been discussion [about] the GE engines... We had a bit of delivery problem with the GE engine, but there's no problem on delivery." He started to mention he didn't know how much I knew. I told him I don't know that much about what's been going on, merely trying to carry information, that I'm a conduit, a telephone, if you will, between you and Otto. He was showing his concern. He said, "There's no problem aside from the slight delivery problem on the engines." It's very difficult to put this in words — he was trying to explain that there were problems, evidently in payoffs.

We know now that there had been a problem, regarding the Turkish airliner that went into the tank in Paris on takeoff, and the initial problem with the DC-10 regarding the rear latch on the door. If it's not closed properly then the door can come out, causing immediate decompression.

— The [sabotaged] Turkish airliner was a couple of years after this, wasn't it? '73 or '74?

The company knew there was a problem. He said, "I know they're concerned about that. I know the Organization is interested in the money alone. They wanted to push theirs, lacking the ability to sell their own, which they were not prepared to do at that time. The A-300 was not ready to fly. They had nothing more than a mockup in '71. So since theirs wasn't ready, then McDonnell-Douglas would pay, since they're the direct competitor. They were looked on more as a competitor than the Boeing, since the Boeing... at that time the 707 had been in service for quite a long time, and they were looking for replacements. It developed that there wasn't real replacement but little more than augmenting the 747 with the A-300, which has sold marginally, and with the [DC-]10 which has done so-so, certainly in light of what has happened.

He finally started talking, searching me out: how much does he know about payments? I'm thinking: payments? What is this about payments? I was a bit puzzled. I said, "Well, what about the payments?" "Well, there seems to be a problem now with Lockheed being investigated for their possible loan and whether they'll get a loan from the U.S. Government; guarantees. There's a little too much heat on the aircraft industry, and they're balking, they're not making payments." He started to explain, in very simple terms, that McDonnell-Douglas had been approached to pay, and was balking because of this investigation and the heat on the industry. I said, "Well, what do you expect me to do?" and he said, "Let Otto know." In retrospect it makes a great deal of sense.

— Could you elaborate on the specifics of the extortion of McDonnell-Douglas prior to this event [the induced crashes of DC-10 aircraft] and, specifically, how it was done, for how long and payments and amounts? You had mentioned that there was an Airbus which was competing, could you explain the whole groundwork on that?

The Airbus was developed and sold through a consortium of French and German manufacturers. They perceived the new generation of aircraft to be middle-range and still large-bodied aircraft, an improvement on the Boeing. They were aware that Lockheed and also Boeing and McDonnell-Douglas were also developing that, however, the costs were deemed too heavy for a single European interest to go it alone and consequently this association was developed. I use this word "developed" and it certainly was encouraged by the German side, who because of the DC-10, which will be explained, wished to profit from this and did not wish to tie up a great deal of their own capital in it.

— When you say "German side," who are you referring to?

Messerschmidt-Volkau-Blum.

— At what point was the decision made, and how was it made, to extort or coerce McDonnell-Douglas?

In the embryonic stages of this, in '71, the German interests did see that the DC-10, the L-1011, the other possible competitors were far advanced, would be direct competition, and they could not go it alone, could not be the first of the new generation of aircraft, and it was decided there were two options. Either through extortion or, if necessary, through the accidents that took place. The [methods] of the accidents as they developed were not known in '71, but they were developing some ideas. The biggest problem in developing an accident is the accident must not appear to be the work of a terrorist because that would not show on the integrity of the aircraft.

— The accidents were to discredit...

The aircraft itself, yes.

— So they decided to start with extortion. How did they start this?

My knowledge is that D., the representative of McDonnell-Douglas in Geneva, who was the direct Organization man on this — had during the development of the DC-10 worked with B., who also had worked with Lockheed, in direct input and output on design. They knew what was happening and when it was happening and how far it was along. They were surprised in one regard when they saw how deliveries were to be made. They were further advanced than the information had been coming. The information had been coming solely through B. and S. directly to the Organization. The multiple options were discussed and it took a while to do it because if they could avoid the 'accidents', they wished to do that. It was not an ego thing, it was dollars and cents, pounds, whatever. They had worked on the extortion from approximately '71 till about '76. Up to '76 it was not considered a problem. They had run a test, one test, done without notification to McDonnell-Douglas. There was no attempt to extort at all, regarding the DC-10 that crashed in Paris. That was well-known to be, at least on the face of it, the failure of the hatch door which caused structural failure of main members in the floor of the aircraft on which passengers were on.

— So the crash in Paris in '74 was a test to see if they had the ability to bring the plane down [Note: 3/3/1974 / Turkish / 346 dead.]

Yes.

— And what did they do at that point?

B. had approached. This was in St. Louis, representatives of the company, I believe top echelon. I don't know the names of the people. It was in the most diplomatic but straight terms. It was put to them that it will cost so much per aircraft to do business. There seemed to be, initially, not a great deal of resistance. It wasn't pay or lose an aircraft. They had approached them with the idea that we have contacts overseas, and we can arrange for sales, and then again it can be your aircraft or another person's aircraft. Now what can you offer us? They did pay per aircraft sold for a limited time.

— *You say payment per aircraft sold. How were the payments arranged and to whom were they made?*

The payments were arranged in cash through a drop in Geneva. The resentment that developed and the balking at payments came at a time when there were congressional investigations developing regarding foreign payments. McDonnell-Douglas felt at this time that everyone was, to use a crude term, coming clean; they wished to cover themselves. They virtually were forced by government pressure in this country to stop. Again, the government thought it was only a matter of payment to sell planes, and they stopped there.

The Organization could care less why it happened. The payments had stopped and they wouldn't resume. After that, the accidents were in earnest, the arranged accidents. S. had corrected some problems that had developed in the ultrasonics system and could be very reliable in arranging that structural failures or cracks could be arranged at any point. They could have it where a crack could be found, reflecting on the aircraft itself, or in the extreme example of the case of the DC-10 in Chicago, they could raise the ultrasonic to such a level that they knew that the natural vibration of the aircraft would complete the work.

Whether it be the DC-10 out of Paris with the problem regarding the cargo door, whether it was the Air New Zealand DC-10, whether it was the Western Airlines DC-10 that crashed on landing in Mexico City, whether it was the DC-10 that crashed at O'Hara Field in Chicago, the one constant that was used in all cases was ultrasonics, leaving no trace. It would be attributed to structural failure of one type or another.

On board the DC-10 out of Chicago, it was learned at the airport that two couriers, members of the Organization were to be on that flight and were to meet with a member of MI5, British intelligence, in Los Angeles, by the name of T. whose front is as a representative of a London newspaper. When they were noticed immediate action was taken to develop the structural crack to such an extent that at certain sound and vibration levels consistent with take-off of the aircraft vibrations necessary to complete structural failure of the aircraft would take place.

The two men on the aircraft, part of the Organization, one K. of Austria and S., who were subsequently killed in the crash.

— *The ultrasonic equipment, could you explain what this is, a possible description of the equipment, how it was used?*

I have never seen the equipment, but from the conversations that I have developed, the equipment sounds a bit like — it's compact, it could be in the seat of a pickup truck or service truck, which indeed it was in the Chicago example, and the actual device that delivered these highly directed waves is through an arrangement where you can direct it, point it, like a... they have these 'guns' you can direct for sound.

— *Now for the Siemans company...*

Their main work is more than just fortunate. A principal facility of Siemans, a facility dealing in the ultrasonics is located very close to the O'Hara Airport. The device that I mentioned could be on the seat [of a car or pickup truck]. The power requirements are relatively large for it. The power requirements were drawn from the ground equipment.

— *At O'Hara, there are some questions of the time frame. You'd mentioned that this was one of the undertakings that the Organization did that was given belated approval because they moved fast. How long before the flight was this imminent defection discovered?*

Less than a day. It was late afternoon, because the information came to me about 11 hours before it happened. Late in the evening, I was in my home when I got a call from a member of the Organization who works for me, and who the Organization is not aware is working for me, and let me know that something was very seriously wrong. It was not a secure line so we had scramblers.

— *Who did these orders come from?*

My man said merely that they came from West Germany. — The order was given to watch them, and they were watched. They were observed at the airport together, talking. No two Organization should ever talk in the open. It was decided, particularly in light of the information about the call to T. in Los Angeles that something had to be done immediately, and they knew that the Organization — these people obviously knew because of Siemans' involvement — that no tears would be shed over a DC-10, and very much, regarding the two men on this flight. Since ultimate authority would come from South America, from Paraguay where the organizational headquarters are, and there was not time to get that approval, then it was decided, then the equipment was brought over from Siemans.

— The destruction of McDonnell-Douglas' planes, the continued extortion — I presume that payments have resumed since the destruction of the planes has stopped... the same drops in Geneva.

Yes.

— Why has McDonnell-Douglas been silent about this? Couldn't they have said, "We're being blackmailed by the Airbus people who've threatened to blow our planes out of the sky... and who have."

The first time they attempted to make the call, they'd be dead before the call was completed. There are people within the corporation who can handle them.

— What did you do after the Paris Airshow?

I took the train that evening back to Madrid, told Otto what had happened, and took the train out again, and during this time — I stayed a couple days at that time — took the train back and forth. I had that thing about not staying in a hotel. After that time I never stayed in a hotel again.

— This is when you went back from Paris?

Yes. He seemed to be very very agitated, and I got the impression that the agitation was almost make-believe. He more or less knew what was taking place, and was merely getting a confirmation that this man S. could be double-dealing. After all, he was known to represent anybody who could pay the price. I had the distinct feeling he wouldn't have sent me in there on something like that if he didn't know. He didn't know me that long. Unless he knew what the answer was going to be, and was merely looking for that confirmation. I passed on the information and he made more sense out of it than I did.

I left, and after that I said, "I've had it." I was so unnerved by what was taking place, that I said that after I got through making [my report]. In fact, this is very unusual — usually things aren't in writing, but this time I put it in writing, handed it in through the mail drop in Munich, and took the first train out just as far as I could go. The farthest place I could go was Bergen, Norway. Takes three days to get there by train.

— You reported to Otto, which obviously had more meaning to Otto than it did to you, and Otto became agitated — and you feel he was putting you on?

Yes. You could tell when he was really upset about something, just that boasting, blustering way that Germans have. He's Austrian, but same thing, Germans and Austrians. He seemed to be upset, but merely as a put-on. He said, "Let's go downstairs" and — we knew those two cars were there — make a great big show of walking — first and only time he did this, walked out to his car, Mercedes, naturally, parked in the driveway. Big show of "How do you do? Hello, goodby," you know, shaking hands, all very ... Take your pick: could they be Spanish police? Could they be his own people? Could they be Mossad? Could they be American? I have no idea.

We picked up where we'd left off, about how he wanted me to spend a little more investigating, after I'd told him about ComSat. I'd mentioned Dillingham, because I'd looked into it a little bit, it was one of my first. I told him that I found it very disturbing, unbelievable, that the majority of Dillingham's assets were in the Ala Moana Shopping Center, and considering how old the company is, 1903 or 1906, and how they controlled, or can control traffic in the island, how everything to the outer islands, outside of Oahu is done by barge. I had noticed in a standard financial report that Dillingham had listed that the business in the barge traffic was severely hampered because the barge broke down, or the tug broke down. This is incredible! I'm not talking about a Ma and Pa hamburger stand, we're talking about a major operation.

They [Dillingham] also got involved in mining ore in Australia, around the Great Barrier Reef, and the Australian government was sticking it to them to such an extent that they had to pull out. It seemed whatever investment they got into was a complete and utter failure, and the only thing that was worth anything was out in Oahu, probably 350-400 million ... supposed to be the largest, or second largest shopping center in the world. They were well-placed, also owning Cal Gas, and they were getting into real estate in Colorado and in California. They were trying to diversify but they were really being inept. I was curious how this was possible, how they could be so inept with all these supposedly experienced [people]. I found out that the board of directors was overlaid with people [with whom] they had made deals to purchase or lease land for construction, and they'd made deals, to keep the costs down, share the profits. For example, when they were developing Waikiki, draining the swamps at the time, the land they would purchase or lease was on the basis of, first of all, we'll make you a director of Dillingham, maybe some Japanese garden farmer or [the owner of] a sushi stand. "You're a director now." They had more directors than General Motors, for God's sake. I told Otto this and how they hadn't done anything, and he found this interesting. I looked at it and said, what would it take to gain effective controlling interest? Controlling interest of a corporation can be done, not by owning 51% of the shares, but by having substantial enough numbers so they have to listen. That would be a good way to start.

I found out how many shares Merrill Lynch had. First you have to know the number of outstanding shares. This is the way they [the

Organization] work, they take their time, they don't rush. Very very low profile.

The plan was to basically take over the corporation. This would be an ideal thing, given what you'd control. They have North Shipping, which is a big shipping company, deals throughout the entire Pacific Basin — not doing anything. That was half and half between them, Dillingham and a partnership basis with Norwegian interests. The idea was to gain effective controlling interest and then full controlling interest. Not, say the outstanding shares are 11 million, to buy all of them or even a majority, but to do it through front companies and various individuals. On the books it appears to be maybe 500 or a thousand different people, but in fact the one entity does the directing.

— Is there anything illegal about that?

Yes, there is. You must report to the SEC when you own over 5% of a corporation.

— So it's very difficult to prosecute, since you do have all these individuals saying, "I own this."

Sure, and I've owned it for a number of years, and I receive the checks, and it goes to their accounts, pay taxes on it. But it's all paid back to the Organization. The Organization gives the word.

— When you have 500 to 1000 people, who between them may own 20%, which is a pretty loud voice in the company, but ostensibly they are individual owners; how can they act in concert? What can they do to impress the company that there is one block talking without compromising their position?

The Dillinghams are more or less the people who are running things for Dillingham. It's done privately: this is the score, and if you want to test it, fine, we'll test it, and show you exactly how much muscle there is.

— They're threatening to dump stock, that's the lever?

Right, and then we'll buy it all and build it up to our own standards. We'd prefer not doing it that way, but...

— Let's talk about the Organization and Dillingham. You show them, through Otto, a corporation in trouble, without direction, but which is potentially a very strong corporation. And the plan is that you, the Organization, could buy a controlling interest through 500 or a thousand people. What happened as a result of that?

They went ahead. As I found out later, the Organization has a number of individuals, American, German, French, British, that they control. These people could tell key personnel that because of their tax situations, they can't afford it, but they want the others to buy some stock and be the nominal owner of it, and this is how they eventually did it. I reported, through the years, on where the major blocks of shares are. They had a relatively small block for trading purposes. Merrill Lynch had something like 300,000 shares on hand that could be obtained at a special price, off the market. It wouldn't be shown as a normal trade, just be transferred from one trader to another, and held in a street name, usually by a bank. The front would be a trust.

— *Did they act on this?*

Yes. I had another meeting — you have copies of notes from that meeting. The first man I spoke to was a P. I believe he is now working for Dean Witter/Reynolds, which is another example of fronts controlling a corporation nominally, but it goes back and back. Dean Witter/Reynolds is supposed to be an American corporation. In fact the principal controlling interest is Arab, and they are in turn controlled by the Germans. It's not in the financial reports, but they are owners of record.

— *Which Arabs are we talking about?*

Kuwait, Saudi Arabia. They're the two principal ones.

— *Then you're saying that Arab control, where it shows up, is German control? That Otto and his people are behind that?*

Yes, and it has been German control since before the war, even.

— *Why do the Saudis and Kuwaitis, who have a great deal of money from their oil, why do they...*

They offer them a false sense of security. The Arabs have a great fear for security, physically, for their positions. I use the term Arab not just to say Saudi Arabia, but Kuwait, Oman, Quatar, Abu Dhabi, United Arab Emirates, these various little potentates. The rulers of the country now, 40 years ago were young men, boys. At that time their education, their beliefs, were very carefully cultivated, knowing that one day they would be in power. The Organization doesn't plan for what they're going to do tomorrow, they plan for the turn of the century, at this point. It's a continuing thing. It's not "Get all we can and skip with it." They want to have permanent effective control, so they've taken this time. It's amazing. The most powerful opposition to the German control of the Arabs is coming from the British, not the Americans. The Americans seem to be pretty content that they control things themselves, but they don't.

— *Let's get back to your personal involvement — were you being paid by Otto for the work you were doing?*

My payment is knowing what's going to happen in the business world, and acting on it.

— *And what year are we talking about?*

'73, '74.

— *And during this six months, what is your function?*

To keep track of what's available. To go through contacts, so when the trader says, "I think we're going to have about 50,000 shares, because someone is about ready to sell," I know that and place the word through the Swiss Bank Corporation, and when it's available, they're there to buy through intermediaries.

— *During this time, were you doing other things for the Organization?*

Basically, just passing on financial information. Texaco, Pan American. One that was very good was Allied Artists. That was a case of getting them to go bankrupt, to take over its assets. The last movie they made, *The Wild Geese,* was the one that did it to them. The movie was done for about two million dollars. Allied Artists — they're very good in a financial sense, they own a lot of monster-type movies from the '50's. They have the rights to most of those. Then once the assets were purchased, they'd be sold. In other words, they picked the company clean.

I had been requested by Otto, during '78 — they were making preparations for control of the gold market, that's the big rush that came in the latter part of '79 — and I started to get information about gold stocks and the commodity of gold, to watch for movement. I contacted D., and the suggestion was about Rustenberg. Another was Troy Gold Industries. These could be picked up for nickels and dimes. The gold market was very stable. The big rush that was expected when Americans could own gold again never came. That worked very well for the Organization, so when I suggested Rustenberg as a relatively obscure thing on the precious metals markets, because when gold moves, silver and platinum move, pretty much in proportion.

— You've just moved from 1971 to 1973 to 1978 and '79...

I was going to go to '75 now. At that time, Otto was generally concerned. He felt that it was time to leave. So he called me back... I had called him and he called me back and told me that he was going to be out of town — that meant he was going to Germany. He usually wouldn't go to Paris. Could we arrange to meet as soon as possible, because there were some things he wanted to discuss with me. When he was in Germany, he sent me a telegram, which I have a copy of — I don't go near the originals, that's part of my safety. He told me that it was time to leave. He said, "Now, this is just between you and me. Even the Organization doesn't know I'm talking to you like this."

We had the meeting and went out. There's a restaurant in Madrid called Horcher's. It was the darling of the Nazi set in Berlin during the war, very luxurious. When the war ended they just picked up bag and baggage, the whole family, moved to Madrid, to be close to their customers. When he walked in — Boom! Served you like you've never seen before. This was very interesting that he was out in the open like this, but he was obviously very agitated about something, and wanted to explain to me that he had to leave. I wasn't to get in contact with him, he'd get in touch with me. We had by that time set up mail drops, contact points, and some of these places that I have here in Sacramento, I can't stand. They really drive me up the wall. One place, I really have a block about this place. On the outskirts of downtown; it's a queer steambath. A hell of a place to have a meeting. I honestly think that Otto likes to see people squirm.

— *So, you went to Horcher's.*

Yes, and he told me not to contact him, he would contact me. I would normally go into, say, E.'s place [a mail drop] quite often. I haven't been there for about a year, now. After he left, I'd gone in there and would have been contacted, normally. He, E., knows where I am most of the time. Sometimes he doesn't know and is not supposed to know: better security, so there can be no leaks from his side. People within the Organization know I work for them, but in what capacity, they're really not all that sure. That's the way Otto prefers it to be, and the way I prefer it.

— *How long was it before he got in touch with you?*

Maybe December '75. He got in touch again about August of '77.

— *About a year and a half. During this time you continued with your reports?*

Yes, that was why we had the meeting. He told me, "You're not supposed to know." So when things happened [Skorzeny's reported death] I was greatly shocked by it. I sent the standard telegram to his widow, and you saw the reply. [Printed card of thanks with painting of Skorzeny.] That was his way of letting me know everything was alright, particularly with the photograph.

— *Are there ways to prove he's alive short of inviting retribution and death? Something a bit less dramatic?*

Well, there's that photograph I told you about, of Otto standing in front of the memorial painting which was commissioned after his "death."

— *During that 18 months, you continued doing Organization business?*

It wasn't orders for Organization business. He knew — he still knows, that I, through my contacts, was able to know what's going on in the business world. Particularly with the Dillingham thing, what developed through contacts there in Hawaii was the fact about Ariyoshi [Governor of Hawaii] being on the take. It was very helpful to know that.

— In March '75, Otto said, "Hang on, because the reports of my death will be somewhat exaggerated," and in December of '75 he got in touch with you again. You got a message?

I had gone into E.'s place, and E. was mentioning that someone was trying to get in touch with me. I knew who that was and I knew how to get down. He had told me in our meeting where he was going. He'd said, "This is the time to get out." I found out later, through normal conversations, that he had gone to Denia, to stay with his friend, who operated a summer camp, something on the Mediterranean.

— Tell me how you got there, and where, in fact, there is.

It's in the north part of Paraguay, the compound. There are a number of ways it can be reached. Get a car, drive down to Mexico, chartering a plane in Mazatlan to Cancun, in Merida. Ostensibly for a rich man's vacation, fishing and all that. You rent a room and keep it, and you keep it for a few weeks, even though you're not there for more than a few days. You establish a pattern that you're out fishing or bumming around, and meanwhile another plane has been chartered to take you from Cancun to Panama City. From Panama City, a plane that will take you the rest of the way, very long range to Asuncion. A plane of the Organization would meet me, yellow and brown twin Cessna, to [take me to] the airstrip that they have. None of this time would normal papers be necessary, so there would be no records or identification on anybody.

— Are there other ways into the compound area?

None.

— About how far is it?

A twin Cessna will go about 225, 250, and the flight was maybe an hour and a half. I'm not saying they went top speed. I was sitting in the back so I wouldn't know. I do a bit of flying, but at that time, I didn't think it was wise to stick my head up there and say, "What's the speed here? What's your heading?"

— You were heading North from Asuncion?

Northwest, actually.

— What happens once you get to the airstrip?

You get taken up to the house. Well, how do you do, shake hands — Oh, God, when he shakes hands. The guy's a monster. Obviously I don't have a muscleman's hand, but it certainly isn't what you would call tiny and dainty, but he can just engulf it. Takes both hands in the shaking. He's big [indicates with his hand above his head]. I'm six feet so he must be six foot six or something like that. Huge great man with meathook hands.

— *Was he the only one there?*

There were security people in the area. Friends, how do you do, fine, let's have dinner, talk about — usually when there are groups of people, friendly patter. One would not give names, real names, but you talk about things that are... I mean, really!

— *Talk about your crimes?*

That's basically what would be done. He asked me about how I first learned about his demise. He wanted the information I had on some of the companies we discussed, and I told him, at that time I had much firmer contacts in Hawaii, about [the governor] and that he could be bought — standard contract. It's amazing how you can talk about these things, matter-of-factly. [The governor], his fee is about $10,000 if you want something done. Somebody you want into the state or somebody out of the state with no trouble, or if you want to conduct business in the state, $10,000 to [the governor] and a sliding scale minimum $8-10,000 for the union, and you can conduct business there. They wanted to develop Hawaii on a long-range basis, inter-island transport, through the air. The principal ones there were Hawaiian Airlines and Aloha Airlines, but also charter airlines, which is good for the Organization when they want to move people around quietly through charters. They developed charters. They were having competition with the hydrofoil. I had mentioned to him the hydrofoil was Boeing, and gave him a list of people involved in operating it and best to be dealt with. I wouldn't deal with them.

— *You were talking to Otto about developing Hawaii as a base?*

Right. And it is being developed very well. I hate to go there.

— *Okay, what else was going on during that visit?*

I mentioned I'd get back to him next time regarding Consolidated Oil & Gas there. It's these American businessmen — it's a listed corporation on the American Stock Exchange — that control Princeville. I said they're hurting for money now. They'd been developing for about five to six years, and it took a little more than even they had. I suggested that as a possibility in the future, said I'll look into it for you. That was basically it. That went over two to three days.

— *You were talking about the compound in Paraguay. You said it was about a dozen buildings. Could you describe the place? For example, starting with the airstrip.*

The airstrip is not a paved way. It's unpaved and well camouflaged, but the camouflage is removed for landing. It's certainly large enough for a twin Cessna fully loaded to land and take off, once the camouflage and obstructions have been removed. You can say 5-6000 feet, approximately.

— *Does a Cessna need that much?*

Fully loaded, it would. If they're having shipments come in, they would. I'll give you an example; one time they had a safe brought in, a very large safe. It was brought in on a DC-6, which was a hell of a time, trying to get the damn thing off the plane.

— *You get off the plane and you're there. What do you see?*

It's maybe a half mile from the main compound. Although there is a path, they don't want to have great access to the airfield. Usually you'll walk. The path is there to bring in heavy equipment, and they can use vehicles, but don't usually. There are obstructions on the path, so if someone could get as far as landing without authorization, then it would be very difficult. The growth around it is very extensive. You'd walk a half mile to the main compound, where there is a large 2-story building, Spanish style. There is a garage with room for about a dozen vehicles in it. There's a large workshop. There's what I like to call a barracks, for soldiers. Army type. Guards. [It sleeps] 100, maybe.

— *This large building that you mentioned, what do you mean by large? Ten rooms? More?*

Let me count. There's a large reception room as you enter through a hallway. Three rooms on the bottom, right next to the reception area. There's a door leading to them, double glass door to get inside. There's secretaries — secretarial offices in the front, on the ground floor. There's a basement. And living quarters on the second floor.

— *How's it decorated inside?*

Call it French Continental, I guess. Nothing as ostentatious as Louis XV, but if you were to furnish a home in French style, with relatively fine furnishings, without the gilt, this is what it would look like. The furniture is a problem because of the moisture there. Very damp, constant warping.

— *What about the colors? Wood?*

Plaster and wallpaper. Very European wallpaper, these little rows of flowers, vertical stripes and flowers. Not effeminate. Blues and greys are predominant. The room that I have is like Dracula's Castle, something from the Victorian era. Not a four-poster bed, but a massive one. I've been in some of the other bedrooms ... large, carved wood, dark.

— *Native labor around? Servants?*

German only. I've seen 25, 35, maybe up to 50 [soldiers] around. Civilian clothes. One thing they do have, the Vietnam combat boots, half leather, half canvas.

— About how much land does the whole compound cover?

I'd say maybe 10 acres, but the buildings are spread out and they're not all in the open. Under cover of trees —there are some very large trees there, or growths.

— What's adjacent to these 10 acres, topologically?

Mountains like the California foothills, a bit steeper, and a bit higher and more heavily overgrown, tropical.

— Does someone own the land adjacent? Is it in use?

No. Not in use.

— Where are the nearest other people?

From what I saw when I was flying in, they're very scattered. There's a river to the west, several miles away ... very small villages ... maybe three huts to a village.

— It's a couple of miles to the river?

More than that.

— And all the traffic in and out is through the air? Can you hack your way in through the jungle?

If you want to try it, go right ahead. Not me. There are sensors that will pick up the movement. Electrically-activated mines, in plastic so there are no metal parts to be detected. They're sufficiently large and sufficiently deep so they couldn't be probed for. In fact, if they got far enough to do that, they'd already be caught on the motion monitors.

— What color is the house?.

Very filthy white. You paint it and probably a month later it looks just as bad as six years later. Never dries sufficiently, so you have this constant bubbling of the paint or whitewash. It's amazingly clean, though, once you're inside. It's all closed up and everything is air-conditioned; you'd think that you were in a nice European country home. It's their touch of home-away-from-home, so to speak.

— With a compound full of SS General Officers, I imagine there would be a tendency to keep it clean. How many permanent residents are there?

Not including guards, maybe 20-25 who live there on a relatively regular basis, or who have rooms there.

— In Paraguay there are people around Otto, people in the Organization. Let's talk about them.

These are Germans in the Organization. To be a true member of the Organization, you must have German blood, to be in the heart of the Organization. Some of the people? Joachim Peiper, another one of the reported deaths. It's very fashionable to "die." Peiper was the head of the unit that killed 83 Americans in the Malmedy Massacre. The War Crimes Tribunal said it was done because they had no place to take them. They were traveling light, so they found it easier to murder 83 men in uniform than to take prisoners. But they had taken prisoners during this period. He also speaks fantastically good English. Otto does not. He's the right-hand man to Otto, very close. D----, Belgian SS, a real lunatic if there ever was one. He's an enforcer, if you will, in the simplest possible terms. Otto Gunch, he was Hitler's SS Adjutant. He spent about 10 years in Russian prisons. Gunch works in the American section, if you want to call it that. In fact he has worked with American publishers translating things into understandable English from German. He has a very good grasp of American idiom. High echelon people in Paraguay, not including guards and security ... about 100.

— Inside the Organization, how many members do you think, worldwide?

Approximately 1000. It just took one to set the whole Napa area on fire in California. Oh, other people presumed dead in the Organization, Adolf Galland, General of the Fighter Army, Luftwaffe. He's very good on transportation...

— Is the Paraguayan government aware of all these people there?

The Paraguayan government are employees of the Organization, nothing more than low-grade employees.

— How about Marty? [Martin Bormann]

They have him in another position. I've never seen him, this one man I mentioned to you is a source of information. The guy [Bormann] is a nut on apple juice. "Dirty sonofabitch trying to get apples..." Apples do not grow in that climate; they have to be brought in.

— Does he live reasonably close to the compound?

Evidently quite close. They don't want him around, sort of like a doddering old grandpa — you don't want the guy around any more. He probably lives in one of the key houses. I tend to believe that he is close by.

— December of '75. You reversed the process and went back up. You worked on those things during the intervening 18 months, and then he got in touch again in August of '77. You got a message to go there again?

Yes, and I did. First of all he asked me how I'd gotten on — evidently he'd done his own investigating. I don't think he ever trusted anyone — but he asked me about how Consolidated Oil & Gas was. He was asking me about Playboy and Columbia Pictures. He asked me, since one of my basic fronts is being into films, since I know a lot of people down there in the business in Los Angeles. Also Lockheed. I made some suggestions on how they could get more stock, and that I would get back to them. I started making preparations shortly after I got back, and went to Dean Witter/Reynolds and spoke to W., who is still with them. For a while he was helping me, purchasing stock through Troy Gold Industries, getting back to the Columbia Films, and — this is interesting — the Gong Show. BCHK stock symbol, it paid very, very very well. Two stock splits and some fantastic dividends.

— When was this?

'78. We'd get together very infrequently to talk about what I have accomplished and what I hope to accomplish by the next meeting, whenever that is, in irregular periods. We've already set up making purchases through the Swiss bank. Once I've delivered information to the Swiss Banking Corporation, the money is there waiting to make the buys. It is held and then transferred over, such as in the case in '79, when the gold thing came about. We were reporting on — like a stockholders' meeting — old business and the new business, and then we'll meet next time. But it was mainly of the purchasing of stock.

— I'd like to ask about the meeting of January '80.

That was more or less a congratulations, with everybody shaking everybody else's hands. That was a celebration, because they'd just sold out their interest with gold price based at 800 and something an ounce.

— Had they also sold Rustenberg?

Everything was sold off. They'd cleared their position.

— Not long before that. I think January was when it hit its peak.

Actually, in February was when it went fffffftt. [indicates straight down]. It hit a high of 852 on the Hong Kong exchange. I think there was some talk of 875, but to my knowledge, it only hit 852.

— They sold at 850, or before that?

From what I gathered, around eight and a quarter. Everything was very quiet — just a big celebration. He wanted to thank me for all I'd done, and I wanted to thank him for all he had done. That kind of profit — you can buy things at 175 — I think the top price they paid for gold was $389, and I had done that myself. I was the foolish one, because a week after the Iranian crisis started I said, "I think I'll hedge a little bit." So instead of buying it directly — I'd buy some directly, actual bullion held in the precious metal account, but on the commodity market, being able to buy much more with little. They hadn't instituted controls at that time. All the playing around that had been done — the Hunts, with the silver, and the gold market being manipulated — the margin was hardly anything. For —

oh, use a figure — for $10,000 invested you could control maybe a million or more dollars in gold. Virtually like owning a million dollars in gold. When it went up, let's say a contract would be at that time 10,000 ounces, I believe was the contracts we were dealing with, if the gold went up, $30-$40 a day, that's $30-$40 an ounce. You're holding a triple contract — each contract is worth 10,000 ounces, so it was worth doing that at $389, even though I didn't buy it, the gold itself.

— In the previous seven to eight months, quite a few events had taken place which were at the instigation of the Organization, starting with, in the period of May '79 through the end of December '79, a series of crashes of the DC-10. In Summer of '79 an agreement was made at Bohemian Grove to run Ronald Reagan as president.

Yes. They decided in '79 that Reagan was going to be elected. A meeting was held, those attending being Alexander Haig, George Bush, Steve Bechtel, Dave Packard, Henry Kissinger and Helmut Schmidt at Bohemian Grove, in which policy was decided for future election of Ronald Reagan, and possible events to follow thereafter. This was merely a preliminary meeting to decide basic goals and to structure the campaign as these American corporate officers would desire to have it structured.

Mr. Bechtel at that time was not in total agreement with certain objectives. To keep him in line a very minor object lesson was made by an attack on Bechtel's holdings in Central America. At that time General Haig wished to have more input, particularly regarding his possible nomination, but acquiesced when told that was not possible at this time. When he continued to balk at his position he was given an object lesson, the attempted bombing of his staff car, which was never meant to explode. It was not radio controlled, it was electronically controlled by wire. It was never meant to kill, merely a lesson to keep him in line. If this Nazi organization can be said to be composed of many godlike mentalities, there can be only one, and General Haig was not meant to be the one. He seemed to the Organization to be pliable, in that he has done many good favors and passed on much information through Helmut Schmidt, information of a political, military and economic nature, who in turn through his own avenues would forward the information to central headquarters in Paraguay.

Shortly thereafter, it was in the final planning stages of the election campaign, it was determined that Reagan was pliable, and could be worked with and dealt with, that there would be no problem. As time grew closer Mr. Reagan was evidently asserting himself in such a way that it was felt that he could not be depended on to follow advice of his subordinates who, in effect, were to be the heads of government. It was determined that he was to be removed. The first operation planned was for

January 11, 1981 at a dinner held as a farewell to close friends in the Los Angeles area. Information was passed through my sources and the operation was stopped. The man who was to have the contract to shoot the president was M., who was a former U.S. Army officer, who was chosen because of his psychological disability and his background. M., during the Arab-Israeli conflicts in the late '60s and early '70s, while still in the Army, requested a discharge so that he may join an Arab legion to fight against the Jews. This was not taken as normal behavior for an Army officer, and he was immediately relieved of his duties and placed in psychiatric care in the Army, where he was examined by both a psychiatrist and, of all people, a rabbi as to his feelings toward the Jewish people. He currently, as his front, operates a small hobby store in Sacramento. He is considered extremely unstable mentally. He is of Russian extraction, he claims proudly that one of his relatives was with the Russian army, a group of Russians that were taken prisoner by the Germans during World War II and who apparently espoused similar ideals regarding the Communists, who were eventually used by the Germans against fellow Russians. His contact in Sacramento is L., who, as a front, operates a jewelry store, who is the section head, the cell leader of KGB in the Sacramento area, and takes his instructions from him. Data from L. is passed through T. who, as a front, operates an antique auction business. My contact was able to prevent this particular contract from being carried out, that is not to say that the contract will not be tried again, as happened in Washington recently.

— Let me ask about the Reagan administration. You said that Reagan was considered to be "pliable" to suggestions from his advisors...

True. He relies on his advisors to run operations.

— Does, for example, Otto tell Helmut Schmidt who tells Haig and Haig says, "Go?" Or are they trusting the instincts of people they feel are allied with them? Are they trusting that Haig is crazy enough to do what they want without prompting?

A little of each, actually. Haig is obviously around-the-bend, but he's just one avenue. The man is so unstable that they don't rely on him solely to give advice to Reagan.

— Could you give examples of the Organization influence, how this has worked?

The petroleum companies, during the Iranian hostage crisis. American oil companies had ordered an embargo against doing business with Iran, and could not purchase oil, not that there was that much to buy. In the early stages, at least, the oil would be loaded on the tankers, out at sea. Papers would be changed. The papers would read that the shipment would be going to the Hague, into Holland, Rotterdam, principally, and it would be going to American refineries on the Gulf Coast.

— It would leave Iran with a bill of lading to Rotterdam? And the bill of lading would be changed?

At sea, as if it were going from Rotterdam to the Gulf Coast refineries, whichever could handle the load. A premium was paid, oh, 40 cents, 50 cents. I heard one time as high as a dollar and a quarter. They called it a commission per barrel.

— Was there much resistance among the oil executives to doing this?

Not at all. Controlling the corporation and having influence is one thing, but ultimately the Organization controlled the flow of funds. It was to their advantage to cooperate. To give you an example, during this time one of the lower rung people wanted to get in on it, and they were contributing a little something, so they were given between 25 cents and 40 cents a barrel. A little something to sweeten it. Considering the capacity of these tankers, it's a nice little touch for making the arrangements. They'd take the fall, if anyone starts investigating, some news organization or government organization that wasn't in the know or wasn't controlled. They'd have to hang somebody's hide to the wall — the guy who's getting the 40 cents commission, because he's doing all the work. He's the recognizable one, he arranged for the shipment, nominally. His name was used, that's more accurate.

— Can you give any other examples?

Eastman Kodak were advised of the manipulation of the silver price far enough in advance to stockpile some rather large amounts of silver. Then, on the announcement of the astronomical prices of silver, going up, they'd announce that we now have to raise our prices. Silver has gone up 10 times over its price in the last 2 months. Now we have to raise our price from $2 a roll to $4 or $5 a roll, when in fact they had silver at the old prices they were using.

— Were the Hunts, who seemed to be at the center of the silver manipulation ...

They weren't. They thought they were screwing the Arabs. It was Arab money that did the buying. So when the bath came, it was the Arabs took the bath. The Hunts got a nice profit for themselves, the Organization got a fantastic profit for themselves, and the Arabs were left sucking eggs. Who took the rap? The Hunts. You notice during the investigation, on paper they supposedly lost, what was it, a billion dollars or so many hundred million ... all on paper....

— How about Columbia Pictures?

There was a contract man at Columbia Pictures, and I'd met with him and discussed investments. I didn't say "The Nazis want to invest with you." Rather, "We'd like to have some input into Columbia." The idea was to get them hyped up about a project that Columbia would merely make profits — somebody else would risk the capital. They liked this very, very much. We were talking about who the best man was, and I suggested, by no accident, that it be R. This was about six months before the Begelman affair developed.

— *What was R.'s function to be?*

To be a star in the motion picture. The Organization would back it.

— *Was this picture produced?*

Never. Never had any intention of being produced.

— *In what way is there profit in this situation?*

That they would schedule — this is another example of long-term planning — around this project, scheduling a release, because they would be acting merely as a distributor for the film. When the film was not delivered in time, that schedule was blown for the next year to eighteen months. That immediately caused a depression in the price of the stock. That was merely manipulation so that they could get the stock in Columbia.

— *Who was supposed to be putting up money for this?*

Nominally, I was. I said I represented European interests that would be interested in investing in this film.

— *So Columbia was scheduling distribution for a film that never got produced. How much of a commitment did they make?*

They made a commitment — we told them they would have worldwide rights to it, and then we told them we would have to shoot such-and-such a place, and they told us, "We like the idea of R., but..." They actually were our best allies in finding problems. In the interim the Begelman affair started up. The Begelman affair helped us, which we were no part of, but it helped drive the price down so we could get into Columbia, which we did at between four and five dollars a share.

— *How did the Allied Artists situation work?*

That was '78, I believe, and representations were made to them, supposedly by a producer who wished to remain anonymous, who wished to rescue them from their plight. They were in trouble for quite a number of years — it didn't just happen in one year. What Allied Artists was told... They had just gotten through producing *Wild Geese* and were in hock about two million dollars, which isn't a great deal for a film company, but for them it was critical. It was what put them over. An agreement had been made to distribute their film and to back any losses they had. The deal had fallen through, particularly when word was leaked to the SEC that the man doing this would be in some violation. He was prevented by some legal maneuvering. SEC was alerted to this, they halted trading immediately in Allied Artists and the company put into receivership and the assets sold off.

— Did the Organization own shares in the company?

Yes. During this period when there was a goosing, this producer — a mythical figure — wanted to buy the company, get them out of their bind. That coincided with the purchase of the shares in the company. When that story started circulating, the Organization had already reached their position in purchasing shares, and the shares had doubled...

— The shares had been purchased and then the offer to purchase the company sent the price of the shares up?

Yes, and then the shares were sold. The company went into receivership and the assets sold off at a profit. Not to Allied Artists. To the Organization.

— Is there a particular attraction to the film industry that the Organization likes?

There are so many ways of hiding profits from the films, basically a type of skimming with creative bookkeeping in some ways akin to the casinos.

— We'd like to get as complete a list as you have in mind of corporations who are involved with the Organization. Not necessarily in accord with them, but which have individuals who are under pressure or in accord.

Companies penetrated by the Organization? Texaco, Polaroid, Pan American, Dillingham, Sun Oil, Standard Oil, Lockheed, Resorts International, Columbia.

— Okay, [...] had asked if there was any overt connection between Rockefeller and other financial biggies and the Organization.

It's interesting that you ask, because Rockefeller, very bluntly, if not too melodramatically, was one of the bitterest enemies of the Organization.

— Was? You mean Nelson?

That's right. David no, but Nelson yes. Nelson worked long and hard during the period when the Germans were currying favor and developing economic and political ties with South America. He was working to knock those ties out. He never did, but they didn't forget that. He was one of the few men that could put the pieces together, and had contacts in

South America that could have blown the whole Organization. At least they looked at that as a distinct possibility. So, far from working with, he worked very heavily against. Not a very endearing personality, I know, but he was a decent person.

— *You had begun to mention that David works with the Organization and that you had some information that Nelson's death was not natural or accidental.*

If I may be permitted, the public is supposed to believe that Nelson was screwing his secretary and merely had a heart attack, instead of it being a case of ... what's the word? Fratricide?

— *You're saying that David had Nelson done in?*

Yes. They considered him too much of a bleeding heart. It must be remembered that Nelson was Roosevelt's man in South America for counteracting the German influence pre- and during WWII. He was probably connected to the Organization, but what's important is that he was one of the few men in a position to hurt the Organization and insulate himself from retaliation. And Kissinger was his advisor, and Kissinger reported to David.

— *We had been talking about Carlos, and you had mentioned that he is always protected by Organization people...*

When he's in Paraguay, yes. I've never seen him. I wouldn't know him if he walked in the door.

— *This door? His reputation is such that he makes a very obvious entry. You'd probably recognize him.*

Grenade first? It was amazing how he just disappears for long periods. That's where he is [in Paraguay] when he disappears. I've never seen him when I've been down there, and I know he's been there on a least one occasion when I was there. An Organization man is with him virtually all the time when he's travelling. The story of his being KGB-trained is untrue.

— *Do you know any of his background with the Organization?*

He is the liaison between the Organization and the terrorists. He's the only one who knows it's coming from the Organization. The Organization provides logistic support, transports him safely to any location, and when he's not on an operation, he's kept safely down there.

— *You mentioned a 1979 meeting at Bohemian Grove where it was decided to elect Ronald Reagan. What was done, specifically, to help elect him? Since you mentioned some involvement with the Iranian hostage situation, was that a part of this plan?*

You must remember that the Shah, the one who died, his father was very pro-Nazi. The German industrial element has very carefully, for many years, cultivated the Middle East countries. There was a time when the royal families were a joke — give them some girls, give them a few fancy parties and they're happy and you can steal their oil for a dollar a barrel. They're now stealing it for forty bucks a barrel. Where do you think the money's going? They get the families to up the price and use the money to invest in the Organization's financial dealings, be it directly in bullion, as I mentioned before. This created a physical shortage of gold, and this was engineered by the Organization. So we're getting back to Iran, and how Iran could help Reagan. Actually, it was supposed to hurt Carter, which it did immensely. People weren't going to vote for Reagan — they were going to vote against Carter. The semantics don't matter. Reagan was elected.

— How was it done?

Information was fed from the Organization to Helmut Schmidt to David Rockefeller to Henry Kissinger. Creating friction leading to an incident and feeding the incident. Very simply, the incident was created by bringing the Shah to the United States. The people in Iran looked at it very simply. Their reaction was predictable.

— What about Organization involvement with the IRA?

The IRA has been funded by this Nazi organization to a great extent. Principally, though, they supply the transmittal of funds and supplying data, supplying logistics, that is, specific materials such as explosives and electronics to accomplish the terrorist acts, such as bombings, burnings and shootings. Among the terrorist acts of the IRA the Organization has supplied the murder of Mountbatten, in which S---- supplied part of the electronics for radio control of the bomb that was set off on Mountbatten's yacht. The Organization continues to supply safe houses for materials to be stored, people to be secreted away, before, during, and after an operation, and to provide safe conduct out of an area. Where it is deemed necessary or advisable, sacrificial lambs are usually given up to the authorities, and the investigation regarding the particular incident would end.

— We haven't really talked about people that you meet and encounter as part of the Organization, the gossip and shop talk, where they happen.

My position is something like Inspector General, and I'm known in certain segments of the Organization, but not all segments. With that unique situation Otto allows me a great deal of freedom. If there's a particular operation that's being planned or is in process, and he feels that he wants an independent observer, I'd be over there. I'd be going two times, three times, four times a year to Europe to observe the operations, as I say, in both planning and operational stage, and then reporting back to him through my drops in Europe. I wouldn't have to directly contact him for that.

— *What sort of operations are these? I know that you've mentioned that the first one was at the Paris Airshow in '71, where you met with S. So, ideally in chronological order, which operations were you overseas for and reported on?*

Most of the principal terrorist operations that took place in Europe, I was there to observe. I'm talking about the hijackings. There was one obscure one — I could never figure out why I was supposed to be there observing it, but I was there to observe the hijacking out of Malmo, Sweden. I was told to contact — I don't know his name, but I was to be on a certain train that ran between Copenhagen and Oslo and crosses over at Heltenborg on a train ferry. At that point a representative would contact me, and know me by sight. It turned out that this man was a representative of Bofors Corporation. They have a number of irons in the fire, sort of a Swedish Mitsubishi Corporation, not just the Bofors guns. He would be filling me in on what had taken place up to the time when I had gotten there, and what was going to take place. Then I would stay in the general vicinity, usually in these little obscure pensiones and hotels, and observe and report back through a mail drop.

— *We'll talk about the other hijacking afterwards, but right now, Malmo. What airline? SAS?*

I don't even recall. It was so obscure and nothing of importance came of it. Was I being tested, were there doubts about my reliability? Was there some facet that I didn't understand? I don't know. But it stuck in my mind even though it wasn't a principal operation to my knowledge.

— *What about the others? I understand it's a burden to say chronologically, going back ten years, but you'd said something about three [hijackings]?*

The Swissair, TWA and Pan American. The ones that were hijacked to the desert, all three of them, and then eventually all blown up. That was the first big operation.

— *That was obviously a major project, but what was the payoff for the Organization in that?*

It indebted the PLO to the Organization through Carlos — it was a Carlos operation. At the same time it got one of the Organization people out that was suspected of, well, the gentleman was going to be picked up on his arrival. Who the gentleman was and what plane he was on and what the destination was, I have no idea. But they evidently had to get a man out.

— *What was the payoff to the PLO?*

Dollars and cents. I was in Paris and was in touch with the people supplying Carlos with the materials for the hijacking. And getting direct reports: I'd be monitoring the frequencies that the communications, during the hijacking, were going out on. During every hijacking operation specific frequencies are assigned because it's known that the Organization will be listening in. This is the way the Organization keeps the PLO honest, if such a thing is possible.

— *Was the Organization involved in the American hijackings?*

Not to my knowledge. Everybody jumps on the bandwagon.

— *Okay, you're sitting there, or standing there, in a comfortable apartment or a dingy warehouse, whatever it is where the monitoring equipment is...*

Crummy pensione on the Right Bank...

— *And you're hearing the reports coming over. Are you talking in between?*

We're talking about: what the hell are they saying? They're speaking in Arabic. There was an Algerian there doing the translating. When I'm in Paris if I need protection I have Algerian bodyguards, the kind of guys who would knock off their mother if the price was right.

— *Was anyone killed in that one?*

No.

— *How about another operation?*

There was one where, of all things, a Lufthansa plane was hijacked, flown to Africa. I believe it was the co-pilot that was shot and thrown out the door. Maybe the pilot.

— *What was your reaction to that?*

Disgusted. Very sorry for this one gentleman who was shot. Especially when it came over that the man was begging on his knees not to be shot, and they just put the gun up to his forehead and psssshhht!

— *I know you were filled in on the Munich massacre, the Black September thing at the Olympics...*

During the 1972 Olympics in Munich, which was one of my first assignments, I tended to collect data and merely be an observer to report to Otto on the events that were taking place. The material, that is, explosives, grenades, weapons were smuggled in through diplomatic pouches.

— *Through which country?*

Kuwait, and through North Sea ports, particularly Hamburg.

— *Were you an observer on [this operation]?*

Directly, on site. This was the first big operation I was involved on, early Summer of '72. I didn't know what was happening until I got there. I was told to get a flight from New York to Brussels, only time I've taken Sabina from New York, and then taking the train from there to Germany. Arriving the following morning in Munich where I was met in a house that had been prepared for me. I was taken to a hofbrau house very close to the city hall, and it was explained to me, the operation was to take place this very afternoon.

— *How much of what was to happen did he tell you?*

That the arms had been moved in, had come through diplomatic pouches, and the operation was due to begin in the early afternoon.

— *How did he describe the operation?*

Taking of hostages from the Israeli part of the compound. The word had gotten out, and [Mark] Spitz was on the list. He would have gotten it if he had stayed longer. They'd take hostages, to disrupt and hopefully end the Olympics.

— *And how long before events actually took place was this briefing?*

A few hours. We went out to the main section. I didn't have much time and after things started popping I didn't have much desire to get into the spirit of the thing, the Olympics. I just wanted to get the hell out of there.

We were there when the shooting started... The buildings are here [indicates] and the freeway comes virtually parallel with the U-bahn, cross the U-bahn station over the freeway here. The big stadium with that ugly plastic cover was here and on the other side was the place for the track meet. Over in this section was where the quarters were and where the action took place. Surrounding it in a semi-crescent was a raised piece of ground where everyone was standing and where we were.

— *Is that the same area where the news camera were shooting from?*

Yes. I had a telephoto lens on my camera and I was viewing through that — it was just as good as binoculars, really. I couldn't really see much of what was taking place. It was more a matter of a personal demonstration to me. Later in the day we went into Munich again, as things were developing, and we'd gone into one of the Lowenbrau beer bars. I said, "I don't know about you, but the first shots I hear, I'm going under the table. I've had it. I want to get the hell out of here."

— *At this time the PLO was still in the quarters?*

Yes, very close to the time when they made the transfer. The word came that they'd made the deal to take them to the airport, then that they'd taken them to the airport. We're following this bit by bit. The news agencies were covering it quite well. Then the news of the shooting and — not bombing, but grenading? I think it's bombing of the helicopters after the German sharpshooters couldn't take them out at not more than 100 yards.

— The event concluded. What did you do then?

I wrote up my report and made my drop in Munich, and it was forwarded. I got the first train I could to the farthest point I could get to. That was the beginning of regular trips to Bergen when things got a little hot.

— You mentioned that there are several projects beginning right now, that are in the works...

One operation underway regarding the problems that England is experiencing, depending on who you listen to, labor problems, racial problems, basically Rightist in origin through the Organization's contacts. This is to lead to a finality. Let me backtrack: when these various IRA men went on their hunger strike in the Mays prison in Northern Ireland, when they died, if anyone was wondering why the reaction hasn't been terribly severe from the IRA they will find out because of the ultimate operation starting to take effect at this time, which would culminate in the assassination of Prince Charles. I was told first that it was to be on the wedding, now I am led to believe through my contacts that within this dissident faction in our organization, the date is being attempted to be moved up considerably to within a week, not more than ten days from today. In any event, whether it be the dissident factions' will that will prevail, or the older generation's ideas that will prevail, they do agree on one point, that Prince Charles will be assassinated through IRA. I believe that it will be by bomb and not by gun. The electronics are already being shipped, and a number of locations are being prepared, since it cannot be absolutely assured because of heavy security on Prince Charles what particular location would be best.

[On November 28, 1992, Reuters New Service reported that an IRA informer had revealed a bomb plot on Prince Charles and Princess Diana that was to have taken place in 1983. There are unsubstantiated accounts of other assassination plots against the Royal couple. — Ed.]

— You mentioned the old faction and the new faction in The Organization; could you cover the differences that they have in attitude towards strategy?

The dissident faction, the youthful faction, differs from the older group in that they wish a more direct, open statement, rather than the subtleties that the older Organization has used. The older Organization will only use assassination when it is in its best interests and necessary; the younger men feel that this should become more policy and not merely a once-in-a-while proposition. The old Organization wishes a very low profile, the younger organization doesn't concern themselves with any kind of a profile, they merely wish to be moving ahead. They haven't seen any appreciable movement, and they wish to be more direct in accomplishing their goals, their goals being more economic than political.

Contacts

Remote Mind Control Technology was reprinted from *Full Disclosure* magazine, Box 903, Libertyville, IL, 60048.

Rumors, Myths and Urban Legends Surrounding the "Death" of Jim Morrison was authored by Thomas Lyttle, editor of *Psychedelic Monographs and Essays,* PO Box 4465, Boynton Beach, FL, 33424.

Behold, A Pale Horse: A Draft of Danny Casolaro's Octopus Manuscript Proposal was provided by Kenn Thomas, the editor of Steamshovel Press, a magazine that examines conspiracies, arcane historcal topics and alternative views of current affairs. Available from 5927 Kingsbury, St. Louis, MO, 63112.

Jim Keith, the editor of *Secret and Suppressed,* is also the editor of *The Gemstone File,* and the author of *Casebook on Alternative 3: UFOs, Secret Societies and World Control,* available from IllumiNet Press, PO Box 2808, Lilburn, GA, 30226. Mr. Keith may be contacted care of IllumiNet Press.

John Aes-Nihil, procurer of the Otto Skorzeny manuscript, runs the Archives of Aesthetic Nihilism. His catalogue documenting obscure and dangerous cultism is available for $5 from Aes-Nihil, 7210 Jordon Ave., B-41, Canoga Park, CA, 91303.

Conspiracy-oriented material may be obtained from the following sources: Prevailing Winds Research, PO Box 23511, Santa Barbara, CA, 93121, Flatland, PO Box 2420, Fort Bragg, CA, 95437, A-Albionic, PO Box 20273, Ferndale, MI, 48220, Loompanics Unlimited, PO Box 1197, Port Townsend, WA, 98368, Wiswell-Ruffin House, PO Box 236, Dresden, NY, 14441.

Mystery object amid the chromosomes

SIR—The very tiny object shown below, much like a fragmented crossword in appearance, was recently found in one of our routine chromosome preparations for prenatal diagnosis following amniocentesis. But what is it?

Is it a man-made device? Packing text as binary coded information on the miniature scale (the scale bar is 10μm) would seem advantageous. Or is it a naturally occurring substance? None of the possibilities we have been able to think of would

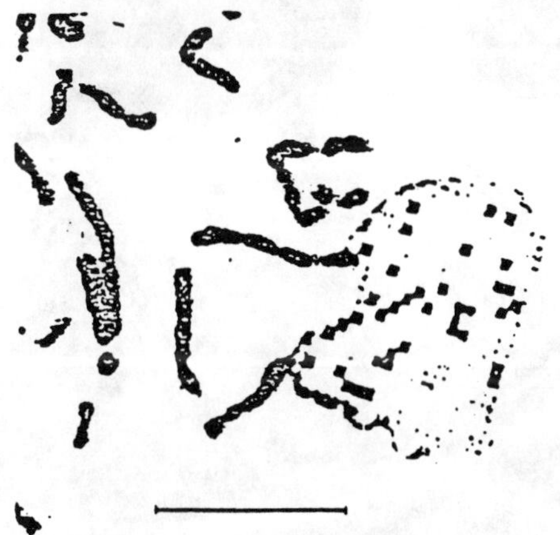

seem to be appropriate for amniotic fluid, so if anybody is able to suggest an answer to this mystery we would like to have it. We are as intrigued as we are ignorant.

JOHN WOLSTENHOLME
IAN HARLOW
GEORGE CLARKE
HILARY SHERIDAN
JON JONASSON
MARK CROCKER
HELEN MATTHEWS
Department of Medical Genetics, Churchill Hospital, Headington, Oxford OX3 7LJ, UK

The AVRO flying disk, collaboratively built in the early 1950s by Canada and the U.S. It was described as both ineffectual "ground effects machine" and high-speed interceptor craft. Would current stories of UFO aliens serve the government's purposes in concealing advanced craft of this sort?

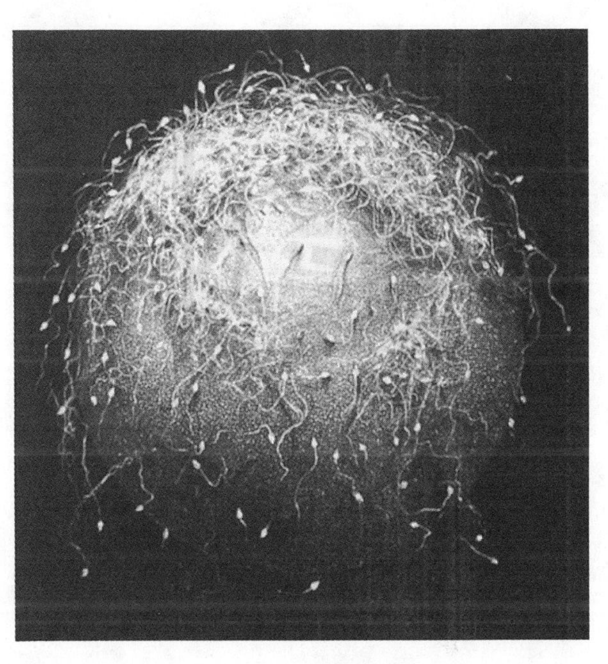

The Law of the Forbidden
Heretical Books from Feral House

Cosmic Retribution
The Infernal art of Joe Coleman

This stunningly designed presentation of Joe Coleman's paintings and illustrations reveals the artist's obsessive visions of outlaws, madness and distressed religious impulses. Includes 32 color pages, 110 black and white pages and an incisive interview conducted by Adam Parfrey. "Coleman unleashes a hallucinatory violence of image and content that is unrelenting and unforgettable." — *Artforum*

$22.95 • Deluxe Paperback Edition • ISBN: 0-922915-06-7

$39.95 • Limited Signed Cloth Edition • ISBN: 0-922915-13-X

CAD: A Handbook For Heels
Edited by Charles Schneider

CAD, my honored wolves is a treasure trove of pictures and information that is likely to turn the most lily-livered sap into a rapacious rogue. Here is the forgotten lore of the red-blooded American male: two-fisted tales, stogies, martinis, beatnik, black velvet pantings, salty gags and last but not least, the most exotic, bewitching, glamorous and glorious girls shown the way nature intended 'em.

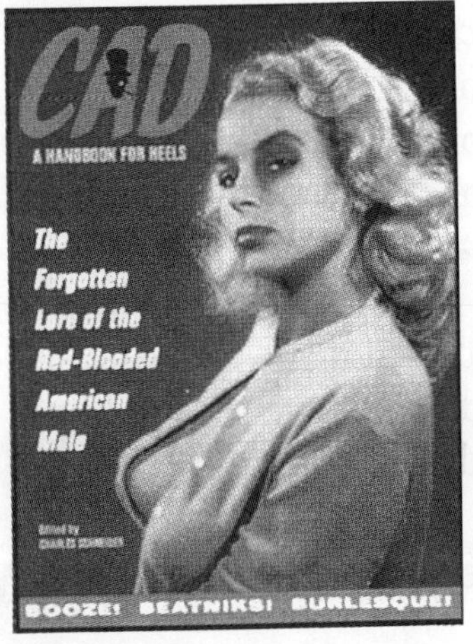

"Get *CAD,* dad, it's BAD!" — *Screw*

$14.95 • Large Format Paperback • ISBN: 0-922915-09-1

The Law of the Forbidden
Heretical Books from Feral House

Apocalypse Culture
Enlarged and Revised Edition
Edited by Adam Parfrey

Eighteen entries enlarge this edition of the influential underground classic that illuminates the dire and phantasmagoric cast of contemporary events. The first half, "Apocalypse Theologies," delineates the symptoms and components of decay; the second half, "The Invisible War," provides theories and analysis on just what is going on. "These are the terminal documents of the twentieth century." — J.G. Ballard

$12.95 • Trade Paperback • ISBN: 0-922915-105-9

Nightmare of Ecstasy
The Life and Art of Edward D. Wood, Jr.
by Rudolph Grey

Rudolph Grey's heralded book, soon to be a motion picture directed by Tim Burton, descends into the shadowy worlds of exploitation movies and pornography to capture Ed Wood's elusive story, revealed here in compelling interviews with those closest to the deranged auteur of *Plan 9 From Outer Space* and *Glen Or Glenda*. Chock-full of rare and amazing photographs, complete with annotated filmography and bibliography, *Nightmare of Ecstasy* is one of those rare books that is as strange, lyrical and hell-bent as its iconoclastic subject.

"Finally the Ed Wood story told in all its naked wonder. *Nightmare of Ecstasy* is an hilarious but heart-breaking portrayal of a brave, eccentric and sometimes insane film director. I stayed up all night reading it with my mouth hanging open." — John Waters

$14.95 • Trade Paperback • ISBN: 0-922915-04-0

The Law of the Forbidden
Heretical Books from Feral House

The Devil's Notebook
by Anton Szandor LaVey

The Devil's Notebook is the first original collection of Anton LaVey's writings to be published in over two decades.

"In a clear polemical style, the good doctor rips into a number of deserving targets ... and imparts wise-ass wisdom that, for me, is worth more than a stack of ancient grimoires. Like *The Satanic Bible, The Devil's Notebook* is a tome only the clever among us will appreciate." — *The Nose*

$10.95 • Trade Paperback • ISBN: 0-922915-11-3

The Secret Life of a Satanist
by Blanche Barton

The definitive biography of Anton LaVey, founder of the notorious Church of Satan. This entertaining account follows the strange and wide-ranging life of the figure declared, " the most dangerous man in America." Includes 24 photos and essential documents never before published. Now available in paperback.

$12.95 • Trade Paperback • ISBN: 0-922915-12-1
$19.95 • Cloth • ISBN: 0-922915-03-2

FERAL HOUSE TITLES ARE DISTRIBUTED TO THE BOOK TRADE BY PUBLISHERS GROUP WEST

To Order Feral House Titles:

Individuals: Send check or money order for cost of book plus $1.75 shipping for first title, $1.25 each additional title. Orders shipped to Canada, add $2.50 shipping for first title, $1.75 each additional title. All other countries: add $4 shipping first title, $3 each additional title for sea mail, or add $10 per title for air mail. All non-U.S. originated orders must include check or international money order for U.S. funds drawn on a U.S. bank

Send SASE for free Feral House catalogue.

Feral House
PO Box 3466
Portland, OR
97208-3466